Towards Equity in Global Communication MacBride Update

THE HAMPTON PRESS COMMUNICATION SERIES
International Communication
Richard C. Vincent, supervisory editor

Goodbye, Gweilo: Public Opinion and the 1997 Problem in Hong Kong
    L. Erwin Atwood and Ann Marie Major

Democratizing Communication?: Comparative Perspectives on
Information and Power
    Mashoed Bailie and Dwayne Winseck, eds.

Global Productions: Labor in the Making of the "Information Society"
    Gerald Sussman and John A. Lent, eds.

Towards Equity in Global Communication: MacBride Update
    Richard C. Vincent, Kaarle Nordenstreng, and Michael Traber, eds.

Reconvergence: A Political Economy of Telecommunications in Canada
    Dwayne Winseck

forthcoming

International Media Monitoring
    Kaarle Nordenstreng and Michael Griffin, eds.

Media and Culture of Singapore: A Theory of Controlled Commodification
    Kokkeong Wong

Towards Equity in Global Communication MacBride Update

edited by

Richard C. Vincent
University of Hawaii, Manoa

Kaarle Nordenstreng
University of Tampere

Michael Traber
World Association of Christian Communication

with editorial assistance by Aphra Kerr (Dublin City University) and
Néster G. Trillo (University of Hawaii)

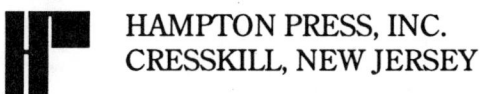

HAMPTON PRESS, INC.
CRESSKILL, NEW JERSEY

Copyright © 1999 by Hampton Press, Inc.

All rights reserved. No part of this publication may be reproduced, stored in a retrieval system, or transmitted in any form or by any means, electronic, mechanical, photocopying, microfilming, recording, or otherwise, without permission of the publisher.

Printed in the United States of America

Library of Congress Cataloging-in-Publication Data

Towards equity in global communication : MacBride update / edited by
    Richard C. Vincent, Kaarle Nordenstreng, Michael Traber : with
    editorial assistance by Aphra Kerr and Nester G. Trillo.
        p.   cm. -- (The Hampton Press communication series.
    international communiation)
    Includes bibliographical references.
    ISBN 1-57273-181-8. -- ISBN 1-57273-182-6
    1. Communication--social aspects. 2. Communication,
International. 3. Mass media--Social aspects. 4. Information
superhighway. I. Vincent, Richard C. II. Nordenstreng, Kaarle.
III. Traber, Michael. IV. Series.
HM258.T69 1999
302.2--dc21   98-56512
                                                               CIP

Contents

Preface
PART I: GLOBAL VISIONS   1

1. State, Capital, and the Civil Society:
   A Problem of Communication
   Johan Galtung   3

2. Where is the New World Order?
   At the End of History or a Clash of Civilizations?
   Majid Tehranian   23

PART II: PROSPECTIVES AND PERSPECTIVES   65

3. Theories and Research to Live By:
   Communications and Information in the 21st Century
   Ramona Rush   67

4. The Cyberright to Communicate:
   A Human Right of the Fourth Generation?
   Wolfgang Kleinwaechter   91

5. Catching Up to Our Digital Future?
   Cyberdemocracy versus Virtual Mercantilism
   Michael R. Ogden   103

6. Democratic Media: The Case for Getting Organized
   Seán Ó Siochrú   139

7. Media as Public Arena: Reconceptualizing the Role
   of Media for a Post-Cold War and Postmodern World
   Dennis K. Davis   155

8. Emancipation from Modernization:
   Development Journalism and New Social Movements
   Hemant Shah   169

9. Is There an Indigenous Seat
   at the Modern Communications Luau?
   Poka Laenui — 187

PART III: EXCURSIONS AROUND NWICO — 201

10. The Concept of "Communicative Democracy"
    and the Flow of Information
    Igor E. Klyukanov — 203

11. Transcending the Dialectic of Culture
    Jeffrey C. Ady — 213

12. Unresearched Assumptions in the MacBride Report
    Michael Basil — 223

PART IV: MacBRIDE LEGACY — 233

13. The Context: Great Media Debate
    Kaarle Nordenstreng — 235

14. "Many More Voices, Another World"
    Looking Back at the MacBride Recommendations
    Allan Hancock and Cees J. Hamelink — 269

15. Sean MacBride: A Short Biography
    Jorg Becker and Kaarle Nordenstreng — 305

APPENDICES: MacBRIDE ROUND TABLE STATEMENTS I - VIII: — 313

Appendix A. The Harare Statement (1989) — 315
Appendix B. The Prague Statement (1990) — 319
Appendix C. The Istanbul Statement (1991) — 323
Appendix D. The Sao Paulo Statement (1992) — 325
Appendix E. The Honolulu Statement (1994) — 331
Appendix F. The Tunis Statement (1995) — 335
Appendix G. The Seoul Statement (1996) — 341
Appendix H. The Boulder Statement (1997) — 347

About the Authors — 353
Author Index — 355
Subject Index — 361

Preface

Historians on every continent are now busily writing the history of the 20th century. Three themes are likely to dominate their efforts. The first is war. The 20th century has created and developed the notion of "total war," with its disregard for civilians and its weapons of large-scale human annihilation. In addition, World War II was followed by the decades of Cold War, which have affected the whole of humankind and from which the world still has not recovered.

The second historical theme is decolonization and how this has changed the map of the world. There are now many more diverse international players than in 1947. Close to a hundred new sovereign states have emerged since then.

And a third theme of 20th century history may well be science and technology, the creation and application of knowledge, and the powers that technologies have unleashed. The technological infrastructure of communication has undergone particularly drastic change, with more in the offing.

This collection of essays on global communication has to do with all these themes. This is particularly true if they are seen from the perspective of a movement that is associated with the name of Sean MacBride: Irish statesman and champion of world peace, international lawyer and human rights activist, advocate of developing nations and international justice.

In 1977 Sean MacBride was chosen to chair UNESCO's International Commission for the Study of Communication Problems. Most of the 15 commissioners were eminent scholars from five continents. They completed their work in 1980 with the publication of a report entitled *Many Voices, One World*. The *MacBride Report,* as it is commonly referred to, constitutes a landmark study of the problems of global communication.

International communication, particularly in the form of radio broadcasting, owes its rapid expansion to the promotion and the pursuit of wars, hot and cold. Propaganda became an unfortunate part of international broadcasting, and in some ways still is. One of the lessons learned from World War II was that radio should never again be used and abused by war-mongering governments as had been the case. UNESCO's *Mass Media Declaration* of 1978 is a bench-mark in this respect, and must be seen as an important precursor to the *MacBride Report*.[1]

Of equal if not greater significance for the MacBride Commission was its concern for the so-called developing countries, or the South. After all, more than half of the commissioners came from the South. Although these countries had achieved political independence, in terms of their economies and cultures they were still treated as colonies.

Another United Nations project, the creation of a New International Economic Order (NIEO), pursued in the early 1970s, was supposed to lead to a more even-handed international trading system and thus to economic decolonization. The decolonization of information and communication was the next logical step. However, the struggle for a New International Information Order (NIIO) was clearly a program of the South and of its Non-Aligned Movement (NAM).[2] It was, in the first instance, the countries of the South that would benefit from "a new, more just and more efficient world information and communication order" (the subtitle of *Many Voices, One World*).

What started as a clear South-North issue soon turned into a quagmire of Cold War politics. In some respect the NWICO was hijacked by the two Cold War superpowers and used to settle their scores, old and new. Thus, the NWICO fell victim to imperial power. The colonial system prevailed in new guises. It did not permit a further emancipation of the South, least of all in the field of communication and culture.

The NWICO is also about science and technology. In the second half of the 20th century technology utterly transformed everyday life in the rich world and, to some extent, even in the poor. Perhaps the most spectacular achievement is the fact that, since the 1960s, radio can reach the remotest villages, thanks to the transistor and the miniaturized long-life battery. Technology allowed the capturing of sound and sight and their distribution in unprecedented ways. The spread of telephony and of computer networks through satellites has given rise to a new lifestyle for the affluent in the North and a small elite in some parts of the South. In general, however, technological resources are now so unevenly distributed that the gap between North and South seems almost unbridgeable, a problem

---

[1] Its full title is "Declaration of Fundamental Principles concerning the Contribution of the Mass Media to Strengthening of Peace and International Understanding, to the Promotion of Human Rights and to Countering Racialism, Apartheid and Incitement to War." For furthur background and details see Kaarle Nordenstreng, *The Mass Media Declaration of UNESCO* (Norwood, NJ: Ablex, 1984).

[2] NIIO later became known as the New World Information and Communication Order, also known by the acronym NWICO.

that the MacBride Report already addressed—at a time when the word Internet had not been invented.

Time will tell whether 20th-century historians will devote to the struggle for the NWICO a chapter, a paragraph, or a footnote. Yet, there are people all over the world who consider the work of the MacBride Commission one of the great landmarks of cultural politics of the 20th century. The NWICO could have been one of the jewels in the crown of UNESCO and the UN system as a whole. Alas, they lost this jewel for the sake of political expediency.

* * *

The MacBride Round Table was conceived and held its first meeting in Harare, Zimbabwe, in 1989. Its expressed purpose was to evaluate world communication at this 10-year mark following the publication of the *MacBride Report*. The inaugural meeting was cosponsored by the Federation of Southern African Journalists, the International Organization of Journalists (IOJ), and the Media Foundation of the Non-Aligned (NAMEDIA). The Round Table urged investments that would help improve the delicate communication infrastructures in the developing world, urged media professionals to set guidelines for operation, and reiterated the belief in a free and responsible press, with a public-interest orientation and without extreme government or commercial control.

Ten Round Tables have been held. Following the Harare meeting in 1989, there was Prague (1990), Istanbul (1991), Sao Paulo (1992), Dublin (1993), Honolulu (1994), Tunis (1995), Seoul (1996), Boulder (1997), and Amman (1998). The Round Table has become an international communication rights advocate with an agenda to accommodate scholars, activists, journalists, and other communication experts devoted to the monitoring of world communication, legal ramifications, and information imbalances, and reporting findings to community groups, UN agencies, nongovernmental organizations, and the news media. Further information on the Round Table may be found at the organization's Website at: http://www2.hawaii.edu/~rvincent/macbride.htm.

The current volume grew out of these Round Table meetings, particularly the one in Honolulu. The chapters that follow offer a look at issues highlighted by the MacBride Commission and thereafter elaborated by the Round Table, on the eve of the 21st century.

The term *MacBride Movement* is no euphemism. What started, historically, with the proposed restructuring of the international information and communication order has grown into an alliance of grassroots organizations, women's groups, ecology networks, social activists, and committed academics. Some now call it a media reform movement, others emphasize media education, and still others focus on the entire cultural environment, of which the mass media are an important part. There is a new NWICO in the making which sees itself as a network of networks based in civil society.

In other words, although many epitaphs have been written on the death of the NWICO, the movement "towards a new, more just and more efficient world information and communication order" is very much alive, although no longer under the same slogans. It has taken on new issues and concerns—the 1995 MacBride Roundtable was on Africa and the Internet—yet it is still steeped in the old NWICO principles.

One of these principles is equity or equality. The concept pertains both to justice and communication. To justice, because communication is an essential precondition to social empowerment. If individuals and groups of people are deprived of communication, or prevented from developing it, they are essentially rendered unequal. Furthermore, genuine communication cannot take place between superiors and inferiors. Masters can shout commands at their servants but they cannot really communicate with them. Communication can only take place if all partners acknowledge, in principle, the equality of all men and women.

This collection of essays treats the issues of equity and equality in communication not merely on the interpersonal but, in the tradition of the *MacBride Report*, on the international or global level. The book thus starts with two chapters proposing a new global vision.

Few international documents on communication have been so unambiguous on freedom and democracy as the *MacBride Report*. In spite of allegations to the contrary, anyone who has actually read *Many Voices, One World* can attest to that. Freedom is the hallmark of all genuine communications and the basis for every democracy. That freedom, however, can only be achieved if communication is truly democratized. The MacBride legacy on freedom and democracy has guided this book. It is also implicit in the call to renew the NWICO debate on new and realistic terms, meeting the requirements of the next century.

Richard C. Vincent, Honolulu, Hawaii, USA
Kaarle Nordenstreng, Tampere, Finland
Michael Traber, London, United Kingdom

PART I

GLOBAL VISIONS

Johan Galtung's seminal chapter argues that all modern societies are built on three pillars: State, capital, and civil society. While there has always been communication between State and civil society, though often weak and tenuous, the economic sphere seems a law unto itself. There are few communication channels between State and capital, and none at all between capital and civil society—a condition causing frustration and repression.

The new world disorder is the subject of Majid Tehranian's chapter. It critiques the current discourses on the new world order and analyzes the global changes taking place, and their implications for communication and democratization. All indicators point to the need to strengthen, through dialogue and new means of self-expression, democratic diversity and cultural pluralism of two-thirds of humankind which hitherto have been objects rather than subjects of history.

1

State, Capital, and the Civil Society: A Problem of Communication

Johan Galtung

MODERN TRIPARTITE SOCIETY, COMMUNICATION, AND CORRUPTION

When the European God reputedly started dying[1] during the Enlightenment, paving the way for secularization, he left behind powerful, feudal successors. The Prince and the Pope, one *rex gratia dei* and the other infallible, praised by courtiers and priests, had long served as personal incarnations. The struggles to gain the upper hand were terrible, with the Prince using his *ultima ratio regis* (arms) and the Pope his *ultima ratio dei* (salvation/damnation). The conclusion was to have the Church officially administer "only" spiritual, not temporal concerns.

Among the temporal concerns were military and political power, as well as economic power, which was increasingly extending its reach, even overseas. As a consequence, early modern European history gave the Prince ultimate control over the East and West India trade, and the Church lost economic power in Protestant countries.[2]

---

[1] Was it really Voltaire who did it single-handedly?
[2] A major and simple reason why the Protestant states became economically strong was that they confiscated Church land and monasteries (that could serve for industries), which could be also a reason why, later on, socialism and social democracy became more important in the Protestant countries than in Northern Europe.

The new industrialist and merchant classes were irrepressible, however, and worked their way up through revolutions (1688, 1789), human rights declarations (1776, 1787, 1789), and above all through a theory (1776) that defined the capital as being omnipresent, omniscient, omnipotent, and benevolent, provided it was left alone as a *causa sua*, equipped with its own Invisible Hand. A new caste of priests, or economists, emerged, praising the infinite, infallible wisdom of the market.

The Prince also gradually receded into the background. Courts became Cabinets with ministers and ministries, and eventually the organization within any modern country known as the State emerged. Once again a caste of new priests emerged, praising the wisdom of the State, laying out in great detail how omnipresence, omniscience, and omnipotence with or without benevolence should be practiced.[3]

These two powerful pillars in the modern social formation are both essentially 19th-century products of the North Atlantic area, now imitated all over the world. But the third pillar, the civil society, that is, people and their associations of sanguinity (family, clan), vicinity (neighborhoods), and affinity (coinciding interests and/or values), was always there, described by sociologists for modern, and by anthropologists for nonmodern, societies (see Figure 1.1). As a result our understanding of social for-

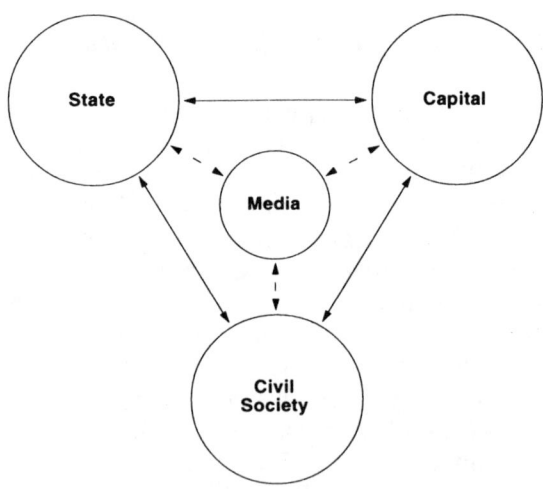

Figure 1.1

---

[3]In Germany that discipline was correctly referred to as *Staatswissenschaft*, the science of the State, closely linked to law and jurisprudence, and highly legitimizing for the State.

mations is fragmented among three or four social sciences, leaving more comprehensive, holistic views to those at the top.[4]

A typology of economic systems can easily be expressed in terms of the relative power of these three parts of modern society, as it emerged (Table 1.1; see Galtung, 1996).

More combinations can be imagined. The extreme cases, strong–strong–strong and weak–weak–weak, are hardly meaningful. Power cannot be everywhere; and there has to be some power somewhere for social cohesiveness. The argument can also be made in favor of an eclectic combination pink–yellow–green, rooted within different niches of the same social formation (see Galtung, 1996).

How the economic system of a social formation shapes up in practice depends, of course, on many structural and cultural factors embedded in the history of that society. However, the logic of international interaction forces a high level of homology on the societies in today's world, meaning not only that they have to have the tripartite structure discussed earlier, but also that the parts have to have some similarities. Thus, the Soviet bloc effort to construct ultra-red societies with a party-run State[5] incorporating capital and suppressing civil society, not only infracted the rights and insulted the needs of the people, but also impeded international interaction. When two societies are homologous each part can find its opposite

Table 1.1. A Typology of Economic Systems.

Color	Term	State	Capital	Civil Society
Blue	Capitalist	weak	strong	medium or weak
Red	Socialist	strong	weak	medium or weak
Pink	Social-democrat	medium	medium	medium
Yellow	Japanist	strong	strong	weak
Green	Localist	weak	weak	strong

---

[4]A social scientist only versed in political science, economics, or sociology is easy prey for a good politician with firsthand experience of the workings of the State, Capital, and Civil Society. The social scientist is rewarded for narrow vision by being given the title *expert*.

[5]It was based originally on confiscating Church property, like in the Protestant countries, not just the property of the Prince (the Tsar) and the princely, or the aristocrats.

number, facilitating international communication and interaction, beyond internal communication.[6] The Soviet Bloc came under double pressure, from within and from without, and imploded in 1989.[7]

China understood this 10 years earlier,[8] creating a capital that was homologous with the Japanese structure, with the civil society being relatively weak (not to be confused with right of assembly and speech, neither of which translates directly into power over State or capital). It is safe to predict that the tripartite structure will prevail worldwide as will problems such as rampant corruption, for example, when capital buys power.[9]

Today this analytical division of modern society is common. But there are precursors with tripartite divisions,[10] such as that defined by Rudolf Steiner (1861–1925). To him society was a totality, a social organism divisible into three different life spheres: the Spiritual-Cultural, Politics–Law and the Economy. They are autonomous yet meaningful when seen as parts of the total social organism. To Steiner all three life spheres were at their best when guided by the three classic slogans of the French revolution: freedom for the spiritual-cultural sphere, equality for the political sphere, and brotherhood for the economic sphere. Thus, education was to him a part of the spiritual-cultural sphere, guided by freedom and independent of the other two spheres. Even if Steiner's spiritual-cultural sphere is not as broad as "civil society," the inclusion of education, and its autonomous administration, makes the concepts sufficiently similar.

Any human being is a member of all three spheres. Take the economic sphere as example: To Steiner the unit of analysis is not the company (with employers and employees), nor the market (with sellers and buyers), but the whole economic cycle comprising producers, distributors,

---

[6]Thus, the hypothesis can be advanced that there is more communication in State–State, Capital–Capital, and Civil Society–Civil Society communities, facilitated not only by IGOs, TNCs, and NGOs, but more importantly by a shared world outlook, than in the State–Capital–Civil Society triad within many societies.

[7]For one theory of how this happened, see Galtung (1992).

[8]After the four years of "debate" following the death of Chairman Mao and the relaunching of the economy associated with the name of Deng Xiaoping from 1980 to present.

[9]Transparency International, the NGO "against corruption in international business transactions," focuses on "the misuse of public power for private profit." "Public power" refers to the people in the State, and the "private profit" usually comes from capital. The money may flow into the pockets not only of State functionaries and top officials (and the remnants of feudal formations that are still around, into the pockets of the Princes), but also into the pockets of the representatives of civil society formally having power over the State—the parliamentarians.

[10]Montesquieu (1689–1755) is rightly famous for his distinction between Legislature, Executive, and Judiciary. But this is actually an intra-State tripartite division, omitting Civil Society and Capital.

and consumers. Together they constitute an association; only in the association can brotherhood (and sisterhood) be realized. The cycle should be neither too small in order to not be too expensive nor too big lest they become opaque to the members. Property is only trusteeship, on behalf of the associations, the true owners.

In practice, however, the cooperation among the three sectors is far from unproblematic. Their logics differ. State logic includes:

- Divine self-perception, partly as wielder of ultimate power (*l'État gendarme*), partly as benevolent provider (*l'État provident*), with the State seen as a mystical entity, a *causa sua*
- Violence monopoly, "to he who has a hammer the world looks like a nail," with a readiness to use force as a self-fulfilling prophecy
- Arrogance, as carrier of ultimate power to kill, rule, and tax, with chief State officers (CSOs) being "Excellencies"
- Expansionism, a general tendency to increase State power
- Enemy construction, a general zero-sum orientation derived from the territorial base, seeing enemies, or cheats, everywhere
- Information monopoly, keeping secret information from lesser humans and internal and external "enemies of the State," with the Geheimrat whispering into the ears of the Prince
- Closed circles, with State officers tending to constitute *a corpus mysticum* disinclined to listen to lesser humans
- Patriarchy, with elements of gerontocracy; typically States are run by older men, usually of the dominant race or nation
- Cosmology driven, enacting, predictably and rigidly, the conventional deep culture of (elite layers) society
- Correspondence, a preference for CSOs whose personalities mirror the deep culture, cosmology, of the society;
- Conventionalism, better to go wrong with actions based on conventional wisdom (meaning cosmology) than on ideology; in the former case the world is wrong, in the second the actor is
- Universalism/specificity, action should be based on intersubjective criteria, that is, either based on cosmology-driven status quo or on time needed to develop a consensual action basis.

Capital logic includes:

- Divine self-perception, as *causa sua*, creators of wealth and profit, problem solvers, and providers of products or jobs
- Drive for monopoly, that is, ever-increasing market shares
- Arrogance, as carrier of ultimate power to run the market, self-image as *causa sua*, chief executive officers (CEOs) as gurus

- Expansionism, a general tendency to increase state power
- Competitor construction, seeing market competitors everywhere
- Information monopoly, keeping information secret from lesser humans and competitors
- Closed circles, executive officers tending to constitute corpus mysticum, being disinclined to listen to lesser humans
- Patriarchy, typically companies are run by men, but not necessarily old and/or of dominant race or nation
- Cosmology driven, being members of the same society.

People logic includes

- Human self-perception, searching for human needs satisfaction including survival, well-being, identity, freedom
- Object-perception, seeing oneself as power objects, even victims
- Subservience, inclined to obey State and Capital
- Status quo: hold on to what one has
- Enemy and friend construction, seeing both everywhere
- Information monopoly and sharing, for empowerment
- Widening circles, networking for empowerment
- Patriarchy, to some extent imitating State and Capital
- Cosmology-driven, inhabiting the same society or culture.

In this chapter State and Capital are discussed on their own terms. State is seen as having a monopoly on military (including police) coercive power and Capital on economic, contractual power, using its power to prey on people whose only power base would be cultural, normative power. The origins in feudalism structurally, and in the occidental religions culturally (with a transcendent male God whose abode is outside the planet, a Father Sky rather than a Mother Earth[11]), are most apparent, that is, this analysis would be less adequate in parts of the world with different histories (but today they all seem to be imitating Western tripartite "modernism").

Much of history can now be seen as a struggle among the three. On the one hand, there is State and Capital preying on people, with the State repressing the inhabitants and Capital exploiting workers and buyers, cheating people in both capacities. In doing so class formations emerge, or are at least reinforced. On the other hand, people fight back, spinning associations, creating a civil society decreasingly based on sanguinity and vicinity and increasingly on affinity. They manage to upgrade themselves from inhabitants to citizens, with rights, holding the State accountable, trying to become producers and consumers, that is, indispensable parts of the economic cycle, rather than dispensable workers and

---

[11] I am indebted to Kelly Kramer for introducing me to this felicitous formulation.

buyers (there are always others around). In the process they may try to conquer the State in a revolution and then have the State run or steer Capital through consumers' associations. And Capital and State may try to capture each other, to impose pure Blue or pure Red solutions.

THREE ENTITIES BUT ONLY ONE CHANNEL OF COMMUNICATION

The basic thesis of this chapter is that many of the problems of modern society derive from a lack of communication in the three bilateral relations: civil society–State, State–Capital, and Capital–civil society. Only in the civil society–State relation is communication (a) transparent to all, (b) institutionalized, (c) two-way and dialogical, (d) used for decisions binding on both parties, and (e) broad or open to any topic. Direct communication between civil society and State is known as a "democracy", and as "parliamentocracy" when communication is indirect, via political parties and parliaments. There is no clear communication channel within the other two pairs, indicating strongly how the total social formation is functioning. However, there are gaps in the social praxis and theory of modern society.

Theoreticians of the right see Capital as a *causa sua* (the way they saw the State some time ago) and efforts to communicate as efforts to control, however dialogical and reciprocal. The market, the centerpiece of Capital, does not like that and will withhold its blessings when controlled, or seek more friendly quarters. "Democracy+free market" focuses on State–civil society, leaving Capital untouched. As "Blue" ideology this is simply not good enough, nor is, the "Red" solution.

The theoreticians of the left, satanizing rather than deifying Capital, will tend to see Capital not as a partner but as something to be controlled by the State (socialism) or by civil society (anarchism). Mature symmetric relations, such as those between State and civil society, are argued by almost no one.

In no way does this mean that the State–civil society channel in modern parliamentocracies is perfect. A third element, the legislature, launched firmly inside the State, supervising or directing the executive, both of which in turn are supervised (to some extent) by the judiciary represents civil society. There is room for argument against indirect power exercised over the executive part of the State by the legislature, which is the reason why the term *democracy* is reserved for countries like Switzerland that frequently use referenda and initiatives (60% of all the nationwide referenda in the world this century took place in that country, having only 1% per million of the world population). And there is room for argument over the nature of the channel for articulating popular sentiment within and outside of the State: Should the constituencies be territorial or nonterritorial (such as people's organizations)? Should the voting be party-, candidate-, or issue-centered? More importantly, there is the problem poised by Ashby's law[12] about the information capacity of any channel: A yes/no referendum contains little information, neither do two-party systems, but frequent referenda and a multiparty system (and particularly the two together) carries considerable information for effective steering of the State.

Moreover, with indirect representation there will always be the problem of whether the elected representatives advocate the interests of the electorate, of the State, of both, or of neither.[13] In addition, the legislature tends to be located in the nation's capital and closer to the executive than the electorate. CSOs (Chief State Offices) are very near, the electorate far away, and the temptations are many.

CAN THE MEDIA FILL THE COMMUNICATION GAP?

To capture better the depth of this problem consider the obvious answer: Isn't this exactly the responsibility of the media?

In principle the media serve as a medium of communication, mediating between the constituent parts of a society, and making for mutual transparency by being intersubjectively visible and/or audible. In principle the media should be able to find out what goes on inside the State, capital, and civil society, making the three transparent to each other, thereby providing at least indirect communication with the five characteristics mentioned earlier. However, it does not necessarily work that way.

First, located in between the three pillars, the media have to be very strong to become a fourth pillar of society. Chances are they will be subservient to one or the other: to State through censorship, subsidies or for fear of being punished by lack of access to sources; to Capital through ownership or advertising money; and to civil society by catering to popular tastes, real or imputed, for violence, sex, and scandal. The three dependencies do not exclude each other; they often come together.

Second, society wants not only information and mutual transparency about events, but institutionalized transparency (not only at the discretion of the editors) and two-way communication with dialogue, leading to

---

[12]Roughly speaking, the information transmitted is only what can be transmitted by the narrowest part of the total channel. In other words, the chain is as strong as the weakest link.

[13]Two important candidates in the case of "neither" are the interests of capital and self-interests. When the two join the gate is wide open for corruption. Thus, the argument can be made for rooting parliamentarians firmly in the State–civil society relation, representing the interests of "both" (but giving civil society the upper hand in cases of incompatibility).

the possibility of influencing events even to the point of decision making. The media can do much to stimulate that dialogue by making information publicly available and by giving representatives of the three pillars space and time to state their views. However, this is not the same as dialogue involved in decision making.

CAN OTHERS FILL THE COMMUNICATION GAP?

Multiple Membership

State and Capital are not abstractions; people operate them, and these people also inhabit civil society. They have double roles, some even triple. There is communication inside persons with multiple memberships. This makes for added competence and insight, but not necessarily for communication in the sense defined earlier. There may be inner dialogues. A person may reflect on whether State or Capital plans will serve human interests in civil society, and the knowledge may weigh so heavily on the conscience that he or she cuts the tie to the two formal pillars of the construction; or, he or she could use inside information gained from State and Capital for personal enrichment.

Pronouncements

Most people would agree that pronouncements from a CSO do not constitute a dialogue, among other reasons because the communication is one way only. A classical Russian *ukas* is intended as nondialogue. Surprisingly many are unable to see advertising or commercials in the mass media for goods and services from capital in the same light, as nondialogical, as one-way communication. An 18-year-old U.S. citizen is reputed, on average, to have seen 340,000 advertisements, each of them nondemocratic, not so much because of content but because of the lost opportunity for having a dialogue. Thus, equal time (TV, radio) or space (papers, magazines) for opposing views would change the nature of the communicative act to an interaction. Why is that space not made available, nor in official bulletins from the State, for that matter? The tentative answer is because the two institutions, being God's successors, are sacred, and God's word is unopposed in Church and Court.[14]

---

[14]The assumption is not that this is a deliberate trick foisted on the population, but that the nondialogical nature of advertising is a carryover from earlier social formations, with God's successors enjoying some of His prerogatives.

People vote with their money. Of course, preference profiles influence production profiles. A CEO from Capital offers products as a supply and takes effective demand as a "yes" vote. But so may an autocratic State executive who offers ideas from the balcony of the State house and measures the mass of people in front of him or her, assuming that no protest means a "yes" vote. They may both be right in saying that people had a choice, they did not have to buy or to show up. They are both wrong in confusing acquiescence with dialogue, not understanding that both could learn from a dialogue, that both may change, that something new and different may emerge from it. To win somebody over to one's side is like winning a debate; in a dialogue both win. Both try to get the citizens or customers hooked on the offer, like a school of fish following the leader. To get those fish on the hook is also what an angler tries to do, but we normally do not refer to that offer of a bait as an act of communication, even if the fish has a choice not to bite, because among other reasons everything is done to limit the choices of the fish. The same holds for the stock market, which in addition is less accessible.

Opinion Surveys

Both State and Capital try to observe the citizens or customers to understand the reasons for the choices they make, voting for the policies of one and buying the goods and services of the other. Obviously, this is not a form of communication: The citizens and customers are not invited to participate in a dialogue as subjects, but are explored, mined for possible inclinations that can be exploited. A dialogue may occasionally happen, but only with selected, closed groups. It is a caricature of democracy.

Trade Unions

Trade unions constitute a communication link between capital and civil society. The link can be institutionalized, made dialogical, and lead to decision making; however, it is not transparent. Meetings with "sensitive negotiations" tend to be behind closed doors. Moreover, the range of topics is limited, in general, to the conditions of work, in no way covering the entire range of issues that would be of interest to civil society in general in its encounters with capital. However, enormous amounts of experience have been gained in this channel of communication, of significance if all five conditions are to be satisfied.[15]

---

[15]There is also an interesting tendency toward transparency by making annual conventions of parties, trade unions, stockholders, and so on open to the public in general and the mass media in particular.

Consumer Unions

Consumer unions exist to articulate some concerns of the members of civil society in their capacity as consumers of the products coming from capital. However, the focus is mainly on quality over price, with analysis of whether one gets one's dollar's worth. The communication is transparent in the sense that what the consumer unions publish is public and often institutionalized in the sense of being published regularly. However, it is far from obvious that there is any dialogue going on. The relation is more like that between artist/author and critic: A product is offered, the critic states a reaction, the artist/author may or may not pay attention, or feign attention, or nonattention. If any decision is made, then that decision is not a joint one. The parties do not really sit down together discussing how the product can be improved or discontinued. That initiative is more likely to come from an interventionist State, maybe as a result of consumers' complaints. The range of issues is limited to quality and price aspects, not to broader aspects.[16]

A Japanese Model

Obviously, a worker is at the same time a consumer; so is a manager for that matter. Both can have inner dialogues about the products they offer on the market, as worker-consumer and manager-consumer. When they meet in a manager–worker context they can feed these two inner dialogues into one outer dialogue, even seeing this as a major part of their commitment to the company. The condition is that they consume the products of their own company, which in general would presuppose that the products are for household consumption because most people only have command over household economies. This communication channel can satisfy all five criteria except one: transparency. The communication will be within the company and not between civil society and capital as such. Yet once again, important experiences are gained that are broader than those of conventional trade unionism; they can be generalized.

---

[16]This is the point at which the whole theory of the externalities of economic action enters (see *Economics in Another Key*). "Consumers" may have interests beyond quality over price, such as whether the company that produces the goods employs women, minorities, has a sound environmental policy, whether the production process stimulates local or national economies, and so on. In no way would this undermine the market; decisions would ultimately be made by the consumers. But the range of concerns behind a decision would be broader, the level of moral consciousness higher (see *Shopping for a Better World*).

A Chinese Model

This Chinese model was discussed during the Cultural Revolution, something that would immediately make it illegitimate in conventional Western debate. The idea was to create a forum in which representatives from all nodes of an economic cycle can meet and discuss the entire economic process: the farmers growing the cotton, the workers/managers in the factories spinning and weaving, the attendants/managers in the shops selling textiles, the customers in those shops, those involved with the production factors, the transportation-communication links, the waste. The idea is close to that of Steiner and realistic in the sense of mirroring how the whole economy works, not just unrealistically focusing on relations between two neighboring nodes.

Lobbying

Two major foci of power such as State and Capital cannot function as parts of a modern society without communication that satisfies most of the five criteria. There has to be dialogue, decision making, and a broad agenda, and it has to be fairly regular. As usual, what can best be sacrificed is what is most needed in a democracy: transparency. Only with transparency can everybody concerned know what is going on and make their own inputs. Communication without transparency is also known as lobbying and is the most important channel used by capital to reach all three branches of the State: executive, legislature and, more rarely, the judiciary. Not only Capital (Japanese and Mexican lobbies) but civil society also makes use of this channel, such as the National Rifle Association and AIPAC in Washington, DC.

The tight cooperation between State (MITI) and capital (Keidanren) in Japan can be conceived of as mutual lobbying; so can the countless meetings of State and Capital in any social democratic country. The ways in which States lobby Capital have been understudied; the focus has most often been on Capital lobbying the State. But the State has great stakes in Capital as carriers of national and class interests, abroad and at home, and as a tax base. Thriving Capital means important spillovers for the State, well worth public money incentives. If an incentive is something A offers B to do what A wants to be done, then it is obviously an exercise of power and may differ from corruption only (which is important) by being transparent and legitimized by a Parliament, that is, by civil society. But the very term, incentive, may be indicative of something.

A MINI-THEORY OF CORRUPTION

Capital will always want something from State such as permissions and contracts, and Capital will be willing to pay a "tip" for the services, ranging from 15% or more. The misuse of public power for private profit, to use again the formula of Transparency International, captures well the temptation of the person in State: he or she has public power, and capital can earn a profit on permits or contracts. Capital may write them off as expenses, and the politician, functionary, judge, official, minister, or even head of State can use this to supplement his or her (sometimes meager) income. As the modern State emerged from feudal social formations in Europe, the vassals and lords who became functionaires were still paid from below with products produced by the serfs rather than from above with salaries financed from taxes paid by those who work for a living. Corruption money was flourishing. As mentioned earlier, in early modern European history, State and Capital merged at the highest levels, setting a pattern for money flowing easily from one pocket to the other. The Third World claims it is now in that phase. What is wrong with this?

First disparaging aspects of European history must not be imitated; at any rate, two wrongs do not make one right. Second, the money that goes into corruption is taken from somewhere, and ultimately the customer or citizen is the one who pays with higher prices or higher taxes . Third, corruption may deform the economy by privileging the wrong projects.[17] Fourth, corruption may deform the country by bringing the wrong people into power. Finally, corruption makes a mockery of democratic decision making.

However, instead of distributing guilt and punishment, society should try to conceive of a structure that would make corruption less likely. For example, other cases can also be interpreted as blocked communication—political protests such as mass demonstrations, hunger strikes, terrorism.

A minority has no doubt about its right to autonomy, even independence, with partial or total control over its own part of some territory on Earth. The problem is that nobody else shares this view; nobody is willing to listen. The case draws, at best, a yawn. A group of consumers has no doubt that a product offered on the market is toxic and of their right to compensation. The group is aware of its duty to warn others and ultimately to get the product withdrawn and the company punished. But nobody listens, or if someone does, his or her listening leaves no trace.

So what does the group do? It resorts to unconventional methods of communication. If that minority group lives within a violent political cul-

---

[17]However, theoretically "incentives" may also help promote the right projects, in a political setting where the public consensus favors the wrong projects. Thus, in an upper-class society with State, Capital, civil society, and the media all dominated by rich people who want to become richer, the right projects, for example, in the sense of eradicating misery, promoting women, and being soft on the environment, would look like the wrong projects. Arguments in their favor would have to be made secretly. Would "incentives" to promote such projects still be corruption? Possibly not if they are made public, and the debate is open for discussion.

ture, it will shoot its way into the rooms where it will be listened to. Given the asymmetries between terrorism that may strike at any point in space and time of its choice, it will succeed in the long run. If the group lives within a nonviolent subculture or is able to develop one, it will probably reach its goal much faster, through gandhian-, kingian-, intifada-type methods. The encounters may not be transparent because of the methods used ("we shall never negotiate with terrorists"), but the outcome will ultimately be transparent.

The same applies to the consumers' group. Sooner or later, using sitdowns outside the company, silent protests, or confronting managers when they exit or enter a building, verbal communication will be established, complete with all five characteristics. Like the minority group it will probably be classified by habitual nonlisteners as "activist," a frequently used term in the United States meaning, by implication, that others are "passivists." In the first case the civil society–State channel does not work, in spite of being the best channel in the triad. The activists engage in extraparliamentarian politics because their representatives do not represent them, having insufficient votes behind them and/or because their issue falls outside the political discourse in the country (as was the case, for a long time, for Blacks, women, and gays). In the second case the State–Capital channel is not deficient; it is nonexistent. In both cases a lack of formal communication leads to informal, extraordinary, sometimes violent communication, or to corruption.

We usually see repressed minorities and poisoned consumers as carriers of legitimate claims, and the corruptors as not. But it is not that clearcut. The majority will see the minority as uppity, unable to see its proper place, using extraparliamentary politics not because legitimate politics is not accessible, but because it does not carry sufficient weight in a majority-held democracy. The company may see its product as just another offering on the market; it is up to the customers to weigh the costs and benefits of the product before deciding to buy it. If they do not like it, they should not buy it. This is an unsatisfactory answer if there are no other affordable products available; moreover, it is completely nondialogical.

Capital may be convinced it has a product for which there will be a demand, arguing it is for the potential customer to decide. What stands in the way is the State. Greasing that channel with corruption money, unblocking the market, is in the interest of the producers, the consumers, and the dealers for whom the market exists (not for the State). The "private profit" is well deserved if that is the price to pay for making market mechanisms work.

In other words, the crook does not necessarily see himself- or herself as a crook. Nevertheless, there is a need for moral judgment, to try to establish standards and rules of conduct that are backed by punishment if infracted, possibly also with some reward when adhered to.

There is another, softer, less legalistic approach—playing up to the potential corruptor as somebody with a communication problem. Imagine all offers from capital to a given country or local community were made public. Imagine local authorities made their standards for accepting an offer public, including not only the quantity and the quality for a given price, but also environmental standards for production and consumption processes, employment generation, and so on. Imagine then that civil society, meaning a variety of consumers' groups, also made its standards public, which may include employment of women and minorities, involvement with the nuclear industry, and so on to bring in some dimensions used by the Council for Economic Priorities in *Shopping for a Better World*. It is not a sign of societal maturity when these issues cannot be explored in open dialogues; communication in this case takes the form of lobbying and bribes, cheating the public, and organized buyers' strikes.

CAPITAL ENTERS THE DIALOGUE: THE WIRTSCHAFTSPARLAMENT

How State, Capital, and civil society act is clear: State will use power, including force; Capital will use money and people; and civil society will use moral power, which ultimately should mean moral behavior (nonviolence) and words. Substituting moral power for military police power and economic power should be a hallmark of societal progress. Efforts to persuade those who possess force and money by means of words, rather than giving in to force or being bribed by money, should be a sign of maturity. However, as mentioned, for dialogue gradually to replace force and money as persuaders, the channel of communication has to be available; if it is not, force, corruption, money, and nonviolent communication such as strikes will be used, which is more than what society can easily afford. Violence not only affects the victims, but also leaves behind traumas that generate cycles, spirals of violence through time and space. The economy will be weakened by strikes and distorted by corruption. Open dialogue seems by far the better approach.

For this to happen the three pillars have to be organized. Civil society is already organized into parties with party spokespersons as representatives. In addition, there is the vast array of nonparty, nonprofit organizations that often may be better carriers of adequate discourses than the political parties. The State is also organized into ministries represented by Ministers as CSOs. And capital is organized into companies represented by CEOs. The components are there. What is missing are the connecting links, like a clutch connecting engine and vehicle for an ever higher level of performance.

Just as there is a minimum requirement for parties, in terms of share of votes, to be represented, a minimum requirement for companies in terms of share of capital and for ministries or other branches of government in terms of share of the State budget may also be argued for. Lest this should lead to serious under-articulation of small companies and ministries, they might be given one representative—the representative of new parties, small business, or small government. Of course there are limits to the numbers of representatives, but larger assemblies are better than none at all, and some clustering or aggregation may be beneficial.

The Capital version of this is today reflected in two bodies: the Chambers of Commerce, with the International Chamber of Commerce (founded in 1920, headquarters in Paris with a staff of 93 persons, national committees in 59 countries, U.N. liaison offices in Geneva and New York), and the World Economic Forum (founded in 1971, headquarters in Geneva with a paid staff of 100, annual public meetings in Davos since 1990). There are important predecessors in European history—the mutual aid societies and guilds, particularly the merchant guilds, which were powerful in the 12th and 13th centuries gradually to be replaced by the crafts guilds, including the traders associated with any particular craft. In the first quarter of this century there was a movement, particularly in England, to restore this type of system. The movement was socialist: the guilds should be controlled by those working, the capital should be put in trust, no large "workers' State" bureaucracy was wanted nor capitalism favored. But very little came of it, and we are still left with a strange tripartite social construction with one part unlinked to the rest.

Neither the basic flaws in the East European socialist approach nor the corporatism associated with fascism in the second quarter of this century should detract from the major concern today: communication and true dialogue. Ideally that dialogue should actually be trilateral in a tripartite society. One could envisage a fairly large building with three assemblies along three of the walls: the party (or civil society) representatives, the representatives of the ministries, and the representatives of the companies, with the latter aggregated into branches. Along the fourth wall would be people, those to whom the process should be transparent, with the media people in the front rows, as is the case today, or in the galleries, as in many national assemblies.

Empty one of the first three walls and we get the setting for the three bilateral dialogues, which is transparent to the people and journalists, who in principle should be the people's eyes and ears (empty one more wall, and we get a convention). In this thought experiment it will be noticed that we do not quite get the legislature of today because there the State is not well represented. The reason is simple: historically the legislature evolved as a way of controlling an unwilling State (*l'etat, c'est moi*, or the modern Yeltsin version, *la democratie, c'est moi*). The State is sometimes present as a minister sitting in a special cubicle, away from the public, journalists, and legislators, listening, talking only when spoken to, with a "we are not amused" facial expression. In a more participatory system each branch of the executive would have their representatives, who would eagerly participate in dialogues within and between both chambers.

What would be typical dialogue themes in the two new channels, possibly organized as dialogical hearings?

For State–Capital there is a wide range of conflict and cooperation themes that are discussed in contemporary modern society, just not in that kind of setting. Any State would like Capital to generate more tax revenue; any capital would like the State to pay infrastructure expenses (or what it sees as infrastructure) and to come up with a plan for generating not only revenue but also employment in a sustainable, that is, reproducible, manner. Why should this only be discussed via parliamentarians who might run the risk of being lost between the two chairs? Why should there not be a prior, but transparent, dialogue between these two mighty pillars of society, with the final decision making being left to the legislature? Democracy as the direct or indirect rule of the society would still exist, only there is a better communication process prior to making final decisions.

In principle this should lead to a reduction of corruption. In some cases Capital gets what it wants because the openly offered arguments are good and are accepted by both the State and the legislature dialogues relatively unscathed. In other cases Capital will not get its way, and the temptation to use bribes in the market will exist. But there is now a much higher level of awareness; moreover, there could be rules to the effect that all deals must first be discussed openly in one, two, or three of these bilateral dialogical fora. The corridors of State and Capital would be more accessible, particularly the shadowy corridors where the two used to meet for illicit deals, with money changing hands.

For civil society–Capital, and perhaps with peoples' organizations rather than parties, as parties will have their say when the dialogue reaches them in the legislature sooner or later. The list of issues would reflect the entire range debated in political economics. Some have been hinted at earlier. But the most important general formula would be popular participation in the development of new products. Why should people not articulate their demands and prompt capital into producing the supply rather than, or in addition to, capital generating a new supply in secrecy, then sneaking up on the people with guerrilla methods to try to get them on the hook as buyers, revealing the new product, launching a barrage of publicity about it, luring people to the marketplace? Why not have a more symmetric approach, particularly if the market is seen as belonging to both the sellers, buyers, and the dealers?

There is something new here: The custom-tailored suit is, after all, made to order. Many products can be ordered, but they are more likely to be specifications of older than newer products. The concern here is with new products, ordered or wanted by groups of people rather than to be used for individual consumption. The demand would go to a branch of capital such as when the State invites bids for public works contract. In no way does this eliminate competition; competition would be enhanced. And why should the State be more entitled to demand a new product than people? Why this indirect way of going about popular demands? Is this commando capitalist way so much better than having the State decide the demand under command socialism? By what theory, if any, is this nondialogical structure justified?

INTERNATIONALIZING THE STATE–CAPITAL–CIVIL SOCIETY DIALOGUE

At the international, or world, level the states are organized into intergovernmental organizations (IGOs), with the most important being the United Nations General Assembly (UNGA) which can also be read as the U.N. Government Assembly). Capital is organized into transnational corporations (TNCs), which can also be aggregated into branches, and the International Chamber of Commerce (and the World Economic Forum) And civil society is increasingly organized into an international civil society (the pan-European version is known as the Helsinki Citizens' Assembly) and international peoples' organizations (IPOs).

PREDICTION

In one generation the U.N. will have a Second Assembly that will be better able to articulate the concerns of people, in other words, a United Nations Peoples Assembly (UNPA), and a Third Assembly more capable of articulating the interests of capital, a United Nations Corporate Assembly (UNCA). Under Article 23 of the U.N. Charter such new organs (of the General Assembly) can be created. There is no need for rewriting the Charter as long as the power relations are the same. This may actually happen internationally long before many countries open such communication channels. The global need, for instance, for a plan from the TNCs for employment generation (they handle a third of the gross world product and one quarter of the trade, but they have generated only 3% of the employment) and for sustainable development is overdue. And there is no substitute for a direct dialogue. Nor is there any substitute for a real-world dialogue about corruption—and this would be the setting.

CONCLUSION

"Tell me how State, Capital and civil society dialogue with each other, and I shall tell you what kind of society you have" is the morale of this chapter. Carriers of overwhelming coercive and contractual power, State and capital can run the entire process alone or jointly, giving rise to different political and economic systems, depending on how they relate to each other. The civil society can use normative countervailing power. The fourth type of power, decision-making power, should balance the three, using civil society to civilize the other two. Today this is done by striking a balance between civil society and the State, leaving Capital alone as if it were represented by either of the other two or were untouchable.

Given the strength of Capital in modern society, the power of the others becomes like the power of the station master in a minor station whose task it is to have the green flag ready when the express train is thundering past. In modern society there may be less class repression because of the possibility of standing up to the State, but much exploitation of classes due to capital is not challenged and made accountable.

The essence of democracy is transparent dialogue as a prologue to decisions for social transformation. Of course, the chiefs of the three meet, for instance, in Rotary clubs. They dialogue and make decisions, but are not held accountable to the public at large. And yet, as John F. Kennedy said: They hold the power to eliminate the human race, and to eliminate poverty. So there is no alternative to joint exploration of cooperative solutions to the major problems of our time. Communication, for dialogue and for progress.

REFERENCES

Galtung, J. (1992). Eastern Europe fall 1989—What happened and why. In *Research in social movements, conflict and change* (Vol 14, pp. 75-97). Greenwich, CT: JAI Press.

Galtung, J. (1996). *Peace by peaceful means*. Thousand Oaks, CA: Sage.

Shopping for a better world. New York: Council for Economic Priorities.

2

Where is the New World Order? At the End of History or a Clash of Civilizations?*

Majid Tehranian

Is there a new world order? The simple answer to that simple question is yes, no, and maybe. *No* because since the end of the Cold War, nothing significant has change the structure of the world *economic* system. *Yes* because something significant has changed in the structure of the world *political* system namely the end of the Soviet Union and the bipolar structure of rivalries between the two superpowers. *Maybe* because the world political economy and its technological, cultural apparatus seem to be in a state of transition that has been characterized differently by a variety of pundits. Francis Fukuyama (1989) labelled it the "End of History"; Samuel Huntington (1993a & 1993b; see also Ajami, Bartley, Binyan, & Mahbubani, 1993) called it the "clash of civilizations."

---

*A shorter version of this chapter appeared in *The Journal of International Communication*, Vol. 1, No. 2, 1994. Copyright 1994 by Majid Tehranian. Reprinted here by permission. Thanks are due to members of the Harvard Seminar on "Ethics, Values, and International Relations" for their helpful comments on an earlier draft.

In addition, an increasing number of scholars have been speculating on the new structures of global economy, polity, and culture under the rubrics of "postindustrial society" (Bell, 1973), "information economy and society" (Masuda, 1981; Porat, 1977), "post-Fordist, flexible accumulation" (Harvey, 1990), "communitarian democracy" (Etzioni, 1993; Tehranian, 1990), "late capitalism" (Mandel 1978), "disorganized capitalism" (Lash & Urry, 1987), "postmodernity" (Docherty, 1993), the "Third Wave" (Toffler, 1980), the "Fourth Discontinuity" (Mazlish 1993), and the "Sixth Modernization" (see later discussion). The *fin de siècle* has also led to an alarming cottage industry of publications on the 21st century, for example, Jacques Attali (1991), Paul Kennedy (1993), and Tehranian and Tehranian (1992).

This chapter offers a critique of the prevailing discourses of the new world order while presenting an alternative reading of the emerging dialectics of globalism and localism or what Robertson (1992, 1994) aptly calls "glocalization." It argues that because of the contradictions and ambiguity of the signals of transition, the discourse has swung from euphoric optimism to dark pessimism, from declarations of a global triumph of liberal-democratic capitalism to forebodings about a coming "clash of civilizations [between] the Christian West and an emerging Confucian-Islamic alliance" (Huntington, 1993a, p. 47). A succession of events has led us from promises to perils, from the end of the Cold War and some vain hopes for "peace dividends" in 1989, to the outbreak of the Gulf War in 1991, the dissolution of the Soviet Union in 1991, and the ensuing civil wars in the former Soviet Union and Yugoslavia, Somalia, and Haiti in 1992–93. Within a very short period of time, the new world order thus has appeared as dismayingly disorderly. Some authors (Singer & Widavsky, 1993) have argued that the real world order consists of "zones of peace" and "zones of turmoil." Although the zones of peace consist of a core of 64 advanced, industrial, liberal democratic countries, the zones of turmoil correspond to a multitude of nations in the rest of the world caught in the agonizing pains of modernization, democratization, or transition from communist to market economies. Although this bipolar division of the world corresponds more realistically to the political and economic realities of a divided world, developed and developing, it fails to account for the center-periphery implosions within each nation and explosions across borders.

The traditional geopolitical or spatial divisions of the world into East and West, North and South, First, Second, Third, and Fourth Worlds, or centers, peripheries, and semi-peripheries no longer ring true.[1] Territories have been deterritorialized. The flows of goods, services, ideas, news, images, and data have increasingly assumed a transnational charac-

---

[1] A new journal, *Public Culture*, has in fact devoted itself entirely to the examination of the transnational cultural flows that cut across such spatial cataegories (see "Editors' comments," 1988).

ter in a global economy and culture that values whatever is novel and affordable. Cheaper goods and novel ideas emerge perhaps as much from the traditional centers as from traditional peripheries. In the meantime, some centers have become peripherized (e.g. New York and Los Angeles slums), and some peripheries have assumed the status of industrial and financial centers (notably the four Asian tigers of South Korea, Singapore, Hong Kong, and Taiwan). This does not mean that a new reign of world democracy has dawned. On the contrary, hard evidence shows that the world has become more differentiated and fragmented along growing gaps in social and economic equality (Maitland, 1994; Tarjanne, 1994; United Nations Development Program (UNDP), 1992). However, the globalization of the world economy has brought about a new deterritorialized system of centers and peripheries based on the levels of science, technology, productivity, consumption, and creativity regardless of location. The new centers and peripheries now reside in transnational organizations and networks.

The dynamics of accelerating, uneven, and self-contradictory, global change can be therefore better understood in light of a longer historical process that is still unfinished. For want of a better terminology, that process may be called *modernization*. Although the term has accumulated a heavy baggage of theoretical biases with which we may not agree, it still continues to have analytic value. I use the concept here to mean a process of change that puts a primary value on scientific, technological, social, economic, political, and cultural innovations in order to achieve progressively higher levels of productivity, democratic participation, and cultural pluralism.

The Western Enlightenment project provides a prime historical example of such modernization, but its fundamental assumptions can be questioned without rejecting modernization as a discourse or practice. A modernization project need not be conditioned, for instance, on the infinite perfectibility of humans, nor on the absolute power of human reason, the need for the human domination of nature, the historical inevitability of progress, and the total rejection of tradition. On the contrary, successful modernization projects have often led to tradition in modernity, nurturing of nature, acceptance of the epistemological limits of human reason, and the recognition of the need for spiritual and mythological foundations in human communities.

Nevertheless, the forces of modernization have proven to be historically cataclysmic forces. They have torn societies asunder in successive acts of creative destruction. Since the 16th century, the project of modernity has gone through at least five phases, including a Fifth Modernization that currently appears to be the dominant trend. In the industrial centers of the world, the cultural resistances to its seemingly irresistible force has ranged from "demodernization" to "postmodernization" movements. In the agrarian and industrializing peripheries of the world, modernization has been largely imposed from above by the colonial masters or the postcolonial elites. It has been thus either zealously sought in "hypermodernization" campaigns to catch up or devoutly resisted in "countermodernization" movements.

If there is a new world order, therefore, it can be better understood in terms of the paradoxes of a situation in which we are increasingly witnessing dazzling technological and economic breakthroughs without corresponding social, political, and normative innovations. These epistemological lags are leading to economic growth without employment, political democratization without political efficacy, and cultural diversity without tolerance and civility. As Adam said to Eve, we are truly in an age of transition. In order to avoid the enormous risks facing us, the challenge lies perhaps in trying to bridge the widening chasms between the exploding technological opportunities and the currently unfulfilled human needs.

DECONSTRUCTING THE DISCOURSE

The discourse of the new world order is not so new. In a computerized search at the University of Hawaii, 125 items were retrieved, including books published around the two world wars, among them, Hitler's *My New Order* (1941). The roots of the discourse can be found in at least four major competing theories of international relations, namely Realism, Liberalism, Marxism, and Communitarianism.

The Realists have primarily focused on the geopolitics of the struggles for power, employed the nation-state as their chief unit of analysis, considered domestic and foreign policy as separate spheres of action, and argued that the pursuit of national interest in the context of a balance of power strategy is the safest and most "realistic" road to international peace and security. Realism is still perhaps the most dominant school of thought both in theory and practice focusing on "peace through national strength."

The Liberals (also known as the Idealists or Neo-Realists), by contrast, have pointed to the integrating forces of the world market as a new "reality" that has created considerable international interdependency in the postwar period. They have argued that increasing levels of free trade, development, and the deepening and broadening of interdependency are the surest path to peace.

The Marxists, although in decline politically, continue to present powerful theoretical arguments that have a great deal of appeal in the peripheries of the world. They view international relations primarily in terms of class relations within and between nations and argue that since the 16th century the advanced capitalist countries have increasingly incorporated the peripheries of the world into a world system of domination and exploitation through imperialism, colonialism, and neocolonialism. The social revolutions in Russia, China, Cuba, Vietnam, and other Third World countries have attempted to break away from the fetters of the world capitalist system. However, they are being reincorporated by an international regime orchestrated by the leading capitalist countries, the World Bank, International Monetary Fund, and the World Trade Organization. In the meantime, the Marxists argue, internal contradictions, wars, and revolutionary struggles will continue to erode the world system.

Finally, the Communitarian perspective has manifested itself in a variety of anticolonial, nationalist, tribalist, localist, ethnic, and religious forms focused on the mobilization of the common historical memories of the peripheries to wage a cultural and political struggle against the centers. The Communitarians thus emphasize the centrality of political community in creating the conditions for a durable peace at local, national, regional, and global levels.

Although each discourse has its own unique set of assumptions and conclusions, reflecting the competing interests in the international community, international communication has forced them into a grudging dialogue. This has resulted in a number of intertextual discourses conducted at international forums. Table 2.1 confines itself only to a genealogy of the more recent discourses and their metanarratives. It demonstrates how, like a chameleon, the slogan of the new world order has historically changed its colors. When a small group of oil exporting countries managed to quadruple the price of crude oil in 1973 through OPEC's collective action, it appeared for a while that the raw material exporting nations could now call for a new world order to redress the deteriorating terms of trade between the developed and developing countries. To the Group of 77 at the United Nations calling for a New World Economic Order in a 1974 General Assembly resolution, the new order meant a revamped international economic system to redress the terms of trade in favor of the less developed countries (LDCs). To UNESCO, which picked up the discourse in the 1970s and 1980s under the banner of a New World Information and Communication Order (NWICO), it meant balance as well as freedom in world news and information flows. The Brandt et al. (1980, 1985) and MacBride et al. (1980) Commission reports that emerged out of these efforts clearly set out those policy agendas.

Following the largely fruitless North–South negotiations of the 1980s, the discourse of the new order was resurrected by President Bush. To mobilize international support for a war effort against Saddam Hussein, Bush employed the slogan at the wake of the Persian Gulf War in 1990–91 with maximum effect. The discourse thus came to mean a new international regime of "law and order" under the aegis of the United Nations supported by the unanimity of the five permanent members of the Security Council. However, the brief consensus on the Gulf War came abruptly to

Table 2.1. The New World Order Discourses and Metanarratives: A Genealogy.

Dates	Labels	Proponents	Opponents
1. The Political Discourses:			
1974-84	New World Economic Order	Group of 77	G 7 led by US

The long-term deteriorating terms of trade between the industrial goods producing countries of the North and the raw material-producing countries of the South have systematically deprived the LDCs of their chances for self-sustaining development. To correct these inequities, a new world economic order is needed to redress the terms of trade by collective bargaining, to provide access for the LDCs to the MDCs markets, and to facilitate transfers of science and technology. Outcomes: the Brandt Report and North-South negotiations at UNCTAD.

1974-84	New World Information & Communication Order	Group of 77	G 7 led by US

The media concentration in the hands of a few transnational corporations from a few advanced industrial countries has created a severe imbalance in the flow of news, images, and data against the LDCs. The consequence of these imbalances is that the LDCs are often stereotyped as places where natural and man-made disasters are rampant. The genuine efforts of the LDCs for development are rarely noted. To correct these imbalances, a new world information and communication order (NWICO) is needed in which the free flow of information is matched by a greater balance. In addition to North-South cooperation, the North has an obligation to assist the LDCs to build up their information and telecommunication infrastructure. Outcomes: The MacBride Report and the establishment of the International Program for the Development of Communication (IPDC) at UNESCO.

1989-93	The New World Order	US & Gulf War Allies	Iraq & Sympathizers

The end of the Cold War has unleashed a variety of new threats to international peace and security by such small or medium powers as Iraq, Libya, Iran, North Korea, and Serbia. To counter this threat and to establish a new regime of international law and order, the Great Powers through the United Nations or independently should police the world by active intervention in situations of conflict. Outcomes: UN intervention in the Persian Gulf War, Somalia, Bosnia, and Haiti. The limited efficacy of such interventions has led to a decline of the discourse of "the New World Order."

WHERE IS THE NEW WORLD ORDER? 29

Table 2.1. The New World Order Discourses and Metanarratives: A Genealogy (con't).

Dates	Labels	Proponents	Opponents
2. The Academic & Policy Discourses:			
1945-present	Modernization Theories	Liberals	Marxists
	As exemplified by the historical experiences of the West, the transition from traditional to modern societies is an inevitable historical process. The LDCs can best succeed by emulating that experience. The best policies to pursue are breaking the traditional cultural barriers to progress, democratizing their polities, liberalizing their markets, and encouraging foreign trade and investment.		
1945-present	Dependency and World System Theories	Marxists	Liberals
	Capitalist penetration of the LDCs has progressively impoverished them materially and culturally, creating a dependency status for most. Some periphery nations such as Japan and S. Korea have escaped this fate by joining the ranks of capitalist nations in a world system primarily run by the transnational corporations. Others also may join the ranks, but the system of capitalist exploitation will continue until socialist revolutions can abolish the class system.		
1973-present	Postindustrial, Information Society Theories	Liberals	Marxists
	In the advanced industrial countries, a progressive shift from manufacturing to service and information sectors has ushered in a new postindustrial society in which the greatest percentage of the labor force is engaged in the production, processing, transmission, and application of knowledge and information. The resulting information economy and society is an international phenomenon facilitated by global transportation and telecommunication technologies. To catch up, the LDCs must follow a strategy of technological leapfrogging by the adoption of the latest industries and technologies.		

Table 2.1. The New World Order Discourses and Metanarratives: A Genealogy (con't.).

Dates	Labels	Proponents	Opponents
1989-present	End of History & Clash of Civilizations Theories	Fukuyama (1989) & Huntington (1993a, 1993b)	

The end of the Cold War, the collapse of the Soviet Union and Eastern European communist regimes, and the introduction of market economies in the remaining of the communist countries signals the global triumph of liberal, democratic capitalism. History as Hegel defined it to be the battlefield of ideas has thus come to an end. The rest will be devoted to the boring details of the global application of the liberal democratic capitalist principles. This process, however, is encountering some resistance from other incompatible civilizations. The next world war may be therefore a war of civilizations between the Christian West and an emerging Confucian-Islamic alliance.

| 1980s-present | Late Capitalism, Postmodernist Theories | | Marxists and Post-Marxists |

Late capitalism is exhibiting a number of features, including global expansion, flexible accumulation, deterritorialization, disorganization, and displacement with postmodern cultural consequences. The process may be viewed either as potentially emancipatory in the unfinished project of the Enlightenment (Habermas) or as a new stage in the development of capitalism in which deconstructionist and anti-narrative strategies are most effective in leaving power no place to hide (Foucault, 1980). Although the former strategy calls for a politics of meaning focused on creating alternative normative structures, the latter implies a politics of anti-politics.

an end by the continuing regime of Saddam Hussein in Iraq and the rise of the civil disorders in some republics of former Soviet Union and Yugoslavia, Somalia, and Haiti, where international dissension and brute force have continued to dominate.

Francis Fukuyama's (1989) essay on "The End of History" belongs to the early phase of post-Cold War optimism. "What we may be witnessing," he argued, "is not just the end of the Cold War, or the passing of a particular period of postwar history, but the End of History as such: that is, the end point of mankind's [sic] ideological evolution and the universalization of Western liberal, democracy as the final form of human government." The Hegelian notion of history as the battlefield of ideas, Fukuyama was proposing, has thus come to an end. All that is left to accomplish now is, according to him, the boring detail of working out the implementation of the liberal-democratic capitalist agenda throughout the world.

The proposition was reminiscent of what Daniel Bell (1960) had argued a generation earlier. Unfortunately for the prophetic merit of both predictions, Bell's (1960) *The End of Ideology* and Fukuyama's (1989) "The End of History" were published just before a new surge of ideological contestations on the world scene. The Cold Wars between the United States and Soviet Union, on the one hand, and between Soviet Union and China, on the other hand, characterized the 1960s. So did the countercultural movements in Europe and the United States. The 1990s are similarly characterized by the reemergence of secular nationalism and religious resurgence to fill the ideological vacuum left by the end of the Cold War. The lesson seems unambiguous. Ideological contestations are a perennial part of human conflict. So long as conflict continues, ideologies will persist in order to adorn material interests with moral legitimacy while providing new myths for social solidarity and action. To be effective, however, ideologies have to cast their own particular myths into universal narratives, hence, the narratives of "End of History" and "clash of civilization." Both these myths, as all myths, have clearly some grounds in "reality."

The "End of History" thesis points to the global expansion of the market economy and its liberal-democratic metanarrative. Huntington's "Clash of Civilizations" comes as the first phase of post-Cold War euphoria is giving way to a new phase of sober realism and even Hobbesian pessimism. He is appropriately skeptical of the triumph of liberal democracy. He ominously forecasts, however, that "the clash of civilizations will dominate global politics. The fault lines between civilizations will be the battle lines of the future. The most prominent form of this cooperation is the Confucian-Islamic connection that has emerged to challenge Western interests, values and power." (p. 22) The religious resurgence in the Judaic, Christian, Islamic, Hindu, and Buddhist traditions, and the increasing economic and political cooperation between East Asian and Islamic countries, provide Huntington's thesis with some plausibility. However, to frame the complex and continuing gaps and conflicts of interests between the deterritorialized centers and peripheries in strictly geopolitical terms is one-dimensional, simplistic, and misleading. It may also serve as a justification for launching another Crusade, notwithstanding Huntington's call for peaceful coexistence. We define our worlds, and our worlds define us.

If the articles by Fukuyama and Huntington were simple expressions of the optimistic and pessimistic temperaments of two solo scholars, there should have been no cause for concern. However, both articles have been celebrated by the U. S. foreign policy establishment (e.g., the Council on Foreign Relations and its quarterly, *Foreign Affairs*; the U.S. Institute of Peace; and a number of conservative, private think-tanks) as major intellectual breakthroughs in defining the post-Cold War era. Although Fukuyama's essay became the focus of much media attention in 1989–90 (Tehranian, 1989), the editors of *Foreign Affairs* compared the significance of Huntington's essay to another article published in that journal in 1945 by a Mr. X (George Kennan). The latter had defined and shaped U.S. policies in the Cold War for the next 45 years. Just as Kennan's proposed "containment" policy hardened the U.S. position vis-á-vis the Soviet Union in the Cold War years, the Fukuyama and Huntington articles seem to propose a U.S. hardening toward China and the Islamic world. The two articles serve several complementary functions. They fill the ideological vacuum left by the decline of communism by identifying a new ideological "enemy." Although Fukuyama argues that the triumph of liberal democratic capitalism is inevitable, Huntington suggests that some residual resistance is still left (Chinese tyranny, Islamic bigotry) against that progressive movement of history.

The academic discourse on the postindustrial, postmodern, post-Fordist, information society has been equally controversial. The optimists and pessimists have similarly dominated the field. Even though liberal analysts such as Daniel Bell, Mark Porat, and Yoneji Masuda provide generally optimistic scenarios, the Marxist world system theorists (e.g., Wallerstein, 1974) present a rather pessimistic view of the emerging world order. At issue is the fate of the peripheries of power, whether situated in the urban ghettoes of the First World or in the rural hinterlands of the Third World. Although the optimists argue that a new phase of "postindustrial, information society " will eventually "trickle down" its benefits to the lower income groups, the Marxists point to the structural impediments that will keep certain regions, societies, and sectors of population perennially underdeveloped (So, 1990).

In the cultural arena, however, the left has become divided between the old and the new left. Although the old left scholars tend to argue that the media conglomerates are homogenizing national cultures into the expanding global capitalist channels of consumer desires (Ewen & Ewen, 1982; Hamelink, 1983; Mattleart, 1983; Schiller, 1976), the new left points to the increasing participation of the peripheries in a global, multicultural, postmodernist pastiche of migrating meanings and identities. To capture the fluidity and irregularity of such transnational exchanges, Appadurai (1990, 1993) has suggested a number of channels, including "ethnoscapes, mediascapes, technoscapes, finanscapes, ideoscapes." In the cultural arena, whereas the old left points to the narrowing of the public sphere of discourse (Habermas, 1983), the new left suggests that power is everywhere to be seized by the deconstructive guerrilla tactics of postmodernism (Foucault, 1980). Although the old left recommends a new politics of meaning focused on creating "ideal speech communities" and "alternative normative structures" (Habermas, 1983), the new left calls for a deconstructive politics of anti-politics (Foucault, 1980).

MAPPING THE NEW WORLD DIS/ORDER

The new world order may be usefully viewed as a new phase in the progressive spatializations of power, that is, as a succession of conquests of space by time (Soja, 1989). If we define modernization as the processes of compression of time and space to achieve progressively higher levels of productivity, the process has now reached nearly all corners of the globe. Time-saving (labor-saving) production techniques (assemblyline, robotics) and space-shrinking technologies (in modern transportation and telecommunication) have diffused modern ideas, technologies, and organizations from the European centers to the rest of the world.

It is appropriate, therefore, to situate the problems of world conflict in the global processes of modernization and democratization that, since the 16th century, have led to growing material and cultural gaps between the centers and peripheries of power. Table 2.2 provides a schematic outline of seven interlocking phases in modernization as experienced by the advanced industrial world. Capitalism initially started with the spatial integration of the modern mercantile cities moving successively on to the nation-state, imperial, global, and increasingly planetary and cyberspatial systems. This and subsequent tables are offered here as statements of the problems brought on by international conflict and communication in the postCold War era. Some of the tables have been more extensively discussed elsewhere (K. Tehranian, 1995; M. Tehranian, 1993a; Tehranian & Tehranian, 1992), but the current phase of modernization and democratization calls for further elaboration here.

Thus viewed, the processes of modernization can no longer be seen as a uniquely European phenomenon, as argued by an earlier generation of modernization theorists. Despite its dramatic results in modern Europe, modernization would also not be considered as an abrupt change in the course of history. History crawls more than it leaps; it evolves rather

Table 2.2. Seven Modernizations and Democratizations: Tidal Waves or Tsunamis in Human History.

Times	Spaces	Economies	Polities	Technologies	Ideologies	Communications
1) 8000 BC –1492 AD	Agrarian Empires	Agrarian Revolution & Multi-National, Bureaucratic Empires;	Feudal Fiefdoms Democratization I: Direct Democracy & Religious Revolutions	Transmission of Information: writing, ploughing, clay tablets, papyrus, roads, postal systems	Anticipatory Modernization: Rationalism vs. Shamanism & Religious Dogmatism	Oral & written: Shamans, Soothsayers, Poets, Prophets Priests, Temples
2) 1492-1648	City-states	Commercial Revolution (aka Mercantile Capitalism)	Rise of City-states; Democratization II: Protestant Reformation & Scientific Revolution	Mechanization of Information: Print, Compass, Oceanfaring ships	Mercantilism vs. Feudalism	Print: Intellectuals, Scientists, Universities
3) 1648-1848	Nation-States	Industrial Revolution (aka Manufacturing Capitalism)	Rise of Nation-States & Colonial Empires; Democratization III: Liberal Democratic Revolutions	Mass Production of Information: Newspapers, Magazines, Books Steam ships, Trains	Liberal Nationalism vs. Monarchical Absolutism	Elite Media: Publicists
4) 1848-1945	Industrial Empires	Banking Revolution (aka Finance Capitalism)	Multipolar World System Democratization IV: Social Democratic & Totalitarian Revolutions	Electrification of Information: Telegraphy, Telephony, Photography, Film, Radio Automobile, Airplane Paper money & banking	Imperialism vs. National Liberation Ideologies	Mass Media: Ideologues
5) 1945-1989	Planet	Managerial Revolution (aka Corporate Capitalism vs. State Capitalism/ Communism)	Bipolar World System Democratization V: National Liberation Revolutions	Digitalization of Information: TV, Computers, Satellites, Transborder Data Flows, Electronic Cash Transfers, Atomic Energy, Space Probes	Globalism (Capitalism vs. Communism) vs. Nationalism	Big/SmallMedia: Technologues vs. Communologues
6) 1989 -present	Cyberspace	Information Revolution (aka Technocratic Capitalism	Multipolar World System & Democratization VI: Localist, Ethnic, Religious, Feminist Revolts	Integration of Information: ISDN & Multimedia DBS, Global Networks (CNN, MTV, Internet)	Ecumenicalism vs. Fundamentalism	Cybermedia: Technologues, Communologues vs. Jestologues
7) Futures	Hyperspace	Space Revolution. (Communitarian vs. Totalitarian Capitalism)	Cyborg Planetary System Democratization VII: Underclass Revolts against Dehumanization	Totalization of Information: Timetravel, Cyborgs, Genetic Engineering, Spaceships & voyages	Totalism vs. Communitarianism	Hypermedia: Shamans, Soothsayers, Visuologues

than makes discrete departures from the past. Modernization should be more properly viewed as an accumulative process of accelerating change achieved by successive applications of scientific and technological knowledge. The pace of that change has historically gained an exponential momentum.

Table 2.2 provides an overview of the accelerations of time, space, and identities achieved by seven successive waves or tsunamis of modernization in the course of a long history. The "wave" or "tsunami" metaphor is perhaps more apt than stages or phases that tend to suggest a kind of discreteness. Tsunamis are caused by earthquakes at the floor of the oceans; they create great cataclysms underneath until they reach the surface, in which case they are utterly devastating to the shorelines. They travel far distances, go back and forth, ebb and flow, and collide on the surfaces of the oceans, while the immensity of the water (in this case, the ocean of human history) remains relatively immutable and constant.

The table draws attention to the dates, spatial loci, economic systems, technologies, and ideologies of modernization in each successive wave. It reveals three distinctly different phenomena. First, time accelerates with each new tsunami leading to progressively shorter intervals. The additive quality of scientific and technological knowledge, and its accelerating effects on change, might possibly explain this phenomenon. Second, space also is compressed with the passage of each tsunami. Thus, modernization incorporates progressively larger spatial domains within its grasp, from the countryside, to the cities, nation-states, empires, globe, cyberspace, and the universe. Third, accelerating time and space lead on to the conjunctures of times, spaces, and identities. In this light, history is more usefully thought of as multilinear and conjunctural than linear and discontinuous. As tsunamis collide on the surface of the ocean, so do civilizations and cultures. They borrow, steal, and adapt elements from their friends and enemies in order to advance their own cause. That is how an uneven world such as ours survives, adapts, and moves forward and backward. An African village could juxtapose some of the signs of premodern, modern, and postmodern lives in a single space, encompassing the plough, the automobile, Coca Cola, and Madonna's pictures and songs.

Sometime around 8000 B.C., a transition from hunting and gathering to agrarian societies must have occurred (Frankfort, 1964). That transition clearly required a higher order of complexity and organization. To tame the land, domestication of animals and invention of agricultural tools were necessary. To assert the rights of individual or collective ownership to land and its fruits, accounting systems were required. Writing and numerology assisted in this process, but to record and transmit such information, the clay tablets and papyrus came into play. Roads and postal systems were built to facilitate market exchange and central government control. However, agrarian societies could not possibly survive without an ideological apparatus of rationalism in which the subject and object were distantiated in the human mind (Frankfort, 1964). That, in turn, facilitated the growth of empirical science and technological innovation. Transmission of information through writing and libraries in such places as Alexandria in ancient Egypt and Gundishapur in ancient Iran became the indispensable tools of knowledge storage and retrieval for successive generations. Despite the enormous diversity of agrarian societies, for the purpose of simplicity, we may consider this long wave of human evolution as the first anticipatory modernization lasting some 10,000 years.

A second wave of modernization began to set in the Western European scene by the 16th century. The important historical watersheds in this tsunami are the Reformation and the Renaissance. Beginning with Martin Luther's posting of 95 theses on the church door at Wittenberg, in 1517, the Protestant revolt against the Catholic Church signaled a religious war that continued through the end of the Thirty-Year War and the Peace of Westphalia in 1648. The Reformation took many different forms in Europe, but its Protestant ethics of frugality, hard work, savings, and investment clearly ushered in a new spirit of capitalism (Weber, 1958; Tawney, 1984). Similarly, the Renaissance lasting from 14th to mid-17th century introduced a new spirit of humanism in arts and letters, scientific exploration, and commerce.

However, the second tsunami of modernization clearly owed its material force to the rise of modern mercantile cities in which the seeds of modern capitalism were sown by the monetization and commercialization of the European economies. Urbanization during the Middle Ages was a very slow process, but it created large cities such as Venice, Florence, Amsterdam, Lisbon, Barcelona, London, and Paris, serving as the centers of a new urbanism. Although large cities were characteristic of the ancient Asian and African civilizations, the new European cities were markedly different in that they enjoyed some measure of municipal autonomy. Whereas Rome, Constantinople, Baghdad, Cairo, Isfahan, Delhi, Beijing, and Timbuktu served as the urban centers of multinational, agrarian empires, the new European cities were breaking from the agrarian past into a new era of mercantile capitalism. The Crusades during the 11th through 13th centuries, technological breakthroughs in ocean transportation, the discovery of the New World in the late 15th century, the flow of newly discovered gold from the New World to the Old World, the scientific revolution of the 17th century, the rise of manufacturing in the new towns, the Enlightenment in the 18th century, and the political revolutions of the 18th and 19th centuries contributed to a transfer of economic and political power from the feudal lords and manors to a new class of merchants in the new mercantile towns and cities under a new capitalist order. Heilbroner (1962) has aptly summarized the process:

> When the travelling merchants stopped, they naturally chose the protected site of a local castle or burg. And we find growing up around the walls of advantageously situated castles—in the focus burgis, whence faubourg, the French word for "suburb"—more or less permanent trading places, which in turn became the inner core of small towns. Nestled close to the castle wall for protection, the new burgs were still not "of" the manor. The inhabitants of the burg—the burgesses, burghers, bourgeois—had at best an anomalous and insecure relation to the manorial world within. As we have seen, there was no way of applying the time-hallowed rule of "ancient customs" in adjudicating their disputes, since there were no ancient customs in the commercial quarters. Neither were there clear-cut rules for their taxation or for the particular degrees of fealty they owed their local masters. Worse yet, some of the growing towns began to surround themselves with walls. By the twelfth century, the commercial burg of Bruges, for example, had already swallowed up the old fortress like a pearl around a grain of sand. (p. 48)

Whereas in the first phase of modernization it was often the countryside that controlled the cities in the form of land-owning feudal aristocracies or tribal invasions, the growth of modern cities signaled a reversal of that role. In fact, the new city's superior technological and organizational abilities for accumulation of capital led, in turn, to a third modernization—the rise of the nation-state system. It is customary to consider the Peace of Westphalia as the beginning of the modern nation-state system. As an island "nation," England led the way in this process, demonstrating, in effect, the advantages of the nation-state as a new form of political and spatial organization. The ideology of the new political-spatial entity was Nationalism; its religion was a national church such as the Church of England and other Protestant churches declaring their independence from the Papacy; its language was no longer Latin, but instead the vernacular languages such as English, French, German, and Italian; its ethos became "the Protestant ethics," which, as Max Weber (1958) argued, emboldened "the spirit of capitalism" toward hard work, frugality, saving, and investment.

Although the Catholic countries (France, Italy, and Spain) did not break away from Rome, they too came increasingly under the impact of a nationalism that fostered the secular spirits of rationality, science, and technology. In comparison to the imperial or city states of the past, the nation-state system clearly supplied a far more homogeneous population, greater defensible natural boundaries, economies of scale, and superior social and political opportunities for mobilizing the population on national missions of consolidation and expansion. The United States was the "first nation" (Lipset, 1963) to come about through a written constitution, demonstrating how the creation of a nation could be realized more through solidarity of ideas than ties of blood. Following the U.S. example, the construction of the nation-state system reached its fruition in Europe during the 19th century with the unifications of the German and Italian states into two new nation-state systems. The system received further impetus following World War I with the breakdown of the Ottoman, Austro-Hungarian, and Russian Empires and the emergence of new nation-states in the Balkans and the Arab world. World War II extended the system to Asia, Africa, and Latin America through the breakdown of the European imperial systems. In 1991, the breakdown of the world's last empire, the Soviet Union, led to a further proliferation of the nation-states.

As old empires were collapsing, however, a new imperialism was being born in the 19th century that may be considered as the Third Modernization. As Hobson (1902/1938) and Lenin (1917/1969) first recognized, the new imperialism was materially different from all empires of the past. It was built on the foundations of the new capitalist order and driven by the search for new sources of raw materials, cheap labor, and consumer markets. Flag followed trade rather than the other way around. Military conquest served only as the last resort for opening up new territories for capitalist exploitation. The shifts from small-scale, entrepreneurial capitalism to large-scale, corporate capitalism, and from manufacturing domination to the supremacy of finance capital, all happening in the second half of the 19th century (Trachtenberg, 1982), made the growth of the new empires both possible and, from a capitalist view, desirable. The two world wars of the 20th century could be, in fact, viewed as the struggles, in the imperialist game, between the old players (England, France, and Russia) and the new players (Japan, Germany, Italy, and the United States).

The Fourth Modernization may be considered to begin with the rise of globalism at the conclusion of World War II in 1945. With the rise of the national liberation movements in the Third World (i.e., the developing countries) and the establishment of the United Nations on the basis of the principle of national self-determination, the old European empires could no longer endure as a viable form of political-spatial organization. As a former colony itself and a new superpower, the United States was well poised to lead the way toward a new principle of globalism. The Bretton Woods Agreements provided the economic basis for such a global capitalist system by creating a World Bank to channel investments from the more to the less developed countries, an International Monetary Fund (IMF) to manage the international currency exchange convertibility, and the General Agreement on Tariffs and Trade (GATT) to encourage world trade by reducing the tariff and nontariff barriers. The United Nations was to provide the political basis for a global economic system through collective security guaranteed by the five permanent members of the Security Council. However, the unanimity needed for such a system to operate broke down with the onset of the Cold War in 1947. The wars in Korea and Vietnam further undermined the principles of globalism by pitting the

First World (i.e., the capitalist countries) against the Second World (i.e., the Communist countries) and the revolutionary parts of the Third World. Nevertheless, globalism continued its irresistible growth through the "global reach" (Barnet & Muller, 1974) of the transnational corporations (TNCs). In their search for new sources of raw material, consumer markets, investment opportunities, low taxes, low rents, low wages, and low government control, the TNCs have devised global strategies that ensure them centralized control but spatial and managerial dispersion. Globalism has also been further strengthened by the reach of global advertising and the culture of mass consumption that it fosters. The seductions of the "soft power" of cultural appeal have proved as powerful as the "hard power" of military might and economic gravity.

The emergence of postmodern architecture and city planning in reaction to the dogmas of modern architecture and urban design may be viewed as part of the transition from the Fourth to the Fifth Modernization. The universalism of the modern international style was challenged by the eclecticism and pastiche quality of postmodern architecture. The utopian cities of the modern world have been similarly giving their place to the "collage cities" of the postmodern world (Rowe & Koetter, 1992). Rejecting the grand utopian visions of total planning and total design, the postmodernists are calling for an eclectic city of many faces and neighborhoods that can accommodate a whole range of utopias in miniature. Postmodernist cultural trends have similarly challenged the metanarratives of modernist culture. Exposure to the diversity of global cultures has challenged the foundations of globalism as an ideology of modernity. It has decentered its universalist claims of the Enlightenment project and created a new sense of cultural relativism. It has also juxtaposed localist cultures and practices alongside the global artifacts of skyscrapers, McDonalds, Coca Cola, and Hilton Hotels. The tension between the global and the local is thus a central political and cultural feature of the Fifth Modernization.

With the demise of the Soviet Union and the more gradual slippage of China into the vortex of world capitalism, globalism seems more irresistible in the 1990s than ever before. However, there are several sources of resistance to its hegemony that deserve careful notice. Nationalism is still a force to be reckoned with. It continues to provide the primary and irreducible principle of spatial-political organization in the world for some 200 recognized states, and holds the promise for hundreds of stateless nationalities in search of political and spatial recognition. Regionalism provides another source of resistance to globalism, which may or may not co-exist with it. Regional organizations such as the European Union (EU), the Association of Southeast Asian Nations (ASEAN), the North American Free Trade Area (NAFTA), and the Asia-Pacific Economic Cooperation (APEC) present actual and potential trading blocs that could turn into fortresses if and when the global system breaks down through economic or political crises. Localism within each large nation-state such as the United States, Russia, India, China, or Brazil also presents sources of resistance to the global hegemony of a capitalist order. Last but not least, Religious Revivalism, in the form of a variety of fundamentalist movements, could disrupt the rule of capital in important parts of the world. The fundamental problem is that although capitalism has unleashed immense productive possibilities in the modern world, it has also created enormous as well as growing disparities among and within nations. The rule of capital has therefore led to prosperity for the privileged sectors of the population but not to peace and justice. The global capitalist system, though ever growing and gaining, continues to be vulnerable.

The vulnerability of global capital is best demonstrated in the dual effects of its technologies in transportation and telecommunication. The new spaces of modernization are the airlanes of modern jet transportation and the cyberspace of modern telecommunication. Both of these technologies have increasingly blared the conventional distinctions between global and local. As the events in the Persian Gulf, Somalia, and Bosnia have demonstrated in recent years, the global conflicts are often localized, and the local conflicts are as often globalized. Similarly, domination and resistance are simultaneously assuming global and local dimensions. The Iranian Revolution, the Iran–Iraq war, the Persian Gulf War, and the bomb explosion at the New York World Trade Center cannot be understood except in terms of an analysis that takes both global and local issues of conflict into account.

The modern and postmodern cities have become the locus of these global–local conflicts. As the greatest symbol and achievement of global capitalism, the city is facing a crisis from within. To understand the roots of the crisis, it is necessary to look both forward and backwards. In the United States, the seeds of the contemporary urban crisis were sown at the turn of the century when the modern capitalist city turned a new corner, from an entrepreneurial to a corporate center, from laissez faire to planning and regulation, and from cultural homogeneity to heterogeneity. Its spatial organization had to accommodate all of these transitions.

Modernization and democratization may be thus viewed as dialectical processes in which the requirements of economic accumulation and political participation are competing for resources (Tehranian, 1990, ch. 9). In the early stages of primitive accumulation, the need for high levels of national savings and investment tend to lead to monopoly capitalism or centralized state planning. This is even more true of the late-comers to industrialization such as Japan, Soviet Union, China, or the two Koreas. In order to catch up, levels of national savings have reached as high as 30% in these countries as compared to the 5%–10% of GDP in the more leisurely pace of economic growth of Western European and North American countries. Sooner or later, however, modernization leads to demands for political participation by those sectors of the population that have been denied increases in their wages. At this stage, the State can choose to democratize and raise wages or repress its citizens. Following long periods of keeping wages down by repressive regimes, the Soviet Union, China, Singapore, Taiwan, and South Korea are currently undergoing such processes of democratization. Conversely, in the face of a mobilized population, democratization can take place without modernization. Many of the LDCs in their postindependence phase of development faced such a dilemma. When resources are meager, the State can be both regressive and repressive, resulting in failures of both modernization and democratization. A more balanced approach to modernization can accommodate the progressive needs for democratization with the requirements of modernization by lowering expectations and leveling incomes, while increasing national savings and investment. Freedoms of speech, assembly, and organization, to the extent that they exist, provide a public sphere of discourse in which the conflicting demands for resources are negotiated and mediated democratically. Table 2.3 provides a few historical examples of modernization with or without democratization.

Typically, however, the course of modernization is characterized by historical cycles from high accumulation to high mobilization. The development of democratic institutions reduces the severity of the cycles by allowing feedback mechanisms to correct the excesses of income inequalities that inevitably occur in the course of capital accumulation. In other words, communicative rationality and public discourse integrate society along more consensual patterns of progress.

A greater problem facing the LDCs is that the more developed world does not wait for them to catch up. Through global communication and advertising, it exposes them to rising political and economic expectations while introducing them to opportunities for production (technological) as well as consumption leapfrogging. As Table 2.4 shows, the modern industrial system has evolved into a succession of different types of capitalism, including the variety known as "Communism" or "State capitalism." Communism or State capitalism has been most likely an appropriate social and economic formation in the early stages of primitive accumulation when lack of infrastructural facilities, heavy capital requirements, and imperfections of the market often called for State planning and investment. However, as economic development reaches higher levels of accumulation and consumption, the complexity of the decisions needed to be made call for a market orientation. The interplay of the forces of supply and demand in the market is far more effective in making the increasingly complex investment and consumption decisions. Moreover, the postwar rise of transnational corporations has facilitated the transfer of science, technology, capital, and management techniques to the less developed areas of the

Table 2.3. Modernization and Democratization: Tradeoffs and Standoffs.

Modernization w/Democratization	Modernization w/o Democratization	Democratization w/o Modernization	No Modernization No Democratization
North America	South Africa	India	Haiti
Western Europe	Soviet Union	Zambia	Somalia
Japan	China	Sri Lanka	Burma
Australia	Cuba	Costa Rica	
New Zealand	Vietnam		
	North Korea		
	Iran		
	Iraq		
	Egypt		
	Algeria		

Table 2.4. A Typology of Emerging Capitalisms: Modes of Production, Regulation, Communication, and Urbanization.

Types of Capitalism	Fordist	Technocratic	Communitarian
Production (Economy)	economies of scale assembly line mass homogeneity Operational manag't big firms goods planned obsolescence mechanical technology long-term employment	economies of scope batch production Taylored heterogeneity strategic manag't medium firms services planned disposability electronic technology short-term employment	economies of status communal work custom-made production community management small firms knowledge/information/signs planned durability indigenous technology life-term employment
Regulation (Polity)	class politics state power monetary and fiscal centralization universal rules	status politics financial power deregulation partial decentralization technical rules	charismatic politics community power re-regulation decentralization indigenous rules
Communication (Culture)	print Ideologues broadcasting clock, map nationalism practical rationality	electronic Technologues narrowcasting computer cosmopolitanism instrumental rationality	multimedia, virtual Jestologues & Communologues interactive-casting MTV, Disney World localism communicative rationality

Table 2.4. A Typology of Emerging Capitalisms: Modes of Production, Regulation, Communication, and Urbanization (con't).

	public vs. private partial surveillance reality orientation	network total surveillance image orientation	connection community surveillance community orientation
Urbanization (City)	urbanization public housing urban renewal form is function internationalism space	suburbanization homelessness urban ghettoization form is fiction eclecticism place	urban dispersion community housing urban revitalization form is meaning vernacular localism community

Source: Adapted from K. Tehranian (1995)

world. No planning commission or Soviet Gosplan can take the place of the numerous investors, producers, and consumers that run a modern, complex, industrial economy. As demonstrated by the rise of market economies in the socialist (i.e., State-capitalist) countries, there is reason to believe that capitalism will continue its evolution and adaptation to new economic, sociocultural, and environmental circumstances. As the latest purchase of a majority share by the United Airlines employers suggests, capitalism may even gradually evolve into a workers' or communitarian capitalism.

The demise of the Soviet Union and the growth of market economies in China, Vietnam, and Cuba may be viewed as continuing efforts in modernization, but democratization is not a necessary outcome. Witness the continuing repression in China and the recent electoral victories of the right in Russia, Germany, France, and Italy. Similarly, the rise of religious ideologies has demonstrated that the processes of modernization are replete with many twists and turns, including the possibility of theocracies that may become themselves carriers of modernization (Juergensmeyer, 1993; Marty & Appleby, 1991, 1992, 1993; Tehranian, 1993b). Contrary to the prevailing interpretations of "fundamentalism" that see it as a reaction against modernization, the current religious resurgence may be alternatively considered as disguised forms of modernization movements to mobilize deeply dislocated, traditional societies. After all, that was what the Reformation and its Protestant offshoots accomplished for the Christian West. What form will modernization take in the future perhaps depends less on the inherent, cosmological features of conflicting civilizations and more on the economic, political, and cultural relations among the world centers and peripheries of power.

The prevailing patterns are full of contradictions. Globalization of the world economy is transforming the major urban centers of the world into a deterritorialized core of technocratic capitalism of corporate and financial headquarters. The semiperipheries (the emerging middle classes) are clamoring for political democracy (in China, South Korea, Taiwan, Latin America). The peripheries are resorting to the primordial, tribal identities of language (India), religion (fundamentalism), race (Africa, the United States), ethnicity (old and new imaginaries), and gender (women) to regain the lost grounds and press for human rights. The neotribalist politics can be and often is intolerant and totalitarian in orientation, but to blame the symptoms without considering the root causes is neither theoretically correct nor practically wise.

The ideological choices of the Sixth and Seventh Modernizations are therefore between dialogue versus clash of civilizations, ecumenicalism versus fundamentalism, communitarian versus totalitarian capitalism, viewing the Planet Earth as a single unified organic system (the Gaia hypothesis) or as a set of clashing civilizations, religions, regional blocs, or warring nations seeking domination. Table 2.4 provides a schematic view of a possible evolutionary process from Fordist to Technocratic and Communitarian forms of capitalism. The table focuses on the main features of production in the economic sphere, regulation in the political sphere, communication in the cultural sphere, and urbanization in the patterns of spatial settlement. Two caveats are in order. First, the distinctions proposed here are of the Weberian "ideal-type" variety and for heuristic purposes only. Moreover, they do not represent any stage theory. As a result, some of the features outlined are more potential than actual, particularly in the case of communitarian capitalism, which might be struggling to be born in some parts of the world by the creation of employee-owned stock companies competing in the national and international markets. Second, the associations suggested are not proof of historical causation. In a typical postmodernist fashion, any system could co-opt the features of the others and juxtapose them with its own. Thus, the homogenization and "Coca-Colanization" of the world is taking place alongside the rise of religious fundamentalisms. Tribalization of politics in the peripheries is taking place partly in reaction to the transnationalization of the economy at the centers (Tehranian, 1990, ch. 1). In the meantime, the material and cultural trappings of modernity such as Holiday Inns, McDonalds, Madonna, Michael Jackson, MTV, CNN, and the Internet are paving the way for a global economy and culture alongside the indigenous economics and cultures.

In its current post-Cold War phase, however, global capitalism is facing severe challenges in the rise of religious revivalisms, regionalisms (EU, NAFTA, ASEAN, ECO, APEC),[3] nationalisms, and localisms (Tehranian, 1993a). These reactions to modernization have historically expressed themselves in a variety of ideological and political movements that may be called hypermodernization, countermodernization, demodernization, and postmodernization. Table 2.5 provides a schematic view of the main features of each reaction, focusing on the stage in the developmental process, the main ideological manifestations, and the best known examples of each in modern history.

The lesson of Table 2.5 is clear without much elaboration. We live in a very uneven world that promises to become even more so in the 21st century (Attali, 1991). The bitter fruits of the growing gaps in the world seem to promise less peace and more violence, less tranquillity and more tension. One of the emerging forms of conflict might be what Huntington

---

[3]The alphabet soup stands for European Union, North American Free Trade Agreement, Association of South East Asian Nations, Economic Cooperation Organization, and Asia-Pacific Economic Cooperation, respectively.

(1993a, 1993b) has called "the clash of civilizations." However, as noted earlier, his ideological casting of the problem is also a recipe for a self-fulfilling prophecy. The encounter of the materially uneven worlds can lead to clashes of cultures and civilizations unless new strategies of modernization are adopted to reduce the gaps and provide bridges of trade, cooperation, dialogue, and understanding. Civilizations are epistemological and knowledge systems. When two civilizations interact, they often develop a third civilization, culture, epistemology, and knowledge system. Out of the worldwide confluence of civilizations, we are developing a global civilization alongside the old regional civilizations as well as national and local cultures. Dialogue is therefore the key to a successful development of a universal, human civilization in whose idiom we all need to speak in order to understand the national and local in the rich variety of human subcultures.

National and global policies can therefore mitigate or exacerbate, regulate or unleash, prolong or resolve conflicts. In this light, modernization and democratization may usefully be viewed as contradictory top-down and bottom-up processes mediated through communication channels. Because all three processes have been significantly transnationalized, Table 2.6 provides a schematic view of the global policy formations with respect to each. The table is based on the following premises: that power is ubiquitous, that even the most powerless have the power to resist, that hegemonic power is never absolute, and that it always has to negotiate with, adjust to, and incorporate the interests of the effective oppositions. The table presents public communication channels as the arena for such mediation and policy negotiations. Broadening the base of global governance and democratization of communication thus go hand in hand.

Reforming global governance may usefully focus on the structures and processes of international relations. The structures of the international system consist of the states, intergovernmental organizations (IGOs), and at least four increasingly powerful non-State actors, including transnational corporations (TNCs), nongovernmental organizations (NGOs), unrepresented nations and peoples organizations (UNPOs), and transnational media organizations (TMCs). The processes of international relations may be viewed in terms of the problems of conflict regulation, conflict management, and conflict resolution. These involve such processes as exchange (trade agreements), negotiation (diplomacy), adjudication, arbitration, mediation, public mis/communication, and violent and nonviolent struggles.

GLOBALIZING THE LOCAL, LOCALIZING THE GLOBAL

A dual process of globalization of the local and localization of the global has thus made isolationism and dissociation virtually impossible for any

Table 2.5. The Periphery's Reactions to Modernization.

	Stage in Development	Ideological Manifestations	Examples
Hypermodernization	Postindependence Postrevolution	Nationalism, Communism, Fascism Crash programs of industrialization to catch up	Russia's Gosplans China's Great Leap Forward. Iran's White Revolution, Hitler's Third Reich
Countermodernization	Early stages of industrialization, Critiques of Industrialism	Romanticism (Rousseau Effect), Transcendentalism (Thoreau Effect), Pacifism-Ruralism (Gandhi Effect)	Russian Narodniks, Jeffersonian Democracy, Gandhian Philosophy
Demodernization	Late-industrial Stage, De-industrialization	Naturalism, Pacifism of the 1960s, Dismantling of the industrial apparatus, Weakening of work ethics, Return to nature	The Flower Revolution, New Ageism
Postmodernization	Postindustrial Stage, Robotics, CAD-CAM, shift from manufacturing to services and knowledge industries	Postmodernism, Relativism, Nihilism	Postmodern Angst of the First World vs. Hypermodernism of the Third World

Table 2.6. The Global Policy Formation Process: A Schematic View.

Resources	Problem Definition	Policy Formulation	Policy Legislation	Policy Legitimation	Policy Implementation, Regulation, Adjudication, & Evaluation
Top-Down Process: Generated by the Interests and policies of the Great Powers and Transnational Corporations					
Natural, Technological, and Human Resources	Think tanks, foundations & commissions, e.g., Rand, Rockefeller, & Trilateral Commission	Great Powers & Transnational Corps, e.g., G 7 + Russia & China, Esso, AT&T, Brit. Telecom, Mitsubishi	National Legislatures & Intergovernmental Organizations (IGOs)	Politicians, publicists, press, & broadcasting	TNCs, IGOs, national govt agencies, regulatory commissions, & the courts
Mediation: Generated by the media constructions of reality and discourses in response to governments & oppositions					
Global Telecom Networks	Global elite press, e.g., International Herald Tribune, Wall St. J., The Economist	Media owners & editors	National media laws, & international covenants on copyright, spectrum & orbit allocation, technical standards	Global media networks, e.g. elite press, CNN, news agencies	Media Associations, e.g., Int. Press Inst., Int. Publishers Ass.
Bottom-Up Process: Generated by the small & medium powers, revolutionary & opposition parties & associations					
Human, Natural, & Technological Resources	Revolutionary movts, NGOs, and related foundations, think tanks, & civil and religious networks, e.g. Amnesty International, World Council of Churches, etc.	Small-medium powers & global lobby groups, e.g., G 77, Physicians for Social Responsibility, American Friends Service Committee, Greenpeace etc.	States in exile, revolutionary movts, e.g., PLO, Tibet govt-in-exile, Unrepresented Peoples Org (UNPO), etc.	The alternative & underground media; the informal networks of gossip, rumor, civic, religious associations	Voluntary associations, labor unions, religious institutions, out of power political parties.

nation—even those that devoutly attempted it for a while such as China, Saudi Arabia, Burma, and Iran. Although globalization is fundamentally a top-down process, localization is a bottom-up one. The agents of transnationalization consist of the global hard and soft networks primarily facilitated by the non-State actors. The hard networks consist of transportation, telecommunication, and tourism (TTT) facilities spun around the globe connecting the core in networks of communication. The soft networks provide the programs that negotiate and integrate the competing interests and values of the global players. These include global broadcasting, advertising, education, and exchanges of information. In the meantime, localization processes are working through their own hard and soft networks, at times employing the core networks and at other times developing their own independent periphery systems. The agents of localization and tribalization consist of the nationalist, religious, and culturalist movements and leaders voicing the peripheries' interests and views. In contrast to the Big Media of the core, they often employ the low-cost, accessible, and elusive small media such as low-powered radios, audiocassettes, portaback videos, copying and fax machines, and personal computer networking. Their software consists of the rich heritage of primordial myths and identities embedded in the traditional religious, nationalist, tribal, and localist ideologies.

However, the infrastructure of a global consciousness is fast growing by the media events and a pop culture orchestrated by such transnational networks as CNN, BBC World TV, Star TV, MTV, the Internet, and nongovernmental organizations (NGOs). Although the first five are largely one-way, top-down channels, the last two provide interactive, bottom-up, international communication channels. The media events (Dayan & Katz, 1992) of the last few decades (e.g., the landing on the Moon, Sadat's visit to Jerusalem, Tiananmen Square, the Gulf War, and the signing of the peace accords between Yitzhak Rabin and Yasser Arafat) have brought about a new global consciousness of a common human destiny.

Since 1985, the steady growth of CNN into the world's first global news network has provided the elites in most parts of the world with a stream of live broadcasts in English, Spanish, Japanese, Polish, and soon French and German. In 1987, to counter the Western bias of its news, CNN started airing the CNN World Report, providing uncensored and unedited news reports from local broadcasters all over the world: "By 1992, 10,000 local news items had been aired on the World Report, originating from a total of 185 news organizations representing 130 countries. CNN's internationally-distributed satellite signal is within reach of 98% of the world's population" (Pai, 1993; see also Flourney, 1992; McPhail, 1993). CNN has thus become more than a news medium. It is also serving as a channel for public diplomacy, working often faster than the private channels of traditional diplomacy. Many heads of states and responsible officials watch CNN during crises in order to directly assess the events abroad while gauging the impact of those events on domestic and international public opinion. Fidel Castro is reported to have been one of the first world leaders to regularly watch the CNN service. During the Gulf Crisis, President Bush indicated at a press conference that he would call up President Ozal of Turkey while the latter was watching CNN's live coverage; the telephone call came through a few minutes later while President Ozal was waiting for it. Peter Arnet's reporting from Baghdad during the Gulf War filled some of the communication gaps between Saddam Hussein and the rest of the world. CNN, however, provides a global picture primarily through a U.S. prism. Britain is trying to emulate the CNN success story through the BBC World Service Television, whereas Japan has considered the establishment of an NHK-led Global News Network (GNN); Lee, 1993). Star Television, acquired by Rupert Murdoch's News Corporation in 1993, covers most of Asia through direct broadcast satellite (DBS).

Similarly, MTV is exporting youthful, whimsical, irreverent, postmodernist, U.S. cultural values into Europe, Asia, Africa, and Latin America. Although possessing universal appeal, MTV is following a localization strategy wherever it goes. Stimulated by the example of a popular program that is promotional in selling the music it plays, local record companies have been quick to take up the challenge. India's Megasound spent only $5,000 to produce a video featuring India's first Hindi rap tune by the local artist Baba Segal:

> The album ended up selling 500,000 copies. Darren Childs, MTV Asia's head of programming, said that the Asian content of its programming has risen from 5% when the channel first aired, to as high as 50% at certain times of the day. The station has 'broken' formerly unknown acts and turned them into regional stars. In addition to the regional stars, the VJ's (Video Jockeys) of MTV Asia are another important reason why viewers tune in. They are all Asian or part Asian and provide Western wackiness while toning down the grungy, streetsmart image of MTV VJ's elsewhere to ensure that local audiences can still identify them. (Lee, 1993)

MTV is thus contributing to the creation of an intended or unintended global, postmodernist subculture with far-reaching consequences.
The Internet is another fast-growing transnational network that connects an estimated 30 million people around the world over 1 million mainframe computers in a global network of networks. One million new users are estimated to be joining the network each month. At that rate, the network will have about 100 million users by the year 2000. If we count the members of such major commercial, online services as Prodigy, American Online, Delphi, Dialogue, and CompuServe logging into the Internet, that figure will be probably soon surpassed. In 1992, *The Whole Internet Users' Guide*

and Catalogue (Krol, 1994) sold 125,000 copies. A dozen other guides currently compete for the market, including *Zen and the Art of Internet* (see "America's information highway," Kehow, 1994). It is no wonder that marketers are viewing the network as a potential electronic gold mine. However, attempts at commercializing the network have faced serious resistance by current users. As Stecklow (1993) notes:

> Residents of "cyberspace," as the on-line computer galaxy is known, are a world apart. They do not take kindly to sales pitches or electronic cold calling. Many view themselves as pioneers of a new and better vehicle for free speech. Unlike television viewers, radio listeners or newspaper readers, they are hooked up to the message sender and other Internet parties interactively—meaning that an offence to their sensibilities can result in quick, embarrassing reports viewed by countless of the network's estimated 15 million users. (p. A1)

This new network nation consists of computer-literate professionals from all continents and all fields, united in the fine arts of chatting, gossiping, exchanging information, and collaborating in a variety of projects from scientific research to lifestyle preferences, dating, financial transactions, and social movements. The National Science Foundation (NSF), which subsidizes the network, has no control over a number of other data lines that are also part of the web. The NSF started phasing out its $11.5 million annual subsidy in 1994. However, the U.S. government and businesses are stepping in. Rupert Murdoch's News Corporation announced it will acquire Delphi Internet Services Inc., an online service that provides Internet access to consumers; Continental Cablevision, the third-largest cable television company in the United States, is offering Internet access to its cable subscribers; and American Telephone and Telegraph Co. is planning to make Internet access available to some data communication customers via a nationwide, toll-free telephone number (Stecklow 1993).

The Clinton Administration has promised that by the year 2000 every school and public facility will have the capability of logging into this vast network. On September 15, 1993, Vice President Al Gore unveiled a plan to coordinate the public and private sector efforts in building a national "electronic superhighway." This has raised the perennial question of the tradeoffs between efficiency and equity in telecommunications. Although the U.S. National Information Infrastructure plans still remain ambiguous, they aim at creating a more efficient flow of communication and information through integrated system digital networks (ISDN). Similar to an earlier drive for the construction of transcontinental, interstate superhighways under the Eisenhower Administration, the metaphor of "electronic superhighways" under the Clinton Administration promises greater mobility and productivity. However, it cannot necessarily guarantee greater equity. Just as the transportation superhighways facilitated the transfer of population and resources from the U.S. Northeast to the South and the West, the new electronic superhighways are also going to redistribute wealth, income, and information access. The transportation superhighways facilitated the industrialization of the South and the West, de-industrialization of the Northeast, the migration of Afro-Americans to the northern cities, the out-migration of upper and middle-income White groups from the cities into the suburbs, the consequent erosion of the urban tax base and urban decay, and the creation of an urban underclass. Unless public policy vigorously pursues the achievement of equity and universal access, an unintended consequence of the new electronic superhighways could be the creation of a permanent information underclass. Similar information superhighways are likely to be constructed by the European Union, Japan, and other major economies. They will also probably bypass the poorer regions of the world and create a global information underclass.

Without telephones, the less developed countries and regions of the world would not be able to log into the global electronic superhighways. Telephones are the linchpin of the new integrated telecommunications systems. Without them it would be impossible to log into the new databases and networks. Yet the global distribution of telephony is more lopsided than any other modern medium. In 1992, some 50 countries accounting for over half the world's population had a teledensity of less than 1, that is, less than one telephone line per 100 inhabitants. Although high-income countries control 71% of the world's 575 million phone main lines, upper-middle-income countries control 15%, lower-middle-income 10%, and low-income only 4% (Tarjanne, 1994). Some newly industrializing countries in East Asia, however, are closing the gap, but many other LDCs are falling behind. On the whole, world telephone distribution patterns have remained relatively unchanged in the last 100 years. In the light of this fact, is information hegemony to replace military domination and repression? Or will the two be mutually reinforcing as in the past?

The new global information marketplace includes four major components: (a) the owners of the highways, the common carriers, paid for by the private or public sectors; (b) the producers of information hardware such as telephones, televisions, and computers; (c) the producers of information software such as the press, broadcasters, libraries, and infopreneurs; and (d) information consumers who demand efficiency, equity, privacy, affordability, and choice. In response to the convergence of information and communication technologies, the U.S. government aims to remove all barriers to entry into any particular sector of the market. This will eventually lead to the full technological and economic integration of the print, film, broadcasting, cable, telephone, cellular phone, computer, and database industries—a process that has already begun with the emergence of giant, multi-media conglomerates.

In another speech on January 11, 1994, Vice President Gore outlined the following five principles that will guide any future U.S. legislation and regulation concerning communication industries. The Administration will (a) encourage private investment, (b) provide and protect competition, (c) provide open access to the Network, (d) take action to avoid creating a society of information haves and have-nots, and (e) encourage flexible and responsive governmental action (CRTNET, #915, January 12, 1994). Given these policy principles, will the coming information superhighway be accessible to everyone regardless of their income? The Vice President had been reassuring on that question (CRTNET, #900, December 22, 1993):

> The principle of universal service has been interpreted in the case of telephone service to mean that what we now have is about 93, 94 percent of all American families have telephone service and it is regarded as affordable to virtually—by virtually everyone. Our definition of universal service, once the cluster of services that are encompassed is agreed upon is that approximately the same percentage should have access to the richer information products as well, so that a school child in my hometown of Carthage, Tennessee, population 2,000, could come home after class and sit down and instead of playing a video game with a cartridge, plug into the Library of Congress and learn at his or her own pace according to the curiosity that seizes that child at the moment—not just in the form of words, but color moving graphics and pictures.

The same concerns for information access and equity have been expressed by an international movement for a New World Information and Communication Order (NWICO) (Galtung & Vincent, 1992; Lee, 1985; Traber & Nordenstreng, 1992). As the advanced industrial world has moved ahead, the gap between the information haves and have-nots has demonstrably grown on a global scale. Except for a handful of East Asian countries (Japan, S. Korea, Singapore, Hong Kong, and Taiwan) and low-population, high-income oil exporting countries (e.g., Saudi Arabia, Kuwait, United Arab Emirates), other LDCs have been thus far unable to catch up. One relatively hopeful sign in this bleak picture is the role that NGOs are playing (Boulding, 1988). The convergence of NGO computer networks and low-cost information technologies is offering opportunities for social movements to develop their own news services and information dissemination systems. In the late 1980s, the Association for Progressive Communication (APC) was established as a nonprofit network to facilitate global communication among the NGOs (see Frederick, 1993). According to Frederick (1993):

> Comprising more than 20,000 subscribers in 95 countries, the APC Networks constitute a veritable honor role of organizations working in

these fields, including Amnesty International, Friends of the Earth, Oxfam, Greenpeace, labor unions and peace organizations. There are APC partner networks in the United Sates, Nicaragua, Brazil, Russia, Australia, the United Kingdom, Canada, Sweden and Germany and affiliated systems in Uruguay, Costa Rica, Czechoslovakia, Bolivia, Kenya and other countries. The APC even has an affiliate network in Cuba providing the first free flow of information between the United States and Cuba in thirty years. Dozens of FidoNet systems connect with the APC through 'gateways' located at the main nodes. (p. 97)

APC affiliates now broadcast more than 20 alternative news agencies, 20 newsletters and magazines, 4 radio station news scripts, and a wide variety of specialist files to which nonconventional voices contribute news and opinion. There are also over 10,000 NGOs enlisting millions of people around the world working for a vast variety of civic goals, from protection of the global environment to the defense of human rights and other endangered species. These social and technological networks together constitute a global civil society that provides, to some degree, a countervailing power to those of national states and transnational corporations.

We need not be technological determinists to recognize the unmistakable links between the communication media and cultural change through history (See Table 2.7 and Tehranian, 1990, ch. 3). Historically, each new medium has created a new communication elite or privileged a particular sector of the old elites. The oral traditions privileged the shamans and soothsayers as the paramount historical memories and voices of the community. The invention of writing created a new class of scribes by the establishment of priesthoods acting as the custodians of the holy scriptures and the newly formed religious institutions. The introduction of print brought about a new secular priesthood in the form of modern intelligentsia challenging the authorities of monarchies and religious institutions. The rise of the mass media (such as newspapers and radio) contributed to the emergence of mass movements in the 19th and 20th centuries led by a new class of ideologues (e.g., Lenin, Hitler, Mussolini, and Roosevelt), providing them with platforms to preach their communist, fascist, or social democratic gospels to mass audiences. The rise of computer technologies and its impact on every aspect of economic and social life has created a new class of technologues. The diffusion of the small media of communication has boosted the power and influence of the traditional communication elites (e.g., the priests, the mullas, the monks, the community activists), that is, the communologues, who can speak in the vernacular languages of common folks. The de-mystifying power of visual media (e.g., television, cable, and VCRs) seems to have led to a new and skeptical generation of communication elite that sees through the pretensions of the ideologues, a new class we may call *jestologues*.

Table 2.7. Premodern, Modern, and Postmodern Worldviews: A Schematic Perspective.

	Premodern	Modern	Postmodern
Time	Circular	Linear	Multilinear
	Eternal	Material	Ephemeral
	Past-oriented	Future-oriented	Present-oriented
Space	Hierarchical	Functional	Anarchical/Playful
	Organic	Designed	Vernacular
	Closed	Enclosed	Open
	Home/Office	Home vs. Office	Home + Office
	Fixed	Fluid	Modular
Being	God the Father	Man/Son	The Holy Ghost
	Supernatural	Natural	Ecological
	Heaven	Society	Community
	Sacred	Secular	Self
	Transcendent	Material	Immanent
Power	Feudalism	Fordism	Flexible Accumulation
	Land	Capital	Knowledge/Information
	Gold	Paper Money	Electronic Money
	Authoritarian	Representative	Participatory
	Matriarchal	Patriarchal	Androgyny
	Mother Church	Fatherland	The Community
Science, Technology, & Aesthetics	Practical Reason	Instrumental Reason	Communicative Reason
	Exegesis	Interpretation	Deconstruction
	Fate	Determinacy	Indeterminacy
	Fusionism	Universalism	Particularism
	Mystification	Rationalization	De-Mystification
	Metaphysics	Paradigm	Syntagm
	The Wheel	The Steam Engine	Telematics
	Form	Multi-Form	Antiform
	The Holy Book	Genre/Boundary	Text/Intertext
	Holy Relic	Art Object	Performance/Happening
	The Creation	Narrative	Anti-Narrative
	Trans-History	Grande Histoire	Petite Histoire
	Classicism	Design	Chance
	Sanctification	Centering	Dispersal
	Divinity	Totalization	Deconstruction
	Logos	Purpose	Play
	Traditional	Modern	Eclectic

Source: Adapted from K. Tehranian (1995)

The culture of postmodernity is relativistic, episodic, antinarrative, despairing, ecstatic, playful, self-mocking, and full of jest. It privileges the jestologues. The battle between communologues and jestologues, between modernity and postmodernity, was sanctified by Ayatollah Khomeini's death warrant on Salman Rushdie. Although the Ayatollah represents the modernists, ideologically committed to the sacred mission of realizing the Kingdom of God on this earth, Salman Rushdie voices the postmodern jester who mocks all sanctities (Tehranian, 1992). Most interpretations of the confrontation have portrayed the Ayatollah as the traditional, religious bigot and Salman Rushdie as the modern, free-thinking intellectual. However, the two figures and what they stand for in the contemporary world can be better understood if we view each in terms of some of the distinctions made between the premodern, modern, and postmodern, as depicted in Table 2.7. The Ayatollah is more of a modernist than traditionalist Islamic leader in his totalizing strategy of fusing the State and the mosque into a single theocratic regime, whereas Salman Rushdie is a postmodern critic in his deconstructionist strategy of mocking the traditional and modern sanctities. The postmodern strategy is to shock, to startle, and to decenter in order to dethrone the sacred and the naturalized. Its paramount medium is the musical video, its message is "Give me my MTV!" Its heroes are the deconstructionist antiheroes (e.g., "Beavis and Butthead"), the new self-mocking shamans of electronic rock music (e.g., Sting or Bono), or the glittering stars of multiple identities and sexualities (e.g., Madonna and Michael Jackson).

The conflict between the premodern, modern, and postmodern is thus part of the cultural landscape of a developmentally uneven, historically schizoid, contemporary world. Table 2.7 presents a schematic view of the contrasting tendencies of premodern, modern, and postmodern cultural orientations. It focuses on the dimensions of time, space, being, science, technology, and aesthetics to suggest a series of differences that, when politicized, can lead to irreconcilable obstacles to communication. That is a central paradox of our time. Increasing channels in international communication have frequently led to increasing dialogues of the deaf.

CONCLUSION

This chapter has critiqued the current discourses on the new world order, presented a historically grounded view of the current global changes and continuities, and drawn out the implications of those changes for modernization, communication, and democratization.

As the absence of a consensus on the shape of the new world order demonstrates, we are in an age of paradigm shifts. Our political and economic institutions are clearly lagging behind the accelerating pace of scientific, technological, and cultural changes. That, in turn, has led to the dramatic breakdown of some political and economic systems such as those in Central and Eastern Europe. As the bombing of the World Trade Center in New York, the Federal Building in Oklahoma City, as well as the nerve gas attack in Tokyo subways have demonstrated in the last few years, the "zones of peace" in MDCs are not as immune from violence as some observers would have us believe. The "zones of turmoil" are spilling over from the peripheries of the peripheries (the rural areas in the LDCs) to the centers of the peripheries (Cairo, Tehran, Bombay, Manila, Mexico City), and into the centers of the centers (New York, Los Angeles, Berlin, Frankfort, London, Tokyo). Complacency (i.e., undue optimism) or alarmism (i.e., undue pessimism) are not warranted in the current transition to a new world order, whatever that turns out to be. In fact, the very fluidity of the situation allows us more room for greater human agency. If wars represent the failures of human imagination, the price of peace is human vision and action.

The future of the world depends, in large measure, on how modernity can be tamed to ensure a continuing production of wealth without disastrous consequences for the global natural, social, and cultural environments. That in turn vitally depends on how humanity can balance its competing and complementary interests in the search for common norms, laws, and sanctions. The emerging world order is caught up in the contradictors of uneven and combined economic, political, and cultural modernizations. Economically, modernization has achieved stunning feats in the establishment of a world market of trade and development that is threatened by increasing environmental pollution, international and intranational inequalities; exclusionary regional blocs; and the political upheavals that may result from those. Politically, modernization has created a multipolar world in which no single great power can rule the world with impunity. It has also unleashed democratic forces that in societies with sizable middle classes have led to the institutionalizations of freedoms of speech, assembly, and organization. Culturally, however, modernization has produced contradictory effects. The history of modernization has been thus far a history of the dominance of instrumental reason as reflected in modern science and technology. The diverse spiritual and cultural traditions of the world provide countervailing perspectives on how to both universalize and localize knowledge. The antagonisms between the global and local, however, have led too frequently to the tyranny of one against the other rather than creative tensions and interactions.

As for international relations, the most significant change of the last few decades appears to be in the stunning expansion of channels of global communication. This has proved to be a mixed blessing. On the one hand, it has led to the hearing of new voices—the Kurds, the Shiites, the

Palestinians, the Tatars, the Tibetans, the Abkhasians, the Uighurs, and hundreds more. On the other hand, it may be producing a communication fatigue leading to a "dialogue of the deaf in international communication" (Tehranian, 1982, p. 21). Marshall McLuhan's "global village" is looking more and more like a neofeudal manor with a highly fortified and opulent castle (centers of industrial, financial, and media power) surrounded by a vast hinterland of working peasants clamoring for survival and recognition.

The debate on NWICO has been largely polarized between those who wish to give new means of self-expression to the peasants and those who consider the media monopoly of the lords to be a greater guarantee of freedom and traditions of civil discourse (Singer & Widavsky, 1993). As in any debate, the two sides may have oversimplified a more complex reality. The new media as the old tend to have dual effects, dispersing and centralizing power, democratizing and controlling. Although the State and corporate institutions use them largely for surveillance, legitimation, and persuasion, the NGOs and UNPOs are employing them to resist, to organize, and to mobilize. As raconteurs of international relations, the media mediate in the top-down and bottom-up processes of global governance and communication (see Table 2.6). They construct the global realities that frame the global events feeding the media constructions of global realities. The emergence of Somalia and Bosnia in the top of the international agenda may be in part considered as the work of Cable News Network International (CNNI). By focusing on the tragedies of famine and ethnic cleansing, the world media forced the governments into taking action. However, the media could not lead them to appropriate actions. In fact, aid and communication fatigue are leading them away from those trouble spots. Setting agendas is a powerful media function, but it does not necessarily lead to resolving agendas.

NWICO can be best constructed by developing communication competence for the voiceless. Pluralism in voices, however, requires pluralism in structures of media access. No single system of media control (governmental, commercial, public, or community) can alone guarantee that plurality of voices. A balance among them might use the expanding channels of communication for an expanding plurality of voices more reflective of the international community. Diverse and autonomous centers of media control are a better guarantee of freedom of speech than the pious wishes of legislatures. However, increasing media monopoly in the hands of a dozen global media conglomerates does not augur well either for a free or balanced flow of information. The project of a new world order calls for a free and balanced flow of communication among the 5.5 billion inhabitants of this planet who are caught up between the imperatives of the premodern, modern, and postmodern worlds to which they belong (see Table 2.7). It calls for a beginning rather than an end of history for the two thirds of humankind who have been hitherto primarily objects rather than subjects of history. It calls for dialogue rather than a clash of civilizations in order to redefine modernity in consonance with the traditions of civility embedded in most world religions and civilizations. The challenge lies in how to tame the forces of modernity for the fulfillment of human needs in rather than against nature, for the celebration of democratic diversity and discussion rather than against it, for cultural pluralism rather than cognitive tyranny

NWICO may be conceived of as a network of networks, among the NGOs, to mobilize the global civil society, to empower the deterritorialized peripheries in the urban centers and rural hinterlands, to enhance their communication competence and media capabilities, to negotiate with the State and non-State actors—the IGOs, TNCs, and TMCs—in order to redress the conditions of dehumanizing poverty and violence, manifest and latent, so characteristic of our world.

REFERENCES

Ajami, F., Bartley, R.L., Binyan, L., & Mahbubani, K. (1993, September/October) Commentaries on the clash of civilizations. *Foreign Affairs*, pp. 2–26.

America's information highway. (1994, December–January). *The Economist*, pp. 35-38.

Appadurai, A. (1990). Disjuncture and difference in the global cultural economy. *Public Culture, 2*(2), 1-22.

Appadurai, A. (1993). Patriotism and its future. *Public Culture, 5*, 411-429.

Attali, J. (1991). *Millenium: Winners and losers in the coming world order.* New York: Times Books.

Barnet, R.J., & Muller, R.E. (1974). *Global reach.* New York: Simon & Schuster.

Bell, D. (1960). *The end of ideology: On the exhaustion of political ideas in the fifties.* Glencoe, IL: The Free Press.

Bell, D. (1973). *The coming of the post-industrial society: A venture in social forecasting.* New York: Basic Books.

Boulding, E. (1988). *Building a global civic culture: Education for an interdependent world.* New York: Teachers College Press.

Brandt, W. et al. (1985). *Common crisis: North-South cooperation for world recovery.* Cambridge, MA: MIT Press.

Brandt, W. et al. (1980) North-South: A program for survival. London: Pan Books.

CRTNET: Communication and research theory. Speech by Vice President Al Gore. #900, December 22, 1993, #915, January 12, 1994.

Dayan, D., & Katz, E. (1992). *Media events: The live broadcasting of history.* Cambridge, MA: Harvard University Press.

Docherty, T. (1993). *Post-modernism: A reader*. New York: Columbia University Press.
Editors' comments. (1988). *Public Culture, 1*(1), 1-4.
Etzioni, A. (1993). *The spirit of community: The reinvention of American society*. New York: Touchstone Books.
Ewen, S., & Ewen, E. (1982). *Channels of desire: Mass images and the shaping of American consciousness*. New York: McGraw-Hill.
Flourney, D. (1992). *CNN world report*. London: John Libbey.
Foucault, M. (1980). *Power/knowledge: Selected interviews and other writings 1972–1977*. New York: Pantheon.
Frankfort, H. (1964). *Before philosophy: the intellectual adventure of ancient man*. Baltimore: Penguin Books. (Original publication date 1949)
Frederick, H.H. (1993). *Global communication and international relations*. Belmont, CA: Wadsworth.
Fukuyama, F. (1989, Summer). The end of history. *National Interest*.
Galtung, J., & Vincent, R. (1992). *Global glasnost: Toward a new information and communication order*. Cresskill, NJ: Hampton Press.
Habermas, J. (1983). *The theory of communicative action* (2 vols.). Boston: Beacon Press.
Hamelink, C.J. (1983). *Cultural autonomy in global communications: Planning national information policy*. New York & London: Longman.
Harvey, D. (1990). *The condition of post-modernity: An inquiry into the origins of cultural change*. Cambridge, MA & Oxford, UK: Blackwell.
Heilbroner, R.L. (1962). *The making of economic society*. Englewood Cliffs, NJ: Prentice Hall.
Hitler, A. (1941). *My new order*. New York: Reynall & Hitchcock.
Hobson, J.A. (1938). *Imperialism: A study*. London: J. Nisbet. (Original work published 1902)
Huntington, S. P. (1993a, Summer). The clash of civilizations. *Foreign Affairs*, p. 24.
Huntington, S.P. (1993b, November–December). The clash of civilizations: A response. *Foreign Affairs*, pp. 2-26.
Juergensmeyer, M. (1993). *The new cold war? Religious nationalism confronts the secular state*. Berkeley: University of California Press.
Kehow, B.P. (1994). *Zen and the art of the internet*. Englewood Cliffs, NJ: PTR Prentice Hall.
Kennedy, P. (1993). *Preparing for the twenty-first century*. New York: Random House.
Krol, E. (1994). *The whole internet users' guide and catalogue*. Sebastopol, CA: O'Reilly & Associates.
Lash, S., & Urry, J. (1987). *The end of organized capitalism*. Madison: University of Wisconsin Press.
Lee, P. (Ed.). (1985). *Communication for all: New world information and communication order*. Maryknoll, NY: Orbis Books.

Lee, Y.C. (1993). *DBS issues in the Asia-Pacific.* Unpublished paper.
Lenin, V.I. (1969). *Imperialism: The highest stage of capitalism.* London: Lawrence & Wishart (Original work published 1917)
Libset, S.M. (1963). *The first new nation: The US in historical and comparative perspective.* New York: Basic Books.
MacBride, S. et al. (1980). *Many voices, one world: Communication and society today and tomorrow.* Paris: UNESCO Press.
Maitland, D. (1994, January 16-20). Forging new links: Focus on developing economies. *Plenary Presentations*, Pacific Telecommunications Council Sixteenth Annual Conference, Honolulu, Hawaii.
Mandel, E. (1978). *Late capitalism.* London: Verso.
Marty, M., & Appleby, S. (Eds.). (1991). *Fundamentalism observed.* Chicago: Chicago University Press.
Marty, M., & Appleby, S. (Eds.). (1992). *Fundamentalism and state.* Chicago: Chicago University Press.
Marty, M., & Appleby, S. (Eds.). (1993). *Fundamentalism and society.* Chicago: Chicago University Press.
Masuda, Y. (1991). *The information society: A post-industrial society.* Washington, DC: World Future Society.
Mattelart, A. (1983). *Transnationals and Third World: The struggle for culture.* South Hadley, MA: Bergin and Garvey.
Mazlish, B. (1993). *The fourth discontinuity.* New Haven, CT: Yale University Press.
McPhail, T. (1993, May 21-23). *Television as an extension of the nation state: CNNI and the Americanization of broadcasting.* Paper presented at the Annual Conference of the French Association of American Studies.
Pai, S. (1993). *The cable news network.* Unpublished paper.
Porat, M. (1977). *The information economy.* Washington, DC: U.S. Office of Telecommunications.
Robertson, R. (1992). *Globalization: Social theory and global culture.* London: Sage.
Robertson, R. (1994). Globalisation or glocalisation. *Journal of International Communication, 1*(1), 33-52.
Rowe, C., & Koetter, F. (1992). *Collage city.* Cambridge, MA: MIT Press.
Schiller, H. (1976). *Communication and cultural domination.* White Plains, NY: International Arts and Sciences.
Singer, M., & Widavsky, A. (1993). *The real world order: Zones of peace/Zones of turmoil.* Chatham, NJ: Chatham House.
So, A. (1990). *Social change and development: Modernization, dependency, and world system theories.* Newbury Park, CA: Sage.
Soja, E.W. (1989). *Postmodern geographies: The reassertion of space in critical social theory.* London: Verso.

Stecklow, S. (1993, September 16). Cyberspace clash: Computer users battle high-tech marketers over soul of internet. *The Wall Street Journal*, p. A1.

Tarjanne, P. (1994, January 16-20). The missing link: Still missing. *Plenary Presentations*, Pacific Telecommunications Council Sixteenth Annual Conference, Honolulu, Hawaii.

Tawney, R.H. (1984). *Religion and the rise of capitalism: A historical study*. New York: Penguin Books.

Tehranian, K. (1995). *Modernity, space, and power: The American city in discourse and practice*. Cresskill, NJ: Hampton Press.

Tehranian, K., & Tehranian, M. (Eds.). (1992). *Restructuring for world peace: On the threshold of the 21st century* (pp. 1-22). Cresskill, NJ: Hampton Press.

Tehranian, M. (1982). International communication: A dialogue of the deaf? *Political Communication and Persuasion, 2*(2), 21-46.

Tehranian, M. (1989, October 7). History finished? It's just begun. *The Honolulu Advertiser*, p. A-11.

Tehranian, M. (1990). *Technologies of power: Information machines and democratic prospects*. Norwood, NJ: Ablex Publishing.

Tehranian, M. (1992). Khomeini's doctrine of legitimacy. In A.J. Parel & R.C. Keith (Eds.), *Comparative political philosophy* (pp. 217-243). New Delhi: Sage.

Tehranian, M. (1993a). Ethnic discourse and the new world dysorder. In C. Roach (Ed.), *Communication and culture in war and peace* (pp. 192-215). Newbury Park: Sage.

Tehranian, M. (1993b). Fundamentalist impact on education and the media: An overview. In M.E. Marty & R.S. Appleby (Eds.), *Fundamentalism and society* (pp. 313-373). Chicago: The University of Chicago Press.

Toffler, A. (1980). *Third wave*. New York: Bantam.

Traber, M., & Nordenstreng, K. (1992). *Few voices, many worlds: Towards a media reform movement*. London: World Association for Christian Communication.

Trachtenberg, A. (1982). *The incorporation of America, Culture and society in the gilded age*. New York: Hill and Wang.

United Nations Development Program (UNDP). (1992). *Human development report*. New York: Oxford University Press.

Wallerstein, I. (1974). *The modern world-system* (Vol. 1). New York: Academic Books.

Weber, M. (1958). *The protestant ethic & the spirit of capitalism* (translated by Talcott Parsens). New York: Scribner.

PART II

PROSPECTIVES AND PERSPECTIVES

Part II takes up some strands in the rope that ties us to the future. Ramona Rush charts a feminist agenda for both women and men. She proposes a new global eco-communication system which is liberatory and can lead to equality and peace. Wolfgang Kleinwaechter analyzes three generations of the right to communicate, and proposes a fourth one: cyber-right for communication in cyber-space. Michael Ogden's chapter also deals with our "digital future," analyzing the political issues that arise from new networking technologies. Seán Ó. Siochrú sees new opportunities for grassroot movements in computer networks but only if they harness and organize people's power.

Next we focus on journalism. Dennis Davis identifies a new role for journalism in postmodern societies, namely, to construct and share culture and provide a bridge between different cultures. Development journalism is then taken up by Hemant Shah. He proposes a normative model that would foster emancipation from modernization.

Finally, Poka Laenui discusses one striking example of communication inequity. His chapter focuses on the communication impasse of indigenous or first people, choosing Hawai'i as a case study.

3

*Theories and Research to Live By: Communications and Information in the 21st Century**

Ramona R. Rush

Parallelisms; territorialities; dualisms; models of scarcity; power and greed; contending theories and realisms about stages of communication, modernization, development, progress, and civilization; exclusionary and enforced silences seem to be what are, and have guided, the mindsets, standpoints, ideologies, worldviews from the time that mankind [sic] swung into the saddle (apologies to R. W. Emerson) to the 21st century.

A powerful example is society's treatment and regard of women, especially concerning women's roles of silence and subservience, including being largely absent from mass media messages. Specifically, women's

---

*An early version of this chapter, "Toward A Humanly Decent Theory of Communication for the 21st Century," by R. Rush, S. Kaufman, and D. Allen, appears in D. Newsom (Ed.), *Silent Voices* (1995, University Press of America). It was developed further by Rush in "Ten Tenets for Deeper Communications: Transforming Communications Theory and Research" for *Women Transforming Communications: Global Intersections*, edited by Allen, Rush, and Kaufman (1996, Sage Publications). The author wishes to thank Pam Creedon, Donna Allen, and Susan Kaufman for support and suggestions in the development of the single-authored manuscript.

issues seem to run parallel with but never intersect the broad agenda of human issues, although both are highlighted by such organizations as the United Nations (Gallagher, 1986). Furthermore, women's issues often tend to lag behind other human rights issues for many reasons.

What follows are suggestions for how to bring global intersections to the so-called superhighway of information—suggestions to assure the silenced that what they say this time will be heard by enough people so that their ideas and knowledge will be remembered and sustained, giving sustainable knowledge. The suggestions include that a theory and its research will:

- be ecologically based, inclusive, and, thus, diverse
- go beyond dualistic thinking and action
- acknowledge human spirituality and sexuality
- be healing and liberatory
- emphasize peace, equality, and justice as dynamic growth forces
- employ realistic frameworks and social action research
- assess the traditional mass media, in their current corporate state, as demographic investigators and reporters of societal trends and progress
- include the alternative, "other" media as scenario sketchers for strategic, social policy surveillance
- develop an envisionary media
- have a global civil society worldview with concern and respect for the information, communication, and integration of its citizens

A Theory and Its Research Will Be Ecologically Based, Inclusive and, thus, Diverse

Each of us is an eco-system. Each of us works within and toward a *global eco-communication system* to bring ourselves into balance (understanding) with the rest of the universe through continual adjustment (communication of information). The more diverse (different) the information, the longer will be the time for adjustment. I envisioned eco-communications (Rush, 1989b, 1992), which stands for the ecology of communications, as the mutual communicative and informative relations among humans, as a species, and between them and their environment:

> Eco-communications is an integrative, realistic, networking force among humans and their concerns for the inclusion and well-being of all planetary species' information and communication systems. The

process of eco-communications as envisioned and when fully operative in a community will help people to secure important and relational places in a changing, ongoing society, challenging and enhancing their unique contributions. A truly integrative eco-communications system will prevent any long-term estrangement or dysfunction or displacement, except for temporary and necessary adjustments, between the individual and its state (of being). A global eco-communications system, in application, provides a map of communication and information flows and gaps, and continually works to improve delivery methods, channels, and content for filling the lacunae. It is what this author has elsewhere called a flow-keeping agenda. [Note: Definition has been changed somewhat since earlier references.] (Rush,1989b, 1996, p. 8)

I see *global* as having at least two meanings. One is the traditional definition of international or intercultural, which has messages, data, or people going across or through some kind of barriers, boundaries, or constraints, whether it be the encoding-decoding process from one human being to another, or the artificial borders between nation-states. The other definition concerns issues that are common enough to any group or groups, of people to transcend traditional boundaries. A good example of this latter definition are women's issues, preferably those defined by women:

> "Women's work is never done." This time, at the turn of this new Century, women's work in its current form must be done. Now is the time for men to begin their hard labor by correcting the structural inequities and societal symbols they have erected, often in the name of God, institution, and knowledge. Men now need to pour *their time, their energy, their money, their knowledge* of the construction and maintenance of structural inequities into disassembling and restructuring those same systems. . . . Many women and some men have discovered *intersystemic connections*, in which a dysfunctional family of nations has symptoms similar to a dysfunctional domestic family, a dysfunctional state contains dysfunctional private and public academic units. Now women, together with the few good men who have kept their sense of moral justice, are prepared to be the architects and on-site supervisors of a new, associative civil society, keeping the best of capitalistic efficiency and democratically channeling it into quality circles and networks of equality.
>
> Women and a few good men must heal themselves of old patriarchal wounds by supervisioning the creation, perhaps for the first time, of structural equality. The perpetrators of territoriality mindsets must heal themselves through the understanding that comes through breaking apart and tearing down their old patterns and reweaving their yarns into a mosaic of inclusiveness, diversity, and equality: an interweave of unique and varied experiences, valuing the whole rather than the parts—holistic. (Rush, 1993, p. 79; emphasis added)

Those who have studied and practice ecofeminist theories largely understand and write about the problems. In sum, there are as many approaches to ecofeminism as there are to feminism as there are to societal structure and ideology (see "Feminism and Ecology", 1993). Those persons who talk and write about the "intersections" of various approaches are working and walking toward "unity through diversity," "walking their talk" toward understanding where the communication commons are located and where are the roads that lead there. The question becomes whether the communication commons will accommodate and facilitate (continually access and adjust through the communication of appropriate and accurate information) the interactive (*not* only interdependent) needs of all species.

The human struggle toward a global, civic society will have a tremendous surge forward once it is relearned or understood that all ecosystems have infinite microcausal as well as microcosmal interconnectivity that ripples outward to become macrocausal and macrocosmal and then back again with rhythms perhaps matching and as strong as the pull of the moon on the tides. In other words, from the microcosmal cell, the individual, the family to the macrocosmal nation-state, multinational corporation, and planet, there are relationships and interactions that affect us going away and coming back: What goes around, comes around.

A Theory and Its Research Will Go Beyond Dualistic Thinking and Action

We now appear to be in a stage of human development in which old reptilian brains—that feature the flight-or-fight syndrome—intervene in progress toward a truly associative civilization. Some powerful members of the human species, through habitual mental views of territoriality and sanctioned violence, are exhibiting societal maladaptation and cultural lag different from those they have artifically induced on "others" in society. The man versus nature and nation-state theories are outworn paradigms in view of the potential of advances in communication technologies, predominantly and not so ironically developed by men in war and boardrooms.

There exists a pollution of the information and communication being sent and received and thus a pollution of the mind. Many persons, individually and collectively, are not getting the kind of information they need when they need it. Nor are they empowered to talk when they think they know what they are saying, or listened to and understood when they are trying to tell others what they think or feel. Certain people and members of species are either endangered or indeed extinct, not only of natural causes but because of the disregard for ecological and environmental distress/breakdowns in planetary communication and information systems. A complete agenda of information and communication that comes from all unique experiences and the collective wisdom needed to survive is not allowed by those currently in power and control.

The first major obstacle to discard is old, outworn paradigms that make many of us Janus-faced humans, habitually thinking and acting in dualistic, competitive, either–or terms. Those paradigms are the consequence of a mechanistic, industrial model of mass production profit and induced scarcity. Few of the planetary species are, or can, work long as factory or military machines. In times of scarce (real or unreal) and/or inequitable distribution of resources (especially those of information) under this dualistic model, people with territorial or survival mindsets are willing to rape, mutilate, torture, or kill each other. Under more stable conditions, progress and modernization have come to mean that resource, health, and information gaps widen under such traditional models and worldviews (see French, 1992).

The second, related obstacle is the segregation of "other" experiences and information/communication channels and messages. "Other" people are primarily those who do not fit, for whatever reason, into a patriarchal, hierarchical, capitalistic, organizational culture. This worldwide system has largely been constructed by elite males, with power extraordinarily greater than their proportional numerical representation in any society. Consumer-poor people, people of color, and women and children mostly belong to "other" groups of people. The largest global demographic groups are comprised of women and children.

Thus, more than half of the world's experiences and information are seriously lacking in major institutions. Because "other" views have not often been included in institutional decision making, advances in technology are often in search of a human condition to fit or hurt, instead of being developed for and improving that same condition. The human species must evolve beyond compounds into communities, beyond shelters into rotating and interconnecting systems, beyond hierarchies into spiraling spheres. Our issues are global and holistic at any level—so must be our theories and research about those issues. They must go beyond capitalism into social democracy; beyond dualism into synthesized trinities, trilogies, and circles; beyond shallow ecology and communications into deep ecology (Naess, 1973, 1992) and global ecocommunications or deeper communications (Rush, 1989b, 1992, 1996).

A theory will be viewed and valued for its circulatory, networking attributes rather than by only its linear aspects, inclusively spherical rather than multilayered, hierarchical qualities. Research methods will at least triangulate a topic/problem under investigation; multimethod approaches will apply a variety of quantitative, qualitative, and demographic methods, for each person is complex and unique in her or his thoughts and actions as is each of our cells as well as that big ecosystem known as the planet. We have to feel, perceive, think, act, speak, and be researched and reconceptualized as deeply and robustly as we exist. Superficial, shallow communication, and ecology is what we have now ("Hi, how are ya?" as the person passes by); deep ecology[1] and global ecocommunications, or deeper communications, are what we need to allow us to take a collective breath of planetary unity. No matter what it is called as long as it is not a co-opted distortion, there will have to be a greening of planetary politics and a feminization and democratization of global communication. This chapter advocates metaenvironmental studies (Orr, 1992) and deeper global ecocommunications (Rush, 1989b, 1992, 1996) as becoming the hub of the planetary universe.

A Theory and Its Research Must Basically be Concerned about Human Spirituality and Sexuality—Sometimes Interchangeably, Often Interactively

If humans are expected to go beyond duality in thinking and action, as was at least theoretically and ideally suggested in the preceding discussion, then our conceptual frameworks and research investigations must acknowledge, explore, and try to understand the dimensions of these two basic human elements. Humans are known to be deeply concerned with both spirituality and sexuality for they are frequently the stuff of legend, mythology, culture, religion, sociology, communications, politics, law, economics. Many modern polling indicators, best-selling books, and other media demonstrate that people in the United States especially are disproportionately involved in, concerned about, and/or affected by violence, sex, and religion. Although many of us believe that structural inequality perpetuated by consumerism and economic dependency could account for a sizable variance in human behavior, it does not necessarily explain the psychology and perpetuation of power, control, and violence (especially against women and children) in global society today.

Miedzian (1991) wrote that "a norm is by definition a standard for judging; it is not itself subject to judgment. So while individual men can be found defective in light of a paradigm of manhood, they cannot be found defective by comparison with women who stand outside the paradigm and are seen as secondary and defective to begin with" (p. 12). According to Miedzian, "since male behavior is the norm, warfare and violence are not only accepted as central, normal part of human experience but they are transformed into heroic, exciting events" (p. 12).

---

[1]"Deep ecology" has a recent dialogue and discussion in " The Philosophy of Ecology," Society and Nature, 1992, including the comments of Arne Naess. "Deeper communication" is based on the suggestions contained with this article on what theories and their research should contain: briefly, deeper communication brings each planetary species into integrative equality through the access of appropriate and accurate information.

Mythologist Joseph Campbell (1988) sees that in order to know ourselves, we must follow our bliss by taking a heroic journey. It is a world of myth out there and we must find our individual places in it. If "there is a commonality of themes in world myths, pointing to a constant requirement in the human psyche for a centering in terms of principles" (p. xvi), then we must see and determine where our skin ends and other boundaries begin. It is a difficult, painful journey here on earth, which is the only eternity we currently know, and we are the only gods and goddesses we *really* know—the here and now—that Campbell writes about.

The phenomenon is the separation of externalities and internalities, the world out there and the world in here, outer and inner peace, with the resolution seemingly some sort of centeredness to bring us out of the uncomfortable "either–or" dualism. Centeredness or balance has to lie somewhere between the fit of cultural norms and myths (often depicted as "knowing the difference between right and wrong") and those we have already experienced for ourselves as a unique individual. When the externalities do not match with our "gut reactions," which have been worked through in our interior dialogues, we have what has been called "cognitive dissonance," something just does not feel right. "Being centered" has to do with each of us feeling comfortable in the integration between our public or external and private or internal systems, between chaos and order. The heroic journey, it would seem, must be continued every minute of every day until each of us has our own worldview, that is, how things work, and who we are, how we fit, most of the time, within all of those dynamic processes known as life and living. Once we know that, we can dance, sing, and write. Yet, if the center of society is based on myths or heroic journeys that are ultimately destructive to all species, then obviously we are in need of new myths and new heroes and need to dispose of outworn paradigms that incorrectly attempt to explain our world and the theories we live by.

Women, then, have been placed in a difficult, often hurtful or deadly position of not knowing whether to digress from, or aggress to, the mean or the norm. It has taken us a long time to understand that that mean, that average, that norm, was not of our own making.

Miedzian (1991) uses an entire chapter to point out why men and women alike will not point the finger at the male populations that conduct the violence:

> Imagine the reaction if close to 90 percent of all violent crimes were committed by women! If tabloid headlines carried stories, with some regularity, of man-hating women leaving behind them cross-country trails of murdered men; bodies of ex-wives, driven by fits of jealousy, killing their former husbands and their children; of groups of women killing each other in rival gang fights. Imagine the scorn that would be heaped on women for killing *each other* off at such high rates! How

quickly such behavior would be perceived as an aberration, a deviation from the norm of male behavior, a 'women's problem' to be dealt with urgently! Think of the fuss made about menstrual emotional stress and menopausal hot flashes as reason for keeping women out of topic political decision-making situations—this in a century which has given us Hitler and Stalin and and more recently Khomeini, Idi Amin, and Saddam Hussein. But when so many men commit violent crimes, or when nations led by men engage endlessly in armed conflict, there is no awareness that we are faced with a "man's problem." (pp. 11–12)

So what does this have to do with sexuality and spirituality? When we know who we are in relation to things and others around us, we each "own our souls," our own spirituality and sexuality. And at that point, they are one and the same, interchangeable, our own humanity.

We become somewhat confused and have "centeredness loss" when we think in terms of "sex" and "religion" instead of sexuality and spirituality. Sex means to divide, cut, as in male/female with reference to our reproductive functions. The current connotations have little to do with that primitive, biological designation. Our worldview now concentrates on social, economic, psychological, and political gender roles and structures that, in large part, have to do with "power sexonomics." That is, there are a powerful few who think they need to be "served" whether it is with sex, food, work, information, money, leisure, or recreation; "others" are expected to be the servers. In order to maintain that distinction, many people have had to be persuaded through "commodification" efforts (e.g., controlled monetary and human resource systems, advertising) that their roles were and are to be that of servers—poor, consumers, prostitutes, maids, welfare mothers, staff assistants. Even the homeless are servers in the sense that the powerbrokers need them to demon-strate and exercise even more control through comparison of their obvious God-given superiority, and, thus, status.

Organized, abstract religion begot the first "go-betweens." Ordained, anointed, and appointed men interpreted for "others" the words of a real but physically removed "king" and the words of a surreal, abstract "god" (i.e., king of kings). These men were indeed the first of many things yet to come: concentrated media owners, advertisers, bureaucrats, chairmen of boards and departments, senators and congressmen, lawyers of the land. Dictionaries are wont to vacillate in their definitions between general definitions that might be interpreted as being personally adaptable and power groups with their externally controlled definitions. (For example, the first definition of *spirituality* is that of "spiritual character, quality, or nature"; the second is that of "the rights, jurisdiction, tithes, etc., belonging to the church or to an ecclesiastic"—Webster's 1988, p. 1293).

Only to the extent that a person's spirituality and sexuality could be separated and owned, controlled by those in power (persuaded that the nuances of particular religious, political, economic, and/or social ideologies meant it to be so), could a mythology of dualism arise. Personal and cultural symbols and accounts of peaceful, cooperative cultures went before these transgressions, including those that recorded the vicious acts of external control that later were conveniently lost, stolen, buried, or burned. Archeomythologists (Gimbutas, 1989) and ecofeminists have vast writings on this violent progression from the time of Indo-European invaders to the present. As they might write, deafening are the silences of those who went before those who are silenced now. Occasionally is heard through mythology the sound of a discordant note that reverberates throughout the others' interior system of belief, sending them into action: The goddess of the Earth, Gaia, has been sending distress signals for centuries. Now her weakened, overtaxed system is gaining sustenance, strength, and sustainability from those who have heard her cries for help. These Earth children are nearly too numbed by and too fearful of violence to cry for help. Our personal centers of security, peace, and justice have either been coopted or are in hiding from the societal centers of controlled violence pollution. Too often today, addiction, cooptation, isolation, or death are the ways these centers can come together.

A Theory and Its Research will be Healing and Liberatory

It is not without reason that self-help books have been so popular through the 1980s into the 1990s. Gloria Steinem's (1992) book on self-esteem, *Revolution from Within*, has perhaps been the crowning touch on this literature of self-actualization. Her book is dedicated to men and women alike, but speaks particularly to women who have had a double bind/standard in being treated as a "minoritized-majority" (Rush, 1989a).

It will be difficult for civilization to advance if more than half of its citizens are wounded in sexual and spiritual skills for survival. bell hooks (1992) offers an explanation for this attribute of healing and liberation. She says simply, *"I came to theory because I was hurting"* (p. 80; emphasis added). She explains how living in childhood without a sense of home with a young black couple of parents, who struggled to realize the patriarchal norm, "theorizing" provided her a sanctuary in which she could imagine possible futures:

> This lived experience of critical thinking, of reflection and analysis, became a place where I worked at explaining that theory could be a healing place. When our lived experience of theorizing is fundamentally linked to processes of self-recovery, of collective liberation, no gap

> exists between theory and practice. But theory is not inherently healing, liberatory, or revolutionary. It fulfills this function only when we ask that it do so and direct our theorizing toward this end. (p. 80)

It might seem strange to expect theory and research to be healing and liberatory, but those who have been victims of societal and individual abuse and those who feel trapped by their human condition will have no trouble understanding this inclusion. As more becomes known about the vast, historical, continuing, and permanent damage done to all species by so few (in comparison) persons entrenched in self-serving societal structures and ideologies, the more people and devices (such as the mass media) will be used to diffuse and distribute empowering, self-actualizing knowledge. Such information pollution includes attributing life-threatening diseases to certain classes of people; generalizing and normalizing scientific information about a few to many, maintaining a tightening loop on elite information and decision making, changing policy under the name of increased and/or different productivity to remove older and more experienced critical thinkers and speakers, and labeling and deriding dissension as "political correctness" and "victimization." Let us count the ways to fragment, objectify, commodify, and media-scapegoat the powerless—all the ways to confuse, divide, conquer, and reconquer those who do not have the necessary resources of all kinds to withstand the feeding-frenzy attack, that speak back to self-serving, constructed models of scarcity.

One solution is for national watchdog groups, accreditation bodies, government (all levels), human resource agencies, and international groups (such as nongovernmental organizations) to publicly demand that public and private employers with documented discrimination put a hold on any policy, production, and employee formulation and changes until the structural inequality/ideology is demonstrably removed. Because of their vastly unrealized potential to educate the leadership of the nation and world, universities and the mass media would be a good place to start the balancing correction through preventive actions such as conflict resolution in the face of emerging communication crises. Enhancement through encouragement, education, and empowerment of the human condition is indeed "free to be . . . you and me" and "being all that I can be." To heal is to set free.

A Theory and Its Research will Emphasize Peace, Equality, and Justice as Dynamic Growth Forces

Peace has been defined as constructive communication; equality as the availability of and information about opportunities in a society, and justice as being treated fairly, including by oneself. Few people would argue against these values, although some might say these definitions of peace and equality overprivilege communication (Hackett, personal communication, November, 1993). The problem becomes to make peace a verb, a dynamic force as powerful as violence. Even nonviolence contains the word of which we are trying to rid ourselves. Our learned behaviors, emanating from competition, sports, military, the entertainment media, the traditional news media, and imitative, repetitive acts from the family and other agencies of socialization, weigh heavily on the side of violence.

We need attitudinal, cognitive, behavioral, and linguistic adjustments that when we think, speak, and act, come from a dynamism of peace, quality, and justice. When some of these adjustments (the civil rights movement, the women's movement, the older citizens' movement, the gay-lesbian-bisexual-transsexual-family diversity movement) gathered force in U.S. society in the 1960s through 1990s, they were finally met with an organized resistance of such ideas politically labeled as "political correctness." Even usually progressive and supportive male leaders in society swung behind this snide commentary on women's and minority studies, sexual and cultural diversity, trying to stereotype a drive to equity as a laughingstock and a societal sham—a continuous derision designed to bring people and programs back under the control of the status quo. In her best selling book, Faludi (1991) branded such behavior toward women as *Backlash*: When women begin to make real progress, it is beat back by a seemingly orchestrated effort (see Introduction, pp. ix-xxiii).

Peace education and conflict resolution skills will help bring about human developmental adjustments. As Rush (1993) notes:

> Important approaches include the integration of conflict resolution and peace education materials into communication curricula, research, and media content.
>
> *Mediation, arbitration, and negotiation skills might well be as important to professionals, professors, and students in our field as are written and oral communication skills.*
>
> The flip side of war and violence is peace and cooperation; we just need to think, act, talk, and write that way and etch these cultural transmissions into our consciences for thousands of years as we have etched the cultural transgressions of abuse, violence, war, and war periods, often cited as historical time demarcations (e.g., "Since World War II").
>
> Along these lines of thinking, we can use terms such as "peace correspondents" instead of "war correspondents" or "global correspondents" instead of "foreign correspondents" [as most women and minorities know, to name or rename is to claim]. (p. 79; italics added)

Theory and research about communication and information will account for and try to integrate many "other" worldviews, for ultimately we must intend, as humans, to interact in ways conducive to a healthy, ecologically, and informationally balanced planet. The Centre for the Study of Communication and Culture's special bibliographic issue of *Communication Research Trends* makes a substantial gain in this direction (Kunst & Witlox, 1993). The attention to peace education and studies is also increasing (e.g., Tehranian & Tehranian, 1992; *Peace and Change: A Journal of Peace Research*.) As Orr (1992) asks: "Why do we spend several hundred billion dollars each year for weapons and preparation to fight wars and a fraction of one percent of that amount on peace research?" (p. 143). Allen (1977) has repeatedly pointed out that male mass media promoted such violence as necessary and did not allow the other side to be heard. Other perspectives are, of course, threatening to the status quo where the loci of domination and control reside.

A Theory will Employ Realistic Frameworks and Social Action Research

Until we can "see" our intersystemic connectivity, we need to take the time and effort to heal our imbalances from being "out of the round" for so long. Social policy research, usually positivist and reductionist, drives much of the United States's social science research agenda; social action research has not received the same attention. The assumption here is that the process of theory and research will be applied to improve the conditions of the human and other species. Moreover, the research must start to toil for those people most in need of the applied results. We would see an emphasis on feminist, critical, qualitative theories and research methods, with quantitative and demographic research rounding out the recirculation of cumulative, sustainable knowledge.

This, of course, does not discount "hard" (a word often and ironically indicative of impersonal approaches and methods) science research or research for the sake of research. It does, however, indicate that what is behind the ivory towers of the increasingly corporate public and certainly private (including religious) universities needs to be rethought. A global, civic society can no longer (and never could) afford predominately patriarchal, hierarchical, administrative, bureaucratic, White male-dominated institutions of higher education, in which top-down decision making has kept theory and research narrow and discriminatory, both in its topics and through its investigators. The millions of public dollars poured into research to enhance the scholarly, military, and commercial reputations and power rewards of a relatively few White males are out of the same pie of associative money that is not being distributed to relatively deprived persons who lack similarly viable opportunities for job training, housing, daycare centers, and other social and economic equities. The same persons who face domestic, societal, and institutional violence everyday need self-esteem rehabilitation from realistic interconnective systems that empower and endow them and their children with self-actualization values and skills.

There now exists a big discrepancy, a big gap, between theory and reality, between theory and application, between theory and social action research, between those who observe and those who are studied. The evaluation component of planetary and human condition research proposals, until society is healthy, will of necessity have to include meta-ecology and global ecocommunication application, demonstration, and action potentials. Along this line, Folbre (1993) took a look at the myth of the middle class and has argued for moving away from focus on class structure and instead studying CRAG, the intersections and interlocking of class, race, age, and gender, in which the conflicts and realities of today are played out. There also appears to be promise in the work coming out of organizational communication applied research in which ideas of chaos and paradoxic encounters further promote the idea of giving up old dysfunctional and often discriminatory models.

We do not have an orderly world, especially when we are going through periods of transitions like the ones in which the civil rights and freedoms of many "other" groups are being forwarded into the mainstream of society. We desperately need models that allow flexibility of civility to be a part of everyday life. How far removed are most of us from presidents or vice chancellors of universities, chairmen, and publishers of boards and organizations? People need to be able to cross rigid lines, to push across constraints and barriers, to seek and find that information most helpful to them when they most need it without being labeled as dissenters, bitches, women's libbers, radicals, or the politically correct. Many persons who are currently isolated and subjected to a continual loss of self-esteem under normal-curve, status quo, group loyalty situations might well be using their talents for ground-breaking initiatives, for community building and collegiality in more chaotic, unstructured, seamless environments.

In large part, it is the old idea of praxis, that is now being picked up and recycled by researchers, including those in communications and especially by those concerned with grassroots, indigenous, and women's issues. Praxis is simply practice, as distinguished from theory. For our purposes here, practice informs theory, and theory informs practice: an interactive cycle. As the 21st Century looms into view, this author currently sees the relationship of practice and theory as where the tire meets the pavement, a friction point instead of a global intersection. Peck (1993) has an interesting standpoint about praxis:

To escape heresy, we must accept paradox. Thinking with integrity is paradoxical thinking. And it is not only necessary that we think with integrity, it's also necessary that we act with integrity. Behaving with integrity is "praxis," a term that was popularized initially by Marxists, and since then has been picked up by liberation theologists. Praxis refers to the integration of your practice with your belief system. As Gandhi said: "What is faith worth if it is not translated into action?" Obviously, we have to integrate our behavior with our theology in order to become people of integrity. Too often that is not done, whatever the religious belief. (p. 209)

A Theory and Its Research will Assess the Traditional Mass Media, in Their Current Corporate State, as Demographic Investigators and Reporters of "Who We Are"

Because concentration of ownership has brought the media under the control and direction of a few corporate owners and diminished the voices of the many publics, reality dictates including and studying what the media do best—sell—which is a tactical role, not a strategic policy orientation. The traditional media through their advertisers and corporate owners have a heavy financial investment and reward structure in counting and understanding consumers, and they do this through expensive marketing research, quite often and well. This kind of information could also be used to help society understand itself through surveillance of social, economic, and political trends that now primarily informs corporations and advertising firms.

Thus, the theory will take into account the global civic responsibility, perhaps a new theory of the press, demonstrated by the media (discussed later). *It is a prosumer approach to a society's knowledge, in which democracy and capitalism can often reside comfortably together.* Efficiency and effectiveness of the mass media do not have to bring with them the damned/praised dualist image if the media would help to deliver equality, empowerment, and diversity along with the entertaining "goods." Again, the externally concentrated and controlled locus of power makes the journalists' center of balance, objectivity, not of their own making, but certainly neither the making of more than half of the world's population. The passion of journalists for fairness and justice has been separated from their praxis because of the market-driven media's imposition of "objectivity" on them—a detached observer standpoint—which allows a hands-off, "business as usual" commercial agenda for the so-called Fourth Estate.

The Alternative, "Other" Media as Scenario Sketchers for Strategic, Social Policy Surveillance

The alternative, women's, minority, critical media will be included in a theory and its research as scenario sketchers for the strategic, or social policy surveillance, role they assume. Although their circulation and distribution are limited because of financial, legal, and institutional restraints, these media describe the reality of about three quarters of the world's population: They carry news and opinions about the human condition not often seen in depth in the mainstream (malestream) media. Their alternative, minoritized-majority roles are seldom theoretically examined for their societal importance, and, thus, such information and communication roles are continually diminished, if included at all, within traditional theories and research.

There are concepts being used similarly to the deeper communication or global ecocommunication that this author advocates and can be applied to communicative and journalistic theories. They include process journalism (Baumann & Siebert, 1993), the media as mediators (Baumann & Siebert, 1992), development journalism as emancipatory movements (Shah, 1993), and environmental or ecological journalism (Galtung & Vincent, 1992).

Galtung and Vincent (1992) offer proposals for a peace-oriented news media—report all sides, clarify the frame of reference, media ownership should not matter, do not overemphasize certain views, enhance the educational side of news, understand the reality of the arms issue, attend to the arms race inner dynamism, realize a weakness of media, consider North–South dynamics, clearly portray peace benefits; and for environment-oriented news media—be aware of cycles, identify all cyclic nodes, demand impact statements, identify long-term impact, identify environmental supporters, name the abusers, help citizens get information, help citizens decide what to do, identify rules broken, conduct follow-ups.

Galtung & Vincent acknowledge that if the news media focus on violence and on events rather than processes, the primacy of newness would direct attention toward direct violence rather than structural violence:

> People will be trained to conceive of the world in terms of the former rather than the latter. In order to see political or economic structural violence at work—commonly referred to as injustice, repression, or exploitation—a higher level of education would be needed to compensate for the difficulties in reporting and conceiving of structural categories undergoing slow processes of change. (p. 15)

A higher level of education could be simply implemented to be more inclusive of and culturally sensitive about women's and others' theories and worldviews.

With proposals such as these to transform communications, it would be a oversight/underslight not to offer the "allow people to speak for themselves," democratic communication philosophy long espoused by Allen (1977) and the Women's Institute for Freedom of the Press:

- People make their judgments on the basis of the information that they have at a given time
- Each person is the best judge of her or his own best interests, not the media for them
- Media owners give people the information they think is important for the public to know
- Media do not mirror society, they represent only the owners' views
- For the public to obtain the information of the majority, people must speak for themselves
- Political power is based on the number of people who can be reached with one's information
- Equalizing power among society would require that all have the means of reaching equal numbers of the public to communicate information when they wish, the way most suitable to the message. (see also Rush, 1989a).

Those of us who have searched for another name for the alternative media because of old paradigm/second-class citizen perceptions were not successful in finding another term. It took a professor of physics two years of random thinking about the problem I posed to her before her suggestion of "parallel press" (or "parallel media") surfaced. Margaret Gallagher (1986) wrote about parallelism in ways similar to the idea of a parallel press. Alternative media carry concurrent news and editorials about society alongside the mainstream press, but seldom do the two intersect (see, e.g., Gutierrez-Villalobos, Hertog, & Rush, 1994). Gallagher found a parallel between the UNESCO-sponsored New World Information and Communication Order (NWICO) goals and actions and those of women. They were like most parallels, she noted, equidistant.

Envisionary Media with New Objectives/Objectivity are Possible: Perhaps a Global Ecocommunication Theory and its Research of Generic (Any Form of Accessible, Usable, and Self-reporting and Correcting Information Channel and Message) Journalism/Communications

It is time for a synergetic "s/heroic" journey into the land of communication, information, and journalism.[2] In fact, it is time to acknowledge that we have (hierarchical and patriarchical as they may be) at least four (five, if intrapersonal—cognitive—is counted) systems of communication that we study: interpersonal, small group, organizational, mass, and global (international/intercultural). A new, generic interconnectivity of sub-disciplines is perhaps in order.

We must also admit that, most of the time, "other voices" are conspicuous by their absences in communication and information, whether in the media or journalism/communication education industries (women's, ethnic, minority, lesbigay voices and images are distorted, not listened to or silenced). We might have a more equitable, holistic approach if we could blend (have parallels intersect) traditional and alternative press. But it is not going to work until there is a global envisioning, accounting, and hearing of all voices "in here and out there." Male authors of most books advocating peace studies and conflict resolution, and even feminist scholarship as a way to these ends, seldom include either the feminists or the feminist scholarship speaking for themselves; we function as if in a half-world and of a half-mind. When the consumer poor are left out of communications, as they almost always are in their own voices, three quarters of the societal iceberg is functionally submerged. When it is also suggested that the voice of Gaia, the earth goddess, be listened to, we hear, "Say what!" Orr (1992), in his listing of academic disciplines with a suggested environmental focus for each, merely leaves out journalism and communication. Galtung and Vincent (1992) state that "a new journalism, a *global* journalism, a problem-conscious, socially conscious journalism, at home in the world as a whole, is still far away" (p. 23).

This author's advocacy of global ecocommunication as a possible theoretical framework/philosophy relies heavily on resolving the dualism, parallelism, cognitive dissonance between individuals and their communities/states/societies/planets. The intersection of capitalism and democracy seems paramount in this integrative paradigm, with keystone reliance on peace studies and conflict resolution. In all of this, however, the focus primarily is on mediation as a constructive communication process, for it is, or can be, the conflict resolution of choice for common people (one in

---

[2]Thanks to Dr. Autumn Grubb-Swetnam for this useful phrase. "Heroic journey" is a phrase found in mythologist Joseph Campbell's writings.

which those wanting conflict resolution are guided, not directed or forced, to make their own decisions; they do not have to be of elite status to participate in this process). It is with this tool, then, that an envisionary media might finally listen to the constructive criticism of Hazel Henderson (1969, 1989), who notes that the mass media have had a role to play in dysfunctional communication for they "are only a poor shadow of what they could be—not for lack of technology, but because of our imperfect understanding of their potential power" (1989, p. 295) As an example, the media can become mediators instead of gladiators. At first blush, it seems to be what the media have purported to be or wanted to do in their quest for "objectivity," but for which they did not appear to have the "communicatively correct" process.

As Baumann and Siebert (1993) point out: "The media mediates conflict, whether it intends to or not" (p. 28). They also urge the media to note that violence is grist for the media—to see the process, not just the outcome: "If violence is an outcome, then the media need to learn much more about the process, or continuum, of conflict leading to such violence" (p. 29). Baumann and Siebert, editor and associate editor, respectively, for the *Cross Times* magazine of Cape Town, South Africa, wrote that "principles of sound mediation are basically principles of sound journalism." (p 29). They noted some of the core principles or lessons that journalists can learn from mediation:

- See the process, not just the outcome
- Move parties beyond positions
- Watch one's language (how misleading or inflammatory it can be—be more aware of culturally exclusive language; of racist, sexist, fascist, militant language, avoiding stereotypes that reinforce pain)
- Learn how to win trust, build credibility, and challenge secrecy and authority at the same time.

The Mediation and Conflict Training for Journalists Project (MPJ) was initiated in early 1990 by the Cross Times Trust:

> The intent behind the MPJ is not to transform journalists into mediators per se, but to make them much more sensitive to conflict dynamics, to the impact of their work, and to the potential for managing conflict—by defining antagonists' mutual interests and getting to the genuine causes of conflicts. Through a series of workshops and publications, we challenge the myth of "objective" journalism, urging journalists to look at the ruts and biases in which they are trapped. (p. 32)

The project urges them to maximize one of their key advantages—nearly unparalleled access to parties in a conflict. They can ask antagonists in a conflict questions that parties would not ask each other. They can promote dialogue. They can widen agendas. They can help manage conflict toward just resolution, rather than merely get the story and run.
Could it be that the *Cross Times* magazine is a rare example of a generic, envisionary medium?

Envisionary media? What we can do is envision what the media might/should be. But they are at once the best of the traditional mainstream channels of communication and information (usually concentrated exclusivity and tactical efficiency), the alternative press (strategic, inclusive policy), the academic journals (concentrated precision and largely reductionistic), the professional press (trend and market analysis), the technological media (unlimited, elite connectivity), and face-to-face and small group discussion (limited, common connectivity).

A Theory and Its Research will have a Global Civil Society Worldview with Concern and Respect for the Information, Communication, and Integration of its Citizens

Several international communication scholars (Frederick, 1993; Galtung & Vincent, 1992; Hamelink, 1991; Rush, 1992, 1996; Tehranian & Tehranian, 1992) are turning toward a new "one world" concept in the sense that advances in technology make possible global conversations and communications. This new/old concept is often called a "global civil society" by John Locke, the English philosopher and political theorist (Frederick, 1993), without the "global" reaches of communications and other technology. The society consists of those individuals and groups who work together, outside and parallel with the operations of the State and corporate business, but always well within the scope of their broad influence, as Frederick (1993) points out. One of the often-cited examples are the nongovernmental organizations (NGOs), groups around the world that share common interests and work together to solve common problems (Boulding, 1988). The NGOs during the 1985 meeting of the U.N. Decade for Women in Nairobi had their own busy and extensive agenda; a later example was the influence of the NGOs during the global environmental meeting in Brazil in 1992. Increasingly important to this associative global society are new technologies, some of them most likely undeveloped or underdeveloped.

Playing important current roles as the 21st century approaches are the VCR, fax machine, and electronic mail. These technologies have the earmarks and some documentation (e.g., about their roles in the dissolution of the former Soviet Union) of envisionary media. Such envisionary media must in some way allow persons to speak for themselves in their own times in their own way about their own needs, hopes, ideas, or worldviews. The electronic mail in the last half of the 1990s held great promise for this kind of envisionary media, but was limited to elite users of computer technology. A global civil society is certainly a reasonable expectation if we have the means with which to share information and try to communicate and cooperate with all of humanity. We are of the same species, even if some do not want to admit it. Sooner or later, our issues are similar because we share human condition concerns. Even if we do not want to be, we are increasingly interactive with each other and the other species with whom we share the Earth.

We desperately need to get rid of our models of scarcity (Henderson, 1996), and replace them with models of sharing. We need to "square off" and "round out" our traditional and status quo notions and theories of "center" and "balance" if we are to arrive at a global civic society having interactive, concentric, and eccentric circle ecosystems. We all want to be balanced and centered and work, live, and play where that occurs much of the time: That is the inner and external peace that so many of us desire. However, "centers" often become urban centers or economic centers or domestic-international power centers, in which being centered means a lot of goods and resources are kept in one place with inequitable distribution to so-called peripheries, where a lot of poor, underprivileged people try to survive.

"Balance," too, is forced into models of scarcity in which often one has to have more than enough of something in order to be "comfortable," such as money, group loyalty, material goods: Lots of people are crowded here under the "normal curve" with little regard for irreverence, dissidence, or difference—the stuff with which artists create brave new worlds and the rest of us might learn something interesting and even exciting.

There is a subtle but important distinction that must be made within the theories of cognitive dissonance and balance, the control concepts of dominance and submission, the economic concepts of power and poverty. A parallel existence in which we are separate but truly equal is better (Rush, 1989a) than the violence and suffering that accompanies the scarcity/competitive model. Many women, feminists, lesbians, and some men are beginning to understand and practice this "concomitant process" (to accompany, have a companion, existence in association). However, a split brain is a dangerous train: The parallel tracks are there but how many of us can envision who will do the switching for the long haul of planetary survival?

Soon the parallel process model must become one of integrative intersections, where we can come together in our commonalities while respecting and learning about and from our differences.

To get to those crossroads of communication, those global intersections, we can ponder these words: "To be together without being afraid of each other—that's the beginning of the revolution" (Flood, 1993).

REFERENCES

Allen, D. (1977). *1977 index/directory of women's media.* Washington, DC: Women's Institute for Freedom of the Press.
Baumann, M., & Siebert, H. (1993, Winter). The media as mediator. *Forum,* pp. 28–30.
Boulding, E. (1988). *Building a global civic culture: Education for an interdependent world.* New York: Teachers College Press, Columbia University.
Campbell, J. (1988). *The power of myth* (with Bill Moyers, Betty Sue Flowers, ed.) New York: Doubleday.
Faludi, S. (1991). *Backlash.* New York: Crown.
Feminism and ecology (1993). *Society and Nature: The International Journal of Political Ecology* [Special issue], *2*(1), 1-162.
Flood, K. (1993, February 28). *Oral sermon.* Lexington, KY: Unitarian Universalist Church.
Folbre, N. (1993, July 16). The center cannot hold. *In These Times,* pp. 14-17.
Frederick, H. (1993). *Global communication and international relations.* Belmont, CA: Wadsworth.
French, M. (1992). *The war against women.* New York: Ballantine Books.
Gallagher, M. (1986). Women and NWICO. In P. Lee (Ed.), *Communication for all: New world information and communication order* (pp. 77-99). Maryknoll, NY: Orbis Books.
Galtung, J., & Vincent. R. (1992). *Global glasnost: Toward a new world information and communication order.* Cresskill, NJ: Hampton Press.
Gimbutas, M. (1989). *The language of the goddess.* New York: Harper & Row.
Gutierrez-Villalobos, S., Hertog, J., & Rush, R. (1994). Press support for the U.S. administration during periods of external conflict: A test of three theories. *Journalism Quarterly, 71*(3), 618-627.
Hamelink, C. J. (1991). Global communication: Place for civil action. In B. Hofsten (Ed.), *Informatics in food and nutrition* (pp. 5-8). Stockholm: Royal Academy of Sciences.
Henderson, H. (1969, Spring). Access to the media: A problem in democracy. *Columbia Journalism Review,* pp. 5-8.

Henderson, H. (1989). Eco-feminism and eco-communication: Toward the feminization of economics. In R. Rush & D. Allen (Eds.), *Communications at the crossroads: The gender gap connection* (pp. 289-304). Norwood, NJ: Ablex.

Henderson, H. (1996). Information: The world's new currency isn't scarce. *Building a win-win world: Life beyond economic warfare* (pp. 196-218). San Francisco: Berrett-Koehler.

hooks, b. (1992, July/August). Out of the academy and into the streets *Ms.*, pp. 80-82.

Kunst, M., & Witlox, N. (Eds.). (1993). *Communication and the environment*. London: Centre for the Study of Communication and Culture.

Miedzian, M. (1991). *Boys will be boys: Breaking the link between masculinity and violence.* New York: Doubleday.

Naess, A. (1992, September-December). Deep ecology and ultimate premises. *Society and Nature: The International Journal of Political Ecology, 1*(2), 108-119.

Naess, A. (1973). The shallow and the deep, long-range ecology movement (a summary). *Inquiry, 16*(1), 95-100. Oslo, Norway: Universitetforlaget, Norweigian Research Council for Science and the Humanities.

Orr, D. (1992). *Ecological literacy: Education and the transition to a postmodern world.* Albany: State University of New York Press.

Peck, M. S. (1993). *Further along the road less travelled.* New York: Simon & Schuster.

Rush, R. (1989a). Communications at the crossroads: The gender gap connection. In R. Rush & D. Allen (Eds.), *Communications at the crossroads: The gender gap connect*ion (pp. 3-19). Norwood, NJ: Ablex.

Rush, R. (1989b, May). *Global eco-communications: Assessing the communication and information environment.* Paper presented to the International Communication Association, San Francisco.

Rush, R. (1992, August). *Global eco-communications: Grounding and re/finding the concepts.* Paper presented to the International Association for Mass Communication Research, Brazil.

Rush, R. (1993). Being all that we can be: Harassment, barriers, prevent progress. *Journalism Educator, 48*(1), 71-79.

Rush, R. (1996). Ten tenets for deeper communications: Transforming communications theory and research, In D. Allen, R. Rush, & S. Kaufman (Eds.), *Women transforming communications: Global intersections.* Thousand Oaks, CA: Sage.

Shah, H. (1994, January). *Development journalism as an emancipatory social movement.* Paper presented at MacBride Round Table, Honolulu.

Steinem, G. (1992). *Revolution from within: A book of self-esteem.* Boston: Little, Brown.

Tehranian, K., & Tehranian, M. (1992). *Restructuring for world peace: On the threshold of the twenty-first century.* Cresskill, NJ: Hampton Press.

Webster's New World Dictionary. (Third College ed.). (1988). New York: Simon & Schuster.

4

The Cyberight to Communicate: A Human Right of the Fourth Generation?

Wolfgang Kleinwaechter

Since the cyberspace has invited millions of individuals to come and to communicate, a new dimension for the human right to freedom of expression has occurred in the history of international communication. The century-old traditional communication frontiers of time and space, which have been gradually reduced already in the last three decades, when satellites opened the door to the global village, have completely disappeared. In a couple of seconds millions of bits of information can be moved around the globe, linking individuals and institutions together into a global community. The loneliness of an isolated island disappears when the undersea fiber-optic cable has reached its shores and offers the possibility to log in, to download information, and to talk with anybody, anywhere, at anytime.

Is this unprecedented opportunity an offer to everybody, or will there be a gatekeeper who asks for an identity card, a special permission and entrance fee if somebody wants to surf on the infobahn? Is there free access, or has only a limited number of info-drivers the right to participate in the global info-race? Is there an individual and collective human right to communicate in the cyberspace? Or do new forms of censorship appear at the invisible horizon of the net of the networks?

When history has reached a turning point, it is always useful to look back and to remember what has happened when the historical process has been reached its last curve. The Internet is not the first technological tool that has challenged the established political and legal frameworks for interpersonal and international communication, although it is certainly the most radical change. A lot can be learned from the past development of communication technology and its political, economic, social, and cultural as well as legal consequences.

The history of human rights freedom of expression, to information and communication itself, is an interesting story that reflects the interrelationship between communication technology development and communication regulation. The birth of the individual right to freedom of expression reflects the invention of a new communication technology—the printing press. This "first generation" of the communication rights was seen mostly as a political and civil individual human right, which also included the freedom of the press. At the end of the 19th century and the beginning of the 20th century, the "second generation" of human rights—social, economic, and cultural rights—put the individual right to freedom of expression in a broader context. Freedom of the press remains an empty concept for people who have no right to education, to learn writing and reading. The "third generation" of communication rights—the concept of the individual and collective right to communicate—emerged with the satellite age, when discussion centered on a "two-way flow of communication" instead of on a "one-way flow of information," on access and participation. This concept was still based on the traditional understanding of sovereignty. Now, with the appearance of the global networks and cyberspace, which is no more linked directly to territory and established legal institutions, the question arises whether special "cyberights" should be established. Will there be a "fourth generation" of human rights to information and communication? Is there a cyberight to communicate?

Let us first look back to history in a more detailed way.

JOHN MILTON'S AEROPAGITICA

John Milton's (1987) call for the individual right to freedom of expression in the early 17th century, when he wrote his famous *Aeropagitica* in which he developed the concept of freedom of information, was nothing more than a reaction toward the invention of the printing press by Johan Gutenberg. Gutenberg's printing press offered for the first time the possibility to duplicate and distribute written ideas and information on a mass basis within and between countries. The ruling elites at this time, both the Catholic church and the feudal absolutists followed this development not only with applause but also with a great portion of mistrust when they discovered that this new wave of information could challenge their absolutist right to "possess the truth," having the potential to undermine the stability of their power structure.

Their reaction was very simple: They took over control of the means of information production and introduced a system of (legally justified) political censorship. Every book that was printed needed permission for its publication. Illegally printed books were put on an "Index," introduced by the Catholic church. The author, the producer, and also the reader of the so-called (dis)qualified book were confronted with much difficulties in their daily lives.

John Milton challenged this system of "regulation." When he wrote *Aeropagitica,* he remembered the old Greek tradition in which the citizens of Athens met every day on the Aeropag, the marketplace, for open public discussions and the exchange of information. At the Aeropag everybody had the right to express him-or herself freely. John Milton argued that the right to freedom of expression is a natural human right of every human being. The publication of ideas with a new technological tool is, according to Milton, nothing else than a broader application of this right, which is not a gift by the government but a natural right of the individual.

However, Milton acknowledged as well that the government has a special interest in this affair, and that the freedom can also be misused. Insofar as some regulations should be accepted that guarantee that the rights and freedoms are used in a responsible manner, and that the rights and freedoms of others are not destroyed, he denied every form of (governmental) censorship that provides a system in which one person (or institution) decides for others what is fit to print. According to Milton, the most ignorant behavior of a government is when it tries to stop the import of the most important resource, the truth, at its ports. Regardless of Milton's logic arguments, there have been a lot of governments since that have chosen to ignore Milton's warning. It could be that because they behaved so ignorantly, they lost sooner, rather than later, the power they wanted to maintain by suppressing the truth.

What Milton proposed was a compromise between individual and public interests. The individual right to freedom of expression was seen, on the one hand, as untouchable, but governments and democratically elected parliaments should have, on the other hand, a right to create a general legal and political framework in the common interest of all individuals and society as a whole. Indeed, the interests of the individual and the interests of the government are not identical, and conflicts and tensions are inevitable. However, conflicts and tensions should not destroy the balance between legitimate individual rights and legitimate public interests. Freedom and responsibility are two sides of one coin and not two different things, contrary to each other. If, on the one hand, governments have an omnipotent power to determine what is "responsible," what is good and bad, individual communication, a classic dictatorship could be the consequence. On the other hand, if rights and freedoms are used in a one-sided and ruthless manner, the "law of the jungle" could create another system of oppression.

FROM THE FIRST AMENDMENT TO THE INTERNATIONAL TELEGRAPH CONVENTION

Milton's call for the right to freedom of expression as a fundamental individual human right played a central role in the revolutions of the 18th century and was translated into the constitutional documents of the new emerging democracies. The U.S. First Amendment to the Constitution, adopted in 1791, says "Congress shall make no law . . . abridging the freedom of speech, or of the press" (see Chamberlain & Brown, 1982). In the French Revolution of 1789, the call for the right to freedom of expression was reflected in Article 4 of the Human Rights Declaration. According to this declaration, individual rights and freedom have its origins on that which the rights and freedoms of others are concerned (see Kleinwachter, 1988).

With the beginning of the Industrial Age, newspapers and journals became open marketplaces of ideas and information. It is interesting to remember that the young Karl Marx used the freedom of the press to develop his theoretical ideas of socialism in numerous critical articles in the *Neue Rheinische Zeitung* and other newspapers. He himself was at this time an enthusiastic supporter of freedom of the press. In one of his early articles (Marx & Engels, 1956), he qualified the freedom of the press as "the open eye of the spirit of a people" (p. 60) and as "the materialized confidence of people in itself" (p. 61). He also drew the attention to the fact that with the coming of mass communication, the question of who owns the means of the production of printing plants and publishing houses was decisive. Marx argued that the owner of a printing press has certainly more possibilities to express him-or herself more freely than an individual who has no access to mass media. Economic censorship could have similar affects such as political censorship.

The emergence of the telegraph in 1837 was the next turning point in the history of international communication. The telegraph created new possibilities for international communication among nations, but communication beyond national frontiers could become a reality only if the technical standards for telegraphy would be supported by all countries in the same way. Twenty-five years after the invention of the telegraph, diplomatic negotiations created a special legislation for the transborder flow of messages. On May 17, 1865, an International Telegraph Convention granted "everybody the right to correspond by means of telegraphs" and obliged the participating states to use the same technical standards. At the same time, however, the "High Contracting Parties" reserved the right "to prevent private telegrams from being transmitted that threatens state security or violate the laws of the country, public order or morals" (Krause, 1960a, p. 62). The states did not react differently to the development of wireless telegraphy at the beginning of the 20th century. The "international Radio Telegraph Convention," adopted in 1906 in Berlin, followed the structure of the telegraph convention created in 1865.

Was this "twin concept" a "balanced compromise" in the spirit of John Milton's *Aeropagitica*? Or was this a disguised attempt by the governments to keep control over (and, under certain circumstances, to censor) the flow of information?

Quoting the German State Secretary for Postal Affairs, Kraetke, from his opening speech in the Berlin Radio Telegraphy Conference in 1906, the "spreading of electrical waves for news transmission by radio-telegraphy will not, however, be stopped by borders, be the place destination within or beyond them" (cited in Krause, 1960a, p. 10). He added: "Therefore radio-telegraphy, more than any other means of news transmission, has an international character right from the beginning which doubtlessly requires an international order" (p. 10).

What was Kreatke's and the German government's understanding of an "international communication order" in 1906? Was it a democratic guarantee for the right to freedom of expression or a disguised legitimation for government censorship? As history has shown, this "twin concept" has been used in the 20th century for both, stimulating free communication and justifying control over the media.

GLOBAL BROADCASTING IN THE SATELLITE GE: FREEDOM VERSUS CENSORSHIP

In the 1920s and 1930s, international short-wave broadcasting spread very fast and opened again broader possibilities for international communication. Negotiations in the League of Nations produced a "Geneva Convention Concerning the Use of Broadcasting in the Cause of Peace," adopted in 1936, which, on the one hand, guaranteed the right to the free dissemination of radio programs internationally, but codified, on the other hand, the right of the state to stop all transmissions that can be seen as dangerous to international peace (Krause, 1960b). The convention was seen (and justified) as a political and legal instrument against the massive misuse of the freedom of information in the history of humanity by the

German Nazi racial and war propaganda. Regardless of the fact that the implementation mechanism of the convention as too complicated and confusing and the procedures—who determines what war propaganda is—remained unclear, the regulation did not work. Nazism and fascism was beaten by other instruments than legally binding convention.

When the first communication satellites were launched on an orbital position in the early 1960s, global negotiations started immediately to create a framework for the use of this new mean of communication. In the Outer Space Committee of the United Nations (COPUOS) and later in UNESCO, the topic became an issue of controversial political discussions. The direct broadcasting of television programs via satellites was seen by dictators as a challenge to their power, by poorer nations as an attack against their cultural identity, by transnational media corporations as opportunity for new markets, and by democratic forces as a new chance to broaden and deepen the individual right to freedom of expression.

When the late Jean d'Arcy (1979) wrote his famous article about developments on satellite television (DBS), he based his ideas in the tradition of the French revolution with its call for an individual right to freedom of expression. However, in his article, he went beyond this individual approach and developed the concept of a right to communicate as a new human right. D'Arcy saw the danger of a deep division of society into active producers and passive receivers of information against the backdrop of the development of communication technology. His alternative proposal—the concept of the right to communicate, based on the individual human right to freedom of expression—was an invitation, in the spirit of the old Greek Aeropag, to use new communication technology for interactive communication among free citizens and free nations.

The discussion on DBS and the right to communicate later became hostage to the ideological debate around the New World Information and Communication Order (NWICO), which overshadowed human rights discussions in the 1970s and the 1980s. A compromise was never reached. All agreements and regulations concerning international communication during these two decades, from the UNESCO Mass Media Declaration (1978) to the UN DBS Resolution (1982), were based on the general "twin concept," which gave both the suppression of information and the misuse of media freedoms a semi-legal international justification.

This "twin concept," which was also adopted by the United Nations in 1966 as Article 19 of the Universal Declaration of Human Rights," referred on the one hand to the individual right to freedom of expression and on the other hand to the right of governments to restrict this individual right in the interests of national security, public order, public health, and public morals, as well as to protect the rights, interests, and reputations of others. (Kleinwaechter, 1990).

Although this "compromise" became the subject of bitter political struggle during the Cold War, both sides could live with this "twin concept" in theory. It gave the "freedom fighters" a right to call for a free flow of information, and it gave the "peace fighters" a justification to stop the free flow of information in the interest of the "maintenance of peace." In practice, the effectiveness of the means of control was reduced permanently. With every new step in the development of communication technology it became more difficult to get the transborder information flow under control. Jamming of "dangerous" radio short-wave broadcasts worked in the 1950s, but jamming of satellite broadcasts, theoretically possible, overstretched the economic capacities of these governments. However, the justification of this "limited and justified censorship" politically did not work. The control of the information flow backfired. Not only did these governments lose their international reputations, but these protectors of "national security" and "public order" from "dangerous information," these surpressers of free communication, could not keep pace with the development of communication technology. The information flow seeped under the "walls." Stupid governments, which prevented, in the sense of Milton, the inflow of truth, lost their power, sooner rather than later.

THE DISAPPEARANCE OF CONTROL OVER SOVEREIGNTY IN CYBERSPACE

The 1980s produced the next tool for global communication, the Internet. By the mid-1990s, there are about 25 million individuals linked together in a global network, which knows no boundaries of time and space. Furthermore, this new tool, which is not linked to a territory, does not know the traditional category of sovereignty. There is no international legislation, besides the standards for interconnectivity and interoperability. No government can control the Internet; there is no one single owner, and no "political qualification" is need to enter cyberspace. As a *New York Times* cartoon with two dogs in front of a computer put it with irony: "In the Internet, nobody knows that you are a dog."

But does the disappearance of classical categories mean that the traditional reaction of governments toward the emergence of new communication technology will disappear as well, that governments will not undertake efforts to get the new tool under control and to put it into a regulatory framework, which provides them the right to interfere if their interests are challenged? And does it mean that there is no need to call for an individual right to communicate because the technology of the Internet per se is a guarantor of this right?

One decade after the Internet escaped from a pilot project of Pentagon (to make the U.S. military communication system invulnerable against Russian nuclear attacks) into the world of academics, which used it for "peaceful" Aeropag-like intellectual debate, it is too early to answer the question with a single yes or no.

On the one hand, the Internet seems to be not only a new step in an endless chain of improvements of international communication, but a totally new mechanism that goes far beyond traditional communication improvements. The decentralized Internet is to a certain degree the most organized chaos in the history of humanity. It is unmanageable and uncontrollable. It is a new dimension, a new culture, a new way of communication. It gives for the first time in history (theoretically) everybody the opportunity "to seek, receive and impart information and ideas of all kinds regardless of frontiers," to use the language of article 19 of the Universal Declaration for Human Rights.

On the other hand, there are numerous efforts to get the Internet politically and economically under control. Governments are interested in knowing what is going on in the information highway. The idea of a clipper chip, which would allow third parties to check individual communications, has not yet disappeared. Pricing is another possibility to erect barriers for the unlimited use for the new technology for free communication. Telecommunications companies can channel the flow of information into "wanted directions" and prevent participation of "everybody."

There are no global negotiations to regulate the Internet thus far. The traditional legal system is not prepared to handle the new challenges. The application of old norms to the new phenomenas will not work. The GATT agreement, reached after eight years of complicated negotiations in December 1993, includes some exceptional clauses, which reserved governments the right to protect national cultural identity. The protection of intellectual property rights was designed to protect a national cultural identity. The protection of intellectual property rights was another key issue of the GATT agreement, relevant to the Internet. But does cyberspace know classic "property right"? How can "virtual property" be defined, and how can it be protected? There are a lot of ideas, some proposals, but no clear legal institutes. Intergovernmental organization are working on this agenda. The World Intellectual Property Organization (WIPO) and the International Telecommunication Union (ITU) are other global organizations trying to create a new legal framework for global communication in the 21st century. And the leading industrial powers of the G7, which have opposed all kinds of regulation in this field within UN and UNESCO in the 1970s and the 1980s, have in the 1990s rediscovered the need for "adequate legislation" for international communication. Legal issues are playing a growing role in all their numerous initiatives from the U.S.-based National Information Infrastructure (NII), to the EU-based "Bangemann Report" and Asian Pacific Information Initiative (APII), to the Global Information Infrastructure Initiative (GIII), which was proposed by U.S.

Vice President Al Gore at the ITU World Telecommunication Development Conference (Buenos Aires, March 1994) and launched by the G7 Summit in Brussels, February 1995 (see Kleinwaechter, 1993). The dilemma is that the states and their governments, which traditionally create international law, are not the main players in the global information society debate. ITU has opened the door for non-state members, which also includes transnational corporations, to participate in international communication law making. The Additional Plenipotentiary Conference of the ITU now has the authority to appoint advisory boards with mixed participation (ITU, 1993).

In the G7 Summit Final Document it is stressed that the regulatory framework of the Global Information Society should "put the user first and meet a variety for complementary societal objectives. It must be designed to allow choice, high quality services and affordable prices." A relevant legal framework must, according to the G7 partners, have to be based "on an environment that encourages dynamic competition, ensures the separation of operating and regulatory functions as well as promotes interconnectivity and interoperability. Open access to networks for service and information suppliers and the mutual enrichment of the citizen through the promotion of diversity, including cultural and linguistic diversity, as well as the free expression of ideas, are essential for the creation of Global Information Society." Competition rules "need to be interpreted and applied in the light of convergence of new entrants and growing global competition" (see Gore & Brown, 1995).

The G7 partners agreed to commit themselves to six objectives:

- Ensure citizens' access through universal service in the respective markets
- Open up markets to allow the development of global systems
- Pursue the interconnectivity of networks and the interoperability of services provide open access to networks and the interoperability of services
- Provide open access to networks for service and information suppliers
- Implement fair and effective licensing and frequency allocation
- Allow for productive forms of cooperation while shielding against anticompetitive behavior (Chair's conclusion, 1995).

However, the new regulations are not yet elaborated, and even the concepts behind forthcoming judicial norms are still unclear and very weak in legal substance. It remains open how such new legal norms and principles will work in practice, how they will affect the individual and collective right to communicate in the cyberspace. What will happen if these regulations remain without any practical affect and fundamental political and economic interests are at stake? Will the argument of a "misuse of the Internet" justify the need for an elaboration of new norms to protect "national security and public order"? Will there be a call for new norms to protect "national security and public order"? Will there be a call for a new "International Network Convention" that would give governments the right to interfere into an unwanted flow of communication? How should governments deal with (organized) criminal activities on the Net? Is the existing system of data protection stable enough to protect privacy? When will a legally binding quota system (with the aim to protect national and cultural identity) be introduced for "video on demand"? How will this affect the freedom to choice and the right to communicate? Is a "cyberpolice" beyond the imagination ("Is anything safe," 1995)? Do we need a new mechanism for disputing resolution? How does one define individual and collective access and participatory rights for driving on the infobahn? Does the cyberight to communicate remain an empty concept? Are the material poor to become also the information poor?

At the moment it seems technologically impossible to bring the unlimited cyberspace under limited governmental control. Clearly defined legal categories for cyberspace that go beyond the concept of national sovereignty will be very difficult to codify and even more difficult to apply and implement. But history tells us that a new communication tool has always produced sooner or later political or economic mechanisms (in legal terms) to use the new technologies as instruments of power or profit, with individual human rights as secondary.

Will it be different with the Internet? Will the waves of regulation, deregulation, and re-regulation come to an end, and does the cyberspace lead to a situation of no regulation, similar to the pre-Gutenberg time, in which Ancient Greece everybody had the natural right to go to Aeropag and to raise their voices. If this will be the case with the cyberspace, then the jump into the information age is truly a revolution.

REFERENCES

d'Arcy, J. (1979). *The right to communicate* (Studies of the Macbride Commission, CIC-Paper no. 36). Paris: UNESCO.

Chair's Conclusion of G7 Information Society Conference. (1995, February 26). Brussels.

Chamberlain, B. E., & Brown, C. J. (1982). *The First Amendment reconsidered: New perspectives on the meaning of freedom of speech and press.* New York & London: Longman.

Gore, A., & Brown, R. (1995, February). *Global information infrastructure agenda for cooperation.* Washington, DC.

International Telecommunication Union (ITU). (1993). *Telecommunication visions of future, A perspective of the World Telecommunications Advisory Council.* Geneva: Author.
Is anything safe in cyberspace? The Growing threats to privacy and property in the information age. (1995, January 23). *Newsweek.*
Kleinwachter, W. (1988). The interrelationship of introduction of new communication technologies and the need for international regulation. In W. Kleinwachter (Ed.), *New communication technology and international law* (p. 7ff.). Prague: IJI.
Kleinwaechter, W. (1990). The birth of article 19—A twin concept of the United States. *Journal of Media Law and Practice, 10*(3), 3.
Kleinwaechter, W. (1993). The search for a world communication order—Hundred years of global negotiations on communication technology. In W. Kleinwaechter & K. Nordenstreng (Eds.), *International security and humanitarian cooperation in the reunited Europe.* Tampere, Finland: Tampere University Press.
Krause, G. (1960a). *Internationaler fernmeldeverein.* Frankfurt.
Krause, G. (1960b). Der rundfunkfriedenpakt von 1936. In *Jahrbuch fur internationales recht* (pp. 31ff.). Kiel.
Marx, K., & Engel, F. (1956). *Werke Band 1.* Berlin.
Milton, J. (1987). *Aeropagitica.* Leipzig: Recam Verlag.

5

Catching Up to Our Digital Future? Cyberdemocracy versus Virtual Mercantilism

Michael R. Ogden

> We reject kings, presidents, and voting. We believe in rough consensus and running code. (Clark, personal communication, November, 1992)

Ready or not, our lives are about to change—quickly! The digital information revolution, which smoldered in academic and industrial test labs throughout most of the 1970s and 1980s, burst on our collective consciousness in the 1990s and caught many people offguard. No longer an abstract concept, the "Information Superhighway" has captured the imagination of the popular press even as continual advances in technology propel the information revolution forward at an astonishing rate. As if in symbiosis with these technical advancements, government, corporate, and individual demand for access to the so-called "Infobahn" has grown at a similar pace.

---

*An earlier version of this chapter was presented at the 6th MacBride Round Table session on Media and New Technologies in an International Setting, January 20-23, 1994, Honolulu, and published in *Futures* (September 1994), *26*(7), 713-729 as "Politics in a Parallel Universe: Is there a Future for Cyberdemocracy?" This chapter is a revised, updated, and expanded version of the earlier work.

Such developments as these are irreversibly changing the way we work, live, and think, what with the sudden proliferation of computers, modems, and communication networks and all the talk of interactive digital libraries, multimedia information on demand, the electronic superhighway, the Internet, Usenet, Gopher, and the World-Wide Web. Such innovations have not of themselves made things better or worse. Rather, they have given us the ability to make changes far more profoundly, dramatically, and—of course—much faster than ever before. As a result, we are now witness to the birth and exponential growth of a "virtual community" (Rheingold, 1993) nearly 107 million strong and adding almost a million new users each month.

However, cyberspace is an "environment" in flux, in which shared values collide with discussions of diversity, in which freedom of expression, freedom of association, and equality are paramount and attempts at censorship are vehemently opposed or simply circumvented. Cyberspace is indeed a "community," one in which the most potent discussions are those that seek to define and delineate this new social environment and the role of the individual in it. As to be expected, this kind of discussion is inherently a political activity. In this case, it is a form of politics on the "electronic frontier," in which the lines are being drawn, decisions made, and actions taken regarding our collective digital future with little input— until recently—from actual governments. However, this is now about to change. As the economic and political forces that control communication technologies begin to impinge on cyberspace, and as "white men in blue suits"—from government ministers to corporate executives (cf. Perry 1995)—talk of an information superhighway crossing national borders and traversing the globe, a narrow window of opportunity is emerging that presents us with a choice: Either we act now to secure communication technologies for the continued facilitation of community formation and interaction among people who could not (or would not) otherwise ever meet "in real life," or through inaction, allow some multimedia conglomerate to take over, restrict the flow of information, and turn it into a giant, fungible, "pay-per-byte" stream of edutainment and vertically marketed, interactive "cybermalls." Such an outcome could effectively destroy cyberspace as an autonomous collective of virtual communities.

What, *exactly*, is "cyberspace"? Is anyone, should anyone, be in control? What will be our digital future? Should we even care? These questions are presently at the heart of a raging debate taking place on Usenet newsgroups and in Internet Relay Chat "rooms" throughout the United States and around the world with no clear resolution in sight. What has become clear is that the potential importance of cyberspace to political liberties and the ways in which virtual communities are likely to change our experience of the real world—as individuals and communities—is not just a function of convergent technologies, but also a function of their intelligent and deliberate use by an informed population. More people must learn about the intellectual, social, commercial, and political leverage presented by participation in the communications revolution that is cyberspace—while the freedom to do so still exists. "The odds are always good that big power and big money will find a way to control access to [cyberspace] . . . . The Net is still out of control in fundamental ways, but it might not stay that way for long" (Rheingold 1993, p. 5). Likewise, present discussions about the future of cyberspace appear to be coalescing around visions of virtual community-centered and network citizen-controlled "Jeffersonian networks" (Kapor, 1992), as opposed to big money and big power in control of the emerging communications technologies,[1] In other words, an evolving grass-roots, participatory cyberdemocracy versus a top-down, repackaged, and corporate-controlled virtual mercantilism. As Rheingold (1993) stated in his seminal book recounting the human side of cyberspace, "what we know and do now is important because it is still possible for people around the world to make sure this new sphere of vital human discourse remains open to the citizens of the planet before the political and economic big boys seize it, censor it, meter it, and sell it back to us" (p. 5).

This chapter is an exploration of these issues. Following a brief exercise in finding a functional definition of what is meant by *cyberspace*, a short historical synopsis of the roots of cyberspace and the beginnings of our transformation into "being digital" (Negroponte, 1995) is provided. Finally, two alternatives will be presented with a discussion of several areas of critical concern that policymakers must contend with in the construction of our digital future. It is vitally important for all to recognize that, at this juncture, the future of cyberspace has become too important to leave to specialists or special interests.

---

[1]This is a tangential reference to Ben Bagdikian's (1983) prediction in his *The Media Monopoly* that soon after the turn of the century there would be no more than a dozen very large corporate conglomerates in control of almost all of the world's important newspapers, magazines, broadcast stations, entertainment production facilities (movies, music, etc.), and, by extension, public access computer networks and databases. To this end, witness media baron Rupert Murdock's acquisition of Delphi, a private computer information network and database, in September 1993. Likewise, since the signing into law of the Telecommunications Act of 1996, mergers and acquisitions in telecommunications, cable television, and media industries are being repeated around the world, with corporations maneuvering for market position.

THE "SPACELESS PLACE"

Cyberspace is a slippery word to define. It has only recently come into common parlance, so any definition remains subjective and illusory. For our purposes cyberspace can be defined as a conceptual "spaceless place" where words, human relationships, data, wealth, status, and power are made manifest by people using computer-mediated communications technology. It has been variously described as a new universe, a parallel universe created and sustained by the world's present and future computers and communication networks. It is accessed through any computer capable of linking into the network; a place, one place, multidimensional, limitless, everywhere, and nowhere; a place where nothing is forgotten and yet everything changes. Cyberspace is the realm of data, of pure information.[2]

However, a mature and immersive cyberspace does not really "exist"—yet—but its genealogy draws from the very history of communication media, from the "invention" of language and writing to communicate across space and time, to "real-time" digital video conferencing between individuals half a world apart. At the same time, cyberspace is an elusive "artifact" of the future, what William Gibson (1984), the science fiction writer who coined the word, has described as "a consensual hallucination experienced daily by billions of legitimate operators, in every nation . . . data abstracted from the banks of every computer in the human system. Unthinkable complexity . . . arranged in the nonspace of the mind [like] clusters and constellations of data" (p. 51). At the core of this, and all other visions of cyberspace, is a matrix of interconnected computers and information systems; in other words, the "Net."

At present, the Net is accessed primarily by means of a telephone cable plugged into a modem connected to a computer. Through the use of such technology, "you are what you type" in cyberspace. But Gibson writes of the possibility in the not too distant future in which individuals will be able to use their brains—directly—through neural plugs. The idea of "jacking in" and interfacing with complex programs that turn computer data into perceptual events appeals to many on the Net, even though there are even more who feel that Gibson has produced works that are not so much science fiction as informed prediction.

---

[2]This definition is a composite of those given to explain "Gibsonian" cyberspace, virtual reality, emergent virtual reality, virtual representation, simulation, telepresence, and computer-mediated communications; that is, networks as social space. Cyberspace has also been variously called the "virtual global village," the "virtual community," and "the Net." In formulating the present composite definition I relied heavily on Michael Benedikt's (1991) influential book *Cyberspace: First Steps*. Also referenced for this purpose was Howard Rheingold's (1993) *The Virtual Community: Homesteading on the Electronic Frontier*, Linda Harasim's (1993) *Global Networks: Computers and International Communications*, and innumerable individuals "on the Net."

The point of this is to illustrate the "immensity" of cyberspace—as a concept and "place"—and the vagueness of its definition. Conceptually, cyberspace's evolution can be said to resemble Indra's Net from Hindu mythology (originally, a metaphor for the infinitely expanding universe): It can thus be seen as a great "net" with a user at each "knot" reflecting every other user like a growing, evolving four-dimensional hologram of itself (cf. McFadden, 1991). Yet in this conceptual "vagueness" lies the empowerment of participating in the definition—as "audience, performer, and scriptwriter . . . in an ongoing improvisation [of a] full-scale subculture . . . growing on the other side of [the] telephone jack" (Rheingold, 1993, p. 2).

So where is cyberspace? Perhaps this is not a very useful question, for "cyberspace is like [the mythical land of] Oz—it is, we get there, but it has no location" (Stenger, 1991, p. 53) no "place." If this is so, then why is cyberspace and how did it come to exist? This may prove more enlightening for cyberspace does have a history (see Appendix A), an accidental history (Rheingold, 1993). What is today referred to as "cyberspace" or "the Net" had its roots in a very different and somewhat apocalyptic purpose more than 20 years ago at the RAND Corporation.

THE BIRTH AND GROWTH OF CYBERSPACE[3]

Mulling over the grim prospect of surviving a nuclear holocaust, the RAND Corporation (at the time, the United States's premiere Cold War think-tank) was faced with a strange problem of strategic importance: How could U.S. authorities successfully communicate in the aftermath of a nuclear exchange, and how would the infrastructure itself be built and controlled? In 1964, the RAND Corporation made public its answer: The proposed network would use existing communication trunk lines, have no central authority, and would be designed from the beginning to operate as if the network was already highly unreliable. Thus, all nodes in the network would be equal in status to all other nodes (no centrally controlled hub to be an easy "first strike" target), and messages would be broken up and transmitted as separately addressed "packets" winding their individual ways through the network until they arrive at their intended destination and were reassembled (Rheingold, 1993). In this way, the communicating computers—not the network itself—were responsible for ensuring that the communication was accomplished (Krol, 1994). This idea of a decentralized, "blastproof," packet-switched, peer-to-peer network was picked up in the late 1960s by the Pentagon's Advanced Research Projects Agency

---

[3]For a brief timeline highlighting some of the key events that helped shape the Internet as we know it today, see Appendix A.

(ARPA) as a way of linking several high-speed supercomputers together for the sake of national research and development projects. By December 1969, four computers were networked together, and the ARPANET was born.

However, by the second year of operation, ARPANET traffic revealed an interesting and unexpected caveat:

> ARPANET's users had warped the computer-sharing network into a dedicated, high-speed, federally subsidized electronic post-office. The main traffic on ARPANET was not long-distance computing [as was originally intended]. Instead, it was news and personal messages. Researchers were using ARPANET to collaborate on projects, to trade notes on work, and eventually, to downright gossip and schmooze. (Sterling, 1993)

As has always been the case, people took a tool developed for one purpose and used it for another totally unintended purpose, much to the surprise—or chagrin—of the original developers. Enthusiasm for this new use of the ARPANET very quickly outgrew that for long-distance computing. Likewise, it was not very long before the invention of topical, electronic distribution lists for the sharing of news and information in a "many-to-many" format with large numbers of like-minded network subscribers began encroaching on the network (a precursor to today's USENET newsgroups). System engineers had to redesign the system again and again to keep up with the exponential growth in network communications traffic (Rheingold, 1993).

Throughout the 1970s, ARPANET continued to grow; its decentralized structure made expansion easy and unlike the typical corporate computer network. The ARPANET could accommodate many different kinds of machines—as long as they could all speak the lingua franca of packet-switching. Researchers involved with the ARPANET began to realize that one future of networking was the interconnecting of dissimilar networks, the development of a "network of networks" (Quarterman, 1993). To facilitate this end, the TCP/IP suite[4] was developed. The Internet Protocol (IP) places data into individually "addressed" packets to be sent out over the network. The "network of networks" that use IP do so primarily with Transmission Control Protocol (TCP), which sets the ground rules for the transport, or "handing off," of the IP packets until they reach their

---

[4]Transmission Control Protocol/Internet Protocol is a set of protocols developed by the U.S. Department of Defense to link dissimilar computers across many kinds of networks, including unreliable ones as well as computers connected to dissimilar Local Area Networks (LANs). TCP/IP's assurance of multivendor connectivity has also made it popular among commercial users (Newton, 1994).

intended destination. Because the TCP/IP software was public domain, and the basic technology was decentralized from its inception, by as early as 1977, TCP/IP was being used by other networks to interconnect with the ARPANET. The beginning of the 1980s marked the expansion of U.S. government agency interest in networking with the connection of the Department of Energy, National Aeronautics and Space Administration (NASA), and the National Science Foundation (NSF) to name a few (Cerf, 1995). In 1983, the military segment broke off and became MILNET (for military operational use), whereas the ARPANET remained a network primarily for education and research support (Rheingold, 1993). ARPANET began to spread, with links from Hawaii to Norway and back again. Both ARPANET and MILNET became wide area backbone networks connecting hundreds and later thousands of local area networks into a global Internet, then called the ARPA Internet (Quarterman, 1993). It is now referred to as just the Internet or the Net, and most recently cyberspace.

Around 1984, proposals were drafted for a national supercomputer access network by the NSF's Office of Advanced Scientific Computing. Deployed in 1986, the new NSFNET became the backbone network in the Internet and set a blistering pace for technical advancement, linking newer and faster supercomputers through faster, larger capacity lines, which expanded twofold in 1988 and again in 1990. Eventually, ARPANET was retired from service in 1989, "a happy victim of its own overwhelming success" (Sterling, 1993), because its link speeds (56 Kbps, or kilobits per second) were considered too obsolete (compared with the NSFNET's 1.544 to 45 Mbps, or megabits per second; at this speed you can send 5,000 pages of text per second or a couple of encyclopedias per minute).

In 1969, there were only four nodes in ARPANET; by 1983, there were around 200. Today, some 20 years after its inception—thanks largely to TCP/IP, continued increases in demand and sustained funding—there are tens of millions of nodes in the Internet, scattered over 42 countries, with more coming online every day.[5] Although the Net was born in the U.S. Department of Defense, the current Internet is much bigger and more diverse than its origins might indicate; military organizations are a small

---

[5]The nodes in this growing network of networks are divided into six basic "domains." Although foreign computers, and a few U.S. ones, choose to be denoted by their geographical locations (e.g., eta.lut.ac.uk, or well.sf.ca.us), others use the following classifications:

.gov	governmental institutions
.mil	military institutions
.edu	educational institutions
.com	commercial institutions
.org	nonprofit organizations
.net	gateways between networks

and shrinking minority on the Internet (Quarterman, 1993). Likewise, in the early to mid-1980s, the NSFNET's high-speed, high-capacity lines, which were known as *the* "Internet Backbone," saw the United States "lording it over" the rest of the Internet (Sterling, 1993). Today, Canada has its own national backbone in the Internet, as does Japan, Australia, New Zealand, the United Kingdom, and several other countries in Europe and Asia (see Figure 5.1). Likewise, "many countries, such as Argentina and South Africa, have international [Internet] links, even though [the Internet] may not have spread far internally yet" (Quarterman, 1993, p. 42). There are also several backbone networks in the Internet that are privately owned and support themselves by charging for access (e.g., ANS, PSINet, AlterNet, and Sprint-Link), and large commercial computer networks such as CompuServe, America Online, and Prodigy—once uninterested in internetworking—are now clamoring to offer Internet access to their subscribers.

Although it is not easy to estimate with accuracy, the Internet's pace of growth in the late 1980s and early 1990s has roughly doubled annually worldwide, whereas the growth rate in Europe has been even faster (Greenbaum, 1993). Dr. Vinton Cerf, Senior Vice President of the Data Services Division of MCI Telecommunications Corporation and former President of the Internet Society, projected some interesting figures in an early 1995 paper titled, "Computer Networking: Global Infrastructure for the 21st Century." According to Cerf (1995):

> The Internet now encompasses an estimated 50,000 networks worldwide [see Figure 5.1] about half of which are in the United States. There are over 5 million computers permanently attached to the Internet [as of 1996 the number is between 10 million and 12 million], plus at least that many portable and desktop systems which are only intermittently online. . . . Traffic rates measured on the recently "retired" NSFNET backbone approached 20 trillion bytes per month in 1995 and was growing at a 100% annual rate.

Quarterman (1993) commented that in the short term such growth rates can be expected to continue. Obviously this kind of growth cannot go on for very long; the planet would run out of people before the year 2000! However, most estimates of Internet growth show little sign of it slowing down significantly in the next few years. One of the likely limiting factors to the phenomenal growth of the Internet will be the number of computer-literate people, or rather the number of network-literate people with computers (and there are estimated to be upwards of 60 million computers in the world already and this number too is growing rapidly). It would therefore appear that learning the Internet now, or at least learning about the Internet, would be a wise move. Some estimate that by the turn

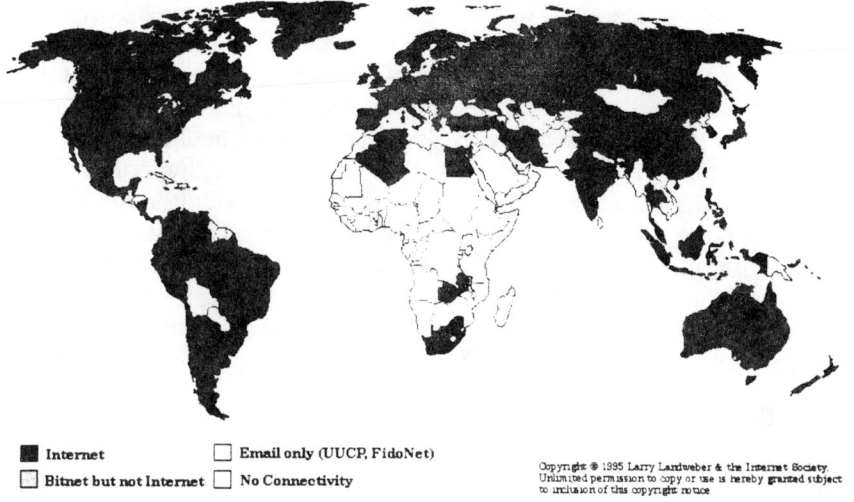

Figure 5.1. International Connectivity Map (Version 13—2/15/95)

of the century, "network literacy," like "computer literacy" before it, will be forcing itself into the very texture of our lives.

FROM "CYBERNAUTS" TO "NETIZENS"

Because of its explosive growth, the Internet has moved out of its original base in military and research institutions and into elementary and secondary schools, public libraries (Lieberman, 1994), and even stylish urban coffeehouses.[6] In fact, the more useful the Internet is proven to be, the more it is regarded as a valuable intellectual resource—or even for casual conversation—the more people there will be who want to get online. Indeed, "if there was any lingering doubt that the computer has become ensconced as a member of the American family, it was dispelled at the turn of the year.... For the first time ever, [U.S.] consumers in 1994 bought $8 billion worth of PCs—just a smidgen away from the $8.3 billion they spent on TVs" (Ratan, 1995, p. 25). Thus, electronic mail, participation in the myriad local, national, and global discussion groups (estimated to be over

---

[6]For example, like a multitude of other coffeehouses in large cities, Cybera is a cafe in London that sells cappuccino and, for the equivalent of about US$2.85, half an hour's access time on the Internet at one of the cafe's 10 computers. Waiters not only serve coffee and hustle for tips, they also provide technical expertise to "newbies" making their first foray into cyberspace (Jackson, 1995).

25,000 on USENET alone), Internet Relay Chat (an online, real-time discussion circle), CUSeeMe (real-time, compressed, desktop-digital video conferencing), Telnet (long-distance computing to access remote databases, CD-ROM collections, library catalogs, and/or to run programs), FTP (file transfer protocol, used mostly for shareware or public domain software and texts),[7] and the World-Wide Web (a networked, hyperlinked, distributed multimedia environment) have come to be widely available and highly desirable Internet services that users expect and depend on! "The spread of the Internet in the 1990s resembles the spread of personal computing in the 1970s, though it is even faster and perhaps more important. More important... because it may give... personal computers a means of cheap, easy storage and access that is truly planetary in scale" (Sterling, 1993).

Perhaps, as computers become more decentralized (a computer on every desk), an emerging countertrend could see computing resources becoming more centralized—in a sense, like a utility. Thus, it may come to pass that in the future "you'll have no more idea of what computer you're using than you have an idea of where your electricity is generated when you turn on the light" (Hillis, quoted in Kay & Hillis, 1994, p. 103). However, one important delimiting factor to accessing the emerging "computing utility" that is the Internet (besides personal computer ownership) may also be an individual's exposure to the Net while attending universities and colleges. This is where most of us have been or will be introduced to cyberspace. If so, "the future [may] see an increasing gap between the information-rich and the information-poor . . . [as] access to the Net and access to college [become] the gateways, everywhere, to a world of communications and information [resources] far beyond what is accessible by traditional media" (Rheingold, 1993, p. 68).

At present, the Internet continues to grow out of control and is spreading almost exponentially throughout the post-Cold War electronic global village. Any computer of sufficient power has become a potential user of the Internet and a window on cyberspace. Such computers sell complete and ready to "net-surf" right out of the box for quite a bit less than US$2,000, and these machines are in the hands of people worldwide.

---

[7]Anonymous access to computers that allow any person to copy his or her public files—free of charge—has become a means of "electronic publication" and distribution of computer programs and resources as well as papers, articles, and other texts. In 1992, there were over a million such public files available to anyone who asks for them, including entire books, all available in a matter of minutes. New Internet programs such as Archie, Veronica, Gopher, WAIS, and the World-Wide-Web have been developed to collect, catalog, display, and explore these enormous archives of material. In fact, several of the resources used by the author in the preparation of this chapter were accessed in this way.

It would therefore seem that the "migration to the Internet by universities, government agencies, community organizations and even business electronic mail users [can be] seen as stirrings of mass appeal for electronic networking beyond the automated teller machine" (Stix, 1993, p. 101). As a result of such "stirrings," the usefulness and market potential of cyberspace has caught the attention of the business community in a big way:

> Every computer company, nearly every publisher, most communication firms, banks, insurance companies and hundreds of mail-order and retail firms are registering their Internet domains and setting up sites on the World Wide Web. They sense that cyberspace will be one of the driving forces—if not the primary one—for economic growth in the 21st century. (Elmer-DeWitt, 1995, p. 6)

As a result, early in June 1991, academic traffic ceased to dominate the Internet; that was the "crossover" date when commercial traffic began to pull ahead (Cerf, 1993). The question now arises, will the Net community take the final step to expand access to include all citizens? This may be the real question of the 1990s as organizations—government, commercial, educational, or otherwise—grapple with the issues arising from the explosive growth of the Internet. Will the expansion process continue beyond the university campus and the business community? Will academics and entrepreneurs fight among themselves for exclusive "ownership"? Or is it likely that governments will step into the chaos and regulate it, or worse, turn it into a tool of "Big Brother"?

This is where "the photon meets the fiber"—so to speak—on the emerging electronic superhighway. One of the main reasons people have begun to flock to the Internet is due to the freedom they experience in cyberspace; it is the freedom of action and association—indeed, the feeling of "pioneering"—on an electronic frontier: "The Internet is a rare example of a true, modern, functional anarchy. There is no 'Internet Inc.' There are no official censors, no bosses, no board of directors [and] no stockholders" (Sterling, 1993). One caveat that has emerged in recent years that has complicated matters is that "several constituent networks connecting to the Internet may indeed have presidents or CEOs, but that's a different issue; the point is that there is no single authority figure for the Internet *as a whole*" (Krol, 1994, p. 16, emphasis added). The Internet is thus an institution that, by its very nature and through its own growth and evolution, has resisted institutionalization. The Net belongs to everyone and no one, and everyone has an opinion about how things ought to be run. As a result, all interest groups on the Net are staking their claim. Businesses want to use the Internet for financial purposes. Governments want the Internet more closely regulated. Academics want to keep it dedicated exclusively to scholarly endeavors, whereas the military want it spy-proof and secure.

Cyberspace fringe groups also have their plans and do not like the present discussions of privatization, commercialization, or regulation of information and/or information flow on the Net (Branscomb, 1991). The hackers, crackers, phrackers, and *otaku*;[8] occupy the cyberspace fringe and push the envelope of existing limits to the free flow of information. They have collectively and at times methodically tested the boundaries of network security, legality, cryptography, civil liberties, activism, and human–computer interaction while simultaneously increasing our legitimate understanding of our emerging "electronic society" and what it may mean to "be digital" through their continued explorations. Yet, like the mountain men on the Western frontier, many of the early "cybernauts" as well as the cyberspace fringe groups (akin to the outlaws and hustlers of old) are being confronted by the advance of other "netizens" (Internet citizens)—including the entrepreneurs—who (like the early pioneers) wish to stake their claims and fence in their private domains.

JEFFERSONIAN NETWORKS VS. DIGITAL GOLD RUSH

From the preceeding discussion, it has perhaps become apparent that there is a need for a "citizens' vision" of the way cyberspace and our individual and collective virtual communities ought to develop—an idea of a preferable or desirable digital future. Perhaps equally obvious, in the absence of such a vision, it is almost guaranteed that the large commercial and political powerholders, currently emerging or already on the scene, will shape our digital future in *their* image—one that may not be in harmony with that of the average netizen. In their book, *The Network Nation* (1978), Starr Roxanne Hiltz and Murray Turoff foresaw many of the human–computer communication developments that we now take for granted. Looking toward the 1990s, they also raised the important question, "what kinds of effects, both good and bad, would this application have on the society as a whole" (Hiltz & Turoff, 1978, p. 468)? In other words, what sort of future (from their vantagepoint in the late 1970s) would be realized?

As it now stands, their visions (and cautions) were not too far off the mark. Clearly, the uses and applications of information technology have continued to grow as we rush to catch up to our digital future. Computers have become increasingly valuable to industries and to citizens

---

[8]*Otaku* is derived from the most formal way of saying "you" in Japanese and the name taken by Japan's newest information age product—socially inept, information-crazed, often brilliant, technological shut-ins; in other words, Japanese hackers. For more information see Seymour, (1992)

and as their inherent potential is realized through future advancements to recognize and simulate speech, generate realistic images, provide accurate models of the physical world, build huge automated libraries, control robots, and help with a myriad of other tasks—they will become invaluable. To accomplish these tasks will require both computing and communications systems many times more powerful than we have today. Ongoing advances in hardware, software, and "wetware" (brain power/knowledge) will constitute the foundation for building the systems and developing the applications that will continue to impact our quality of life. In reality, the information revolution has only just begun.

Today—perhaps, in part, influenced by such earlier perspectives—there appear to be two different visions of a cyberspatial future emerging in the online debates: one I call cyberdemocracy, and the other virtual mercantilism. This is not to say that other, alternative visions have not emerged; one has but to "lurk" on such discussion groups as "alt.cyberspace" or "alt.politics.datahighway" (among others) on USENET to obtain a sampling of the broad spectrum of opinions. However, the two that will be compared and discussed here represent the shared visions of a large number of netizens and have attracted the most attention and debate.

What does either vision of the future of cyberspace look like? Are they truly incompatible, or are there any commonalties that can be built on? Perhaps at the outset it is important to realize that—whatever the answers might be today—one thing is for certain, our digital future will probably bare very little resemblance to today's plans. But before examining these two visions, it may be helpful to look first at what instigated the present debate over our future in cyberspace.

NREN and the NII

No doubt much to the annoyance of today's "keyboard cowboys" and "cyberoutlaws," who presently forage on the "frontier" of our digital future, the Internet would not exist if it were not for U.S. government sponsorship of the technologies that made it possible. Although the government certainly did not build the Net, the information technology and the information industry were driven forward in large measure by the ideas and people that flowed from the ARPA and NSF programs and research. Today, the National Information Infrastructure (NII), a proposed fiber-optic-based digital superhighway, has emerged as the "first great infrastructure project of the twenty-first century" (Biesada, 1993, p. 59) and perhaps the first really new infrastructure to develop in nearly a century (Cerf, 1995). The proposed NII became a priority item with the Clinton Administration and was highlighted as being of strategic importance to ensuring the United States continued preeminence in information technology well into the 21st century. Much of the potential of the NII is seen as being directly linked to the development of new hardware and protocols for substantially higher communication speeds than the NSFNet has been able to achieve thus far. The intention, therefore, is to create a 5 Gigabyte or better network capable of sending CAT scans, real-time, full-motion video, and entire Libraries-of-Congress-per-minute worth of text crosscountry all on the same fiber-optic backbone.

To facilitate the development of such a network, the High Performance Computing Act of 1991 was signed into law by then President Bush. This piece of legislation provided federal assistance, in collaboration with industry and academia, for development of advanced computer hardware and software, as well as networking technologies needed to route data at gigabit speeds. Following close behind were two strategic planning documents, *National Information Infrastructure: An Agenda for Action* (The White House, 1993) and *America in the Age of Information* (The White House, 1994). Produced by President Clinton's Administration, these documents set forth a high-level strategy for the U.S. federal government's research and development investment in information and communications technologies and identifies areas for strategic focus that are aligned with U.S. national goals.

Today, the High Performance Computing and Communications Initiative (HPCCI)—an outgrowth of the 1991 Act—has become the multiagency cooperative effort under which the Clinton Administration's strategic plans are to move forward. Led by the National Coordination Office, HPCCI became the founding initiative for the formation and operation of the National Research and Education Network (NREN), seen by many as being the necessary first step in the implementation of the NII. NREN, designed to be a five-year US$2 billion project (Sterling, 1993) involving three agencies (the NSF, NASA, and the Department of Health and Human Services), is expected to extend U.S. technological leadership in computer communications through research in, and development of, high-speed supercomputing. As David Lytel of the White House Office of Science and Technology Policy stated, "NSFNET is to the Internet what NREN is to the NII" (quoted in Biesada, 1993, p. 62). Such programs as HPCCI and NREN—particularly with their increasing emphasis on enabling broad-based future use of the information infrastructure—have earned the support of the U.S. Congress and of large segments of the U.S. populace. However, if the NII is to be an outgrowth of the Internet, and the government's role is to be the same as it was in the early days of ARPANET and NSFNET, then the HPCCI and NREN have spurred a heated debate on whether the government should be so heavily involved in the building of the NII.

Complicating matters was the fact that, until recently, the basic telecommunications "law of the land" in the United States, the Communications Act of 1934, was over 60 years old; predating television, transistors, computers, satellites, lasers, fiber optics, and cellular telephones. "In light of the dynamic growth and development of telecommunication and its strategic importance, the lack of contemporary and current laws [was] almost a national disgrace" (Pelton & Bender, 1995, p. 47). The Telecommunications Act of 1996, signed into law by President Clinton in February 1996, is the first attempt to rectify the situation. The Act was crafted ostensibly to advance the public good by promoting competition and reducing regulation. However, in its present form it has been criticized as being in violation of rights protecting the freedom of speech through the banning of nebulously defined "indecent" or "obscene" communications.[9] Furthermore, certain provisions repealed price controls on cable and phone rates and permitted greater concentration of media ownership—worrying many consumer advocacy groups. Neither does there appear to be adequate public quid pro quo in the Act as it now stands. Many voice disappointment over a lost opportunity to formulate a truly visionary telecommunications and information policy foundation:

> Although the Telecommunications Act of 1996 was generally welcomed as being long overdue, none of the parties to it were completely satisfied with the results. Arrived at through the course of intense Congressional lobbying, the law that was eventually adopted represented a carefully crafted compromise rather than a bold blueprint for the future. (Garcia, 1996, p. 44)

---

[9]As reported by the Electronic Frontier Foundation (EFF), on June 14, 1995, the U.S. Senate approved by a vote of 84–16 an amendment to the Senate's omnibus telecommunications deregulation bill that raises grave Constitutional questions and poses great risks for the future of freedom of speech on the nation's computer-communications forums. Sponsored by Sen. Jim Exon (D-Nebraska), the amendment originated as an independent bill titled "Communications Decency Act of 1995," and is intended, according to its sponsor, both to prohibit "the [computer] equivalent of obscene telephone calls" and to prohibit the distribution to children of materials with sexual content. As drafted, however, the legislation not only fails to solve the problems it is intended to address, but it also imposes content restrictions on computer communications that would chill First Amendment-protected speech and, in effect, restrict adults in the public forums of computer networks to writing and reading only such content suitable for children. Furthermore, it puts the onus of responsibility for monitoring such behavior and content on the service provider—essentially deputizing network access providers and allowing them to eavesdrop on private messages in order to report wrong-doing. For additional information on this and other pieces of legislation (both domestic and foreign), see the EFF's "Action Alerts" (URL: http://www.eff.org/pub/Alerts/).

Still, the conventional wisdom in Washington is that if all unnecessary legal and regulatory barriers are removed (see Table 5.1 for an abridged list of legislation), then private interests will step in to build it. "But there's a catch. For the full economic potential of the NII to be realized, longtime NII proponent Vice President Al Gore argues that all Americans must be able to 'connect' at an affordable price" (Biesada, 1993, p. 59). According to Vice President Gore (1991), the Federal dollars authorized for NREN "represent an initial, rather than ongoing, investment, intended to spark the development that will create the demand for [the NII] as a commercial enterprise" (p. 153). In a speech made to the National Press Club in December 1993, Vice President Gore further clarified the government's position on the NII, stating that:

> This Administration intends to create an environment that stimulates a private system of free-flowing information conduits. . . . Our goal is not to design the market of the future. It is to provide the principles that shape that market. And it is to provide the rules governing this difficult transition to an open market for information. We are committed in that transition to protecting the availability, affordability, and diversity of information and information technology, as market forces replace regulations and judicial models that are no longer appropriate.

However, many on the Net are as suspicious about private enterprise building the NII as they are of direct government involvement in its construction and/or administration: "Although the Internet as it now exists grew to epic proportions by fostering 'open' TCP/IP standards and protocols, there's no guarantee that the [future] digital superhighway will follow the same pattern. Openness isn't what made Ma Bell rich" (Biesada, 1993, p. 59). As if to realize the worst fears of Internet denizens, the NSF announced in 1993 that it was turning over three of the most important administrative functions of Internet management to private enterprise. The assigning of Internet addresses (and thus the ability to act as "gatekeeper" of access) went to Network Solutions. Maintaining directory and database services (keeping track of people and resources) went to AT&T. And the maintenance of information services provided to Internet users (information "tools" for making use of the Net) went to General Atomics (Rheingold, 1993). Many individuals keyed in on a troubling sentence in the NSF press release that subsequently set the Net aflame with controversy:

> Consistent with FNC guidelines on obtaining *reasonable cost recovery* from users of NREN networks, the NSF has determined that the INTERNIC Information Services provider [those listed above plus MCI and IBM from an earlier transfer] *may charge users* beyond the US research and education community for any services provided. (Rheingold, 1993, p. 88, emphasis added)

Table 5.1. Legislating Our Digital Future In Cyberspace (103rd & 104th US Congress).

Bill: Title	Sponsor	Status	Description
(103) HR 523:	Constance Morella (R-MD)	Pending	Would allow federal agencies to copy right computer software produced by the government.
(103) HR 707: Emerging Telecom. Tech. Act of 1993	John Dingell (D-Mich.)	Became law Sept. 1993	Establishes procedures to improve the allocation and assignment of the electromagnetic spectrum for private use.
(103) HR 1328 (S 564): Government Printing Office Electronic Info. Access Enhancement Act of 1993	Sen. Wendell Ford (D-Ky.) Ted Stevens (R-Ak.)	Became law June 1993	Requires Congressional Record and Federal Resister to be available electronically.
(103) HR 1757: National Information Infrastructure Act of 1993[a]	Rick Boucher (D-VA)	Passed House July 1993	Spurs the development of the applications that will be available over NII
(103) S 4: Title VI National Competitiveness Act of 1993	John Rockefeller (D-WV) Ernest Hollings (D-SC)	Reported in Senate	Would accelerate the development of NII by funding in conjunction with the private sector, the R&D needed for applications.
(103) S 1086: Telecoms. Infrastructure 1993	John C. Danforth (R-MO) Daniel Inouye (D-Hawaii)	Became H.B. 1822	Fosters furthur development of nation's telecommunications Infrastructure Act of through enhancement of competition.

Table 5.1. Legislating Our Digital Future In Cyberspace (103rd & 104th US Congress) (con't).

Bill: Tile	Sponsor	Status	Description
(103) S 1822: Communications Act of 1994	Same as Above plus others		Evolved into S.652 of 104th Congress
(104) HR 1004: Companion Bill to S 314	Tim Johnson (D-SD)	Introduced in House	Essentially the same as S 314
(104) HR 1555: Communications Act of 1995	Thomas Bliley, Jr. (R-VA)	Passed House August 1995	To promote competition and reduce regulation in telecommunications and encourage the rapid deployment of new telecommunications technologies
(104) S 314: Communication Decency	Jim Exon (D-Neb.)	Incorporated as Title V, S 652	To protect the public from the misuse of the telecommunications network and telecommunications devices and facilities
(104) S 652: Telecommunication Competition & Deregulation Act of 1995[b]	Larry Pressler (R-SD)	Passed Senate June 1995	To provide for a pro-competitive, deregulatory national policy framework for advanced telecommunications and information technologies

[a]Formerly known as the High Performance Computing & High-Speed Networking Applications Act of 1993.
[b]Signed into law as the "Telecommunications Act of 1996" by President Clinton on February 8, 1996.
Sources: Data compiled from "Legislating Your Digital Future" [Table], December 1993, *UnixWorld*, p. 60; and *THOMAS: Legislative Information on the Internet*[World Wide Web site], June 1995, Washington, DC: Library of Congress URL: http://thomas.loc.gov/.

Is this the first turning of the Internet to metered services? Is this an attempt to control the extension of the Internet to the "grassroots" of computing—so dear to the heart of all utopian populists—through access pricing? Or is it only the beginning of a well-thought-out process of privatizing a technology that long ago outgrew its government sponsors?

There is still much contention surrounding the respective roles government and business should play in the building of the NII. The online debates remain polarizing over these issues. It is certain that actions taken over the next few years will, in many ways, determine the political and economic structure of cyberspace—and our digital future—for decades to come. Gordon Cook (1992), a well-known Net gadfly and publisher of an electronically distributed newsletter focusing on the political and policy issues related to the emerging NII, pointed out that, "it is questionable whether the US government should be involved in the building of [the NII] backbone. What [President Clinton's] Administration must make clear is that it will do whatever is necessary to ensure affordable access to the network. It must also help to educate Congress concerning the policy implications behind the network." Perhaps this is where the real challenges lay on the route to our digital future.

A Vision of CyberDemocracy[10]

For now, the Internet is still largely free of metered services and restricted access. However, even as the debates rage, restrictive legislation looms over the Net like a thunderstorm while commercial traffic encroaches and cable television and telephone companies jockey for potential market position and the necessary "clout" to have a major say in defining future access, pricing, and content policies on the NII. Yet, if we are to believe in the vision of cyberspace described by some, then "[life] in cyberspace . . . [could] shape up [to be] exactly like Thomas Jefferson would have wanted: founded on the primacy of individual liberty and the commitment to pluralism, diversity, and community" (Kapor, 1992).

---

[10]This particular description of cyberdemocracy draws from several sources besides my own ideas and intuition. First, the *National Information Infrastructure: Agenda for Action* (The White House, 1993) paints a very glowing picture of democracy in the Information Age. Second, and perhaps more important, there are discussions and reactions by various Internet denizens (particularly in the USENET newsgroups "comp.org.eff.talk;" "comp.society.futures;" "alt.culture.internet;" and "alt.cyberpunk") to such traditional media reports as the September 1991 issue of *Scientific American's* Special Report devoted to the topic of "Communications, Computers and Networks: How to Work, Play and Thrive in Cyberspace" as well as the followup article in *Scientific American* by G. Stix (1993). And finally, there is the vision of what cyberspace's potential future could be as described in the publications and deliberations of the Electronic Frontier Foundation.

In this vision of a cyberdemocracy, people can live (physically) almost anywhere they want without foregoing opportunities of association or useful and fulfilling employment by "telecommuting" to their "virtual offices" or gathering at "Cyberspace Inns" (Coate, 1992) all on the electronic superhighway. The best "schools" (such as they would exist on the Net), teachers, courses, and vast storehouses of information would be available to all students without regard to geography, distance, resources, or disability. Students would be able to take virtual field trips that would allow them to visit the Louvre in Paris or explore volcanoes in Hawaii, the rainforests of Belize, or even the ocean floor.[11] Computers and network access in the schools would help prepare students for the job market of the future, which will demand a labor force that is well informed and computer literate.

In a similar vein, services that would improve health care and respond to other important social needs would all be available "online," without waiting "in line," whenever and wherever you need them. Such digitally delivered services will reduce health care costs while increasing the quality of care, especially in underserved areas: "Experts have [already] concluded that nationwide use of information technologies could reduce health care costs by $36 billion every year. [Present] pilot efforts in Georgia, Texas, West Virginia, and other states [demonstrate] that telemedicine can effectively bring specialists' services to rural areas" (The White House, 1993). When fully implemented, this will extend to rural and remote areas the same benefits that urban dwellers have come to take for granted in health care, not to mention access to libraries, government information, cultural resources, and entertainment.

Furthermore, because of the free flow of information across local, state, regional, and national boundaries, access to government information at all levels becomes a "right" of all netizens in the facilitation of their informed participation in the democratic process at whichever level they

---

[11]The JASON Project is the first step in realizing this type of an educational environment that is expected to become the norm in the future. Founded in 1989 by Dr. Robert D. Ballard, the JASON Project conducts a two-week scientific expedition each year in a remote part of the world and broadcasts in real-time, using state-of-the-art technology, to a network of educational, research, and cultural institutions in the United States, Canada, Bermuda, and the United Kingdom. The JASON Project provides teacher training and a curriculum specially developed to highlight the science, technology, engineering, and social studies of the year's expedition. Participating students at the interactive downlink sites have the ability through telepresence to "go live" to the expedition, to operate the scientific equipment being used, and to talk directly with the scientists at the expedition site. One such expedition, "JASON VI: Island Earth," took students on a voyage to the volcanoes, observatories, and unique environments of Hawaii from February 27–March 11, 1995. For more information, see URL:http://seawifs.gsfc.nasa.gov/scripts/JASON.html.

so choose.¹² Empowered U.S. citizens will most likely vote by modem, and there will be much greater participation in the political process than there is today, thanks to computers and network technology becoming the enablers and propagators of democracy. By putting politics online, Washington has the potential of becoming a "virtual capital" in which "US Representatives and Senators could participate from their states or districts while citizens would have any information, debate or proceeding at their fingertips" (Phillips, 1995, p. 68).¹³ This vision of cyberdemocracy would likewise see access to governmental and political processes extended to the traditionally underserved, including the poor, minorities, rural residents, and disabled individuals.

Finally, information technology is lending a competitive advantage to manufacturers who wish to tighten the connections to their suppliers, producers, and customers. They also want to outpace their competition by shrinking the time needed to design and bring new products to market, slashing inventories, building products to order instead of according to forecasts, and tapping new markets (Bartholomew, 1995). Therefore, through the strategic application of information technology, small manufacturers get orders from all over the world electronically, and with detailed specifications, in a form that the machines could use to produce the items (a vision of Alvin Toffler's, 1981, "prosumer"). Individual netizens would also have access to new and/or enhanced products and services such as "video on demand," the hottest video games, or banking and shopping from the comfort of their own home whenever they chose.

This may come about not so much because of the phenomenal progress in making computers faster, more powerful, and better able to augment the human mind, but because the most important resources on the world's networks are still people (Stapleton, 1992). Likewise, people on

---

¹²It appears that much of the thinking in this area has been influenced by the resurgence of "electronic town hall" meetings made popular by H. Ross Perot and Bill Clinton during the 1992 U.S. presidential campaign. This idea of "electronic democracy" has a history that parallels that of radio (F. D. Roosevelt's "fireside chats") and television (Nixon–Kennedy debates) and a fair bit of practice as well. (e.g., Elgin, 1991; Kirschner, 1991; Toregas, 1989; Van Tassel, 1994; Varley, 1991; Westin, 1971; Wittig, 1991). For a cautionary statement about the possible darkside to electronic democracy, see Golding & Murdoch (1989) and Schwartz (1994).

¹³Through the Library of Congress supported "THOMAS: Legislative Information on the Internet" service (URL: http://thomas.loc.gov/), the "White House Home Page" (URL: http://www.whitehouse.gov/), the "FedWorld Information Network" (URL: http://www.fedworld.gov/), and the ability to e-mail your congressional representatives through the "Interactive Democracy" home page (URL: http://www.teleport.com/~pcllgn/id.html), part of this vision of cyberdemocracy is already materializing.

the Net tend to gravitate toward electronic communities based on common interests and shared affinities rather than dwelling on the technologies involved in bringing them together. Thus, through "an investment in time, community resources, and our own reeducation, we learn to perceive ourselves as members of the global electronic community" (Stapleton, 1992, p. 96). As a result of this "reeducation" and new "perceiving," people will begin to define what they want from cyberspace. And what they apparently want is more freedom to do what they want when they want within their virtual communities!

However, most netizens who aspire to this view are not computer-literate "pollyannas." Many realize that communities—virtual or otherwise—are usually governed by laws, or at the very least, a code of ethical values representing the group (thus, the emergence of "netiquette"—rules of "acceptable" conduct on the Net). There are still some obstacles that must be overcome. Competitive pressures could lead infrastructure builders to bypass rural and low-income communities, thereby widening the gap between rich and poor. The same technology that is able to identify and link citizens and political institutions could also facilitate nationwide identification systems and increased governmental surveillance. It has become widely recognized, therefore, that protections need to be in place to guarantee privacy and intellectual property. With the rise to eminence of network technologies, how people and businesses exchange information and entertainment products and services and how copyrighted works are created, reproduced, distributed, displayed, adapted, and sold become critical issues that should be monitored carefully if we are to avoid neo-Orwellian potholes in the information superhighway. Furthermore, the virtual communities of cyberspace—which in many cases cross state and national boundaries—beg the question of whether laws and/or code of ethical values that govern conduct in cyberspace should be those of geographic location or electronic locus (Branscomb, 1991, p. 158).

The increasing use of the Internet and its explosive growth have raised questions about the application of the law to communication in cyberspace (Appelman, 1995). How do we resolve conflict, protect civil liberties, and prevent computer crime? What about the rights of "electronic personnae" and the shielding of the physical, individual human being from certain types of liability or exposure (Karnow, 1994)? Perhaps one way to address these issues is to first "articulate the kinds of values we want to see protected in the electronic society we are now shaping and to make an agenda for preserving the civil liberties that are central to that society" (Kapor, 1991, p. 160). In other words, we might begin now outlining the vision of a future cyber democracy (see Appendix B for a list of possible public interest principles; see also Connolly & Webster, 1993a, for a model policy statement about rights and responsibilities in cyberspace) and work toward its fulfillment.

The "Brave New World" of Virtual Mercantilism

Have we not seen and heard this before, the promise of an education and information cornucopia pouring forth from the end of an electrical wire? Remember the promises of broadcast and cable television? Now the telecommunications and cable TV executives are seeking to allay concerns over their proposed megamergers, insisting that the melding of telecommunications and entertainment giants presages the coming of an electronic superhighway that will connect students with learning resources, provide a forum for political discourse, increase economic competitiveness, and speed us into the multimedia information age (Kapor & Berman, 1993).

However, if the private sector is to build the information superhighway (and some think it should), is it likely that it would voluntarily relinquish control over the terms of access, use, and content? Are we to believe that the megamergers taking place between large media and telecommunications corporations are benevolent, dynamic and wholesome change? Or is it really a case of "robber barons redux" (Lapham, 1994)?

Following this tack for a moment, a likely scenario would see communication "confederations" (because no single company has the resources to build, program and operate anything as complex as the information superhighway) building a network with fiber-optic or some other high-capacity "conduit" running into the home, providing gigabytes of information (a combination of 500 channels of TV, video on demand, Internet, or World-Wide Web-like computer services and local and long-distance telephone services) cheaply and easily. Yet this would primarily be a single-directional flow; it can carry plenty of information into the home, but very little out. In this scenario, any information coming out of the home beyond a telephone conversation would be carried at mere modem speeds. Anyone interested in providing anything more than a few simple message back to the larger Net community would need to contract with the owners and operators of the networks—for if everyone can be a provider of information, the communication confederacies would lose business.

Indeed, it may already be too late, for Time Warner, US West, and Silicon Graphics have partnered to build their version of the information superhighway; as have cable giants TCI, Cox, and Comcast joined forces with the long-distance company Sprint for the same purpose. Each of about half a dozen similar partnerships are all hoping to develop a design for a seamless nationwide system for delivering cable and telephone services to every home in the United States (Greenwald, 1995) and eventually to the world. However, it appears that the potential for commercial exploitation of the Net was perhaps always there. With 30% of the Fortune 500 already on the Internet, and two thirds of Internet users working for major corporations (Littman, 1993), "the die hath been cast." From the perspective of the communication confederacies, the Net is just waiting for them to master its quirks, gain a competitive edge, and then ascertain how much to charge and the best way to collect.

However, if bringing the Net to everyone is too important a matter to be left to the private market alone, then the government might take control of the process, or—in the extreme view—build the Net itself. Therefore, this vision of the not-too-distant future would see the setting up of legally enforced monopolies dependent on government subsidies and patronage—in the form of licenses and franchises assigning public property to private use—to build a network that would be much more closed than open.[14] Law enforcement efforts would concentrate on censoring transborder information flow and setting up market entry barriers: "Content [would] be supplied only by a carefully chosen set of providers, barriers to entry [would] be created for everyone else. Programming [would] seek the least common denominator, and the population [would become] divided by income into information haves and have-nots" (Kapor, 1992). Some believe that if our politicians proceed down this path, then they will be "setting the stage for the last half of the '90s to be a lot like the last half of the '60s" (Winer, 1995). It appears obvious that the potential of cyberspace to significantly restructure the balance of power in society, and to hasten our transition to "becoming digital," has struck fear into the hearts of those with a vested interest in the status quo. Thus, they will try to convince governments to "shut down whole avenues of creative expression in the name of 'decency' and the bottom line. So what if the next generation is deprived of its right to explore, discover, and contribute to humanity" (Winer, 1995)? We must only hope that we remain vigilant. If we can mange this, perhaps they will not succeed.

IS IT "CRUNCH TIME" IN CYBERSPACE?

Perhaps the future of cyberdemocracy lies somewhere between "cyberutopia" and Huxley's "Brave New World." Before the current wave of publicity spurred by the Clinton Administration's repeated references to the "Information Highway," the Internet only doubled in size annually. Now it doubles in size every nine months or better (Poole, 1993). Increased user demand is the primary reason. Thus, it would appear that cyberspace has already begun to force itself on our consciousness, demanding our attention, requiring us to act. As well, the recent debate over

---

[14]For a rather entertaining if not dystopic view of possible rewrites to the Bill of Rights in such a scenario see Barlow (1993).

whether or not the government should build the NII has been meaningless because the simple fact is, government can't afford the hundreds of billions of dollars it would cost to lay fiber to every home, office, school, factory, hospital, and library in the United States. Fiscal reality dictates that the creation of the NII will be a joint effort between the government and the private sector. (Biesada, 1993, p. 59)

The present U.S. Administration hopes that by establishing protocols, standards, and testbed projects, private industry will be encouraged to do the rest (Gore, 1994). However, before the government commits to any policy, it must first arm itself with an understanding of the situation at hand and the commitment to seek intervention for redress of private enterprise's failures should such action be warranted.

In an attempt to promote awareness of the need for a public-interest perspective on the NII, a coalition of nonprofit and public interest organizations that calls itself the "Telecommunications Policy Roundtable" met in Washington, DC in the summer of 1993. Recognizing that policy decisions made during the next few years will have repercussions that impact public policy for decades to come, this coalition admonished policymakers to move beyond narrow and short-term interests and to instead embrace diversity, openness, participation, and discussion as guiding principles in the formulation of the NII. In order to guarantee future generations inherit an information infrastructure that enhances the quality of life for everyone, the Telecommunications Policy Roundtable produced a set of principles (see Appendix B) that they identified as "sacrosanct" to their vision of the NII, which include universal access, freedom to communicate, and the assurance of privacy. These principles are intended to steer present and future planning of the NII and to be used for evaluating its success.

In a somewhat parallel effort, the Electronic Frontier Foundation, a nonprofit group that promotes civil liberties in computer mediated communications, highlight the following as possible areas of focus and debate:

- Competition and diversity should be encouraged whereas government intervention should be kept to a minimum
- Everyone who wants to should be able to connect at an affordable rate—those too economically disadvantaged should be subsidized
- Users should be able to directly participate in determining the content of the system
- People should be able to choose the roles they wish to play, whether as consumers, providers, or both
- Networks must be built as open systems with a series of interoperable components and well-defined publishing interfaces that permit maximum third-party competition

- Constitutional protections of personal privacy and freedom of expression should be extended to the emerging networks.

Of course, with any declaration of cyberspacial rights also come responsibilities; we as civic minded netizens should be prepared to shoulder our burdens. As an initiative of the American Association of Higher Education—building on a 1989 project to analyze the impact of NREN on society—a model policy statement on the rights and responsibilities of individuals and institutions in cyberspace (focusing on education) was offered as a "work in progress" (Connolly & Webster, 1993a, 1993b). The principles contained in this document are based on the recognition that the electronic community is a complex subsystem of a larger community and is therefore founded on the cultural values espoused by that community. It is further recognized that as new technologies modify the electronic community and further empowers individuals, "new values and responsibilities will change this culture" (Connolly & Webster, 1993a, p. 25). Thus, the goal of any "Bill of Rights" for electronic citizens should be to articulate these emerging values as well as the fundamental rights and obligations that accompany them.

The intention of the committee that drafted the *Bill of Rights and Responsibilities for Electronic Learners* was that it be referred to and used as a guide by other electronic communities in the drafting of similar statements. Could this be construed as the infant stirrings of possible future electronic emancipation? Perhaps, for as Mitch Kapor (1993) of the Electronic Frontier Foundation stated rather succinctly, the Jeffersonian ideal of cyberdemocracy espoused by many is one that "promotes grassroots democracy, diversity of users and manufacturers, true communications among the people, and all the dazzling goodies of home shopping, movies on demand, teleconferencing, and cheap, instant databases.... It's our choice to make. Let's not blow it."

Ultimately, the protection of our cherished democratic principles in the future will depend on the debate generated by the efforts of such advocacy groups and whether ordinary citizens are up to the task of making sound judgments about the day-to-day decision of government in the emerging computer-mediated "agora" of cyberspace (Ogden, 1996)

> A key question is whether we should trust the wisdom of citizens to guide our [democracy] into the future. An important insight into this question emerged from George Gallup, who reviewed his experience in polling American public opinion over half a century and found the collective judgment of citizens to be "extraordinarily sound." Gallup discovered that citizens are often ahead of their elected leaders in accepting innovations. (Elgin, 1991, p. 29)

If today's citizens are to exercise greater civic responsibility in the future cyberdemocracy, they must also acquire greater civic competence in cyberspace.

As we stand at the brink of the 21st century, we can no longer pretend to be naive about the consequences of technology. Neither can we afford to be ignorant of the "power politics" invoked by technology's application. Therefore, the political issues raised by the new networking technologies that now link individuals, groups, and organizations in virtual communities of affinity are issues at the very core of our evolving "digital future" that must be grappled with even as we teeter on the very edge of the next millennium.

APPENDIX A:
AN INTERNET TIME LINE

The following timeline is, in part, adapted from Robert H. Zakon's "Hobbes' Internet Timeline v.2.5" (1996) hosted by the Internet Society (URL: http:// info.isoc.org/guest/zakon/Internet/History/HIT.html).

- 1969 ARPANET commissioned by Department of Defense (DoD) for research into networking; first node at UCLA and soon after at Stanford Research Institute (SRI), UCSB, and University of Utah.
- 1971 ARPANET grows to 15 nodes (23 hosts).
- 1972 Invention of e-mail program to send messages across a distributed network.
- 1973 First international connections to the ARPANET: England and Norway.
- 1976 UUCP (Unix-to-Unix Copy Protocol) developed at AT&T Bell Labs.
- 1979 USENET established using UUCP between Duke and UNC.
- 1981 BITNET, the "Because Its Time NETwork", started as a cooperative network at the City University of New York to provide electronic mail servers to distribute information. CSNE (Computer Science NETwork) built through seed money granted by NSF to provide networking services to university scientists with no access to ARPANET.
- 1982 Transmission Control Protocol and Internet Protocol commonly known as TCP/IP, established as the protocol suite for ARPANET.
- 1983 Name server developed at University of Wisconsin, no longer requiring users to know the exact path to other systems.

ARPANET split into ARPANET and MILNET. EARN (European Academic and Research Network) established, very similar to BITNET.

1984 Domain Name Server (DNS) introduced. Number of hosts breaks 1,000.

1986 NSFNET created (backbone speed of 56Kbps) and establishes 5 super-computing centers (JVNC@Princeton, PSC@Pittsburgh, SDSC@UCSD, NCSA@UIUC, Theory Center@Cornell) with the aid of NASA and DOE facilitating an explosion of universities to become connected.

1987 NSF signs a cooperative agreement to manage the NSFNET backbone with Merit Network, Inc. (Merit, IBM, and MCI later founded ANS). Number of hosts breaks 10,000, whereas number of BITNET hosts breaks 1,000.

1988 Internet worm burrows through the Net wrecking havoc in network computing community.

1989 Number of hosts breaks 100,000. NSFNET backbone upgraded to T1 (1.544Mbps). First relay between a commercial electronic mail carrier (CompuServe) and the Internet allowed.

1990 ARPANET retired. Second relay between a commercial electronic mail carrier (MCI Mail) and the Internet through the Corporation for the National Research Initiative (CNRI).

1991 WAIS released by Thinking Machines Corporation. Gopher released by University of Minnesota. U.S. High Performance Computing Act (Sponsor, Sen. Gore) establishes the National Research and Education Network (NREN).

1992 World-Wide Web released by CERN. Number of hosts breaks 1,000,000.
NSFNET backbone upgraded to T3 (44.736 Mbps).

1993 InterNIC created by NSF to provide specific Internet services:
- directory and database services (AT&T)
- registration services (Network Solutions Inc.)
- information services (General Atomics/CERFnet)

U.S. White House, United Nations, and World Bank come online. Mosaic takes the Internet by storm; WWW proliferates at a 341,634% annual growth rate of service traffic.

1994 Communities begin to be wired directly to the Internet. US Senate and House provide information servers. First flower shop takes orders via the Internet. Shopping malls arrive soon after. Mass marketing finds its way to the Internet with mass e-mailings ("spamming"). Worms of a new kind find their way around the Net—WWW Worms (W4), joined by Spiders, Wanderers, Crawlers, and Snakes as information search engines.

1995 NSFNET reverts back to a research network as main U.S. backbone traffic is routed through interconnected network providers. First official Internet wiretap successfully in helping U.S. Secret Service & Drug Enforcement Agency apprehend group illegally manufacturing and selling cell phone cloning equipment.
1996 Internet 1996 World Exposition—the first World's Fair to take place on the Internet.

- Restrictions on the Internet use around the world:
- *United States* passes controversial Communication Decency Act in order to prohibit distribution of indecent materials over the Internet.
- *China* requires users & Internet Service Providers to register with the police.
- *Germany* cuts off access to some newsgroups carried on CompuServe.
- *Saudi Arabia* confines Internet access to universities and hospitals.
- *New Zealand* classifies computer disks as "publications" that can be censored and/or seized.
- *Vietnam* prevents most state agencies from releasing information on the Internet and requires diplomats and foreign organization to seek approval from the foreign & culture ministries to transmit information online. Approval would be given in the form a license.

APPENDIX B:
PUBLIC INTEREST PRINCIPLES

A coalition of organizations, which calls itself the Telecommunications Policy Roundtable, met in Washington, DC for a couple of months during the late summer of 1993 to promote the need for a public-interest perspective on the U.S. National Information Infrastructure (NII). This group produced the following set of public-interest principles to serve as guidelines for planning the NII and for evaluating its success. (Please send inquiries further to these statements to the Center for Media Education, cme@access.digex.net.)

RENEWING THE COMMITMENT TO A PUBLIC INTEREST TELECOMMUNICATIONS POLICY

Telecommunications Policy Roundtable
September 1, 1993

A communications revolution is underway as profound as the introduction of the printing press. A new "National Information Infrastructure" is rapidly moving into place—which will carry video, audio, and data information into homes and offices across the country. Its emergence will produce fundamental shifts in American life, transforming everything from work to education to government to culture. Because the health of our democracy is inextricably linked to the nature of our communications system, this new information infrastructure raises far-reaching questions about our country and its transition into the next century: Who will own these networks? Who will have access to them? What steps will be taken to preserve public institutions?

Policy decisions made during the next few years will shape the communications system for decades to come. Enlightened policies could harness the power of these new technologies to ameliorate many of our nation's most critical problems by revitalizing civic institutions, expanding educational opportunities, enhancing access to health care services, and improving job training. However, without a clear commitment to public goals, this promise will never be fulfilled. Instead, many of the shortcomings of our present telecommunications system will be intensified and a host of more serious problems created. There is already a growing disparity between the technologically affluent and the technologically disenfranchised that endangers our social fabric.

Policy makers must ensure that the development of the information infrastructure reflects the public interest spirit that has long guided our country's communications policies: our commitment to a national telephone system available to all gave rise to the concept of "universal service," enabling those in the most remote parts of the nation to have access to the means of communication; our commitment to making noncommercial educational, arts, and public affairs programming available to all Americans led to the creation of a public broadcasting system.

Our government has the responsibility as public trustee to ensure that new communications technologies serve the democratic and social needs of our country. The rise of new technologies and new businesses has increased the importance of this responsibility. The convergence of once separate industries requires a new policy framework for the information infrastructure, rooted in the shared values of our country and dedicated to the common good.

We call on the President and the Congress to pursue a broad and public interest vision for the National Information Infrastructure. We must move beyond narrow and short-term interests and embrace a view that reflects the great diversity and richness of our country. Our policies should reflect the values of a democratic government—openness, participation, and discussion. They must be inclusive and generous in spirit, ensuring that all segments of our pluralistic society have meaningful access to the telecommunications system. These are the principles on which a great nation has been built.

As representatives of many nonprofit and public interest organizations, we believe that the following principles must guide policy making in order to ensure that future generations inherit an information infrastructure which enhances the quality of life for everyone.

1. UNIVERSAL ACCESS
All people should have affordable access to the information infrastructure.

Fundamental to life, liberty, and the pursuit of happiness in the Information Age is access to video, audio, and data networks that provide a broad range of news, public affairs, education, health, and government information and services. Such services should be provided in a user-friendly format, widely available to everyone, including persons with disabilities. Information that is essential in order to fully participate in a democratic society should be provided free.

2. FREEDOM TO COMMUNICATE
The information infrastructure should enable all people to effectively exercise their fundamental right to communicate.

Freedom of speech should be protected and fostered by the new information infrastructure, guaranteeing the right of every person to communicate easily, affordably, and effectively. The design of the infrastructure should facilitate two-way, audio and video communication from anyone to any individual, group, or network. The rights of creators must be protected, while accommodating the needs of users and libraries. Telecommunication carriers should not be permitted to constrain the free flow of information protected by the First Amendment.

3. VITAL CIVIC SECTOR
The information infrastructure must have a vital civic sector at its core.

For our democracy to flourish in the 21st Century, there must be a vital civic sector which enables the meaningful participation of all segments of our pluralistic society. Just as we have established public libraries and public highways, we must create public arenas or "electronic commons" in the media landscape. This will require the active involvement of a broad range of civic institutions—schools, universities, and libraries, not-for-profit groups, and governmental organizations. It will also require vibrant public telecommunications networks at the national, regional, and state level.

4. DIVERSE AND COMPETITIVE MARKETPLACE
The information infrastructure should ensure competition among ideas and information providers.

The information infrastructure must be designed to foster a healthy marketplace of ideas, where a full range of viewpoints is expressed and robust debate is stimulated. Individuals, nonprofits, and for-profit information providers need ready access to this marketplace if it is to thrive. To ensure competition among information providers, policies should be developed to lower barriers to entry (particularly for small and independent services); telecommunications carriers should not be permitted to control programming; and antitrust policies should be vigorously enforced to prevent market dominance by vertically-integrated media monopolies.

5. EQUITABLE WORKPLACE
New technologies should be used to enhance the quality of work and to promote equity in the workplace.

Because the information infrastructure will transform the content and conduct of work, policies should be developed to ensure that electronic technologies are utilized to improve the work environment rather than dehumanize it. Workers should share the benefits of the increased productivity that those technologies make possible. The rights and protections that workers now enjoy should be preserved and enhanced. To encourage nondiscriminatory practices throughout the information marketplace, public policy should promote greater representation of women, people of color, and persons with disabilities at all levels of management.

6. PRIVACY
Privacy should be carefully protected and extended.

A comprehensive set of policies should be developed to ensure that the privacy of all people is adequately protected. The collection of personal data should be strictly limited to the minimum necessary to provide specific services. Sharing data collected from individuals should only be permitted with their informed consent, freely given without coercion. Individuals should have the right to inspect and correct data files about them. Innovative billing practices should be developed that increase individual privacy.

7. DEMOCRATIC POLICYMAKING
The public should be fully involved in policy making for the information infrastructure.

The public must be fully involved in all stages of the development and ongoing regulation of the information infrastructure. The issues are not narrow technical matters which will only affect us as consumers; they are fundamental questions that will have profound effects on us as citizens and could reshape our democracy. Extensive efforts should be made to fully inform the public about what is at stake, and to encourage broad discussion and debate. The policy process should be conducted in an open manner with full press scrutiny. Effective mechanisms should be established to ensure continued public participation in telecommunications policy making.

REFERENCES

Appelman, D. (1995, June). The law and the Internet: Emerging legal issues. In *INET'95* (URL: http://inet.nttam.com/HMP/PAPER/222/abst.html). Honolulu, HI.

Bagdikian, B. (1992). *The media monopoly* (4th ed.). Boston: Beacon Press.

Barlow, J. (1993). Bill o' Rights. *Mondo 2000, 11*, 16-19.

Bartholomew, D. (1995, June 19). Blue-collar computing. *InformationWeek, 532*, 34-43.

Benedikt, M. (Ed.). (1991). *Cyberspace: First steps.* Cambridge, MA: MIT Press.

Biesada, A. (1993). Paving the digital superhighway. *UnixWorld, 10*(12), 58-62.

Branscomb, A. (1991). Common law for the electronic frontier. *Scientific American, 256*(3), 154-158.

Cerf, V. (1993, August). The past, present, and future Internet. A look at the growth of the Internet. In *2nd ONE BBSCON.* Colorado Springs, CO: One, Inc. (Electronic copy obtained via e-mail request from onebbscon@boardwatch.com).

Cerf, V. (1995). Computer networking: Global infrastructure for the 21st century. In E. Lazowska (Ed.), *Computing research: Driving information technology and the information industry forward* (URL: http://www.cs.washington.edu/homes/lazowska/cra/networks.html). Computing Research Association.

Coate, J. (1992). *Cyberspace innkeeping: Building online community.* Electronic publication obtained from the WELL via gopher.well.sf.ca.us.

Connolly, F., & Webster, S. (1993a). Bill of rights & responsibilites for electronic learners. *Educom Review, 28*(3), 24-27.

Connolly, F., & Webster, S. (1993b) New policies for an evolving future. *Educom Review, 28*(3), 28-30.

Cook, G. (1992). NSFnet "privatization" and the public interest: Can misguided policy be corrected? (Executive Summary). *COOK Report on Internet—NREN, 1* (10 & 11). (Electronic copy obtained from ietf-request@ietf.cnri.reston.va.us via gopher).

Elgin, D. (1991). Conscious democracy through electronic town meetings. *WholeEarth Review, 71,* 28-29.

Elmer-DeWitt, P. (1995). Welcome to cyberspace [Special issue]. *Time 145*(12), 4-11.

Garcia, L. (1996). The failure of telecom reform. *Telecommunications* [Americas Edition], *30*(9), 43-50.

Gibson, W. (1984). *Neuromancer.* New York: Ace.

Golding, P., & Murdoch, G. (1989). Pulling the plugs on democracy. *New Statesman and Society, 2*(56), 10-11.

Gore, A. (1991). Infrastructure for the global village. *Scientific American, 256*(3), 150-153.

Gore, A. (1993, December 21). Remarks by Vice President Al Gore at National Press Club. In *The White House: Office of the Vice President.* Washington, DC. (Electronic copy obtained from Almanac Information Server via e-mail document request to almanac@ace.esusda.gov).

Gore, A. (1994, January 11). Remarks prepared for delivery by Vice President Al Gore at Royce Hall, UCLA, Los Angeles. In *White House: Office of the Vice President.* Washington, DC. (Electronic copy obtained via FTP from ftp.eff.org).

Greenbaum, J. (1993). Internet in Europe. *UnixWorld, 10*(12), 37-38.

Greenwald, J. (1995). Battle for remote control [Special issue]. *Time,* 145(12), 69-71.

Harasim, L. (Ed.). (1993). *Global networks: Computers and international communication.* Cambridge, MA: MIT Press.

Hiltz, S.R., & Turoff, M. (1978). *The network nation: Human communication via computer.* Reading, MA: Addison-Wesley.

Jackson, J. (1995). It's a wired, wired world [Special issue]. *Time, 145*(12), 80-82.
Kapor, M. (1991). Civil liberties in cyberspace. *Scientific American, 256*(3), 158-164.
Kapor, M. (1992). Where is the digital highway really heading? The case for a Jeffersonian information policy. *WiReD, 1*(3). (Electronic copy obtained from WiReD InfoBot via gopher.wired.com).
Kapor, M., & Berman, J. (1993, November 24). A superhighway through the wasteland? *New York Times*, op-ed page. (Electronic copy obtained from the Electronic Frontier Foundation via gopher.eff.org).
Karnow, C. (1994). The electronic persona: A new legal entity. *Virtual Reality World, 2*(1), 37-40.
Kay, A., & Hillis, D. (1994). Kay + Hillis. *WiReD, 2*(1), 103-105, 148-149.
Kirschner, B. (1991, Fall). Electronic democracy in the 21st century. *National Civic Review*, pp. 406-412.
Krol, E. (1994). *The whole Internet user's guide & catalog* (2nd ed.). Sebastopol, CA: O'Reilly & Associates.
Lapham, L. (1994). Robber barons redux. *Harper's, 288*(1724), 7-11.
Legislating your digital future. (1993, December). *Unixworld*, p. 60.
Lieberman, D. (1994). Teens for telnet: K–12 and the Internet. *InternetWorld, 5*(1), 38-40, 42.
Littman, J. (1993). Commerce on the Internet: The digital gold rush. *UnixWorld, 10*(12), 42-48.
McFadden, T. (1991). Notes on the structure of cyberspace and the ballistic actors model. In M. Benedikt (Ed.), *Cyberspace: First steps* (pp. 335-362). Cambridge, MA: MIT Press.
Negroponte, N. (1995). *Being digital*. New York: Knopf.
Newton, H. (1994). *Newton's telecom dictionary* (8th ed.). New York: Flatiron.
Ogden, M. (1996). Electronic power to the people: Who is technology's keeper on the cyberspace frontier? *Technological Forecasting & Social Change, 52*(2 & 3), 119-133.
Pelton, J., & Bender, G. (1995). Breaking the NII gridlock: Is it time for a new action agenda? *Telecommunications, 29*(5), 47-50.
Perry, S. (1995, February 28). Ministers have firmer grip on information society issues. *G7 Live Home Page* (URL: http://www.ibm.com/Sponsor/g7live/30016.html).
Phillips, K. (1995). Virtual Washington [Special issue]. *Time, 145*(12), 65-68.
Poole, G. (1993). It's crunch-time in cyberspace. *UnixWorld, 10*(12), 52-56.
Quarterman, J. (1993). The global matrix of minds. In L. Harasim (Ed.), *Global networks: Computers and international communication* (pp. 35-56). Cambridge, MA: MIT Press.

Ratan, S. (1995). A new divide between haves and have-nots? *Time, 145*(12) [Special issue], 25-26.
Rheingold, H. (1985). *Tools for thought: The people and ideas behind the next computer revolution.* New York: Simon & Schuster.
Rheingold, H. (1991). Electronic democracy. *WholeEarth Review, 71,* 4-11.
Rheingold, H. (1993). *The virtual community: Homesteading on the electronic frontier.* New York: Addison-Wesley.
Schwartz, E. (1994). Direct democracy. *WiReD, 2*(1), 74-75.
Seymour, C. (1992, May). The incredibly strange mutant creatures who rule the universe of alienated zombie computer nerds. *Tokyo Journal, 5,* 24-31.
Stapleton, R. (1992, July). Opening doors in the global village. *Computer, 25*(7), 94-96.
Stenger, N. (1991). Mind is a leaking rainbow. In M. Benedikt (Ed.), *Cyberspace: First steps* (pp. 49-58). Cambridge, MA: MIT Press.
Sterling, B. (1993, February). Internet. *The Magazine of Fantasy and Science Fiction.* (Electronic copy obtained and used with author's permission from gopher well.sf.ca.us).
Stix, G. (1993). Domesticating cyberspace. *Scientific American, 261*(2), 100-110.
Toffler, A. (1981). *The third wave.* New York: William Morrow.
Toregas, C. (1989). Electronic democracy: Some definitions and a battle cry. *Public Management, 71*(11), 2-3.
Van Tassel, J. (1994). Yakety-yak, do talk back! *WiReD, 2*(1), 78-80.
Varley, P. (1991). Electronic democracy. *Technology Review, 94*(8), 43-51.
Westin, A. (Ed.). (1971). *Information technology in a democracy.* Cambridge, MA: Harvard University Press.
White House, (1993, September). *The national information infrastructure: Agenda for action.* Washington, DC: U.S. Government. (Electronic copy obtained from Almanic Information Server via email document request to almanac@ace.esusda.gov).
White House. (1994). *America in the age of information.* Washington, DC: U.S. Government. (URL:http://www.whitehouse.gov/WhiteHouse/EOP/OSTP/NSTC/html/cic/cic-plan.html.
Winer, D. (1995, June 16). "I hope I die before I get old." *HotWiReD.* (URL: http://www.hotwired.com/Signal/DaveNet/).
Wittig, M. (1991). Electronic city hall. *WholeEarth Review, 71,* 24-27.
Zakon, R. (1996). *Hobbes' Internet timeline v.2.5.* The Internet Society. (URL: http://info.isoc.org/guest/zakon/Internet/History/HIT.html).

6

Democratic Media: The Case for Getting Organized*

Seán Ó Siochrú

The last number of years has seen significant growth in democratic media initiatives around the world: alternative, usually community-based media that are motivated not by profit, but by solidarity, the struggle for survival or creative expression; media that empower not pacify, that create not simply repeat (see, e.g., Lewis, 1993, for a diverse review). The swelling of the ranks of community media is evident from the rapid growth among international Nongovernmental organizations (NGOs) representing them. To name just a few: AMARC, an elder among them, was founded in 1983 as a partnership of community radio stations and now counts its members in the thousands; Vidéazimut, founded in 1990, has grown to over 70 members active in community video and access television, many of which represent national federations of dozens of members; and APC (Association for Progressive Communication) has since 1987 brought together dozens of members and associates providing Internet access for the NGO sector in every continent. Similarly, any observer of the scene will have noticed a huge increase in the number of regional and international conferences, festivals, and other events on community and democratic media.

*An earlier version of this chapter appeared in *Media Development*, No. 3, 1996. Copyright 1996 by WACC, London. Reprinted by permission

The emergence on this scale, and from sometimes desperate circumstances, of people striving to articulate a voice, to create an identity and broadcast an image, offers inspiration to all those who believe that the media can and must be a force for democracy and development. However, it is also important not to overstate the facts. The fragile and often sporadic nature of democratic media is demonstrated by the many initiatives that emerge with great hopes, only to disappear through lack of a permanent sustainable base and adverse circumstances beyond their control. It would be a mistake to underestimate the scale of the task ahead for democratic media if they are to become a significant force in peoples' lives, from local to global levels. Building beyond isolated, often spontaneous and self-sacrificing media projects toward an enduring and mutually sustaining democratic media sector is going to demand a qualitatively new level of organization.

This is already happening within specific media at the national level and internationally with AMARC, Vidéazimut, APC, and other NGOs. Yet a further level of solidarity and common action is required before these sectoral activities can create a platform for sustained growth. The current growth in community holds forth an opportunity to develop a strategy for democratic media as a whole, to pull together the different stands around the central theme of media participation and democracy, transcending individual media to what they hold in common.

This chapter contributes to a debate emerging on what a strategy to promote democratic media might look like, one that on the one hand consciously counters the commercial mass media now sweeping all before them on the global stage, and, on the other hand develops its own sense of identity, dynamic, and destiny. (see, e.g., Ambrosi, 1996; Mohr, 1996; Raboy, 1996). The chapter considers: (a) the strengths and weaknesses of both democratic media alternatives and of global commercial media; (b) some basic building blocks for developing a successful collective strategy for democratic media; and (c) a few tentative short-term strategic goals that might be pursued, raising in particular the opportunities created ironically by the process of media neo-liberalization.

A premise is that the democratic media movement cannot strategically be content simply to pursue its own activities, filling what niches are available to it, but remaining oblivious to the continuing growth of the great forces of the commercial sector. For much of the growth in democratic media has, consciously or unconsciously, been in response to pressures emanating from the commercialization, privatization and commodification of communication. As Lewis (1993) put it, illustrating that this is not new:

> Some fifteen years ago I described alternative media as "antibodies produced . . . as a protection against the neglect, insensitivity, and insanity of the conventional media." The intervening years have con-

> firmed the general truth of a metaphor which suggests that inadequate or repressive mass media systems (and, one would want to add, the societies that produce them) seem inevitably to generate alternative media. (p. 15)

The trend away from public service goals and toward market mediation of output, and the homogenization of form and content of the mainstream media, are documented well enough to need no review here. Many local alternatives emerge in direct response to these trends, reclaiming a space that has become alien to local populations and disconnected from their needs. They attempt to compensate for the distortion of media space and communication processes and somehow wrest back control over content, production, and the ultimate purpose of the media.

Thus, the democratic media movement is essentially local in outlook and emerges often not from a positive agenda, but in opposition to a self-confident and aggressive mainstream that recognizes no boundaries. Insofar as it is created as antithesis, community media must go further and invent its own proper identity. If it is to achieve self-sustaining growth, it must generate a dynamic of its own, a collective dynamic beyond individual efforts and isolated opposition. This chapter therefore argues that democratic media cannot but set itself against, in every sense, commercial media. It must compare and contrast its strengths and weakness and set out deliberately to develop a coherent, viable, and rapidly expanding sphere of democratization.

STRENGTHS AND WEAKNESSES

The recent success of privately owned empires, and of commercial media as a whole, is the result of a coincidence of a diverse set of factors. A significant role can be attributed to the following.

First, commercial media operate at all geographical levels. Intra-or intercorporate connections exchange content and generate economies of scale and scope from local to national and global levels. However, commercial media collectively and individually also lobby hard, bringing strategic influence to bear on intergovernmental organizations, national governments, and even at the local level.

Second, there are numerous cross-connections between the different strands of commercial media (film, video, television, telecommunications, newspapers, etc.), not just in ownership, but also in terms of cross-marketing, strategic goals, lobbying, and other mutually reinforcing strategies.

Third, commercial media appeal to real desires of people and are in a position to constantly reinforce those desires and deepen their "markets."

Fourth, each medium projects a clear identity, purpose, and aim into the public sphere, and although each is different, they are all more and more associated with a single distinct set of characteristics and lifestyles that espouses consumption as the key to fulfillment.

Fifth, they have a sustainable and secure economic base and supporting economic structures, and finally, they have a clear strategy, both individually and collectively. Competition between them, sometimes fierce, does not distract them from recognizing and acting on their common interests, with little need for direct collaboration, either overt or covert.

Contrasting starkly are the democratic media (see Table 6.1).

Table 6.1. Contrasting Commercial and Community Media.

Dimension	Commercial Media	Democratic Media
Territorial	Global: creation, delivery, lobbying	Local: activities and advocacy
Cross Media Links	Numerous: ownership/ control, content, promotion/marketing	Few.
Appeal	Established need for passive entertainment	Suppressed need for participation and creativity in communication
Public Identity	Clear identity: For each medium, and all (consumerism)	Only exceptionally, even for individual media
Economic Base	Sustainable and secure	Insecure, temporary
Strategy	Global: for single TNCs and whole sector	National: emerging global strategy in individual media

First, they originate locally, and usually remain at that level. Second, often isolated from each other, different media maintain relatively few interactions and exchanges. Third, they sometimes suffer from existential doubt, motivated by broad political and social concerns or narrow local issues and having to work hard to develop or retain links to local realities.

Fourth, only exceptionally can democratic media individually develop a clear identity among the public, even amongst those with whom they come in direct contact; and collectively they have virtually no easily discernible unifying thread. Fifth, they have no secure economic base, relying on scarce local resources and temporary external support, and, finally, democratic media seldom engage in strategic planning, individually or collectively, although there is evidence that this is changing.

Of course, this is not to suggest that democratic media should, to achieve their aims, be structured in a manner similar to commercial media. Indeed, what is a strength to one can be a weakness to the other. The preceeding factors must thus be filtered through the priorities of commercial and democratic media, the former motivated by profit and sometimes megalomania, the latter engaged in a process of empowerment and democratization.

Most fundamentally, commercial media can relate to people only as consumers of commodities and command their loyalty only to the extent that these commodities are seen as desirable and continue to be delivered. Democratic media, however, are open and participative, needing to ensure accountability at every level. People can identify with the common objectives and collaborate in the struggle to achieve them, enabling community media to draw on much deeper resources. Similarly, commercial media command people's attention as a separate and discrete part of their lives, often walled off from other aspects of social and economic reality, whereas democratic media enable people to engage more closely with their broader realities.

Nevertheless, these factors, suitably modified, can offer long-term strategic milestones in terms of indicating the maturity of democratic media.

BUILDING BLOCKS

This section explores what might be required to build a movement for democratic media in terms of the factors described earlier.

The Need for a Global Dimension

At the global level, mainstream commercial media enjoy free reign, virtually immune from national structures that until a decade or two ago constrained their activities. They face a weakened, often floundering, intergovernmental system, in general meekly subservient to the major powers that in turn have virtually identified their own national interests with those of their roving multinational corporations and of neoliberalization. Media conglomerates can enter almost any country, confident of their clear identity, universal appeal, and saleability of wares, often backed by powerful national governments. Their intergovernmental agents such as WTO and IMF smooth the way by negotiating irresistible deals with corrupt or desperate politicians to gain "market access."

Democratic media cannot afford to ignore this dominance of mainstream media, not simply because of the resultant sterilization and homogenization of media content, but because in very practical ways it curtails their growth and room for maneuver, and their access to resources. For instance, in telecommunications, new standards for Digital Audio Broadcasting (DAB) may seriously affect the cost for community radio to get involved in this area; for community and democratic TV, the gradual scaling down and elimination of the development role of Intelsat affects the extent to which low-cost transponders are available; and the implementation of a neoliberal agenda in telecommunications by the WTO, the World Bank, and others could threaten universal service in many rural and poorer areas of developing countries, including their access to e-mail and other services with development and democratic potential.

Anterior to the hegemony of neoliberal ideas is the lack of a coherent alternative. A major success of the commercial media and their attendants has been to present their own version of the way forward, the commercialization and globalization of the media, as the only feasible one. In the realm of ideas, as well as in direct influence, community democratic media thus have a major task ahead.

Finally, democratic media have yet to establish any major voice beyond local and national levels to match those of direct broadcast television, of news agencies, and of publishers. The potential value of sharing and distributing content and resources, and of reaching larger audiences, is undoubtedly also great in democratic media. Although in less than global terms, this is illustrated, for example, in television by Deep Dish and the proposed Mondiale Satellite Channel, and in news agencies by IPS and AMARC's more recent initiative for radio news in Latin America, Pulsar. But none imagines they seriously rival the commercial conglomerates or are yet in a position to profit from the same economies of scale. The need for a global dimension thus exists at policy, ideological and at practical levels.

Cross-Fertilization of Media

There are huge commercial gains to be derived from linkages between the different media, especially film, video, magazines, books, and increasingly computer software. Such cross-marketing of brands and output, manipulating the desire for identification amid growing surface-level diversification, is hardly an aspiration of democratic media. However, collaboration between the different media is valuable in a number of ways. For instance, in terms of output, e-mail and Internet services can be used as a means to exchange written radio news, audiotapes, and even video clips for later broadcast. In terms of sharing, national or regional support organizations, providing resource centers, newsletters, training, and so forth, can share facilities. Most important, in terms of consciousness-raising and collaborative action, the exchange of information among practitioners working in different areas of democratic media can clarify what they have in common and can reinforce the trend toward cooperative action and strategic development.

Collaboration should extend beyond the media sector per se to find its strength in numbers. More general movements for democracy in communications, academic associations, and others pursuing the right to communicate are natural allies and can broaden the effective sphere of influence for democratic media.

Clarifying Aims and Objectives

Individual initiatives in democratic media usually have clear aims and objectives, arising from specific, often time-bound, contexts. Even organizations at the international level that represent a specific medium can after some time and internal development be reasonably clear on what they intend to achieve.

However, there has been little attention devoted to the role of democratic media as a whole, beyond simply the cumulation of individual initiatives. Although rightly railing against the commercialization of media and the reduction of output to mass-entertainment commodities, democratic media must be clear on what they are proposing in their place, how they see their role and that of others. Are democratic media proposing themselves as an alternative to mainstream media, with aspirations to supplant them? How are democratic media really different from local commercial media? Can they seriously expect ever to occupy anything but a minor role, useful especially to oppressed groups at a certain stage of development? Or are they an active niche area that complement the passive mainstream? Can they be a harbinger of a future mainstream media, of a truly participative society? Can commercial media be reformed in any significant ways?

These questions will require answers if a broad democratic media and communication movement is to grow in self-understanding and direction.

Creating an Identity

Such a movement will also require a clear identity that all people can recognize as distinct from commercial media, in the form both of individual media such as a local community radio station and of democratic media in general. Knowing what it stands for is the first step in supporting any organization, and such knowledge must be both concrete (the right to participate in your local station and to demand that it listen to your views) as well as abstract (the right to communicate and engage in democratic processes).

Creating this identity will, of course, hinge on questions of participation and the relationship between the "audience" and the medium. Radio offers a useful example. Local commercial radio stations, multiplying under liberalizing regimes, often claim (fearing the loss of advertising revenue) that they operate in effect as community radio. Hence, they argue, there is no need for a distinct license category, for instance, for nonprofit stations, to address community needs. However, what really distinguishes them is not whether they are profit oriented, but rather their relationship with the "listeners." Commercial local radio requires only that people listen or engage in "pseudo-participative" entertainment and news programming. Democratic community radio, however, must open its objectives, staffing, programming, and all other aspects to its constituents, no longer simply listeners but now active participants.

It is thus not only on the basis of content, but also of process that democratic media must construct an identity, with each specific medium interpreting this in its own way.

There is also a deeper, long-term issue surrounding identity. Although the tendency of global commercial media to homogenize, and ultimately destroy, local cultures has been the subject of much debate, policy responses have often been at the national level, for instance, with attempts to resist external influence and to strengthen the national culture. Indeed, in doing so, champions of national culture often adopt the language of commercialization, focusing on culture as commodity and the need to bolster "cultural industries." The European Union's response to the domination of U.S. media in film and television would fall into this category.

Community media offer an alternative, drawing their efficacy and legitimacy from the ultimate source of culture: local community interaction, variety, and creativity. As a source of cultural reflection and renewal, supporting democratic media has much to recommend it over propping up state-sponsored cultural symbols. Democratic media might here find a major long-term vocation. And it should be noted that the "local community" in this context encompasses the idea of "community of interest" with effective proximity or "localness" generated via, for instance, e-mail, video, or television distribution. Such communities of interest can span the global, geographically, while remaining essentially local in character, offering some hope of rescuing the notion of the global village and global village culture.

Addressing Real Needs

Commercial media appeal to atomized people, fragmented from each other and seeking some respite from daily struggles—dreams of release and riches, no matter how unlikely, are better than none at all.

The "appeal" of democratic media is fundamentally different. There are no easy solutions to offer, no "quick fixes." Indeed, what is offered is often a struggle, first to understand the nature of the media, then to use them to challenge the order in which people seek solace in dreams in the first place. They also offer the excitement of learning new ideas and skills, of exploring social relationships, and of engaging in effective collective action.

This is a far cry from relaxing to "Neighbours" and "Dallas," one demanding a high level of commitment from the "audience" and a determined effort by the media organizations themselves. Nevertheless, although democratic media might also (hopefully) offer entertainment, it is only by maintaining the primary focus on real needs and struggles that they can strike a distinct chord with people.

As Hamelink (1994) put it:

> Today's world communication disempowers people through attractive and effective forms of social control. However, some day the system will run out of luck and its clients will discover that ultimate human fulfillment is not the "triple D satisfaction" of deodorants, diets and detergents.... It is the continuous anxiety of the "mandarins of world communication" that people decide one day that "enough is enough." This revolt requires an active self-organizing global civil society, that organizes the protection of its interests against the hegemonic, expansionist forces of states and transnational organizations. This means that we interpret civil society not only as a defensive and reactive force, but also as a pro-active movement. (p. 147)

Addressing real needs engenders, as a natural continuum, such a proactive movement.

Creating a Secure Economic Base

Because democratic media cannot afford the luxury of chasing the most lucrative and wealthiest segments of the market, but must instead address pressing human needs, a secure economic base will always represent a challenge. Those most in need of a voice are usually those least able to pay for it.

Yet a stable economic base is essential for long-term growth. Development-oriented NGOs and national aid agencies have traditionally provided a level of support, but cannot, and should not, be relied on to continue supporting initiatives indefinitely.

Rather, a secure economic base must be forthcoming, both through fund-raising and an income-generating capacity of the media themselves and also, crucially, through securing legitimate, publicly supported, long-term income from national and regional government (and possibly, in the future, global governmental systems).

Developing a Strategic Capacity

Finally, none of these can be achieved in the absence of a strong strategic capacity, from grass-roots initiatives to media sectors to democratic media as a whole.

Commercial media engage simultaneously in competitive activities with their rivals and in "collective" (although largely autonomous) activities to support the sector as a whole through constantly recreating and expanding the territory (geographic, economic, and human) that they dominate. The strength of democratic media, by contrast, must be in explicit cooperation and collaboration.

A strategic capacity at the global level does not come quickly and easily, especially when one is concerned with the participative nature of the process. Learning to intervene effectively to influence governments, intergovernmental organizations, public opinion, and indeed the commercial media requires a slow accumulation of experience at all levels, methodically exchanged with others through formal and informal means. Lessons can be learned outside the communication sector, for instance, from the environmental and gender movements. Slow or not, conscious and deliberate effort must be invested in developing and nurturing a strategic capacity among democratic media.

STARTING POINTS

Reordering the preceding factors, they can be summarized as a set of long-term strategic goals for the democratic media movement:

- Clarify the potential and role for democratic media and aims and objectives
- Develop a strategic capacity, building from individual initiatives to global organizations
- Engage with the issues at all levels, from local to global
- Create a clear identity for democratic media, both individually and collectively, that all people can readily understand
- Maintain the focus on people's needs in their real lives, not on competing with mainstream media
- Seek a long-term economic base, at project, national, and international levels.

Given the present state of affairs, achieving these must remain beyond the visible horizon for some time yet. Nevertheless, they offer direction in terms of focusing immediate actions on long-term goals.

Needless to say, the main priority for democratic media is to continue to create innovative, sometimes alternative, media at the grass-roots level, experimenting and consolidating achievements. This is the wellspring of a movement. The following sections focus above this level, suggesting priorities for immediate action that address, in interconnected ways, the preceeding goals. Although necessarily presented in general form (they require tailoring to specific circumstances), they are intended to be realistic in scope and achievable within the foreseeable future.

Create a Democratic Media Alliance

A democratic media alliance, initially comprising an informal grouping of international NGOs then possibly national ones, could form the basis for a deepening of understanding within and between specific media. Over time and based on progress, this could gradually evolve toward a specific entity, representing in certain domains democratic media as a whole and acting as a central point of contact and collaboration.

Such an alliance or organization would assist progress on a number of fronts, among them:

- It would offer an arena in which to debate the role of democratic media as a whole and strategies to promote it

- It would facilitate networking and sharing of resources and collaboration on ongoing issues
- It could comprise a hub of information on all aspects of democratic media, both for those involved and for others, and even undertake its own research activities
- The process of formulating a specific identity could be initiated, and in the longer term this identity could be promoted
- It would offer a single point of contact for lobbying intergovernmental and other organizations, simplifying the logistics of developing such relationships.

The first steps of such an alliance would proceed on the basis of mutually beneficial, practical, and realizable goals.

Build and Experiment with Democratic Structures

Many of the preceeding factors hinge, naturally enough, on developing democratic structures. Participative structures are central to constructing and projecting a unique identity and to building intimate sustainable links with people ("audience," "clients," "users," etc.). The strategic capacity to influence any democratic medium will be determined by its ability to mobilize people, which in turn depends on how deeply people are committed. Such commitment also supports a major pillar of sustainable economic existence. Another economic pillar, government funding, in turn also demands transparent and democratic structures to achieve public legitimacy.

Developing democratic structures is therefore not simply a matter of principle, but a matter of central necessity. Creating them within the nongovernmental sector, however, is not easy, and there are few enough models of relevance. Democratic and participative structures must exist not only at the ground level, but also, and sometimes more problematically, at the national and international levels. Such structures would ensure that the centrality of grass roots realities is not lost in international actions—the NGO always risks, in proportion to its success, incorporation into and compromise by more powerful structures of interest.

There is an urgent task to develop and formalize participative models of community radio, video, television, and the other media and to devise innovative models for national and international organizations. Much can be learned from past experience within, and indeed outside, the media sector.

Intervene in Policy Fora

Public policy creates both the constraints and the opportunities within which democratic media operate. Effective intervention into policy formation is critical to the growth of the sector. National (sometimes regional)-level policy is still the most important, but the global level, via intergovernmental or multilateral organizations, is increasing in influence, especially in the context of neoliberalization.

Effective lobbying requires clear, well-constructed ideas and a coherent effective voice. Nationally, this can be assisted significantly through the various democratic media collaborating to understand the issues, explore policy options, and influence the outcome. International exchanges of information can also be of use, comparing developments in different countries in terms of policies and lobbying strategies.

At the international level, transnational alliances are essential. Most intergovernmental organizations will listen only to international organizations, referring others to national governments. Here there are currently major policy developments of relevance to the future of community media and access to infrastructure and airwaves. Yet, at this level, democratic media have virtually no presence. Establishing relations with the ITU, the WTO, and UNESCO would be a first step (in 1995 UNESCO published its World Commission on Culture and Development report, arguing for a "global commons" that offers free satellite radio and television signals). However, activities of organizations such as the World Bank, the IMF, OECD, and G7 intertwine to influence virtually all domains, including the media, with impetus added in the context of the "information society." Such organizations could also be the subject of observation, analysis, and intervention.

In practical terms, then, a strategy should be devised to support national lobbying and construct vehicles for intergovernmental influence. The focus should not, however, be solely on securing greater influence for the democratic media sector. Of equal importance is pressing to democratize structures of governance in relation to all aspects, and at all levels, of media policy development and implementation. It might be noted here that the democratic media sector, like the NGO sector in general, cannot perceive itself as an alternative to democratic government. Rather, it is both a means to supplement global, national, and regional governments where they are restrained and compromised and a force to deepen democracy within existing structures of governance.

Exploit the Opportunity of Liberalization

The state is also a potential source of permanent funding for democratic media, and, ironically, the process of neoliberalization of the media and regulations governing them offers a significant opportunity for levering state funding through effective lobbying.

In principle, a state that relies on market forces and private ownership as the principle motive for economic development has an obligation to ensure that profits are not generated at the expense of essential aspects of human life and dignity. Establishing the right to communicate as one such essential aspect, and securing support for its instruments, democratic media, is of course a major struggle with the state and private interests, a struggle rendered seemingly more difficult under neo-liberal policies.

Neoliberalization, a term used here to denote commercialization, privatization, commodification of production, and the reduction of regulatory restrictions on media activity, essentially represents a movement away from democratic control by means of political structures toward increased private sector power. The effect is an atomization and stratification of the influence of people and their transformation into consumers. Their democratic choice is reduced to whether they purchase one commodity or another—if they can afford either.

Given the long-standing public service role of the media, such changes do not occur without resistance. The relatively visible erosion of the social good and the "public service ethic" inherent in the liberalization process (affecting, for instance, television, radio, telecommunications, newspapers, and even film sectors), combined with the patent inability of its protector, the state, to renew its role from within its own resources, creates a "democratic deficit." This void can be occupied by proponents of democratic media as a lever to secure an economic basis for the sector. In other words, the possibility is that the "public-service ethic," hitherto occupied by a more or less benign top-down state, can now be taken by the alternative media sector and democratized. A central source of legitimacy in this argument is that democratic media are open, participative, and accountable to the people. Without this, they become simply another interest group, with no rights to any special status.

Thus, for example, democratic (or community) radio may argue for state support, especially if they decline a right to advertise; democratic video and television can demand production and transmission facilities (already achieved in many countries); and development-oriented Internet use can demand local access and support for training, equipment, and so forth as part of universal service policies.

At a global level, a similar argument can be made, although the structures are less amenable to influence. Certainly, issues ranging from radio spectrum allocation and cross-subsidies for global universal service (where the divisions between countries are far greater than those within them) to the right to protect cultural diversity against profit maximization fall victim to the global agenda of neoliberalization. Counterarguments must be forcefully articulated and alternative structures proposed.

Not all countries are subject to neoliberal policies, and when they are, such an opening may not always exist. Nevertheless, this "silver lining" of neoliberalization is the kind of opportunity that a democratic media movement must grasp as a means to build its future. Such a campaign plays to the strengths of the media movement, with its roots in democracy. It also underlines the value of strategic planning, collective action, and developing an identity as a means to influence policy objectives.

CONCLUSION

Long ago, Karl Marx pointed out that capitalism transforms all before it into its own image, the image of the commodity bought and sold for a price. The transformation of the media has taken longer than most, and they continue to resist the process because the media are central to society's own image and sense of identity. To surrender them to the market is to lose a fundamental aspect of our being. Opposition has thus been real and sustained, sometimes with the help of a state stepping in forcefully on behalf of the people.

Even in mature economies, the state is now in a weakened condition, its power base under threat and its legitimacy in the area of media under siege by a resurgent private sector.

The New World Information and Communication Order carried the issue to the global stage, but in the end it was also defeated, partly because it lacked roots in real, ground-level struggles. The democratic media sector now emerges as the alternative, or at least one alternative, that firmly reasserts the centrality of people, their dignity, and creativity. Although still in its early stages, those committed to the right to communicate, both as creation and reception, have a responsibility and an opportunity to organize their activities beyond immediate concerns, directing ideas and energies toward the broader context. The opportunities to do so are there now. This is the only way for democratic media to come in from the margins and help shape the future.

REFERENCES

Ambrosi, A. (1996). Les Chemins de traverse de la communication démocratique. In *Multimédia et communication a usage humain*. Paris: FPH.
Hamelink, C. (1994). *Trends in world communication*. Penang: Southbound.
Lewis, P. (Ed.). (1993) *Alternative media: Linking global and local*. Paris: UNESCO.
Mohr, L. (1996, April). *Riding the tide or swimming against the current*. (Clips, No. 10). Montreal: Vidéazimut.
Ó Siochrú, S. (1995, October). Universal service in the global information society: Problems and prospects. *TELECOM '95*. Geneva: ITU.
Raboy, M. (1996, April). *Towards a global framework for democratic media* (Clips, No. 10). Montreal: Vidéazimut.
UNESCO. (1995). *Our creative diversity: Report from the World Commission on Culture and Development*. Paris: Author.

7

Media as Public Arena: Reconceptualizing the Role of Media for a Post-Cold War and Postmodern World

Dennis K. Davis

We have reached a time of considerable uncertainty in world politics and communications. Media pundits and politicians have tried to label this era but none has been successful. Some have celebrated an information age and the emergence of a new international order. The signs of these changes are said to be everywhere. They point out that information production and distribution is becoming more and more important to modern economies. The old international order based on superpower confrontation has ended. Communication-related industries are expanding. But this is also an age of disinformation and disorder. Public knowledge and understanding of international or domestic politics have not increased even though more information is available. Racial and ethnic prejudice and cultural misunderstanding are clearly increasing in many parts of the world. Conflicts within and between nations persist.

We have come through one of the most eventful decades in human history, and it will be many decades before its consequences are apparent. The end of the Cold War was not simply the end of superpower confrontation. It had much more profound cultural implications that we are just beginning to understand. What makes this era especially challenging is that so many old cultural and social trends have ended abruptly. Although most of these trends were quite problematic, their disappearance has left a cultural void. New trends may take decades if not centuries to become established. The most striking example of the consequences of cultural upheaval can be found in Eastern Europe. There the collapse of the old social order has been followed by the renewal of ancient ethnic conflicts.

At a time when the very basis of social order may be eroding, we have developed very powerful new communication media. With these media, we can span space and time as never before. Complex messages can be sent instantaneously around the world, but there is little evidence that these media will be used to address our cultural problems. In the United States much of the current planning for new media involves sophisticated entertainment services for wealthy consumers. Delivery of these commodities to this market is said to be necessary to pay for development of the media. Thus, although our ability to understand culture and the human condition has never been greater, and even though powerful new communication technologies are at hand, we seem unlikely to use this knowledge to stem conflict and use new media wisely.

In this chapter, I base my arguments on the work of postmodernist theorists, who have argued that the central defining feature of our global community today is the decline of modernism. Everywhere we are confronted by growing evidence that modernism is losing its ability to structure human action. Rising levels of violence and gang activity on the one hand and the resurgence of traditional forms of culture on the other are only the most obvious indicators of the decline in modernism. But how are we to interpret this evidence and what should we do? Some believe that we have no choice but to sustain modernism despite its increasingly evident faults. Others call for radical change but are unable to explain what the consequences of these changes will be.

This chapter offers no easy answers to the dilemmas posed by the decline of modernism. It offers a way of interpreting the decline of modernism and then uses this interpretation to evaluate the societal role of news media. News media are viewed as a very central institution in the perpetuation of modern social orders. They flourished along with modernism, and they will be severely affected by its decline. If this view is correct, the problems faced by journalists will intensify over the next decade in certain predictable ways. This could lead to a radical transformation of news media or to their gradual disappearance.

Unlike some analysts (Christians, Ferre, & Fackler, 1993), I am not deeply troubled by the prospect of a world without news industries. I am all too aware of the many limitations of modern journalism. As explained later, this industry has become increasingly devoted to the production and distribution of news as a saleable commodity. Its commitment to social service has eroded. Like most modern institutions, it is caught up in the serious contradictions of modern values. Ultimately, it is constrained by its bureaucratic social structure, its collaboration with other modern social institutions, and the relationship it has established with its consumers.

Thus, I find it hard to imagine how existing news media could be reformed so that they will play a constructive role in the development of postmodern social orders. In this chapter, I consider the purposes to be served by postmodern media. However, I recognize that it is unlikely that existing news media can or will serve these purposes. In all likelihood, new media will need to be developed that are more closely grounded within the communities they serve. These media, in turn, might be linked into larger networks that serve to bridge communities.

A DEFINITION OF MODERNITY

Elsewhere (Davis, 1995) I have traced the rise of modernism and identified reasons for its decline. From its inception during the 16th century, modernism has been an especially virulent and hegemonic worldview. The most threatening aspect of modernity is its inherent assumption that it is not just another form of culture. Rather, modernity has been assumed by its proponents to represent a culmination in cultural evolution. It is quite simply a Culture to end all cultures. It can only evolve but can never be superseded. It is Civilization, Natural Order, Knowledge, and Truth. Like the laws of science, it is assumed to be universally valid and eternal. All other forms of culture must be subordinated to it because they are necessarily incomplete, transitory, parochial, and primitive. As it evolved, modernism moved from being grounded in Christianity to grounding in science. Several competing forms of modernism emerged, including communism, socialism, and capitalism. All shared a common strategy for imposing order on human action: a) the use of science to develop powerful new technologies to span or bind space and time (Giddens, 1990), and (b) development of large-scale bureaucratic social institutions.

Bureaucracy provided a very powerful means of structuring social order. It proved so powerful that it could constrain and manipulate culture to reach bureaucratic objectives. Bureaucracies have two means of control—technology and coercion. With these tools, they are able to extend their power over vast reaches of time and space.

One of the most important strategies used by bureaucracies to impose social order has been the construction and dissemination of powerful visions of social reality. These visions lead most people to view modern culture and bureaucracy as essential features of the social world and fostered their dependency on them. For example, bureaucracies excel at the mass production and distribution of consumer goods. By fostering dependency on such goods, bureaucracies assure their survival.

There are many ironies in the way that modernism has emerged as a worldwide, hegemonic culture. Although it is grounded on quite naive notions of individualism and places supreme value on individual autonomy, all modern social orders have found quite effective strategies for manipulating individuals and limiting the possibility for autonomous action. By promoting individualism, bureaucracies effectively isolate people from one another and discourage the rise of competing forms of social organization such as social movements. Alternate forms of social organization are frequently presented as interfering with the rights of individuals and as a threat to democracy (Davis, 1993). But, in actuality, it is bureaucracies that restrict individuals and limit the scope of democratic government. Every modern social order is a centralized political state in which authority is wielded by technocrats who govern various bureaucracies. Modern social orders have provided social stability. But this stability comes with a heavy price—marginalization or active suppression of a broad range of grassroots, culture construction efforts. Modernity by its very nature is simply unable to accommodate significant levels of cultural pluralism, no matter how much pluralist values are espoused in modernist writing.

MODERNISM AND THE SUPPRESION OF CULTURE CONSTRUCTION

By nature, human beings are constantly imposing meaning and order on the psychological, social, and physical world. They are motivated to construct forms of culture that can structure their experience and enable them to live in meaningful association with others. Everywhere on this planet, cultures arose out of this need to live in a world that one knows and experiences as meaningful. Traditionally, folk communities arose out of this innate motivation toward shared meaning and order. Such communities declined when they failed to provide sufficient meaning and order. Culture construction efforts are inherently innovative and unpredictable. Although at any given point in time they must build on existing forms of culture, they are always open to significant, qualitative changes. Change is especially likely when a wide range of existing social practices, expectations, and definitions cease to be useful in conceptualizing, working toward, and achieving objectives experienced as meaningful.

Modernism is unable to accommodate much freedom in culture construction by social groups. It demands that all persons accept the cultural forms necessary for the effective operation of large bureaucracies. A variety of techniques are used to suppress cultural experimentation and marginalize groups that engage in it. Within bureaucracies, culture construction is limited by a hierarchical order that requires that most significant cultural innovations originate from the top. Authority to create culture is based on position in the hierarchy or technocratic training not on an individuals skill in developing innovative, more useful forms of culture.

Bureaucracies prize ritual and perpetuate stereotypes as a means of maintaining control over culture. Bureaucratic authority is reverenced in routinized ways. Time is tightly controlled—specifically defined tasks must be accomplished within certain time limits. There is little spare time for creating and transmitting alternate definitions. Persons who defy the rituals are easily identified and dismissed or marginalized.

This view of modernism explains why every expansion of modernism has been accompanied by the extermination of indigenous cultures. Modernism cannot tolerate the existence of alternative cultures that might provide alternate ways of conceiving and experiencing the physical and social world. This highlights another tragic irony of modernism. Although cultural pluralism is a central value of modernism, this pluralism is quite limited. Superficial forms of cultural diversity are permitted or even encouraged (i.e., variation in clothing, hair styles, music) but severe limitations are placed on cultures that foster inherently different worldviews. Thus, on the surface modern social orders can appear to be culturally diverse. But this diversity hides significant discrimination against any forms of culture and social organization that could challenge and undermine bureaucratic control.

As a form of culture, there is growing evidence that modernism has exhausted much of its potential for creating meaning. Its visions of human nature, social order, and even the physical universe have become inherently contradictory and ambiguous (Davis & Jasinski, 1990). These perspectives have been explored in detail over four centuries. Once powerful rituals have become empty exercises with little ability to compel attention and structure experience. Increasingly, social order is maintained through bribery and coercion, not by culture. Cooperation with bureaucracy is rewarded with consumer goods and challenges to bureaucracy are punished with marginalization.

News Media as Agents of Modernity

The decline of modernism is not something that will be explained and interpreted by newspapers. Although journalists dutifully report the events that signal this decline, they can provide only a superficial analysis of them. There are many reasons for this, but the most fundamental of them is that journalism is itself a modern bureaucratic social institution (Davis, 1995). As such, it is incapable of providing a radical criticism of itself and its role within modern social orders. News media operate in cooperation with the other bureaucratic social institutions that structure the modern world. Journalists report news events from the point of view of these institutions and enable them to maintain the status quo (Gans, 1979).

Since the beginning of modernism, news media have been recognized as playing a central role in politics. Libertarian thinkers envisioned media as a public forum in which various political ideas could be presented and debated. They believed that in a free and open contest between ideas, truth would win out, public decisions could be based on it. Thus, by establishing various forms of communication freedom, the best public decisions would be made. In time an ideal social order would be created. This belief was ideally suited to bridging the cultural diversity that plagued the early libertarians. To create a broad-based social movement, they needed to bring together very different social groups. These groups were effectively promised that their views could become part of the dominant culture if those views were found to be true. But early libertarians were not necessarily committed to long-term cultural diversity and pluralism. Many expected that the one, true, natural cultural and social order would emerge soon after the artificial restrains of medieval culture and its social institutions were overcome. Thus, from its early history, modernism has had an ambiguous commitment to pluralism. Routine suppression of indigenous peoples around the world demonstrated just how limited the libertarian vision of cultural diversity was.

Libertarian notions became the primary means of legitimizing most modern forms of mass media. If a free and open exchange of ideas is essential to modernity, then media can serve society by institutionalizing a public forum for such ideas. By providing a public space for airing diverse points of view and by supplying information in support of these ideas, news media could serve as an engine of democracy. In most modern social orders, journalists have succeeded in enshrining press freedom as a basic right. But this right is premised on the increasingly dubious notion that the type of public forum provided by bureaucratized news media will permit discovery of truth and enable progress toward an ideal social order. Even many defenders of modern news media admit that they have failed to give sufficient priority to sustaining a useful public forum.

As modern social orders evolved, news media developed in a manner that was completely consistent with other modern social institutions. News media became centralized and bureaucratized. They developed and utilized powerful technologies to span space and time. In the United States they evolved into industries devoted to the packaging and marketing of information commodities. They formed alliances with other social institutions to serve their own interests and provide overall support for modernism. To the extent that a public forum was maintained, it became increasingly structured and elitist. Radically different cultures were excluded. Public debate was limited to a narrow spectrum of modern ideas. For example, the voice of native peoples was effectively excluded from U.S. media. This exclusion facilitated marginalization and virtual extermination of their cultures.

The rise of modernism generated many rationales for narrowing the scope of the ideas to be considered in the public forum. Intense competition between various forms of modernism (i.e., capitalism, socialism, or communism) forced these ideas to be excluded and their proponents marginalized. Through a bizarre reinterpretation of libertarian notions at the end of the 19th century, the conception of media as public forum for ideas was transformed into media as a "marketplace" for ideas. Well-packaged true ideas would not only drive out bad ideas but could be sold at a profit. This view legitimized increasing emphasis on the sale of information commodities to mass audiences (Shiller, 1981; Schudson, 1978). Journalists adopted strategies used in other businesses devoted to the mass production and marketing of goods. They became another type of technocrat— skilled at managing vast bureaucracies devoted to packaging, distributing, and selling information commodities. These commodities were increasingly decontextualized from the everyday culture of the persons who consumed them.

In order to earn the highest profits, media corporations focused on two objectives: (a) packaging content to make it as attractive as possible for large audiences, and (b) maximizing the ability of their medium to serve as an effective vehicle for advertising. The strong emphasis on packaging led to important shifts in how news was defined and the manner in which news was presented. For example, the modern definition of news as brief, accurate, balanced reports of discrete events is quite consistent with the desire to market news to the largest audience and make this audience available to advertisers. These decontextualized reports do not offend persons from different cultural, ethnic or racial backgrounds. Similarly, Edward Epstein (1973) documented how network television news directors chose to prioritize coverage of events that would provide visually attractive or compelling pictures. Other research found that most news stories are structured using stereotypical themes that mass audiences find easy to understand (Bennett, 1988; Gans, 1979).

However, attractive packaging has done little to increase the ability of news media to transmit useful information. Public knowledge of politics has not increased, whereas public alienation and political cynicism have risen. If critics like Neil Postman (1985) are right, packaging may well interfere with the transmission of serious information. The marketplace of ideas becomes the marketplace of information commodities. The links between sale of these commodities and the operation of our political system have become quite ambiguous. Critics have developed quite persuasive arguments that blame badly packaged information for a variety of problems in our political system (Entman, 1989; Postman, 1985).

News media have also evolved to serve advertisers as effectively as possible. Since the 1870s, the majority of revenue earned by urban newspapers has come from advertising. Again and again, advertisers have demonstrated that they have little loyalty to specific media and will not subsidize a medium that cannot effectively transmit their messages no matter how valuable it may be to society at large. The rapid demise of mass circulation magazines in favor of television during the 1950s serves as a chilling example of what can happen when a medium ceases to be the most cost-effective means of delivering advertising. News media are forced to compete alongside all other media for advertising revenue, and this competition shapes them in subtle, and not so subtle, ways that are becoming evident. For example, during the 1970s and 1980s, many urban newspapers made an effort to rid themselves of the types of readers who were not of interest to urban advertisers (i.e., poor people or rural residents). Newspapers ceased to serve these segments of the public on economic not political or ethical grounds.

Thus, it is possible to conceptualize news media as very active and biased agents in the promulgation of the modern worldview and support for other social institutions (Herman & Chomsky, 1988). This argument notes the close association between the rise of news media and the triumph of modernism over the past century.

Previous Research on News Media

The ambiguous role of news media and the increasing priority given to marketing of information commodities has not gone unnoticed by academic researchers. Social scientists from several disciplines have studied these changes. Some have done so from the perspective of various normative theories. For example, it is common to question whether news media are meeting their social responsibilities as implied by some form of democratic theory (Christians et al., 1993). Others have attempted to observe and measure news production, transmission, and reception. Persuasive evidence is marshaled to demonstrate that news media are failing to support democracy. News coverage of politics is found to be intrusive and disruptive (Patterson, 1993; Davis, 1990). News stories are found to pander to popular tastes while obscuring or ignoring important social or political events (Bennett, 1988). These stories are built around information from official sources and serve largely to reinforce the status quo (Gans, 1979). When alternate points of view are presented, they tend to be inadequately covered or unfairly represented. Often these points of view are placed in stories as part of a ritualistic exercise to give them the appearance of balance and objectivity (Tuchman, 1978). Distribution of news stories through powerful media technologies does little to affect the level of public knowledge about politics (Robinson & Davis, 1990). The ability and motivation of average persons to participate in politics is marginal at best. The most attractive and widely known news stories are typically of little use to people in making sense of politics or their role in it (Davis & Robinson, 1989).

There has come to be widespread agreement among news researchers concerning the need to reform a broad range of news production practices. Research has documented serious limitations in these practices (Epstein, 1973; Fishman, 1980; Gans, 1979; Tuchman, 1978). Content analysis has identified many problems in the narrative structure and themes found in news stories (Bennett, 1988). Audience comprehension research has identified many reasons why people find it difficult to learn from news, make many errors, and quickly forget what they do learn (Davis & Robinson, 1989; Graber, 1987; Gunter, 1987; Robinson & Levy, 1986). These problems apply to all forms of news coverage, but they are especially prevalent for coverage of international issues, events, and politics (Galtung & Vincent, 1992). International news coverage dwells on "bad" news—news about natural disasters, political crises, violent crimes, and bizarre happenings. Constructive social change and other cultural perspectives are considered too boring or complex to be newsworthy. But another explanation for this coverage may be the modernist biases of Western journalists.

Research-Based Critiques of Journalism

It has become popular among some political scientists to argue that U.S. politics would be better if political institutions were freer to operate and evolve according to their own internal dynamics without so much interference from news media. Patterson (1980, 1993) and others have argued that news media have played an especially disruptive role in politics since the 1960s. But these criticisms imply that we should leave politics to the political technocrats who dominate modern political institutions. We must trust that they will do their job better if they do not have to cope with constraints placed on them by news industries. This critique appears to place too much trust in modern political institutions.

Researchers who study the flow of news and how people learn from news media tend to rely on classical democratic theory and libertarian assumptions. They assume that if the flow of useful news can be increased and if this news can be made more accessible to people, then political and social conditions will improve. There are many difficulties with this perspective. How should the utility of news be determined? How could popular but useless forms of news be eliminated if these are necessary for news media to be profitable? Journalists argue that they are doing the best they can under difficult circumstances. Why should they adopt the innovative news values of academics when they have a long-established tradition that guides them?

Is Reform of News Media Possible?

At this moment in time, radical reform of news media appears unlikely. Pressures from other social institutions are either insufficient or unlikely to result in meaningful reform. News media are increasingly engaged in an all-out competition for the mass audience. Competitive pressures are likely to distract journalists from making reforms. New communications technologies permit competing media to be developed at a low cost. Readership of major urban newspapers has been in a steady decline for over a decade. Young readers are being lured away from printed news reports. As news audiences come to practice more diverse cultures and their commitment to modernism weakens, traditional forms of news content become less and less relevant. News media may respond by changing news production practices, but this seems likely to be of very limited social value.

The Emergence of Postmodern Culture

If postmodern theory is correct, we are entering a period of cultural ferment that could well persist for centuries. There are few historical precedents for this type of radical cultural change. Modern culture itself arose over a period of two centuries, and during this time there was constant turmoil. The medieval world-view did not suddenly fade away, nor did medieval social institutions suddenly collapse. Medieval elites struggled to preserve their power against a very diverse array of modern counterelites.

The essential features of postmodern culture remain to be defined. Most of what has been defined is based on a rejection of elements of modernism. Various forms of postmodernism can be differentiated by the aspects of modern culture that are found to be problematic. Early libertarianism found its essential values in a rejection of medieval community and feudal authority. In time a coherent alternate perspective developed, and alternate social institutions were formed. It is unclear which of the various critiques of modernism will permit a coherent vision of society to be constructed.

POSTMODERN THEMES AND MEDIA REFORM

One common theme in postmodernism is rejection of the individual as the basic unit of society. The basic unit is viewed as the community—groups of people capable of creating and sharing culture (Davis & Jasinski, 1993). Individual experience is the product of enculturation. Individuals are created by communities, but this theme can lead to quite diverse conclusions. Increasingly, it is being viewed as a basis for restoring modernism itself. If individualism is the fatal flaw in modernism, then all we need to do is place more emphasis on community. Ironically, this effort to restore modernism could actually accelerate its decline. It fails to recognize how great a role individualism plays in the success of modern institutions. If strong communities are encouraged, they are likely to create alternate forms of culture that will make it more difficult for them to be controlled by modern institutions.

An interesting recent effort for journalism reform can be interpreted as a move to preserve modernism in this way (Rosen, 1993). Jay Rosen proposed what he terms "public journalism" and "community connectedness" as a means of enhancing public life. Rosen accepts the criticism that newspapers no longer serve societal purposes assigned to them by libertarian thinkers. However, he believes that many journalists still are committed to these purposes. If practical strategies can be developed that permit these purposes to be served by newspapers, then journalists will adopt them. Modern democracy will be saved. But how will "community connectedness" differ from what journalists already do? News media are well connected to the other social institutions that dominate modern society. Their ability to create and manage an effective public forum in which a broad range of ideas can be considered is questionable.

Another central theme in postmodernism is culture as a means of constructing radically different yet profoundly meaningful perspectives on the social world. This perspective on culture differs in a very important way from the modernist view of cultural pluralism. Modernists accept the existence of other cultures; however, they assume that these cultures can somehow be adapted to modernism. It is assumed that modern values and norms can structure public life for everyone. Other cultures can structure private life.

Some postmodernists reject the possibility of public life and public culture. They argue that any culture that attempts to bridge other cultures will be inherently hegemonic. They believe that the very conception of public culture is inherently modernist and must be rejected for that reason.

Thus, it will not be easy to develop a postmodern conception of the social role of communication when there is such disagreement over postmodernism itself. My preference is to seek a middle course between one set of strategies that essentially seek to restore modernism by revitalizing modern social institutions (e.g., Christians et al., 1993; Rosen, 1993) and laissez-faire, nihilistic approaches that are content to await the collapse of modernism.

Communication in a Postmodern World

Two overall objectives can be envisioned for communication in a pluralistic, postmodern world: (a) communication as a means of culture construction and sharing, and (b) communication as a means of bridging diverse cultures. A postmodern world is likely to be characterized by the rapid proliferation of culture. As the constraints on culture production imposed by modern social institutions erode, many news forms of culture will appear. Many will be linear extensions of existing cultures. Some will be synthetic; they will weave together elements from many other cultures. Some will seek to revive dead or dying cultures. Others will be innovative.

The first of these objectives is relatively unproblematic. Our understanding of the many ways that communication can be used to create and share culture is expanding exponentially. New insights are being produced across a broad range of disciplines in the humanities and social sciences. Even business schools have begun to investigate corporate or organizational cultures. Psychological counselors, especially group therapists, increasingly conceptualize their work in terms of culture construction. People are discovering how to work with others to redefine themselves and fundamentally alter their experience of the social world.

The second possible objective for communication is more problematic. If we are successful in using communication to construct powerful, compelling forms of culture, these cultures could easily be very divisive. Throughout human history, people practicing intensely meaningful local cultures have tended to deeply distrust outsiders. There are some who see the postmodern world as a return to tribalism; a world where all of our most meaningful experiences will be derived from a very limited set of relationships. Is it possible to construct highly meaningful local cultures and still have enough people who are motivated to join associations or movements that bridge and give perspective to these local communities?

My own vision of the postmodern world is optimistic. I think it likely that people will want to be active in more than one local community, and that they will be drawn to movements or associations that bridge these communities. But if this is to occur, it is important that communication media serve to deepen people's understanding of culture construction within communities and make them aware of the value of participation in groups that bridge these communities. Although I am optimistic that communication media could be used in these ways, I recognize that it is unlikely that existing media industries will serve these purposes. Even if public journalism envisioned by Rosen were successful, it would provide only limited understanding and awareness.

It will be necessary to envision a new type of public arena quite different from the public forum imagined by libertarians. In this arena, entire cultures are open to examination. No contest occurs over isolated ideas or bits of information. Rather, the arena would permit alternate cultures to be explored, their values appreciated, their experiences examined and imagined. There is no expectation that an ideal form of culture or social order will emerge out of this arena. No linear progress toward truth is expected. Instead, it would serve a range of purposes. Most importantly, it would provide legitimation for cultural diversity.

REFERENCES

Bennett, W.L. (1988). *News: The politics of illusion*. (2nd ed.). New York: Longman.

Christians, C.G., Ferre, J.P., & Fackler, P. M. (1993). *Good news: Social ethics & the press*. New York: Oxford University Press.

Davis, D.K. (1990). News and politics. In D.L. Swanson & D. Nimmo (Eds.), *New directions in political communication*. (pp. 147-184). Newbury Park, CA: Sage.

Davis, D.K. (1993, April). *News coverage of social movements: From discovery to decline*. Paper presented at the Central States Speech Association, Lexington, KY.

Davis, D.K. (1995). Media and modernity: The future of journalism in a post cold war & postmodern world. In P.C. Wasburn (Ed.), *Research in political sociology* (pp. 325-353). Greenwich, CT: JAI Press.

Davis, D.K., & Jasinski, J. (1993). Beyond the culture wars: An agenda for research on communication and culture. *Journal of Communication*, *43*(3), 141-149.

Davis, D.K., & Robinson, J.P. (1986). The social role of television news: Theoretical perspectives. In J.P. Robinson & M. Levy (Eds.), *The main source: Learning from television news* (pp. 29-56). Beverly Hills: Sage.

Davis, D.K., & Robinson, J.P. (1989). Newsflow and democratic society in an age of electronic media. In G. Comstock (Ed.), *Public communication and behavior* (Vol. 3, pp. 59-102). New York: Academic Press.

Entman, R. M. (1989). *Democracy without citizens: Media and the decay of American politics*. New York: Oxford University Press.

Epstein, E. J. (1973). *News from nowhere: Television and the news.* New York: Random House.

Fishman, M. (1980). *Manufacturing the news.* Austin: University of Texas Press.

Galtung, J., & Vincent, R. C. (1992). *Global glasnost, toward a new world information and communication order?* Cresskill, NJ: Hampton Press.

Gans, H. (1979). *Deciding what's news.* New York: Pantheon.

Giddens, A. (1990). *The consequences of modernity.* Cambridge, England: Polity Press.

Graber, D. (1987). *Processing the news* (2nd ed.). New York: Longman.

Gunter, B. (1987). *Poor reception: Misunderstanding and forgetting broadcast news.* Hillsdale, NJ: Erlbaum.

Herman, E. S., & Chomsky, N. (1988). *Manufacturing consent: The political economy of the mass media.* New York: Pantheon Books.

Jasinski, J., & Davis, D.K. (1990, September). *Political communication and politics: A theory of public culture.* Paper presented at the Political Communication Division of the American Political Science Association, San Francisco, CA.

Patterson, T. E. (1980). *The mass media election: How Americans choose their president.* New York: Praeger.

Patterson, T. E. (1993). *Out of order.* New York: Knopf.

Postman, N. (1985). *Amusing ourselves to death: Public discourse in the age of show business.* New York: Penguin Books.

Robinson, J.P., & Davis, D.K. (1990). Television news and the informed public: Not the main source. *Journal of Communication, 40,* 106-119.

Robinson, J.P., & Levy, M., with Davis, D.K. (Eds.). (1986). *The main source: Learning from television news.* Newbury Park, CA: Sage.

Rosen, J. (1993). *Community connectedness passwords for public journalism.* St. Petersburg, FL: The Poynter Institute for Media Studies.

Schudson, M. (1978). *Discovering the news: A social history of American newspapers.* New York: Basic Books.

Shiller, D. (1981). *Objectivity and the news: The public and the rise of commercial journalism.* Philadelphia: University of Pennsylvania Press.

Tuchman, G. (1978). *Making news: A study in the construction of reality.* New York: Free Press.

8

Emancipation from Modernization: Development Journalism and New Social Movements

Hemant Shah

For more than two decades, development journalism has been criticized, delegitimized, and declared a failed project by observers "steeped in libertarian capitalist press culture" (Murphy, 1993, p. 2). In reality, development journalism was conceptualized in the early 1960s as independent, critical journalism that provided constructive criticism of governments and established development bureaucracies from an adversarial stance. This idea was appropriated by a handful of government leaders and used as a rationale to take control of mass media to promote State policies. As a result, all forms of government and communication in the Third World were conflated into "a ghostly demon that persecuted journalists, distorted media forms and conspired against free speech" (Murphy, 1993, p. 4). Thus, the "debate" over development journalism boiled down to a simplistic dichotomy: Western, commercial mass media were free, whereas Third World mass media were strictly controlled and manipulated by elites.

The intent of this chapter, however, is not to carry out a critique of the pluses and minuses of the free press/controlled press debate. I contend that this debate diverts attention from the important problem of discovering ways that communication can contribute to participatory democracy, security, peace, and other humanistic principles that are at the core of the discourse on modernity and advocated by, among others, the MacBride Commission (Commission for the Study of Communication Problems, 1980).

The disagreements about development journalism have taken place within a more general debate about the relationship between mass communication and national development. The so-called dominant paradigm of mass communication and national development studies, an intellectual tradition rooted in the ideology of modernization, has come under attack from a variety of intellectual directions (see e.g., Golding, 1974; Rogers, 1976; Samarajiwa, 1987; Servaes, 1990). The criticisms include charges that the dominant paradigm emphasizes top-down flow of information, pays little attention to concerns of people at the grass-roots level, is interested primarily in economic growth, and severs the connections between the spatial and temporal dimensions of people's lives in ways that leave them disoriented, alienated, uprooted, and unable to resist the negative effects of modernization.

Some critics of the dominant paradigm have proposed an alternative model for mass communication and national development called "another development," which is rooted in an ideology of communitarianism (Tehranian, 1995). This model emphasizes democratic communication involving two-way and horizontal flows of information, gives voice to people at the grass-roots level, and suggests a reconfiguration of the spatial and temporal dimensions of human relationships that allows people to reclaim a sense of rootedness. However, even though the "another development" paradigm is to be commended for its commitment to counteracting the negative effects of modernization, few specific details are offered regarding how mass communication can encourage more democratic communication.

This chapter provides some specific guidelines about how development journalism can contribute to more democratic communication in the process of humane development. First, the chapter briefly discusses the dominant model of mass communication and national development, paying particular attention to the ways that mass communication was expected to reconfigure spatial and temporal relationships to bring about a "modern" Third World. Next, it outlines the actual individual and societal effects of efforts to apply the dominant model in the Third World, highlighting the negative impact on the spatial and temporal dimensions of people's lives. Then the chapter examines the concept of emancipation and its relationship to new social movements that can help reestablish spatial and temporal security as a basis for structural transformation. Next, using the characteristics of "new social movements" as a basis, a normative model for the role of development journalism in fostering democratic communication for emancipation from modernization is outlined. The relationship between development journalism and social change is considered in the final section.

MASS COMMUNICATION AND NATIONAL DEVELOPMENT

Expectations of the Dominant Paradigm

In the most general terms, the dominant paradigm promised happiness and security that was supposedly enjoyed in abundance in the West. The process of modernization, emphasizing economic growth through industrialization and urbanization, was the theoretical engine that drove research and policy making through the 1960s and 1970s. Although Rogers (1976) declared that the dominant paradigm had passed, it still informs much research and policy making related to mass communication and national development.

The role of journalism in the process of Third World development has been discussed since the earliest treatments of mass communication and national development (see Lerner, 1958, Passin, 1963; Pye, 1967; Schramm, 1964). Journalism, along with all other forms of mass communication, was supposed to help reconfigure the temporal and spatial organization of people's everyday lives in ways that would move small or large communities (including nations) away from tradition and toward modernity. Researchers assumed news could help direct people toward modernization by depicting images of rational decision making, popular democratic participation, and the technological sophistication of modern life in the West. It was assumed that people exposed to these images would want to emulate the modern (Western) lifestyle.

Actual Impact of the Dominant Paradigm

Western-style modernization did come to the Third World. Productivity, health care, education, transportation, and mass communication all improved. However, the price was a growing structural inequality that had an impact on the spatial organization of life. For example, inequity led not only to the economic but physical marginalization of laborers, who were forced to live in the outskirts of metropolitan areas or to eke out a living as landless laborers in the countryside. Although the number of people living in absolute poverty on the margins of society grew, there was an increasing concentration of power in the hands of rural and urban elites. Policies of modernization also led to the creation of new international spatial relationships in which the West represented the center of power and the Third World represented the periphery and semiperiphery. The temporal dimension of this new relationship lay in the denial of the unique histories of Third World countries. The assumption was that current conditions in the

Third World were like the past of the West and the future of the Third World was like the West's present.

There was a human dimension to these structural-level effects of modernization. More and more people were hungry, malnourished, homeless, unable to read or write, and unable to live in dignity. For many individuals, modernization processes created profound crises related to the formation of self-identity. For example, one of the spatiotemporal consequences of modernization (and modernity generally) was the separation of spatial and temporal dimensions of human existence. In "premodern" communities human communication occurred in a context of face-to-face interaction in which individuals shared the same spatial and temporal location; that is, they talked to each other in each other's physical presence. The history of modernity shows a gradual but continuing separation of time and space, a process Giddens (1990) refers to as "time-space distanciation." Modernization, the post-World War II theoretical and policy offspring of modernity, brought with it the technological ability to completely sever the connection between the spatial and temporal dimensions of human interaction. Individuals no longer had to share the same space or the same temporal moment to communicate with one another (Giddens, 1990). Communication could take place over a phone, information could be stored and retrieved in different places and times, and mass media could bring images of places and times never before imagined.

As a result, localized and interpersonal social relationships with family and friends were "disembedded" (Giddens, 1990) and replaced by ones that were physically distant and impersonal. The information, ideas, and images from unfamiliar spaces and times intensified "reflexivity," the drive to contemplate all aspects of social life and subject them to revision and alteration in light of new information and knowledge (Giddens, 1991). These processes of disembedding and reflexivity then created existential anxiety and a sense of alienation for those living through the process of modernization.

Journalism and mass communications seemed to reinforce these processes and exacerbate their effects. Institutions of journalism and mass communication were controlled by ruling elites and were biased spatially toward the West (and urban areas) and its cultural tastes and temporally toward the future represented by the West. This orientation stretched the spatial and temporal horizons of the "premodern" community and undermined its characteristic connections between physical setting and social interaction (Giddens, 1991; Gregory, 1989; Meyrowitz, 1985).

News organizations presented little information about development. When they did, it focused on events rather than processes and dramatic personalities rather than structural analysis (see, e.g., Dilawari, Stewart, & Flournoy, 1991; Encanto, 1982; McDaniel, 1986). Thus, development news provided little historical (i.e., temporal) background or structural orientation (i.e., spatial orientation because structure organizes the management and use of space) that could help readers contextualize the modernization processes through which they were living. Development news came from the top down, emphasizing official, bureaucratic views and pronouncements and did not represent the interests, priorities and aspirations of the poorest and most marginalized (see, e.g., Ogan, Fair, & Shah, 1984; Ogan & Rush, 1985; Shah & Gayatri, 1994). The "technocentricity" of modernization (Luke, 1990) was reflected by the science and technology emphasis of development news (see, e.g., Haque, 1986; McKay, 1992; Shah, 1990, 1988), which helped intensify reflexivity by undermining local and traditional ways of knowing and dealing with agriculture, social organization, the environment, and so on. Furthermore, access to information was extremely unequal, and gaps in knowledge grew between the haves and have-nots, creating separate cultural spaces within which these groups learned about and constructed their social realities.

It is clear that modernization in the Third World is a process full of contradiction. For example, increased productivity and economic growth was accompanied by poverty and inequality; technological and organizational innovation was accompanied by corporate retrenchment, which led to massive unemployment; and the ability to communicate over large distances and spans of time was accompanied by a sense of dislocation and disorientation. The benefits of modernization—such as they were—did not reach a vast majority of Third World inhabitants. There is a clear need, therefore, to emancipate the large number of Third World inhabitants who have been marginalized to the periphery, trapped there by modernization—often in absolute poverty—with neither "sense of place" (Meyrowitz, 1985) nor identity.

EMANCIPATION AND NEW SOCIAL MOVEMENTS

Emancipation involves "collective actions which seek to level and disperse power, or seek to install more inclusive values than the prevailing ones" (Pieterse, 1992, p. 32). Emancipation requires, first, a basis for establishing spatial and temporal security, which involves a reorientation to material surroundings and establishing a sense of belonging to a body of traditions and history. The process creates "locales"—symbolic settings that help constitute social activity—where individuals can again experience the (not necessarily physical) presence of people with whom they are interacting and gain a sense of community or "place" (Giddens, 1990). A place for localized relations can counteract the consequences of modernization because it represents a reconnection between temporal and spatial elements of life. Reorientation to physical surroundings may require what

Jameson (1984) calls cognitive mapping, a "situational representation" that illuminates and provides individuals with an understanding of their place within society by coordinating "existential data (the empirical position of the subject) with unlived, abstract conceptions of the . . . totality" (p. 90). Establishing connections to cultural tradition and history requires construction and reconstruction of premodernization ideologies that can be retrieved and expressed as histories or projected as normative models representing alternative forms of social organization (Apter, 1987).

Second, emancipation requires a basis for reconstructing cultural identities (Verhelst, 1987), that is, not a nostalgic reconstruction rooted in a longing for the way things were, but the creation of new identities that reflect and reconcile the ambivalence of Western-style modernization. The reconstruction of cultural identities involves a resistance and accommodation dynamic. Resistance may include establishing autonomy for formulating definitions of self, nation, and development and creating a vocabulary for articulating critique. Accommodation may include acculturation into some elements of the culture of modernization (Marcus, 1992) or possibly the "indigenization" of foreign products, values, or practices (Appadurai, 1990).

The third requirement is transforming the relationships between social action and social control; that is, the constraints structure imposes on agency. Such transformations, although they are fundamentally political, are not based solely in class struggle. They also are characterized by their connection to formations of cultural identities (Aronowitz, 1992). The transformations have as their immediate goal "changing hegemony and expanding civil society" rather than total structural reform (Pieterse, 1992, p. 21). This self-limiting characteristic of emancipation is rooted in the idea that "in social relations everything is not subject to the calculus of an absolute rationality" and the need to remember "the dark side of modern myths like progress, liberation and revolution" (Melucci, 1992, p. 73).[1]

---

[1] Emancipation must be distinguished from three similar ideas—participation, empowerment, and resistance. Participation usually means democratic involvement, but discussions often revolve around how to integrate marginalized groups into the mainstream rather to define the conditions under which they will participate (Pieterse, 1992). Empowerment refers to a participatory approach to social change, but the direction of change is often unspecified or vague. Empowerment also implies the gaining of power, but often the difference "between 'power to' (ability) and 'power over' (control)" is not spelled out (p. 10). One of the primary goals of resistance is establishing autonomy to create self-definition as a basis for collective action. Resistance can be negative, as when progressivism becomes "identified with saying no" (p. 11). It can be affirmative when it is understood as critique that creates an opening for change, but most versions of resistance imply only reaction to repression or injustice. The potentially proactive and transformative elements of resistance are generally not elaborated (p. 12).

Collective actions aimed at emancipation from modernization can be understood as "new social movements" (NSMs). NSMs are characterized by their unique ideology, base of support, motivations of members to participate, organizational structure, and political style (Dalton & Kuechler, 1990). The ideology of an NSM usually will advocate social organizing on grounds other than purely economic. In the context of Third World modernization, emancipatory NSMs may question the emphasis on economic growth and advocate greater attention to issues related to culture and quality of life such as increasing the opportunities for social, economic, and other forms of participation. Participants in NSMs are not drawn solely from the ranks of the poor or from repressed minorities. Instead NSMs draw their support from socially diffuse sets of individuals who nevertheless represent a like-minded community with a common goal. In the Third World, NSMs may draw their support not only from those marginalized by modernization, but also from intellectuals, students, enlightened members of the middle class, journalists, and so on.

The goals of a NSM often involve instrumental and collective goals that cannot be restricted to any one group. Supporters may be drawn to an NSM to help accomplish, for example, the practical goal of providing specific kinds of basic needs to a specific dispossessed community, but also by the broader political and philosophical issues of equity and emancipation. The structure of NSMs are decentralized, open, and broadly democratic. This loose structure reflects the "diffuse and fluid social base" (Dalton & Kuechler, 1990, p. 14) of NSMs' base of support. Finally, NSMs use pragmatic and perhaps unconventional methods of direct action such as carefully planned uses of mass media to influence public opinion.

DEVELOPMENT JOURNALISM AND EMANCIPATION

The characteristics of NSMs provide a basis for generating a normative model of development journalism. Four principles sketch out the broad parameters of the model. The first three concern journalism per se (that is the practice of reporting and writing) and the last involves the role of journalists in emancipation from modernization.

Participation, empowerment, and resistance clearly are part of a process of emancipation. Yet emancipation is more than just the sum of participation, empowerment, and resistance as they are commonly understood. Emancipation implies involvement, but on terms defined by the participants. Emancipation means securing the ability to make progressive change. Emancipation means having the autonomy to formulate self-definitions, but in a way that is proactive and transformative.

First, development journalism should be concerned with social, cultural, and political aspects of development, in addition to economic aspects. The emancipatory goal of development journalism should be to promote and contribute to humane development, which focuses on (a) meeting material basic needs such as food, shelter, clothing, as well as nonmaterial needs such as dignity and a sense of security; (b) empowering people so they may articulate and manage their own development; and (c) ameliorating structural obstacles to humane development such as inequity, rigid caste, race, and gender divisions, and corrupt bureaucracies (Jamias, 1987; Webster, 1984).

Second, development journalism should be democratic and emphasize communication from the "bottom up." Development journalism should involve reporting that includes people affected by modernization, values their perspectives, consults them as sources, and publicizes their needs and their plight. Development journalism should seek out and emphasize local knowledge and discussion of the development process rather than the views of officials. By providing an outlet for the voice of people at the grass-roots level, development journalism helps them articulate their own views and priorities for development, thereby resisting definitions imposed by the West or by urban elites. For example, reporters at the *Hindustan Times* in New Delhi "adopted" a village and wrote weekly stories about issues and concerns voiced by the residents (Verghese, 1976). In Gauhati, the capital city of the Indian state of Assam, newspapers assessed the type of development-related information desired by their readers and wrote stories on those topics (Mazumdar, 1985).

Third, development journalism should be pragmatic and unconventional in its approach to reporting. Even though traditional journalism reports facts perceived to be the truth and makes a conscious effort to remain detached from the subject of the story, development journalism should make explicit efforts to promote reform and encourage social action. Development journalism can encourage action, for example, by providing information that makes people aware of services, opportunities, and problems that need attention. Readers can then act immediately and personally on information salient to their needs. Development journalism can encourage reform, for example, by keeping the problems related to development on the agendas of policymakers so that they may be forced to take action leading to emancipatory social change. One of the results of the *Hindustan Times* experiment in development journalism (Verghese, 1976) was that government officials were forced into action by the negative publicity generated by news stories of government neglect of villages and villagers.

However, the pragmatism of development journalism should not be understood as driven purely by practicality or simple cost-benefit calculations. Development journalism is a normative model rooted in the principles of humane development. It should give people a chance to meet their material and nonmaterial basic needs and try to reconstruct a secure sense of place and history (i.e., an orientation in space and time) within which people can satisfy their needs and which provides a basis for reformation of cultural identities, self-expression and critique; and, ultimately, transformation and emancipation.

Thus, development journalism represents a new and unconventional model of journalism (from the perspective of the West, at least) that emphasizes process over events, explanation over description, bottom-up over top-down flow of information, and a wide range of sources over officials and experts. Development journalism should be based on non-Western news values. Development journalists should replace the dry, mechanical recitation of "facts" with reporting of contextualized narratives and interpretation. They should obliterate the false division between news and editorial that is derived from the myth of objectivity. This type of reporting requires immersion in social movements and commitment to the goal of emancipatory change.

The three principles of development journalism articulated thus far can be summarized as journalism that uses a holistic approach, is people-oriented, and emphasizes advocacy (Shah, 1992). The holistic approach can provide a basis for providing spatial and temporal security. An orientation toward the day-to-day conditions of people can play an important role in the process of reconstructing cultural identities. An emphasis on advocacy can help promote and help mobilize support for transformation.

A holistic approach to development journalism implies a recognition that development is a process and not an event. Changes in one part of a system have effects in other parts of the system, and the effects may occur over time. Furthermore, parts within a given system and the system itself have historical trajectories that impinge on the ways interaction within the system takes place. Thus, development is a complicated process occurring in a global system of domination and dependence. The enormous complexity of the situation may contribute to feelings of alienation and anxiety for those living through the modernization process. Development journalism may help to counteract these forces by providing the cognitive mapping necessary to establish a sense of physical and cultural belonging. To create this sense of physical belonging, development journalism may, for example, compare the development process with similar processes in other regions or countries and point out the unique needs and accomplishments of the local community. To establish a sense of cultural belonging, development journalism can discuss the development process in the context of its cultural relevance and historical significance, point out the cultural implications and consequences of change; assess how (and if) people's needs are being met; and propose culturally relevant models for future development plans.

The people orientation of development journalism can help facilitate reconstruction of cultural identities by fueling the resistance-and-accommodation dynamic. Through the broadly democratic nature of development journalism, local communities develop a set of concepts and theories that provide the basis not only for understanding the contradictions of modernization, but also for critiquing them and proposing alternatives. The alternative visions may include the terms on which certain elements of modernization are to be adopted (if at all), in a culturally relevant manner.

The reconstruction of cultural identities based on the resistance-accommodation dynamic takes place within a locale. It is within this symbolic or physical place that people converge to interact and perhaps collectively confront (what is perceived to be) an "outside" threat such as the State or the West (Apter, 1987). The advocacy emphasis of development journalism helps to maintain and strengthen this space for autonomy and resistance. Development journalism can help create, maintain, and strengthen a mobilization space with news that helps recreate situationally relevant myths of the past and propose visions of the future to make significant the current battles for autonomy, integrity, and security.

Table 8.1 summarizes the development journalism reporting strategy just outlined in the form of 10 prescriptive guidelines adopted from Shah (1988). Galtung and Vincent (1993) suggested similar proposals for "development-oriented news media" and provide several examples of good development news reporting.

Finally, Development journalists should take on the role of movement intellectuals. An important part of any social movement is its organic intellectuals. They provide energy for collective action by helping create a space for awareness and action. Organic intellectuals are "individuals who through their activities articulate the knowledge interests and cognitive identity of social movements" (Eyerman & Jamison, 1991, p. 98). They are organic intellectuals because their role is created in the very process of creating social movements; their identity and the identity of the social movement they lead are created interactively.

Development journalists—the practitioners of development journalism—can be understood as organic intellectuals if they are able, first, to disidentify themselves with dominant Western practices and values and identify themselves with the Other—in this case those marginalized by modernization (Pieterse, 1992). Then, they should examine and understand the conditions of modernization and its effects on the Third World and "articulate the concerns of emergent forms of protest, putting them into broader frameworks," showing their "deeper meaning and significance" (Eyerman & Jamison, 1991, p. 98).

Social movements provide opportunities for professionals of many kinds to apply their knowledge to new, politicized contexts, making it possible for some of them to become movement intellectuals (Eyerman &

TABLE 8.1. Development News Reporting Guidelines

1. Emphasize development as a process rather than as events. Stories should reflect complexity rather than focusing on ribbon-cuttings and press conferences.

2. Discuss success stories about citizen action, government response, problem solving, etc., but provide critique when needed.

3. Discuss the relevance of development issues to local needs. Stories should explain how specific projects and plans are related to people's needs.

4. Provide contextual or background information about the development process. Readers should understand how development-related issues evolved into their current status.

5. Discuss implications and consequences of the development process. Readers should understand the potential structural impacts (e.g., distribution of wealth, migration, demographics) of specific projects, plans or policies.

6. Discuss the personal impact of development. Reporters should explain the effects of policies on personal earning power, physical, and social mobility, health, etc.

7. Discuss and compare the development process in other regions or countries. This information helps provide larger contexts within which to make sense of local development processes but also provides examples to emulate and lessons about what to avoid.

8. Compare the development process with original goals and with claims of success to help ensure a measure of accountability in the process of planning and implementing development plans.

9. Discuss the development process in the context of people's aspirations and goals. Show readers how (and if) their desires are reflected in ongoing development processes.

10. Allow people to articulate their concerns and views about development in their own words. Dialogues and conversations about development should be reported to reveal in an authentic "voice" the views of people affected by development.

Source: Adapted with permission from "Development news on All India Radio: Assessment of quantity and quality," by H. Shah, 1988, *Journalism Quarterly*, 65, pp. 1034-1041. © 1988.

Jamison, 1991). From this perspective, journalists committed to emancipatory journalism may be understood as professional movement intellectuals for social movements oriented toward emancipation from modernization. The journalists, using their skills in the space created by social movements, provide a communicative capability that contributes to reconstructing cultural identities, expressing autonomous critique, and facilitating transformation (see Downing, 1984; Manca, 1989). Although neither the journalists nor the emancipatory journalism they write is solely responsible for social change, they both are of central importance in struggles for emancipation from modernization (Butalia, 1993). However, the emancipatory journalist's role is not to blindly support social movements. Rather, the emancipatory journalist is critically supportive by providing feedback that points out problems with the directions, orientations, priorities, and leadership of the movements.

Surveys of journalists in Algeria (Kirat, 1987), India (Eapen, 1969; Shah, 1989), and Nigeria (Dare, 1983) show that many respondents acknowledge and attach some importance to development journalism. Further evidence of the commitment to development journalism is the more than 1,000 journalists from around the world who listed their names in the *International Directory of Development Journalists* (1987).

DEVELOPMENT JOURNALISM AND SOCIAL CHANGE

Social change is intimately related to social control, and control is related to gathering, nurturing, and applying power. According to Fiske (1993), there are two kinds of power: (a) a top-down "imperializing" power that operates through technologies and bureaucratic mechanisms controlled by the State and that works to maintain the social order, and (b) a weaker, bottom-up "localizing power" that aims to manage immediate social conditions by producing and holding on to places that can be controlled by subordinated groups.

Modernization is a type of imperializing power. The forces of modernization that emerged from the West after World War II claimed the whole of the Third World as its territory and under the rubric of humanitarianism began to transform Asian, African, and Latin American countries into replicas of the West. This process—essentially one of imposing social control—was justified by two temporally based discourses. On the one hand, a discourse of tradition suggested that Third World views and values were from a backward and primitive time of the past and needed to be replaced by a worldview that could be provided only by modernization. This discourse provided the justification for introducing education systems, religions, and communication styles of the West into the Third

World. On the other hand, a discourse of nation suggested that benefits accruing from the establishment of a modern nation-state would trickle down to even the most dispossessed inhabitants of the Third World. This discourse justified the imposition of Western (supposedly advanced) styles of governing, methods of bureaucratic organization, and ideas of meritocracy into the Third World.

The enclosure of Third World territorial space and the temporal discourses of tradition and nation also helped justify other methods of social control. One argument was that because Third World "natives" are primitive, they must be watched, categorized, trained, mobilized, coerced, indoctrinated, and so on. The rhetoric of the inclusive nation-state was, in reality, based on elite interests represented as national interests. The voices of those who refused to accept those interests were ignored, and their bodies and cultures were marginalized. The mass media, including journalism, participated in creating the illusion of modernization as choice, access, participation, and emancipation for all.

Development journalism is a localizing power. It represents an attempt to help people establish local control over their immediate social conditions. Development journalism can facilitate local control by (a) showing how needs can be satisfied within a context of imperializing power, (b) revealing contradictions and problems within the discourse of modernization, and (c) providing temporal and spatial security from which action for change can be initiated. However, the localizing power of development journalism will not bring about a comprehensive overhaul of imperializing power. Development journalism (as conceptualized in this chapter) and other types of localizing power primarily are geared toward providing people with resources to challenge the equations of power (i.e., how much power is in the hands of various groups and individuals), not necessarily the relations of power (i.e., which collectivity is dominant and which is subordinate; see Jacobson, 1993; Wartenberg, 1990). Any journalist potentially can contribute, even inadvertently, to conditions that stimulate challenge to the existing equations of power (see Bruck, 1989; Eliasoph, 1988; Meyers, 1992; Shah, 1994). But the development journalism movement and development journalists, the movement's organic intellectuals, actively, explicitly, and purposefully try to expand the opportunity to emancipate the Third World from modernization.

REFERENCES

Appadurai, A. (1990). Disjuncture and difference in the global cultural economy. *Public Culture, 2*, 1-24.
Apter, D. (1987). *Rethinking development: Modernization, dependency and postmodern politics.* Newbury Park, CA: Sage.
Aronowitz, S. (1992). *The politics of identity: Class, culture, social movements.* London: Routledge.
Bruck, P. (1989). Strategies for peace, strategies for news research. *Journal of Communication, 39*, 108-129.
Butalia, U. (1993). Women and alternative media (India). In P. Lewis (Ed.), *Alternative media: Linking local and global* (pp. 51-60). Paris: UNESCO.
Commission for the Study of Communication Problems. (1980). *Many voices, one world.* Paris: UNESCO.
Dalton, R.J., & Kuechler, M. (1990). *Challenging the political order: New social and political movements in Western democracies.* New York: Oxford University Press.
Dare, O. (1983). *The News Agency of Nigeria: A study of its impact on the flow of news and role conception of its staffers.* Unpublished doctoral dissertation, Indiana University.
Dilawari, S.R., Stewart, R., & Flournoy, D. (1991). Development news on CNN world report. *Gazette, 47*, 121-137.
Downing, J. (1984). *Radical media: The political experience of alternative communication.* Boston: South End Press.
Eapen, K.E. (1969). *Journalism as a profession in India: A study of two states and two cities.* Unpublished doctoral dissertation, University of Wisconsin-Madison.
Eliasoph, N. (1988). Routines and the making of oppositional news. *Critical Studies in Mass Communication, 5*, 313-334.
Encanto, G. (1982). Development journalism in the Philippines. In E. Atwood, S. Bullion, & S. Murphy (Eds.), *International perspectives on news* (pp. 33-48). Carbondale: Southern Illinois University press.
Eyerman, R., & Jamison A. (1991). *Social movements: A cognitive approach.* University Park: Pennsylvania State University Press.
Fiske, J. (1993). *Power plays, power works.* London: Routledge.
Galtung, J., & Vincent, R. (1993). *Global glasnost: Toward a new world information and communication order?* Cresskill, NJ: Hampton Press.
Giddens, A. (1991). *Modernity and self-identity: Self and society in the late modern age.* Cambridge, MA: Polity Press.
Giddens, A. (1990). *The consequences of modernity.* Stanford, CA: Stanford University Press.
Golding, P. (1974). Media role in national development: Critique of a theoretical orthodoxy. *Journal of Communication, 24*, 39-53.

Gregory, D. (1989). Presences and absences: Time-space relations and structuration theory. In D. Held & J. B. Thompson (Eds.), *Social theory and modern societies: Anthony Giddens and his critics* (pp. 185-214). Cambridge, MA: Cambridge University Press.

Jacobson, T. L. (1993). A pragmatist account of participatory communication research for national development. *Communication Theory, 3,* 214-230.

Jameson, F. (1984). Postmodernism, or the cultural logic of late capitalism. *New Left Review, 146,* 53-92.

Jamias, J.F. (1987, March). Humane goal for development journalism. *Philippines Communications Journal,* pp. 21-26.

Haque, M. (1986). Is development news more salient than human interest stories in Indian elite press? *Gazette, 38,* 83-99

International Directory of Development Journalists (1987). New York: United Nations Development Program, Division for Economic and Social Information.

Kirat, M. (1987). *The Algerian newspeople: A study of their backgrounds, professional orientations and working conditions.* Unpublished doctoral dissertation, Indiana University.

Lerner, D. (1958). *The passing of traditional society: Modernization in the Middle East.* New York: Free Press.

Luke, S. (1990). *Social theory and modernity: Critique, dissent, and revolution.* Newbury Park, CA: Sage.

Manca, L. (1989). Journalism, advocacy, and a communication model for democracy. In M. Raboy & P. Bruck (Eds.), *Communication for and against democracy* (pp. 163-173). Montreal: Black Rose Books.

Marcus, G. (1992). Past, present and emergent identities: Requirements for ethnographies of late twentieth-century modernity worldwide. In S. Lash & J. Friedman (Eds.), *Modernity and identity* (pp. 309-330). Oxford: Basil Blackwell.

Mazumdar, A. (1985, May). *Development communication through press: A case study of newspapers of Assam.* Paper presented at the International and Intercultural Division of the International Communication Association, Honolulu.

McDaniel, D. (1986). Development news in two Asian nations. *Journalism Quarterly, 63,* 167-170.

McKay, F. (1992, August). *Development journalism in an Asian setting: A study of Depth news.* Paper presented at the Intercultural Communication Division, Association for Education in Journalism and Mass Communication, Montreal.

Melucci, A. (1992). Liberation or meaning? Social movement, culture and democracy. *Development and Change, 23,* 42-77.

Meyers, M. (1992). Reporters and beats: The making of oppositional news. *Critical Studies in Mass Communication, 9,* 75-90.

Meyrowitz, J. (1985). *No sense of place.* New York: Oxford.
Murphy, B.K. (1993, December). *Independent development journalism: The case of southern Africa.* Paper presented at the African Studies Association, Boston.
Ogan, C., Fair, J.E., & Shah, H. (1984). "A little good news": The treatment of development news in selected world newspapers. *Gazette, 33,* 173-191.
Ogan, C., & Rush, R. (1985). Development news in CANA and Interlink. In W.C. Soderlund & S.H. Surlin (Eds.), *Media in Latin America and the Caribbean: Domestic and international perspectives* (pp. 95-119). Windsor, Ontario: Ontario Cooperative Program in Latin American and Caribbean Studies.
Passin, H. (1963). Writer and journalist in transitional society. In L. Pye (Ed.), *Communications and political development* (pp. 82-123). Princeton, NJ: Princeton University Press.
Pieterse, J.N. (1992). Emancipations, modern and postmodern. *Development and Change, 23,* 5-41.
Pye, L. (1967). Communication, institution building, and the reach of authority. In D. Lerner & W. Schramm (Eds.), *Communication and change in the developing countries* (pp. 35-55). Honolulu: East-West Center Press
Rogers, E. (1976). Communication and development—The passing of the dominant paradigm. In E.M. Rogers (Ed.), *Communication and development: Critical perspectives* (pp. 121-148). Beverly Hills: Sage.
Samarajiwa, R. (1987). The murky beginnings of the communication and development field: Voice of America and the passing of traditional society. In N. Jayaweera & S. Amunugama (Eds.), *Rethinking development communication* (pp. 3-19). Singapore: Asian Mass Communication Research and Information Center.
Schramm, W. (1964). *Mass media and national development.* Stanford, CA: Stanford University Press.
Servaes, J. (1990). Rethinking development communication: One world, many cultures. *Journal of Development Communication, 1,* 35-45.
Shah, H. (1988). Development news on All India Radio: Assessment of quantity and quality. *Journalism Quarterly, 65,* 25-430.
Shah, H. (1989). A preliminary examination of journalistic roles and development reporting at three Indian newspapers. *Media Asia, 16,* 128-131.
Shah, H. (1990). Factors influencing development news reporting at three Indian dailies. *Journalism Quarterly, 67,* 1034-1041.
Shah, H. (1992). Development news: Its potential and limitations in the rural United States. *Journal of Development Communication, 3,* 9-15.

Shah, H. (1994). News and the self-production of society: Times of India coverage of caste conflict and job reservations in India. *Journalism Monographs*, No. 144.

Shah, H., & Gayatri G. (1994). Development news in elite and non-elite newspapers in Indonesia. *Journalism Quarterly, 71,* 411-420.

Tehranian, M. (1995). Communication and development. In D. Crowley & D. Mitchell (Eds.), *Communication theory today* (pp. 274-306). Stanford, CA: Stanford University Press.

Verghese, G. (1976). *Project Chhatera: An experiment in development journalism* (AMIC Occasional Paper No. 4). Singapore: Asian Mass Communication and Information Center.

Verhelst, T. (1987). *No life without roots.* London: Zed.

Wartenberg, T.E. (1990). *The forms of power: From domination to transformation.* Philadelphia, PA: Temple.

Webster. A. (1984). *Introduction to the sociology of development.* Atlantic Highlands, NJ: Humanities Press International.

9

Is There an Indigenous Seat at the Modern Communications Luau?

P. Laenui

Galtung, in his opening chapter, presents a model of modern society, divided into three components: State, Capital, and Civil Society. Essentially, his conclusion is that a healthy society depends on the interaction among the three; if one dominates one or both of the others, serious societal distortions easily emerge.

The task of communications, he says, is to reveal the deeper connections between these three components. His standard for communicative links between these three parts is that they be ongoing, institutionalized dialogue aiming at joint problem solving, and transparent to others. The question that must be posed here is: How do indigenous people fit within this scheme?

The indigenous people I am speaking of do not fit. They are marginalized from civil society, usually unseen and unheard. They tend to be the last in the society to have communications opportunities via the State, Capital, and even in Civil Society.

Perhaps we need to ask who the indigenous people are in the first place. I present a description of indigenous people from the U.N.'s Martinez-Cobo Report:

> Indigenous communities, peoples and nations are those which, having a historical continuity with pre-invasion and pre-colonial societies that developed on their territories, consider themselves distinct from other sectors of the societies now prevailing in those territories, or parts of them.
>
> They form at present non-dominant sectors of society and are determined to preserve, develop and transmit to future generations their ancestral territories, and their ethnic identity, as the basis of their continued existence as peoples, in accordance with their own cultural patterns, social institutions and legal systems. (1986, p. 29)

According to the United Nations and the International Labour Organization, a specialized agency of the U.N. that has taken a particular interest and has worked specifically on the issue of indigenous peoples, there are approximately 300 million indigenous people who live in more than 70 countries on five continents. I suggest that they are undercounting these people because they refuse to count the "dalits" or those who are sometimes referred to as the untouchables in India who number approximately 200 million. Indigenous peoples are not only on continents but on islands as well.

The vast majority of indigenous people are in Asia. Of the 300 million estimated by the U.N., 150 million live in Asia; 60 million are the adivasi, or scheduled tribes of India. With another 200 million dalits, certainly India must be seen as the largest concentration of indigenous people. China counts their indigenous people at 90 million, and like many other places, there are always more who claim that they too are indigenous and should be included in the count. Pacific peoples make up 1.5 million. In Scandinavia, the Saami counts for 80,000, and in the former Soviet Union, there are 1 million indigenous people. In Africa, there are about 15 million.

Often when one thinks of indigenous people, the American continents come to mind. There are roughly 30 million in South and Central America, including Mexico, where in several countries indigenous people make up the majority. In North America, there are about 1.5 million (IWGIA, 1991).

Indigenous peoples are as varied as the environments they inhabit. They are forest dwellers, desert nomads, fisher folks, farmers, as well as urban inhabitants. Their cultural practices are just as diverse. They seem to share some common traits, however, which is a bond of spiritual depth and meaning with their traditional territories. The World Council of Indigenous Peoples describes the indigenous people's relationship to land as follows:

> The earth is the foundation of indigenous peoples. It is the seat of spirituality, the fountain from which our cultures and languages flourish. The earth is our historian, the keeper of events and the cradle for the bones of our ancestors. It provides us food, medicine, shelter and clothing. It is the source of our independence. It is our mother. We do not dominate her, we harmonize with her. (1985, p. 1)

Because of such a close kinship between indigenous peoples and their traditional parts of the Earth, and especially because they often inhabit some of the planet's most vulnerable ecosystems, tropical rain forests, and coastal zones, the Arctic indigenous peoples are among the first to be affected by environmental degradation. Their lands are among the world's most valuable. This includes Australia's aborigines and Burma's ethnic nationalities territories loaded with mineral deposits, tropical forests in Malaysia that are logged for lucrative export and for converting those areas for grazing and agriculture, and land seen as quick solutions to the problem of overpopulation such as the Chittagong Hill Tracts of Bangladesh as well as East Timor and West Papua.

Over these past 40 years, the State, Capital, and "Civil" Society have all looked to indigenous territories to meet the growing demands of high-consumption industrialized societies and fast-swelling populations in developing countries and developed countries. The results for indigenous peoples have been disastrous.

Deforestation has caused flooding, desertification, destruction of sacred sites, and disruption of traditional economic activities, including fishing, agriculture, and hunting. Mercury used by gold miners have poisoned nearly 1,500 kilometers of the Amazon river systems. Diseases brought in by miners have killed thousands of Yanomami in Brazil and Venezuela. Dams and hydroelectric projects have displaced millions in Asia, the Arctic, and in North America. Toxic waste dumping in Canada, acid rain in Northern Europe, and nuclear testing in the Pacific have also affected indigenous peoples.

The International Labour Organization (ILO), in recent years, has tried to respond to the predicament of indigenous peoples. It recently adopted the convention concerning indigenous peoples (ILO, 1989) making provisions to define and protect land rights as well as setting forth the right of self-determination. Conventions, however, are not binding on countries that do not ratify them, and at present, less than 13 countries have done so (Roy, 1998).

The United Nations has also tried to respond to the plight of indigenous peoples. The U.N. Working Group on Indigenous Populations, consisting of "independent experts" appointed by governments, has been working for over 10 years to draft a declaration of rights. The task has been finally completed and the document forwarded for eventual adoption by the U.N. General Assembly. As a matter of binding law, however, it holds no promise for indigenous peoples because a declaration merely stands as an aspirational statement of rights, nothing more. Ratification itself is not available for sympathetic countries.

Thus, the two major movements in the international arena that hold the most hope for indigenous peoples are inconsequential. Societal distortions, from the bottom view of indigenous peoples, will continue to their great disadvantage in the foreseeable future. This leads us to the question of whether there is any promise in the field of communications to aid indigenous peoples in bringing about greater equity in the relationship between the modern and their traditional societies.

There is nothing visible on the horizon for indigenous peoples. Remember, indigenous peoples are often the poorest of the poor, those most marginalized from the society, from whom slavery and debt bondage may be commonplace. Those few indigenous people who have become professional within modern society and yet maintain a bond to their own people are simply unable to compete in modern society on their people's behalf. A recent article appearing in the *Hawaii Investor* (Jokiel, 1993), reported on an attorney working in the Commonwealth of the Northern Marianas Islands. He was a member of a law firm whose central office was located in Hawaii, and that had branch offices in California and in Washington, DC. Through this network of offices, he was able to take advantage of time differences, massive numbers of attorneys, computer modem and fax transmissions, and computer research so that overnight he could get a completed pleading or motion into the U.S. Supreme Court on a land controversy in Saipan, while a Chamoru attorney representing his people had not even begun his research at the local law library for he is still waiting for it to open.

Not only are the disadvantages extremely great in competition with those in the modern society because of the economic disadvantages and the lack of technological sophistication, but indigenous peoples are also just as disadvantaged in being able to establish among themselves ongoing methods of communications. They are generally not hired by the media, and, if hired, certainly not able to report on or to indigenous people. Therefore, in order to communicate, they must develop their own forms of communication. A number of failed attempts reflect the great difficulty in carrying on serious, long-term communication among indigenous people.

Two organizations that come out of Asia have been unable to carry out any consistent form of communication—the Pacific Asia Council of Indigenous Peoples (PACIP) formed in 1987 and Asia Pact formed a few years later. PACIP's failure is largely a lack of resources as well as the technological sophistication to maintain a communication system. The Pact has received some financial assistance from churches and produced a few informative documents, but this assistance has not continued.

In South America in the mid-1970s, the Indian Council of South America (CISA) was formed in the hope of uniting the indigenous people of that continent. Financed by European and Canadian governments, CISA operated under the concept that indigenous people's practice of self-determination should mean control over their own economic, social, and political development. They believed that this should include not only the digging of wells and holding of classes, but also being able to communicate with one another. CISA was able to sustain a monthly bulletin as well as a bimonthly magazine entitled *Pueblo Indio*, distributed throughout its membership. However, allegations of misuse of funds and internal organizational disagreements led to the drying up of funds at the end of the 1980s.

Mexico and Central American Indians formed their own regional organization, CORPI and, like CISA, was also able to obtain funds from Canadian and European governments and churches. Apparently they too have not been able to maintain an ongoing publication. The North American Indians have failed to maintain a single regional organization across the Canadian/U.S. border. The World Council of Indigenous Peoples operating out of Canada and the International Indian Treaty Council out of the United States have not been able to maintain a consistent, long-term publication.

There are numerous non-indigenous organizations that have written about and have incorporated indigenous writings within their own publications. The International Work Group for Indigenous Affairs (IWGIA) operating out of Denmark is probably the most noteworthy for having maintained a consistent publication and a yearbook of indigenous peoples. Its board members are European, which is also the source of their funding. Other efforts can be found in Survival International, which has a central office in England, and Cultural Survival, which is based in the United States. Both have written consistently about and advocated for indigenous peoples. Thus, we have a situation in which indigenous peoples are not participants in communications with either State, Capital, or Civil Society. Because of their circumstances, as a collective, they have been marginalized from the sharing of power among the others.

The United Nations General Assembly had declared the year 1993 as the International Year for the World's Indigenous People, under the theme, "A New Partnership." At the end of the year, having heard the complaints of indigenous people that the year was essentially too short to make any meaningful change in bringing about a new partnership, the General Assembly then declared the international decade for the world's indigenous people.

A CASE STUDY: HAWAI'I

The indigenous people of Hawaii, the native Hawaiians, reflect, although to a lesser extent, the marginalized conditions of indigenous peoples of the world. As early as the reign of Kamehameha I (1779–1819), Hawaii was recognized in the international community as a sovereign nation. She was trading with China, England, and the United States and was generally dealing with many other nations of the world on a regular basis. By 1887, Hawaii had treaties and conventions with Belgium, Bremen, Denmark, France, the German Empire, Great Britain, Hamburg, Hong Kong, Italy, Japan, the Netherlands, New South Wales, Portugal, Russia, Samoa, Spain, the Swiss Confederation, Sweden, Norway, Tahiti, and the United States (Book, 1887). Indeed, Hawaii had entered into at least five treaties or conventions with the United States[1] (Bevens, 1957).

Hawaii was a member of the Universal Postal Union, the forerunner of the League of Nations and later the United Nations. Hawaii had established approximately a hundred diplomatic and consular posts around the world (Husted, 1892). Hawaii's independence was so firmly recognized that on November 28, 1843, Great Britain and France joined in a Declaration recognizing its independence and pledging never to take possession of Hawaii (U.S. Senate Ex. Doc. 52, 1843). When the United States was invited to join in this declaration, J.C. Calhoun, United States Secretary of State, replied that the President adhered completely to the spirit of disinterestedness and self-denial that breathed in that declaration: "He had already, for his part taken a similar engagement in the message which he had addressed to Congress on December 31, 1842" (Pageot, 1844). Immigrants from all parts of the world came to Hawaii, many renouncing their former national allegiance and taking up Hawaiian citizenship. For example, in 1844, John Ricord renounced his allegiance to the United States and took the oath of allegiance to Kamehameha III. He was later appointed Attorney General for Hawaii (Kuykendall, 1967). By 1892, Hawaii was a multiracial, multicultural nation of Hawaiians.

On December 18, 1893, the U.S. President Grover Cleveland delivered his message to the joint houses of the U.S. Congress in which he declared:

> By an act of war, committed with the participation of a diplomatic representative of the United States and without authority of Congress, the

---

[1]These treaties include: Treaty of Commerce, December 24, 1826; Treaty of Friendship, Commerce and Navigation, August 24, 1850; Rights of Neutrals at Sea, March 26, 1855; Treaty of Commercial Reciprocity, September 9, 1876; and Treaty of Commercial Reciprocity, November 9, 1887.

Government of a feeble but friendly and confiding people has been overthrown. A substantial wrong has thus been done which a due regard for our national character as well as the rights of the injured people requires we should endeavor to repair....

[Hawai`i's Queen Liliuokalani] knew that she could not withstand the power of the United States, but believed that she might safely trust to its justice. She surrendered not to the provisional government, but to the United States. She surrendered not absolutely and permanently, but temporarily and conditionally until such time as the facts could be considered by the United States [and it can] undo the action of its representative and reinstate her in the authority she claimed as the constitutional sovereign of the Hawaiian Islands.

In summarizing the events, President Cleveland wrote:

The lawful Government of Hawaii was overthrown without the drawing of a sword or the firing of a shot by a process every step of which, it may be safely asserted, is directly traceable to and dependent for its success upon the agency of the United States acting through its diplomatic and naval representatives.

But for the notorious predilections of the United States Minister for annexation, the Committee of Safety, which should be called the Committee of Annexation, would never have existed.

But for the landing of the United States forces upon false pretexts respecting the danger to life and property the committee would never have exposed themselves to the pains and penalties of treason by undertaking the subversion of the Queen's Government.

But for the presence of the United States forces in the immediate vicinity and in position to afford all needed protection and support the committee would not have proclaimed the provisional government from the steps of the Government building.

And finally, but for the lawless occupation of Honolulu under false pretexts by the United States forces, and but for Minister Stevens' recognition of the provisional government when the United States forces were its sole support and constituted its only military strength, the Queen and her Government would never have yielded to the provisional government, even for a time and for the sole purpose of submitting her case to the enlightened justice of the United States.

[T]he law of nations is founded upon reason and justice, and the rules of conduct governing individual relations between citizens or subjects of a civilized state are equally applicable as between enlightened nations. The considerations that international law is without a court for its enforcement, and that obedience to its commands practically depends upon good faith, instead of upon the mandate of a superior tribunal, only give additional sanction to the law itself and brand any deliberate infraction of it not merely as a wrong but as a disgrace. (pp. 5901-5903)

Cleveland, although filled with principled words, failed to take any active step to restore the Hawaiian government. When William McKinley replaced Cleveland as President, the provisional government that had since adopted a constitution and proclaimed a new government, rushed an emissary to Washington, DC to negotiate a treaty of annexation with the new administration. The "Republic of Hawaii" ceded "absolutely and without reserve to the United States of America all rights of sovereignty of whatsoever kind in and over the Hawaiian Islands" (Thurston, 1904, Article 1, p. 248). A "treaty of annexation" was signed. Realizing the "treaty" would not get the two thirds Senate approval required for ratification under the U.S. Constitution (Article 2, Section 2, Clause 2), the conspirators circumvented that requirement through a joint resolution of Congress (Newlands Resolution, 1898). Hawaiians were never given a choice in this matter.

The United States set up a territorial government naming Sanford Dole, previously the President of the Provisional Government and of the Republic of Hawaii, as Governor of the Territory of Hawaii (The Organic Act, 1900). The Organic Act declared that all citizens of the Republic of Hawaii (which the Republic's "constitution" declared to be all citizens of the nation of Hawaii) were automatically U.S. citizens and citizens of the Territory of Hawaii. Hawaiians were given no voice in their citizenship "changes."

Following his appointment as territorial governor, Dole provided government positions and lucrative government contracts to his friends, allowing monopolies in shipping, finance, and communications. The Big Five, a coalition of five business entities, comprising not more than a dozen men, all finding their roots in the missionary party, controlled every aspect of business, media, and politics in Hawaii. Beginning with sugar, they took steps to control transportation, hotels, utilities, banks, insurance agencies, and many small wholesale and retail businesses. When they teamed up with the Republican party and the U. S. Navy, there was virtually nothing left unexploited.

The list of social atrocities is long. Paramount among these was a massive propaganda program undertaken to convince Hawaiians that the United States was the legitimate ruler and that Hawaiians were no longer Hawaiians but Americans.

Children were forced to attend U.S. schools and were taught to pledge their allegiance to the United States, trained in the foreign laws, told to adopt foreign morality, to speak no language but the foreign one (English), and to adopt the foreign (U.S.) lifestyle. Official government proceedings were to be conducted in English and not Hawaiian. In the schools and college campuses, the language of Hawaii was, if at all, taught through the foreign language departments.

The customs, traditions, and even the cultural names of the people were suppressed in this recycling effort. The arts and sciences of Hawaiian ancestors were driven to near extinction. The advanced psychology practices, including the techniques of healing were driven into the back countryside. The *oli* (chants) offered to ancestors who had not yet jumped into the eternal *po* (darkness, creation) were no longer passed to younger generations. The art of communicating from island to island through the power of thought, of seeing through walls or over mountains and breaking even the barrier of time, were no longer practiced and today are almost extinct. The Hawaiian people were being ground to extinction.

The United States was able to bring in a whole new population. Hawaii witnessed a tide of U.S. citizens flooding into Hawaii, bringing with them their barrage of "cultural," "moral," "religious," and political concepts. Hawaiians were urged to mimic U.S. ways, idolizing their heroes, adopting their living styles and believing they too were U.S. citizens. As Americans transmigrated, they took choice jobs with government agencies or management positions with business interests. They became owners of the best lands of Hawaii. They gained power in Hawaii, controlled greater chunks of the economy, and the public media, and entrenched themselves in politics.

The military turned Hawaii into their pacific fortress, turning Pearl Harbor from a coaling and fueling station to a major naval port, bombing islands, evicting families from their traditional homes, destroying sacred Hawaii heirlooms, and building naval communication towers that emitted radiation and ammunition depots, which in recent decades have been used for hiding nuclear weapons. They declared martial law at will and imposed military conscription over the Hawaiian citizens.

Freedom of trade was stopped. The U.S. Congress took over foreign relations. Hawaii could buy only U.S. goods or foreign goods the U.S. approved. Complicating this even further was the Big Five control over shipping.

Children were forced into the "educational" system. The irrelevance of the education they received made them unfit for the world they actually lived in, making them strangers to their own heritage and believers in the myth that Hawaii's sovereignty is dead (Fuchs, 1961).

Every aspect of Hawaii was "Americanized." Military show of strength was constant. Trade was totally controlled. Education and media were regulated. The secret ballot was a farce. Hawaii, that melting pot of cultures, races, languages, and lore, changed from a reality to an advertisement slogan for politicians and business people.

Statehood 1959

After 60 years of indoctrination, the people in Hawaii were given a chance to be equal U.S. citizens. The United States placed the following question to the "qualified" voters (U.S. citizens who were residents of Hawaii for at least 1 year) in Hawaii: Shall Hawaii immediately be admitted into the Union as a State (The Admission Act of 1959)?

All who considered themselves U.S. citizens voted. This included the thousands of people who arrived from the United States under their infiltration policy of colonization. It consisted of the thousands of military personnel who considered themselves residents of Hawaii. Included also were the thousands who had been brainwashed through generations of socialization to accept the U.S. domination as a fact accomplished with no possibility of freedom.

The United States had so delicately structured the method of voting that there was no practical choice. Those who resisted U.S. domination and insisted on their Hawaiian citizenship could not reach the voting booth. They had to declare themselves U.S. citizens before being allowed to vote. Even those willing to accept the "American" brand were to chose between the frying pan and the fire, between Territorial domination or Statehood. The question, "Should Hawaii be free?", was never asked. "Hawaii" chose Statehood.

Post "Statehood" Land

Land today is bartered back and forth with no regard to its spiritual and cultural values or the economic needs of the people. Much of it is investor (many foreign)-owned, locked up by those simply waiting to maximize their profit. There is minimal concern for the needs of the local people. Giant buildings are raised over taro (the staple food, *Colocasia esculenta*) patches or beaches fronting abundant fishing grounds. Apartment units, mostly empty, are being sold in foreign markets at prices far above the people's abilities to pay. Meanwhile, many Hawaiian people are sleeping in cars or parks hoping to avoid arrest before the morning.

Even areas previously ignored by the middle society, sites to which Hawaiians unable to afford housing turned, were recently (in 1994) declared major parks (Moku Anuenue, Sand Island, and Makua beach). The inhabitants were evicted, their homes bulldozed and their leadership charged as criminals.

Economic Dependence

With much of Hawaii's land investor-owned, today there is very little land to provide the necessary food for the Hawaiian population. Hawaii's people have thus adopted a dependence on the United States for its food. Where ancestors could well feed a population as large as the present without any importation, today almost all food consumed in Hawaii is imported. Whenever rumors of a waterfront strike is spread, Hawaii undergoes panic buying, store shelves are short-stocked and basic food items rationed.

Dependence on the U.S. military, the tourist industry, and now to a lesser extent sugar and pineapple to provide the purchasing power of U.S. goods has developed. In a call in the 1980s to return one of the eight major islands, Kahoolawe, from military control to civilian control, the Governor refused to support such a move, giving as his only excuse his fear of military spending loss. Kahoolawe was eventually returned to the State of Hawaii in 1992.

Military Dependence and Hawaiian Brainwashing

Today Hawaii's mountains and valleys are filled with nuclear and nonnuclear weapons. A major island, Kahoolawe, had for decades been used for the exclusive use of military training. Indeed, one-fourth of the island of Oahu, by far the most populated island of the Hawaiian islands, is occupied by the military.

Another casualty is found in the Hawaiian citizens, who today have no knowledge of their birthright as an independent people. Youths are first to join in military service to fight for "liberty and justice for all," never asking when that honorable principle would also be applied to themselves.

Hawaiian Entry into Media

The entry of the Hawaiian people, as an indigenous people, into Hawai'i's media is paltry. There have been small independent efforts to print Hawaiian newspapers in the last 10 years, but those efforts have never been sustained. The Office of Hawaiian Affairs (OHA), a government-funded entity created out of the Hawaiian State Constitution, however, has been able to maintain an organizational newspaper for the past 12 years. However, when an independent organization, Hui Na'auao, consisting of over 50 Hawaiian organizations, banded together to educate the Hawaiians on the issue of Hawaiian sovereignty by attempting to print an article on alternative economics for Hawaii, the article was suppressed apparently because it was not consistent with the position of OHA. OHA, however, is by far the best funded organization in Hawaii and is able to deliver an assimilationist point of view to the Hawaiian people under the guise of a Hawaiian voice.

There is no Hawaiian-controlled radio station in a local market of dozens of radio stations. Neither is there a Hawaiian-controlled television station. The Hawaiian National Broadcast Corporation, a small nonprofit corporation, has attempted to develop Hawaiian broadcasting, using

Hawaii Public Radio stations. Funding, however, is nonexistent so all programming is done on a volunteer basis, and out-of-pocket costs are generally met by the handful of people forming the corporation.

There is currently no hope of change in sight. Those corporations funding public broadcasting are at best resistant to the message of native Hawaiians. Most of these corporations have histories deeply involved in the overthrow and/or profit from that crime. The two major newspapers are owned by outside interests who use newspapers primarily for their investment value as opposed to public service. The *Honolulu Advertiser* with the largest circulation for a daily edition, was only recently sold to Gannett by owner Thurston Twigg-Smith, grandson of Lorrin A. Thurston, mastermind behind the overthrow of the Hawaiian government.

CONCLUSION

One of the goals of the decade should be to set aside 2% of the world's communications resources for capacitation building of indigenous peoples of the world. This capacitation building should include not only education and training, but also the provisions of facilities, equipment, and supplies to enhance the goals of indigenous communities. The fulfillment of these aspirations should enable indigenous communities to become active participants in communicating for themselves, to carry on their ongoing, institutionalized dialogue aimed at joint problem solving, a dialogue that is transparent to others in society.

REFERENCES

The Admission Act of March 18, 1959, Pub L 86-3, 73 Stat 4.

Bevans, C. I. (Ed.). (1957). *Treaties and other international agreements of the United States of America* (Vol. 8, pp. 861-877). Washington, DC: Department of State.

Book, E. (1887). *Treaties and conventions concluded between the Hawaiian Kingdom and other powers since 1825.* Honolulu: Author.

Cleveland, G. (1893, December 18). Special messages, To the Senate and House of Representatives. In *A compilation of the messages and papers of the Presidents* (Vol. XIII, pp. 5892-5904). New York: Bureau of National Literature.

Fuch, L. H. (1961). *Hawaii pono.* New York: Harcourt Brace.

Husted, F. M. (1892). *Directory and handbook of the kingdom of Hawaii* (pp. 48-51). Oakland: The Pacific Press.

International Labour Organization (ILO). (1989, June). *ILO Convention 169*. Geneva, Switzerland: Author.
International Work Group for Indigenous Affairs (IWGIA). (1991). *Yearbook*. Copenhagen, Denmark: Author.
Jokiel, L. (1993, December). Doing the deal. *Hawaii Investor*, 29-30, 44-46.
Kuykendall, R. S. (1967). *Hawaiian kingdom, 1778-1854*. Honolulu: University of Hawaii Press.
Newlands Resolution of July 7, 1898; 30 Stat. 750; 2 Supp. R.S. 895.
The Organic Act of April 30, 1900, C 339, 31 Stat 141.
Pageot, French representative in Washington, dispatch to Guizot, French minister of Foreign Affairs. (1844, June 11). AMAE No. 55. Paris.
Roy, C. (1988, May 26). ILO: Total of 13 countries have ratified [Data via email from Chandra Roy, ILO, roy@ilo.org].
Thurston, L. A. (Ed. & Indexer). (1904). Fundamental Law of Hawaii. (Article 1 of Resolution of the Senate of Hawaii ratifying the Treaty of Annexation, September 9, 1897). *Hawaiian Gazette*, pp. 247-250.
United States Senate (1843). Ex. Doc., 52 Cong., 2 Sess., No. 57, p. 13.

PART III

EXCURSIONS AROUND NWICO

A critical look at NWICO is the subject of Part III. Igor Klyukanov examines the epistemological foundations of NWICO, and pleads for a general ecology of knowledge which would make communicative democracy possible. The need for taking culture seriously from a dual materialist and structuralist perspective is analyzed by Jeffrey Ady. That discourse often overlooks the reality of the nation state which persists in spite of the globalization, and forgets that nations may have radically different views about communication policies. Michael Basil's chapter provides another critical look at NWICO. He comes to the conclusion that the *MacBride Report* has made assumptions about powerful social roles of the media, often empirically based, which have not been substantiated.

10

The Concept of "Communicative Democracy" and the Flow of Information

Igor E. Klyukanov

The main focus of this chapter is on the conceptual work behind the New World Information and Communication Order (NWICO). It has always had a strong rhetorical base of popular universalism. At the same time, the very essence of NWICO, that of information and communication, seems to have been treated in insufficient depth. As a result, the key concepts discussed within the framework of NWICO such as imperialism, control, context, delinkage, and so on often carry a somewhat metaphorical connotation; for example, "the notion of 'cultural' or 'media' imperialism was always to a certain extent metaphorical" (Sparks & Roach, 1990, p. 276). Most of these, or related, concepts have been thoroughly analyzed by a number of communication and information theorists, by which they have been assigned strictly defined meanings.

EPISTEMOLOGICAL FOUNDATIONS OF THE NWICO

One such concept that is not given adequate treatment in NWICO discussions is that of *knowledge*. At the same time, this notion is absolutely crucial for our understanding of information and communication processes. It is essential to discuss this notion because "there is a general inclination in the West to see knowledge in terms of atomism and deductivism, a tendency to present reality in a fragmented, scattered way, dividing it into small bits that can be understood and 'digested' one at a time" (Galtung & Vincent, 1992, p. 14). This tendency is especially evident in the analysis of news media, in which "atomism, the basic detachability of events, is the basic message... No connection, not even the report that some people suspect a connection is presented via the news media" (p. 14).

It is necessary to oppose this view, providing NWCIO with a firm epistemological foundation. This foundation can be best developed within the framework of the General Systems Theory as a broad approach to knowledge based on the systems concept (Ruben & Kim, 1975).

The most important system principle is that of wholeness and interdependence. It means that the world must be viewed as a whole because its parts (individuals, cultures, sectors of the globe, etc.) interrelate and cannot be understood separately. This pattern of interdependence is what creates organization in the system. Armed with this basic principle, we can now address the question of "imperialism" from epistemological positions.

The prevailing epistemology of today splits systems as symbiotic wholes into supposedly independent "things" (me/you, East/West, etc.). According to this view, a line can be drawn between a system and its environment. However, "the line drawn between 'organism' and 'environment' by our conventional model of reality . . . is a fiction. Unfortunately, we think that it is real" (Wilden, 1980, p. 219). This is a tragic epistemological error that "feeds pollution, racism, alienation, exploitation, oppression, and all other forms of pathological communication" (p. 210). This is an epistemology of biosocial imperialism that serves as a justification of the increasing power of the transnational corporations, growing gaps in telecommunications between different regions of the world, and so on. This pathological mentality allows our culture to replace the complementary systemic relations on which it depends with the linear relationships of dominance and subservience between unequal socioeconomic subjects.

This closed-systems mentality is especially evident and precarious in dealing with cultural environments. The expansion of cultural imperialism continues unabated, at the expense of smaller and less powerful cultures. The imperialist transnational corporations are driven by short-sighted pragmatic considerations, and all the calls to think of the consequences of this policy fall on deaf ears. However, even those trying to foster cultural identities do not seem to fully realize those ramifications. Those engaged in the discussion "about the accelerating disappearance of indigenous cultures as our Coca-Cola civilization spreads over the world" (Diamond, 1993, p. 78), are missing the main point. They lament the fact that little attention "has been paid to the disappearance of languages themselves and to their essential role in the survival of those indigenous cultures" (p. 78; emphasis added). It is a big mistake to discuss the fate of "those" cultures as organisms (systems) existing in isolation from ours.

The essence of the epistemology of biosocial imperialism is a failure to understand what might be called the Boomerang Effect. A socioeconomic subject (a person, a group, a corporation, a region, a country) cannot exploit its environment without upsetting the balance between itself and the other systems that ultimately will affect the subject itself. The same thing can be said of biosocial imperialism as of any other war: The next worst thing to having lost a war is having won it.

This mentality can be described in terms of "action mode versus interaction mode. The action mode probably relates to a process of dehumanization of the adversary to the point where the 'Other' is seen as either a thing or as totally autistic, incapable of interaction, locked into a standard stereotyped reaction to anything coming out of 'Self'" (Galtung & Vincent, 1992, p. 127). The task of the information flow, represented in the first place by news media, is to break through this distortion and replace the action mode with the interaction mode.

The theory of imperialism, developed within the Marxist tradition, explains the economic and political structures. At the same time, some scholars point to "a close relationship between the experiences of economic and political imperialism and major features of cultural life" (Sparks & Roach, 1990, p. 276). This relationship cannot be denied because of the *isomorphism* existing between different models of the world as a system in relation to its communicative pattern. It is communication, as a model of existence of humankind, that brings together cultural, political, and economic structures and allows them to be viewed as isomorphic.

Once again, this view is based on the systems view of the world made up of interacting and interdependent parts. This approach makes it possible to underscore the fact that the information flow in the world at present is largely a form of pathological communication. The main problem of today is to stop this dangerous tendency and to replace the relationships of power and free competition with the complementary relationships of cooperation. This task makes NWICO even more meaningful in the world today as a forum for promoting the ideas of information-flow equity and multicultural peaceful environments.

THE CONVERGENCE/DIVERGENCE MODEL OF INFORMATION FLOW

Information flow is a well-chosen term. It suggests an active exchange of knowledge structures between different systems in the world as a suprasystem. The information "flows" only if there is a constant interaction between the systems, which, in turn, depends on a difference of potential between them. The phrase "information and communication order" might suggest, to a nonspecialist, the idea of something cast in stone, achieved and imposed on the system once and for all. This is an oversimplification as it overlooks the dialectic and dynamic nature of "order" as an unsteady state that has to be constantly maintained in the system by the interaction of its parts.

Any individual system has to process vast amounts of information every day. Organizing communicative behavior, that is, maintaining order in the system, becomes more and more difficult. Under such circumstances, a communicative system faces two options.

One option is to decrease the amount of knowledge by simplifying and reducing the number of various information structures. In essence, this means, in effect, putting the information flow in reverse. Examples of this tendency are quite numerous. Take, for instance, adolescents' communication with its limited context-bound vocabulary and grammar that sometimes is little different from that of "paleolithic man," who "had a set of folk images of his cave, the surrounding woods, the people in his own and other bands," and which was quite accurate "because of very rapid feedback" (Boulding, 1975, p. 134). The information flow between the adolescents as parts of a social system is characterized by a limited number of structures and a high degree of convergence over time on a common domain of meaning (e.g., "that's cool", "yeah," "totally," etc.). Such systems develop in the direction of less resistance to the environment. This method of dealing with an information flow can be called the Reader's Digest Syndrome of Communication.

On a societal level, this tendency is nowhere more evident than in the countries previously subject to a monolithic and ideologically guided policy. The leaders of those countries found the easiest way to handle the information flow is specifically, to simply block it by putting down an iron curtain or erecting a wall between themselves and the rest of the world. It is known how difficult and dangerous it can be to gain access to outside information in a society where foreign radio stations are jammed, undesirable books are banned, and the State ideology reigns supreme. The implications of such a "dead-levelism" approach to the flow of information can be tragic. The closed system with one common code and all the channels of new inputs of information cut off will move toward a steady state and eventually stop functioning, or else it will explode into a number of new systems. The fate of the former Soviet Union is a good example of this tendency of convergence, or a tight control over the flow of information. It did not become the "melting pot" envisaged by its leaders, but instead developed along the lines of a "salad bowl" model, with different systems embracing old cultural identities or asserting new ones.

Ironically, it is along these same lines that the second danger facing the information flow lies. This approach, equated with progress (in its modern understanding), implies further refinement of information and social structures. Unlike the first approach, decreasing the potential of communication, this one puts special emphasis on the information flow as a conceptualizing device helping us control reality more and more fully.

The growing freedom of symbolic representation has its downside as well. Organizing experiences with the help of symbolic communicative tools may be an obstacle rather that help in solving problems, as we abstract certain properties from a situation, that is, a continuum of experience. This mild ailment, known as "verbal forgery" (Hertzler, 1965, p. 52), does not exist in animal communicative behavior, but, unfortunately, is very much in evidence in human exchange of information. More serious are different forms of lying, miscommunication, and so on that cannot be avoided due to different frames of reference of communicators.

Taken to its extreme, the information flow may become overorganized, and overorganization threatens the survival of a human ecosystem, leading to social disorder (Wilden, 1980). In other words, communication becomes more and more differentiated, comprises more and more structures, and sometimes may go beyond our control. In this case, differences between two systems, each with its own highly complex organization, cannot be overcome, and the information does not flow but breaks down, which may have far-reaching sorrowful implications, especially in a situation with little contact between the systems. A good example is the well-known phrase said by Nikita Khruschev at the U.N. session, "We will bury you!", understood by citizens of the United States by its literal meaning, although meant in Russian as "We will catch up with you and pass you by."

The United States is another example of this ruinous trend that manifests itself in a new tribalism. The "salad bowl" model seems to be in jeopardy, as the United States is being hyphenated and split apart by different groups demanding preferential treatment over individual rights. More and more often the warning is heard against tribalism and the issue of "identity crisis" is being heatedly debated.

Any communicative system, therefore, is in constant danger from two sides. Left to itself without any information inputs from the outside, it will move toward destructuring; otherwise, interacting with more and more other systems, it may reach the critical point of overorganization, and also disintegrate. That is why it is absolutely essential to constantly maintain order in the information flow, preventing the communicative system from reaching these two extremes. The communicative system is ordered only when the information flows freely between these two extremes, never reaching either of them.

This pattern of information equity fits very well into the Convergence Model of Communication developed by Kincaid (1983).

According to this model, groups that come to share more and more information are said to have convergence, and groups that share less and less information are said to have divergence. The main point here is that both tendencies take place at the same time, and that is why order in the system is always unsteady and dynamic. This principle of communication can be called the Pendulum Principle: The information flows as long as the pendulum keeps swinging back and forth, and the order in the system can be equated with its position in the middle, even though it never really stops there.

Once again, on a global level, the flow of information can break down if either of these tendencies is taken to its extreme. The state of convergence into a steady equilibrium can be reached from both a lack of diversity (underorganization), or too much diversity (overorganization). Coming back to the epistemology of biosocial imperialism discussed earlier, it is now clear why any system (person, group, corporation, culture, etc.) with imperialist ambitions will eventually find itself in a situation of political-economic-cultural isolation, leading, eventually, to its death. However, different systems can diverge to the point where no information is shared, which is also ruinous for a communicative system. That is why empires stagnate, and multicultural societies with a harmonious flow of information flourish.

The convergence/divergence model of information flow throws new light on the issue of "delinkage" discussed within the NWICO framework. It is notable, for example, that of the two authors of the editorial on NWICO in one of the volumes of *Media, Culture, and Society*, one believes that the call for delinkage must be given a new priority, while her co-editor disagrees profoundly (Sparks & Roach, 1990; see also, Roach, 1990). The dialectics of the information flow mean that delinkage cannot exist without integration; these are two sides of one coin, which is why both co-editors are right in their own way.

The convergence/divergence model can also explain the rivalry between the two competing acronyms—NIIO (New International Information Order) and NWICO. It is easy to see that the former puts emphasis on divergence of different systems and their interaction (international order), whereas the latter emphasizes convergence of different systems into one world order. Given that the pattern of convergence is more important, NWICO seems to be a better choice; it is no coincidence, obviously, that this acronym is now favored by everybody, almost without exception.

TOWARD A GENERAL ECOLOGY OF KNOWLEDGE

Finally, the dialectical approach to information flow highlights another important issue involved in communication, that of *control*. NWICO was built on a tenet that communication is a basic human right and an individual need. Today it seems to be necessary to underscore the fact that not only is communication a basic human right, but it is also a responsibility of an individual. If we look at the way communication is developing in the world today, it can be readily seen that the matter of information-flow equity is far from being resolved, and that the information and communication order is not quite in order. Nowhere is this more evident than in news media and entertainment. In the current "Decade of Culture," ironically, we witness violence and the degradation of minorities and women made popular in songs, film, television programs, and computer games. All this calls for a scientific control of the information flow in the world, meaning by "scientific" the system approach to communication discussed earlier.

To this end, we must welcome any regulations of the information flow that can take the forms of standard dictionaries, normative grammars, educational programs, legal establishments such as anti-pornography laws, and so on. This must not be seen as infringement on individual freedom because what "is often referred to as 'freedom' is, in fact, "that ongoing production, distribution, and consumption of distortions of reality of which one is not even aware" (Galtung & Vincent, 1992, p. 160). The key concept in this approach to information flow must be that of "communicative order," or what is right for the communicative system.

We must constantly answer the question, "What does it mean to do the right thing?", in our daily lives, as well as in momentous affairs of nations. The moral code that seeks to regulate human communicative behavior and applies very well to the control of information flow is the Brazen Rule discussed in the Game Theory. This rule reads, using the words of Confucius, "Repay kindness with kindness, but evil with justice" (Sagan, 1993, p. 14), and it justifies the use of any regulations imposed on the communicative system for the benefit of its parts, that is, for its own benefit.

This rule is the basis for the most effective communicative strategy in normal (not pathological) exchange of information. It is called "Tit-for-Tat":

> It is very simple: You start out cooperating and, in each subsequent round, simply do what your opponent did the last time. You punish defections, but once the other player cooperates, you are willing to let bygones be bygones. At first it seems to garner only mediocre success. But as time goes on, the other strategies defeat themselves—from too much kindness or too much cruelty—and this middle way pulls ahead. (Sagan, 1993, p. 14)

This happy medium is what can be called Communicative Democracy. It avoids the danger of the "communicative dictatorship" that manifests itself in a limited number of structures and a high degree of convergence on a common domain of meaning. Examples of this "pragmatic myopia" extend from the communicative behavior of adolescents to closed societies, in which case the disease begins with the symptoms of political, economic, and cultural provincialism and ends in either death or revolution. However, communicative democracy steers clear of "communicative anarchy" with its danger of too much freedom due to a high degree of divergence.

The concept of communicative democracy represents order in the flow of information that has to be constantly created and maintained by cooperating parts of the system. It also makes indispensable the control mechanism that seeks any deviations and imbalances in the information flow and neutralizes or transforms them. In this context, the concept of "information and communication order" acquires its literal meaning. Also, such terms as *communication equity, human rights*, and so on take on a new, strictly defined, meaning.

Unfortunately, there is a gap between this scientific and everyday mentality, which brings us back to the epistemological foundations of NWICO. Until the time when every part of the system, that is, every socioeconomic subject, fully realizes the true nature and significance of knowledge, and the systemic organization of information in the world, the matter of communication-flow equity, will not be completely resolved. To this end, the gap between the two paradigms of knowledge has to be bridged. That is why it is urgent to get on with a massive educational program of systems education that deals with a general ecology of knowledge. This term is used to mean:

> The study of patterns of interrelationships among the various 'species' (subsystems, sub-subsystems, etc.) or fields and subfields of knowledge with emphasis on: a). preserving the condition of dynamic balance between the 'species' and their environment; and b). optimizing the overall, symbiotic fruits of synergistic interactions among them. (Clark, 1972, p. 168)

The urgency of redesigning curricula in general and communication curricula in particular, determined by pressures stemming from threats to our civilization, is experienced today more than ever. One such curriculum project in general ecology of knowledge proposed more than 20 years ago included such topics as "systems approach," "game theory," "predictive simulation," "the control process," "utopian models," "societal engineering," "the psychology of mass movement," "designing games for global grass-root involvement," and many others (Clark, 1972). Even though this project has not yet received widespread support, some encouraging steps have been made in that direction (see Liska & Cronkhite, 1995).

The intellectual track in the MacBride movement introduced many important issues into the political track. We must not think of projects in the epistemological sphere, such as the one just mentioned, as merely intellectual exercises. We need to think about the relationship between academic work and the political process, which calls for an intellectual rethinking of the theory behind NWICO, incorporating its ideas as part of a curriculum in as many educational institutions as possible.

All this makes NWICO even more meaningful as a forum for dealing with information and communication on a global level. Through the analysis of news media, information technologies, cultural and civil movements in the world, NWICO has to strive to convey the message that the general ecology of knowledge is "dynamic, action-oriented, organismic, relative, nonlinear, open-ended, value-conscious, holistic, and interdependent" (Clark, 1972, p. 168). This is a challenging task, yet to solve it is vital for the world's survival.

This task can be solved only through "global glasnost," an apt term coined by Galtung and Vincent (1992). At the same time, it must be emphasized that "glasnost," or openness, goes hand in hand with "perestroika," or restructuring. In our case, we must discuss not the economic but the epistemological restructuring of the sociocultural subjects in the world, or "global perestroika," that is, changes in the mentality of the individual systems. We will have every right to speak about the new world information and communication order only if and when every individual, as a part of the world suprasystem, realizes the true nature of knowledge and learns how to use it for the benefit of the system and for his or her own benefit. In this context it is hard to overestimate what NWICO has been doing in the sphere of social movements for democratizing communication, giving voice to those who, for one reason or another, have been deprived of this basic right. These endeavors are consistent with the Principle of Multiple Collective Action discussed by Galtung and Vincent (1992). It is through this civic involvement that the epistemological restructuring can take place and a transition can be made from the mentality of biosocial imperialism to the concept of communicative democracy.

REFERENCES

Boulding, K.E. (1975). General systems theory—The skeleton of science. In B. Ruben & J. Kim (Eds.), *General systems theory and human communication* (pp. 21-32). NJ: Hayden Book.

Clark, J. W. (1972). The general ecology of knowledge in curriculums of the future. In E. Laszlo (Ed.), *The relevance of general systems theory* (pp. 163-180). New York: Braziller.

Diamond, J. (1993, February). Speaking with a single tongue. *Discovery*, pp. 78- 85.

Galtung, J., & Vincent, R. (1992). *Global glasnost: Toward a new world information and communication order?* New Jersey: Hampton Press.

Hertzler, J. (1965). *A sociology of language.* New York: Random House.

Kincaid, D.L. (1983). Communication technology and cultural diversity. *Informatologia Yugoslavica, 15*(1-2), 71-82.

Liska, J., & Cronkhite, G. (1995). *An ecological perspective on human communication theory.* Fort Worth, TX: Harcourt Brace College.

Roach, C. (1990). The movement for a new world information and communication order: A second wave? *Media, Culture and Society, 12*, 283-307.

Ruben, B., & Kim, J. (Eds.). (1975). *General systems theory and human communication.* NJ: Hayden Book.

Sagan, C. (1993, November). A new way to think about rules to live by. *Parade Magazine*, pp. 12-14.

Sparks, C., & Roach, C. (1990). Editorial. *Media, Culture and Society, 12*, 275-281.

Wilden, A. (1980). *System and structure: Essays in communication and exchange.* New York: Tavistock.

11

Transcending the Dialectic of Culture

Jeffrey C. Ady

Were the efforts that birthed the MacBride Report successful? Did the Report result in policies and transformative forces that achieved the recommendations of the Report? Has the NWICO movement enjoyed success in the intervening years, and is it on course to enable a truly global and equitable information suprasystem? The answer offered is that the movement toward a new world information and communication order has enjoyed limited success. Few, if anyone, would contest this. But the focus of this chapter is to explore a reason for this conundrum of culture.

Evidence abounds as to the marginal impact the MacBride Report had on restructuring international communications relations (Thomas, 1996). The MacBride Commission and the NWICO movement as a whole have viewed the problem and formulated recommendations in ways that have not adequately addressed the issue of culture as it interfaces with communication policy (Barnett, 1996; Golding & Harris, 1996; Hamelink, 1996; Thomas, 1996).

THE DIALECTIC OF CULTURE

The movement may have not addressed the problem of culture squarely perhaps because of a less than balanced view of culture. The movement's perspective on culture is arguably very materialist in nature. The prevailing view of culture and of communication problems in general in NWICO discourse has been based in a Western liberalist morality and ethic with the result of blindness to local, non-Western, realities; the great attention to imbalance, dependency, and the destructive forces of media mercantilism exemplifies this trend. The characteristic focus on class, imperialism, and conspiracy (Thomas, 1996) defines culture as superstructure over the base of production much as did Marx (Sahlins, 1976); culture is framed, vis-a-vis communication, as media products and technologies.

Although the problems identified through such analysis are of utmost importance, the lack of a more structuralist analysis of culture—a perspective that places inherent meaning in the ways in which people groups live, think, and communicate, approaching them as existing on their own terms—eliminates from discussion a host of pressing issues and, in fact, precludes a more successful addressing of the problems identified through materialist analysis. Although the materialist and structuralist views of culture are not the only ones, they represent a major division—a paradigmatic opposition, in Sahlins's (1976) words—on the construct of culture in a variety of literatures. Certainly the narrative that follows does not do justice to the many authors who have engaged in compelling and original thought on the subject, but it is intended to associate names that are familiar to many along the lines of a dialectic between materialist and structuralist views of culture.

The division began with different reactions from Marx and Franz Boas to the same stimulus: Enlightenment mechanistic materialism, the assumption of an objective nature in human culture, realized either directly or mystically, whether through external nature or human form. Marx disagreed with this assumption, arguing that "even the objects of the simplest 'sensuous certainty' are only given . . . through social development, industry and commercial intercourse" (Marx & Engels, 1936/1965, p.57). Marx's exit from mechanistic materialism was the appeal to "practice, and to the structures of reality built up from concrete and present action, in historically specified ways, of sensuous human beings" (Sahlins, 1976, p. 66). Boas took the same problem of mechanical materialism, working from there to discover the "historical specification of the acting subject" (Sahlins, 1976: 66), that is, the structuring power of tradition and ideas on human existence. The human construction of experience was situated by Boas, first at the psychological and later at the cultural level.

Marx's departure from Enlightenment materialism was historical materialism; Boas's exit was the germ of the structuralist anthropological concept of culture. For Marx, and those who follow in his ideological line—including, significantly, Lewis Henry Morgan—human practice always follows directly from praxis (Sahlins, 1976). For Boas and his students, the conceptual scheme always mediates between praxis and practice (Lévi-Strauss, 1966).

From this point the two streams of thought were developed and sharpened. Lewis Henry Morgan's description of human history as "an appendage of natural history, its law of motion merely forms of appearance of biological laws" has been equated with Marxist materialism (Schmidt, 1971, p. 47). Soviet author and critic Georgei Plekhanov critiqued artistic forms as symptomatic of bourgeois decadence, echoed by his compatriots Andrey Zhdanov and Karl Radek at the 1934 Soviet Writers' Congress (Milner, 1993). Soviet Marxism, attempting to dissociate itself from prolific cultural expression in the West, thus revealed its thought on culture in the 1930s. British Marxist critics Ralph Fox and Christopher Caudwell followed a similar thread in the 1940s, with the latter writing that culture is a "secretion" from the "economic base" (Milner, 1993, p. 8). Malinowski's work on culture eliminated symbol and system from cultural practices and rendered culture unable to be analyzed as a thing in itself (Sahlins, 1976), leading to an ultrautilitarian view that disavowed any inherent meaning in cultural practices or products.

In later years, reaction to a modernist movement generated from the influence of, among others, Lévi-Strauss, and Geertz took the form of a reevaluation of structuralist thought on culture (Friedman, 1994). The commonalities between British cultural materialism, Foucault's "genealogy," Bourdieu's cultural sociology, and Habermas's theory of communicative action are such that these streams can be termed "roughly equivalent" (Milner, 1993, p. 105), for all three sought to distance themselves as much from structuralism as they did from poststructuralists such as Derrida and Barthes.

The end of this lengthy ideological stream of NWICO discourse on culture is that culture is viewed according to a materialist perspective as something that is determined by the order of production, secondary in importance—and in order of urgency—to the social structuration of power. Thus, culture, when not discussed as a part of a hegemonistic force of politicoeconomic dominance, is treated as a nonentity with no substance of its own worthy of consideration.

The other stream of thought, of course, follows the structuralist and relativist tradition of Boas, Durkheim, the Harvard anthropological venture, and its product, Clifford Geertz. Durkheim attacked economism with his concept of the social fact, arguing that it had primary powers over economy. He advocated the notion of social convention in itself over the liberal economist tenet of society as an outcome of private interest (Sahlins, 1976). Boas's notion of culture as "an abstractable packet of signs, symbols tools and beliefs" (Friedman, 1994, p. 68) became systematized and developed through the work of Alfred Kroeber, Julian Steward, and Leslie White into something positivist and self-styled as descriptive. Lévi-Strauss (1963) rejected the analysis of "institutions" in favor of the consideration of "societies". This was taken further in the United States through the cooperation of Kroeber, Clyde Kluckholn, and Talcott Parsons. The outcome was a Harvard anthropology of the "systems of meaning, symbolism, [and] cognitive categories" (Friedman, 1994, p. 68), which was further sharpened and heralded by Clifford Geertz, who saw culture as a "publicly accessible text" based in the time and space of social life with immanent, inherent meaning.

In the end there remains a division between naturalism/functionalism and strucuralism—certainly neither absolute nor exclusive, but inescapable nonetheless—and it divided Marx and Morgan from Boas, Malinowski from Radlcliffe-Brown, the Manchester and Frankfurt schools from Lévi-Strauss and Harvard social science (Friedman, 1994; Sahlins, 1976). Both streams addressed different problems and offered divergent solutions, hence, the problematic for the NWICO movement's preference for the former over the latter.

THE CONSEQUENCES OF A DIVIDED EPISTEME OF CULTURE FOR THE MOVEMENT

Interestingly, the dialectic between the materialist and structuralist views of culture finds expression in NWICO discourse as broad language devoted to the recognition of culture gives way, by sheer force of weight, to observations and recommendations of a materialist nature.

On the one hand, culture has been described as worthy of preservation, on the local level, at all costs. Nongovernmental organizations (NGOs) and NWICO advocates have espoused this position regarding NWICO. The Prague Statement of the MacBride Round Table on Communication (1990) states that "the ideas of the NWICO . . . should be applied in accordance with specific cultural values, historical traditions and social needs of particular countries and regions" (p. 2). The International Organization of Journalists (1993) echoes this concern, arguing that "it is imperative that people get to know each other, share their experiences and their knowledge for the benefit of common prosperity and finally to respect the diversity of cultural values, each of which are worthy of preservation" (p. 3). Mowlana (1993) argues that any discussion of a new world order "must take into account the broader ecological/communication context as well as the diversities of global culture" (p. 395). Martín-Barbero (1993) attacks transnationalism as "the dislocation of the centers that articulate the universe of each [local] culture" (p. 145). These views offer an excellent sample of what, within NWICO advocacy, has been argument for the preservation of local cultures against dominance or change by outside sources.

On the other hand, another thread of culture conceptualization in NWICO discourse reveals a preponderent materialist orientation, preponderent because the spirit of a large portion of policy recommendations reflects that intellectual tradition. Culture is seen as a product of the media; it is treated as a social phenomenon whose first cause is media content. Roach's (1992) analysis suggests this second perspective on culture in the call for analysis of the way "mass media shape and change cultural environments," according great social power to "the media." The urge for "new cultural policies" that would "foster cultural identities that are tolerant of and non-threatening to other peoples" (p. 11) suggest a view of culture that is quite different from that of the structuralist anthropological view of culture as something that is quite difficult for any one agency to change. Vincent (1996) offers similar language in asserting that communication media can reverse the trend to which they have contributed in stopping the Westernization of non-Western societies "through a campaign of awareness and consciousness-raising, and local culture image production" (p. 199). The view of culture described here is consistent with the materialist conception of culture as part of the ideological superstructure and as an agent of imperialism. More central to the materialist tradition, though, it implies that the media, as means of economic production, are larger than culture, a "first cause" to cultural development, so to speak, with the capability of radically changing a culture at its most fundamental level in a short period of time. They are the practice that proceeds directly from praxis without the intervention of the Lévi-Straussian component of social concept; hence, rendering culture largely irrelevant to the calculus of communication policy.

The NWICO movement's preference for the materialist episteme, as asserted earlier, has been unbalanced in that the lack of a structuralist-relativist appreciation for the problems of culture regarding international communication policy has meant the development of blindspots. There are numerous examples of how the phenomena best described by a structuralist episteme have continued to spawn challenges to the advance of a new world information and communication order.

The MacBride Report called for the creation of policies aimed at the fostering of cultural identity and creativity, the involvement of the media in such efforts while safeguarding national culture development and promoting knowledge of other cultures. But the national cultural policies recommended in the MacBride Report "have not emerged . . . the media have become rather more involved in the creation of global than local culture, and . . . there are few indications of a more intensive cultural dialogue in the world" (Hamelink, 1996, p. 81).

The challenges encountered in discovering how to synthesize, implement, and enforce a global information and communication order evidenced thus far are symptomatic of the cultural dialectic. On the one hand, as has been shown, calls for the preservation of local cultures are expressed. On the other hand, it is assumed that there is an emergent global, cosmopolitan superculture as well as calls for a cultural struggle, the result of which is a global culture reflecting certain values ostensibly making global policy viable. The result is language such as that from Vincent, (1996):

> The principles of the New World Information and Communication Order were basically good ones, and we should not allow them to be lost in the quest for greater industrial development and self-serving national politics. If we can sacrifice our societal rights to communication use and access, then many other freedoms are certain to succumb. (p. 207)

Vincent sets "self-serving national politics" against the preservation of "societal rights to communication use and access"; arguably, such juxtaposition leaves the definition of society vague, for only a global society in this case would make the contradistinction logically allowable. A smaller unit of analysis regarding society leaves one with a contradiction. Materialistically speaking, societies preserve their "rights to communication use and access" through "self-serving national politics." What is most intriguing is that, in fact, societies are still defined by increasingly diverse cultures and enduring nation-state entities (Nordenstreng, 1993). Vincent (1996) also states "the essence of a democracy is the ability for all to communicate" (p. 193), yet other scholarship (Frank, 1993) demonstrates that "democracy" is by no means universally recognized as functionally the same, particularly regarding what communication is to be used for and who has the right to say what. We are inescapably returned, then, to the fundamental questions of "whose rights?" and "whose democracy?", questions that gave rise to the MacBride Commission's work in the first place.

As long as cultures remain as diverse as they are and the evidence points to increasing divergence, not the opposite, a structuralist analysis will be needed. Although processes and forces of globalization are in operation (Galtung & Vincent, 1992; Hamelink, 1993), they operate in favor of and promote the nation-state as a social unit conducive to commercial transnationalism (Hamelink, 1993). Cultures throughout the world need no such encouragement to remain diverse. Culture by nature is self-perpetuating, and human beings are, by psychological necessity, ethnocentric (Brislin, 1993).

As Falk (1993) noted:

> Britain's inability to insulate [Salman] Rushdie is an extreme instance of a wider reality, the spread of cultural images in a world of antagonistic cultures, not geographically separable. International law cannot address these challenges in any conventional manner, that is, by positing standards, procedures, sanctions. Perhaps, cross-cultural dialogue can work toward a position of mutual greater respect and tolerance

over time, but the point here is that the world is confronted with a new kind of profound challenge, a response to which it has not even started to fashion. (p. 425)

Hamelink (1993) argues that the world's citizens have hardly begun to address the problems of the global coexistence of races and cultures. In reality, "the potentially explosive multiethnic encounter on the municipal level has not been even satisfactorily resolved" (p. 377). Noting that most of the world's population still face resolution of their most basic needs, Hamelink (1993) asserts "it would seem that, as people are themselves insecure, they are reluctant to trust 'strangers' and to accept" a diversity of lifestyles as a good thing in an emerging multicultural society. Mowlana (1993) echoes Falk's greater hope for interpersonal rapprochement in the face of international intransigence: "the way *people* relate to each other in a world of 'internationalized' culture and consciousness may be more important than how nation-states relate" (p. 218; emphasis in original). But there is no likelihood, realistically, that interpersonal bridges are any less fraught with danger; Brislin's (1993) earlier referenced dismantling of this myth ought to be remembered here.

The movement's frame of reference was excessively focused on the mass media; center versus periphery, North versus South, imperialists versus dependants were the star players in a drama written around the issue of cultural imperialism that could not adequately address the real concerns of culture, identity, and globalization (Golding & Harris, 1996). In Golding and Harris's (1996) words, "the confusion between political project and the stubborn verities of economic and cultural existence is substantial" (p. 8).

How would this persistent cultural division work itself out in terms of information and communication policy? Although materialist analysis identifies conflicts of interest, "what have not been recorded, registered, let alone understood, are the reasons animating these conflicts of interests. . . . The resurgence and resistances embodied in shared local categories (i.e., caste, religion, sub-cultural affiliation, etc.)" (Thomas, 1996, p. 164). In politicoeconomic discussions regarding Africa, materialist analysis was given center stage at the expense of consideration of cultural factors. The exclusion of culture "was not surprising in view of the way it was used as a catch-all variable in modernization theory and reduced to an economically determined false consciousness by some Marxists" (Barnett, 1996, p. 48n). Another case in point is Mowlana's (1993) treatment of the question of information and communication policy in the Islamic world. A disparity exists between the Islamic world and the West concerning information and communication, and the nature of that clash is cultural. Although information is seen as a commodity in the West, Mowlana argues (1993), "throughout Islamic history, especially in the early centuries, information was not a commodity but a moral and ethical imperative" (p. 396). There is a fundamental disagreement at the cultural level concerning the nature and social locus of information between the West and the Islamic world which is not bridgeable through semantic gymnastics. "In a number of fundamental ways," Mowlana asserts, "the notion of the Information Society Paradigm and the emerging global information community runs counter to the basic conception of Islamic community and a number of principal tenets of Islam" (p. 398).

Should the importance of the Islamic world be minimized, Mowlana asks, "And who are on the periphery side of this equation? Notably, the more than one billion Muslim people who constitute one-fourth of the world's population" (1993, p. 407). What has been described here as a "case in point" is said to affect such a huge proportion of the world's population that the "case in point" designation is an embarrassing understatement. It also demonstrates that the cultural forces in the world not only persist as forces larger than information technologies and practices, but they also actively militate (in the preceding case, very likely literally so) against a new world information and communication order which would ostensibly challenge cultural norms. More importantly, though, it illustrates the limits of a materialist view of international communication policy: As far as it goes, it runs into Golding and Harris's (1996) "stubborn cultural verities." That is where structuralist analysis may provide some assistance.

TRANSCENDING THE DIALECTIC OF CULTURE

The NWICO movement has encountered quandaries in its approach to culture; hence, the "limited success" alluded to at the beginning of this chapter. But limited success should not be read to suggest failure. Indeed, that the movement continues toward the end of its second decade, and that the dialogue has been both lively and consciousness-raising, speaks of success. It may be argued that Gramsci's ideal of working-class intellectuals leading members of their class "in the battle for counter-hegemony" (Milner, 1993, p. 55) has foretold the heart and soul of the movement.

In order for NWICO to move past the tension between epistemologies of culture that have produced the crisis described in this chapter, the movement must understand that, just as the structuralist view of culture neither sees the importance of means of production nor appreciates how its products may be used to legitimate existing social order, the materialist take on culture both fails to adequately capture the scope and depth of culture and misses the fact that cultural "superstructures" are just as material as the bases of economic production (Milner, 1993). A union of the two perspectives would allow the understanding that many, if not most, people in the world may not operate according to a European positivist-materialist logic and would help the movement to grasp why there has been resistance, of various forms, to much of the movement's efforts. The movement must find a way, within its definition of the problems and possibilities of international communication, to bring the two perspectives together.

Such a union is not without precedent in social theory. Milner (1993) recognizes both class and culture in his critical approach and argues that people create their own cultures but leaves room for emancipatory politics. Williams (1977) follows Gramsci in arguing that culture can be viewed as a whole, beyond superstructure, and still be wedded with an interest in ideology. Friedman (1994) also constructs a bridge between the two. Sahlins (1976) argues that culture "is a new object, created by symbolic valuation and synthesis of the objective reality" (p. 64), effectively bringing together the materialist and structuralist into a complementary union.

Such a bridge is essential for the future relevance and success of the movement. The definition of freedom, justice, participation, and access must incorporate openness to local- and culture-specific ways of approaching communication problems (Thomas, 1996). This need places the locus for change not in the goals of NWICO but in the philosophical premises that frame and animate the movement's policy and actions. It is a key ingredient in the future success of the movement and will continue to be so for as long as cultures continue to differ in meaningful ways.

REFERENCES

Barnett, T. (1996). States of the state and third worlds. In P. Golding & P. Harris (Eds.), *Beyond cultural imperialism: The new world order* (pp. 25-48). London: Sage.

Brislin, R. (1993). *Understanding culture's influence on behavior.* Orlando: Harcourt Brace.

Falk, R. (1993). Rethinking the agenda of international law. In K. Nordenstreng & H. Schiller (Eds.), *Beyond national sovereignty: International communication in the 1990s* (pp. 418-431). Norwood, NJ: Ablex.

Frank, A. (1993). No end to history! History to no end? In K. Nordenstreng & H. Schiller (Eds.), *Beyond national sovereignty: International communication in the 1990s* (pp. 3-28). Norwood, NJ: Ablex.

Friedman, J. (1994). *Cultural identity and global process.* London: Sage.

Galtung, J., & Vincent, R. (1992). *Global glasnost: Toward a new world information and communication order?* Cresskill, NJ: Hampton Press.

Golding, P., & Harris, P. (1996). Introduction. In P. Golding & P. Harris (Eds.), *Beyond cultural imperialism: The new world order* (pp. 1-9). London: Sage.

Hamelink, C. (1993). Globalism and national sovereignty. In K. Nordenstreng & H. Schiller (Eds.), *Beyond national sovereignty: International communication in the 1990s* (pp. 371-393). Norwood, NJ: Ablex.

Hamelink, C. (1996). MacBride with hindsight. In P. Golding & P. Harris (Eds.), *Beyond cultural imperialism: The new world order* (pp. 69-93). London: Sage.

International Organization of Journalists. (1993, June). Declaration of the International Organization of Journalists at the World Conference on Human Rights, Vienna, Austria.

Lévi-Strauss, C. (1963). *Structural anthropology*. New York: Basic Books.

Lévi-Strauss, C. (1966). *The savage mind*. Chicago: University of Chicago Press.

Martín-Barbero, J. (1993). Modernity, nationalism, and communication in Latin America. In K. Nordenstreng & H. Schiller (Eds.), *Beyond national sovereignty: International communication in the 1990s* (pp. 132-147). Norwood, NJ: Ablex.

Marx, K., & Engels, F. (1965). *Correspondence: 1846-1895*. New York: International Publishers. (Original work published in 1936)

Milner, A. (1993). *Cultural materialism*. Melbourne: Melbourne University Press.

Mowlana, (1993). New global order and cultural ecology. In K. Nordenstreng & H. Schiller (Eds.), *Beyond national sovereignty: International communication in the 1990s* (pp. 394-417). Norwood, NJ: Ablex.

Nordenstreng, K. (1993). Sovereignty and beyond. In K. Nordenstreng & H. Schiller (Eds.), *Beyond national sovereignty: International communication in the 1990s* (pp. 461-463). Norwood, NJ: Ablex.

Prague Statement of the MacBride Round Table on Communication. (1990, September 20-21). Prague, Czechoslovakia.

Roach, C. (1992, August 21). Report of the Fourth MacBride Round Table, Guaruja, Brazil.

Sahlins, M. (1976). *Culture and practical reason*. Chicago: University of Chicago Press.

Schmidt, A. (1971). *The concept of nature in Marx*. London: NLB.

Thomas, P. (1996). An inclusive NWICO: Cultural resilience and popular resistance. In P. Golding & P. Harris (Eds.), *Beyond cultural imperialism: The new world order* (pp. 163-174). London: Sage.

Vincent, R. (1996). The future of the debate: Setting an agenda for a new world information and communication order; ten axioms. In P. Golding & P. Harris (Eds.), *Beyond cultural imperialism: The new world order* (pp. 175-207). London: Sage.

Williams, A. (1977). *Marxism and literature*. Oxford: Oxford University Press.

12

Unresearched Assumptions in the MacBride Report

Michael Basil

I am interested in the effects of communication and the process under which these effects occur. In reading the MacBride report, I became interested in the changes that have occurred in the concept "right to communicate" and in many of the underlying assumptions of the report. Although this concept originally appeared to represent free speech and freedom of the press (Richstad & Harms, 1977), this movement appears to have also embraced access to technology or control of that technology. Although I understand the natural connection of these ideas, I believe that the inclusion of access to technologies in the "right to communicate" has introduced several dangerous assumptions. Most importantly, I am interested in the assumptions of how positive effects are hoped to accrue through access to those technologies.

My discussion here focuses on "media effects" underlying the MacBride Commission report. I offer these ideas in support of the important aims of the MacBride movement. Perhaps by uncovering and examining these assumptions and understanding that may be problematic, the movement can help focus on which rights to communicate may be most important.

I am bothered by six serious assumptions in the MacBride report and the MacBride movement. Three of these I have categorized as assumptions about large effects of communication and three as positive effects. In sum, these assumptions are predicting large, positive effects of communication technology. Although these are not necessarily fatal assumptions behind the right to communicate and the New World Information and Communication Order (NWICO) movement, they are, at least, very optimistic. I will work through these assumptions and suggest an approach that would avoid pitfalls.

ASSUMPTIONS OF LARGE EFFECTS

In the MacBride report (MacBride et al., 1980) there appears to be three assumptions that lead to an unexpressed conclusion that communication technology causes things to happen. These assumptions are based on how the technology of communication shapes society. Although these assumptions are not necessarily wrong, I hope that pointing them out may help adherents of the MacBride movement to more accurately define the how and why under which communication technologies may affect our lives. This, in turn, may provide insights into which rights, technologies, or aspects of those technologies may play a role in bettering civil society.

Technology Drives Society

The first serious assumption in the MacBride report is one of causality. The report assumes that technological development drives societal development (Campeanu, 1977). Clearly, the MacBride report falls on the side of Karl Marx and Marshall MacLuhan, who felt that technology drives society. That is, the report appears to assume that "tools" determine how we think. For example, in the Stone Age, a technological determinist would propose that stone tools shaped our lifestyles. The MacBride report assumes that communication technologies shape how we communicate. Our lives are shaped by the communication technologies around us.

There is, however, an opposite point of view. The other side feels that society drives technology. These views can be seen in the writings of Max Weber. These societal determinists feel that our needs determine our tools. In the Stone Age, for example, the technological determinists would propose that we needed tools, so we developed them. This point of view would suggest that our needs to communicate shape our communication technologies. If a group of people is given a fax machine, they would not necessarily use it. This issue was raised as far back as 1978 (Fisher, 1982).

Because the MacBride report follows the technology determinist ideology, it assumes that technology drives society. As a result, the

MacBride report appears to advocate that having or using an advanced technology will lead to a more technologically developed society. Sociologists have not, however, solved the problem of causality in 100 years. Current theories suggest that causality may involve some of both (Schement & Curtis, 1995). That is, like teaching, only when people are ready for a technology will they use it. There is no benefit to providing it beforehand. I think, therefore, that MacBride adherents should consider a society's need or readiness for a technology before assuming that the presence of that technology will change the society.

We should also be aware of the antecedent conditions in civil society. It is possible that access to media technology, before a society feels the need, would simply result in a waste of resources. It is also possible that providing a people with media technology earlier than they would otherwise have access to it could result in their sidestepping, or even missing, the development of other important societal conditions. Although the MacBride report suggests that access to communication technology will lead to democracy, it is possible that technology before democracy could lead to censorship, arrests, and even exile of those who would use that technology to advocate societal change. In such a scenario, it is possible that using communication technologies could enhance the government's ability to locate and identify dissidents. This appears to have occurred in China after the Tiananamen Square uprising, where leaders of the student movement were quickly identified and, if possible, jailed.

Communication is a Defining Technology

The second serious assumption in the MacBride report is that communication technology is a "defining" technology as defined by Winner (1977). This view holds that communication technologies are one of the most important technologies of this century. They have the ability to shape societies. This view, when combined with the technological determinist assumptions discussed, leads to the view that communication technologies and access shape societies (McLuhan, 1964; Toffler, 1980). That is, this assumption holds that nations are a particular way because of their use of tools. Communication and lifestyles are the way they are because of the way we communicate.

The MacBride report assumes that communication technologies are so powerful their use will result in changes to the structure of the societies that use them. The argument is often assembled from data comparing developed and developing nations, as in Part II of the report (MacBride et al., 1980). This assumption holds that, for example, an African nation will be changed if it gets a computer, regardless of whether it has electricity. Clearly, not only must the antecedent conditions such as electricity be present, but so must other needs for the output of that machine. Specifically, what will be the computer input and output, and how will that play a role in the existing social order? A high-power parallel computer would likely be put to different use by a Marxist dictatorship than a capitalist democracy.

Providing communication technologies may not necessarily improve the lot of indigenous peoples in the developing world. If communication technologies are not defining technologies, then providing them may make no difference in everyday life. A few affluent people may divert money to their purchase, while the majority of the population would not. Even if communications devices are defining technologies, providing television transmitters may result in the diversion of resources to the purchase of receiving sets and the diversion of labor from otherwise fruitful activities to leisure.

More and Newer Technology is Better

A third assumption in the MacBride report is that more or newer technology is inherently better than less or older technology. This assumption is that the more communication technology is available to an individual or a nation, the more information, or the more access a people have to technological things, the more "developed" and democratic they will be. Again, this assumption is based on the first two—that the major industrial nations are that way because of their communication media. It ignores the antecedent conditions and the desires of the government.

The argument that more advanced technologies are better is equally problematic. One of the principle technologies that have made social movements possible appears to be the mimeograph machine. It allowed people to get out information in a short time very cheaply. Many of the newer technologies, including video and multimedia, do not have those advantages. Producing multiple videos requires access to duplicating facilities. Multimedia, meanwhile, is expensive and requires considerable start-up costs. Therefore, insuring that people have access to these forms of media does not insure they have any more power.

The logical flaw in that line of reasoning that more is better or that newer is better is one of causality. If you look at current conditions, more advanced nations have more advanced communication technology. The assumption is that the higher level of technology and the newer forms of technology made these places more developed or democratic. As Mueller (1993) observed, taken to the logical extreme, this position would hold that to make a company more successful, all you need to do is buy more telephones. This is clearly untenable at extreme levels. At some point the company will not benefit, but will go broke. I believe that this position is also untenable at the levels of technology suggested in the MacBride report. In many instances buying technology will have no appreciable effect on either an individual's life, on a society, or on civil society in general.

In general, the MacBride report assumes that infusing more and newer communication technologies will result in more developed, advanced, democratic, and financially secure people. This result, however, assumes three other things. First, it assumes that the money cannot be better spent on other items and commodities. I leave this argument to economists. Second, it implies that the technologies will lead to development or satisfaction. This assumption seems strange given the amount of time that people in developed countries devote to television entertainment. Third, it assumes that the advantages outweigh the disadvantages. It is possible, however, that communication technologies provide more problems than solutions. It is possible for example, that the decay of the family, local culture, and values and a decline in the value of education has accompanied the introduction of television in many countries.

I address next this last set of assumptions—that the technologies will lead to satisfaction or development—and that the advantages of communication media outweigh the disadvantages. Stated differently, the MacBride report seems to assume only positive effects of communication technologies.

ASSUMPTIONS OF POSITIVE EFFECTS

In addition to the three questions of large effects, there are three assumptions referring to overwhelmingly positive effects of communication or of communication media. These assumptions appear to suggest that civil society's access or ownership of these media will affect society in positive, and not negative, ways. They appear to be largely unfounded.

No Negative Effects on Interpersonal Communication

The first assumption of positive effects in the MacBride report is that these new media will not usurp interpersonal communication. This assumption, however, appears to be challenged even within the report. At various times in the report the problem of indigenous peoples is raised. Several "critical" theorists in media, myths and narratives (Carey, 1988) have proposed that television has taken the place of fireside conversation. The participants in that seminar believed that television situation comedies and news displace cultural myths. As such, they see electronic communication, at least access to television receivers, as potentially disruptive.

Similarly, McCombs and Shaw's (1972) agenda-setting theory proposes that what electronic media talk about suggests what should be important to us. Perhaps the same can be said for other technologies. Perhaps these new technologies, or access to them, will allow other people to impose their agendas on our conversations.

Even more extremely, Noelle-Neumann (1984) believes that electronic media quiet the minority. Communication channels can quiet others. Perhaps the former Soviet Union and Pinochet survived because they silenced the minority through control of the media. Providing access to these technologies may accidentally insure that a large part of people's everyday communication would consist of political indoctrination. Perhaps, again, the use of newer technologies would allow the government greater access to what was said.

Although the MacBride Commission views communication as a possible vehicle for increasing political interest and participation, a contrasting view is that they do just the opposite. Unlimited access to news and other political information may actually provide a "narcotizing dysfunction," in which people spend so much time observing what is happening that they have no time to actually participate. As a result, people spend their efforts in surveillance instead of participation. This effect appears most likely in the case of television news (Lazarsfeld & Merton, 1971). The MacBride Commission appears to have ignored this possible downside to information—information to the point of inaction.

No Negative Effects on Local Culture

The second assumption about effects is that mass media will usurp local culture. Even statements in the MacBride report propose that television allows U.S. culture to overpower local culture. This cultural imperialism view holds that communication technology allows larger and more technologically developed cultures to dominate smaller ones. This effect is even more evident when the second culture the enabling technologies such as television and films (Mattelart, 1979; Schiller, 1976; Wells, 1972; Tunstall, 1977).

Although we often think of this effect in terms of undeveloped countries, the effect is not limited to them. Even France, a country with a very advanced film industry, and one known for the production of some of the best critically acclaimed films in the world, fears that their language and culture are being diminished by U.S. films and television shows. This, again, occurs in a country where they already have an active film industry. Yet the dominance of U.S. films seems almost inevitable, even with intervention. What chance does a country with an undeveloped industry have? Many feel that this is a matter of "education" of the masses to alternative fare. Most free-market media experiments such as independent broadcasting in Britain have resulted in people choosing higher production quality, low brow fare. This effect may even be enhanced by the production costs of newer media such as interactive cable and multimedia.

Another example can be seen in "public access" cable. Although cable companies provide this forum to viewers, very few viewers take advantage. Instead, most opt for the slicker productions on commercial television. One may also look at the history of the BBC for similar concerns. When they were without competition the BBC produced generally high-quality fare. With the introduction of independent stations, which often aired U.S. programs, the BBC was faced with the possibility of "competing" by lowering the standard on some of their programming (Gelb, 1993; Tusa, 1994). In the United States, public broadcasting, in search of viewers, has increased the number of British "soap operas" to encourage listeners. In sum, providing a vehicle for local programming does not necessarily result in viewers watching local programming, as Vincent (1996a) suggests in his discussion of local production and program popularity.

More Positive than Negative Effects

Over the years, media effects researchers have spent more effort examining the negative effects of the mass media. Generally, they have spent more effort examining violence than examining the positive effects of "Sesame Street" or "Mr. Rogers' Neighborhood." Of yet we have no reason to believe that the positive effects outweigh the negative. Perhaps this is a question that should be addressed with additional research.

The MacBride report seems to assume that there are more positive than negative effects. But what if all the diffusion of communication technologies helps insure that there are more children out there imitating "Rambo" than "Mr. Rogers?" Increasing access to this "enabling" technology, then, may make the people more isolated, culturally dominated, and even violent. In the United States, as news media are driven by market forces, there is an increase in the amount of gratuitous violence. Fast-paced fires, murder, and mayhem often take a front seat to more insightful news. Even comparing across the news media in the United States, it appears that newer technologies such as radio and television focus more energies on sensational stories than older media such as newspapers and newsmagazines.

Cultivation theory proposes that what we see on television shapes how we indeed see the world (Gerbner, Gross, Morgan & Signorelli, 1994). Directly to the point of negative effects, studies of cultivation show a relationship between the violence on television and the violence in society. Perhaps by insuring people's access to communication technologies, and their content, we may also be insuring a more violent society. Perhaps a government-controlled media, although logically inconsistent with the approach of the MacBride Commission, would actually provide a healthier, safer society. This is a viewpoint that would not fit well with the market liberalization and privitization forces currently espoused by many in the West (Vincent, 1996b).

CONCLUSION

Overall, these six assumptions are based on two basic myths of communication. The first assumption is that communication is either good or bad. Generally, "breakdowns" and manipulation is bad, other forms of communication are good. Locally held, democratically controlled communication is seen as good, whereas larger, profit-based communication is seen as bad. This simple dichotomy, however, may not always be true. The good or bad potential may not depend so much on the technology as on the use to which that technology is put. In the United States, for example, television is put to both commercial entertainment and noncommercials educational ends.

The second myth underlying some of the MacBride Commission assumptions is that more communication can "fix" anything. In families and developmental communication the myth appears to be that all you need to do to make things better is communicate, and communicate often. There are some problems here. Economic development and distributions of wealth may well be two of them (Shaw, 1977). Providing access to communication technologies may not result in desired changes. In fact, redistribution of communication technology and access to that technology may actually be a "bone" to appease people.

I am not trying to suggest that diffusion of technologies is inevitably bad. I am suggesting, however, that the effects are not inevitable, and they are not inevitably good. Instead, I suggest that some effort should be devoted to discovering the conditions that yield the most positive effects from communication technology—open dialogue, economic well-being, and satisfaction among people. We do not know whether this will occur under conditions in which there is a guarantee of free speech, in which the communication is government or independently controlled, or whether particular media have the most beneficial effects. But we should attempt to discover those conditions, and in addition to distributing technologies, try to insure that those conditions coexist with the technologies. I doubt that the MacBride Commission would have proposed improving access to communication if they believed it would result in more entertainment, pornography, and violence programming that is becoming more and more prominent today. The relaxation of controls can, unfortunately, very well lead to such outcomes.

REFERENCES

Campeanu, P. (1977). A sociologist's view of the right to communicate. In L. S. Harms and J. Richstad (Eds.), *Evolving perspective on the right to communicate* (pp. 237-246). Honolulu: East-West Center.

Carey, J. W. (1988). *Media, myth, and narratives: Television and the press.* Newbury Park, CA: Sage.

Fisher, D. (1982). *The right to communicate: A status report.* Paris: UNESCO.

Gelb, N. (1993). Trouble at the BBC: John Birt's revolution. *The New Leader, 76,* 3-5.

Gerbner, G., Gross, L., Morgan, M., & Signorelli, N. (1994). Growing up with television: The cultivation perspective. In J. Bryant & D. Zillmann (Eds.), *Media effects: Advances in theory and research* (pp. 17-41). Hillsdale, NJ: Erlbaum.

Lazarsfeld, P. F., & Merton, R. K. (1971). Mass communication, popular taste, and organized social action. In W. Schramm & D. F. Roberts (Eds.), *Process and effects of mass communication* (pp. 554-578). Urbana: University of Illinois Press.

MacBride, S., Abel, E., Omu, F. I. A., Beuve-Mery, H., Osolnik, B., Ekenzo, E. M., Oteifi, G. E., Marquez, G. G., Pronk, J. P., Losev, S., Somavia, J., Lubis, M., Verghese, B. G., Masmoudi, M., Zimmerman, B., & Nagai, M. (1980). *Many voices, one world.* New York: Unipub.

Mattelart, A. (1979). *Multi-national corporations and the control of culture.* Atlantic Highlands, NJ: Humanities Press.

McCombs, M. E., & Shaw, D. L. (1972). The agenda-setting function of mass media. *Public Opinion Quarterly, 36,* 176-187.

McLuhan, M. (1964). *Understanding media: The extentions of man.* New York: New American Library.

Mueller, M. (1993). Communications as infrastructure: A sceptical view. *Journal of Communication, 43,* 147-159.

Noelle-Neumann, E. (1984). *The spiral of silence: Public opinion—our social skin.* Chicago: University of Chicago Press.

Richstad, J., & Harms, L. S. (1977). Preface: Dynamics of the right to communicate—A brief history of the concept. In L. S. Harms & J. Richstad (Eds.), *Evolving perspective on the right to communicate* (pp. 1-14). Honolulu: East-West Center.

Schement, J. R., & Curtis, T. (1995). *Tendencies and tensions of the information age.* New Brunswick, NJ: Transaction Publishers.

Schiller, H. (1976). *Communication and cultural domination.* New York: International Arts & Sciences.

Shaw, C. (1977). The right to communicate. In L. S. Harms & J. Richstad (Eds.), *Evolving perspective on the right to communicate* (pp. 277-285). Honolulu: East-West Center.

Toffler, A. (1980). *The third wave.* New York: William Morrow.
Tunstall, J. (1977). *The media are American.* New York: Columbia University Press.
Tusa, J. (1994). Implications of recent changes at the BBC. *Political Quarterly, 65,* 6-11.
Vincent, R. (1996a). The future of the debate: Setting an agenda for a new world information and communication order, ten proposals. In P. Golding & P. Harris (Eds.), *Beyond cultural imperialism* (pp. 175-207). London: Sage.
Vincent, R. (1996b). The New World Information and Communication Order (NWICO) in the context of the information superhighway. In D. Winseck & M. Bailie (Eds.), *Democratizing communication?* (pp. 335-404). Cresskill, NJ: Hampton Press.
Wells, A. (1972). *Picture tube imperialism?* New York: Maryknoll.
Winner, L. (1977). *Autonomous technology: Technics-out-of-control as a theme in political thought.* Cambridge, MA: MIT Press.

PART IV

MACBRIDE LEGACY

The final section is directly devoted to the MacBride legacy. Kaarle Nordenstreng reviews the great media debate—the context of the movement from the early 1970s to the late 1990s. Alan Hancock and Cees Hamelink evaluate the recommendations of the *MacBride Report* in terms of their significance for today's world and the measures that have, or have not, been taken toward their implementation. This analysis sets a new agenda, namely, of policies and tasks that still need to be pursued with various degrees of urgency. The section ends with a brief biography of Sean MacBride, set out by Jorg Becker and Kaarle Nordenstreng.

13

The Context: Great Media Debate

Kaarle Nordenstreng

The MacBride Commission and its report belong to a passage of history, which has become to be known among communication experts as the "global media debate" (Gerbner, Mowlana, & Nordenstreng, 1993). Actually the debate got at times so political and high profile that it is justified to call it "great" as done in the title of this review. The debate was simultaneously on several topics, including the worldwide imbalance of media facilities and flows as well as the lack of accuracy and fairness in international news reporting, particularly concerning the developing countries in the Western media. (The news bias aspect is bypassed in this review; it is well covered in works such as Galtung & Vincent, 1992; Richstad & Anderson, 1981; Sreberny-Mohammadi, Nordenstreng, Stevenson, & Ugboajah, 1984; Yadava, 1984.)

The following review is made through the most pervasive concept of the debate: the New World Information and Communication Order (NWICO). As such it provides a repeat and update of already well-cultivated literature, rather than a new angle or shaking discoveries. (The review here is a mini version of a textbook unit prepared for an MA in Mass Communication by distance learning, administered by the Center for Mass Communication Research, University of Leicester, UK, and edited by Oliver Boyd-Barrett in 1995.)

HISTORY

The roots of the debate reviewed here can be traced as far back as the prewar League of Nations (Nordenstreng, 1993a). Most of the so-called "international instruments" by which the international community has expressed its political and legal orientation with regard to the media can be listed as elements of NWICO. Tens of such pieces of international law existed by the late 1970s, including 44 standard-setting instruments with more or less direct reference to the performance of the mass media (Nordenstreng, 1984).

Given such a heritage, it can be argued that little in NWICO was in fact new; its essence was made up of old ideas and established principles that were brought together under a new umbrella. For example, the problem of global imbalance of information structures was recognized by the United Nations (UN) long before any great debate on NWICO. The UN's Economic and Social Council, ECOSOC, addressed the problem as early as 1961. One year later, the UN General Assembly expressed its concern over the fact that "70 percent of the population of the world lack adequate information facilities and are thus denied effective enjoyment of the right to information," and it invited the governments of developed countries "to cooperate with less developed countries in connection with this program for the development of independent national information media, with due regard for the culture of each country." Moreover, as early as 1952, a UN General Assembly resolution considered that "it is essential for a proper development of public opinion in under-developed countries that independent domestic information enterprises should be given facilities and assistance in order that they may be enabled to contribute to the spread of information, to the development of national culture and to international understanding" and continued that "the time has arrived for the elaboration of a concrete program and plan of action in this respect" (Nordenstreng, 1984, p. 4).

It is ironic that it took nearly 30 years before the UN system, through UNESCO, reacted to this appeal by mobilizing a major international program for the development of communication (IPDC). Why did it take so long before major action was taken on a problem that had been recognized for decades? The key to this question lies in the gradual but fundamental change in the relations of social, economic, and political forces in the world, beginning with the establishment of the socialist countries and ending with the process of decolonization, which created the developing countries of the so-called Third World. In this situation the capitalist countries of the West had gone on the defensive, faced with an overall challenge that was articulated in demands for a new order—in the field of international communications as well as in the world economy. Thus, NWICO became an issue not so much because of the emergence of some drastically new phenomena (such as communications technology), but fundamentally because a sufficiently strong coalition of social forces had accumulated to enforce a new order—at least as a political program, even if not as an immediate reality.

In a historical perspective, NWICO also means the revival of political projects that had been introduced at the second session of the UN General Assembly in 1947 and at the UN Conference on Freedom of Information held in Geneva in 1948, but which were then paralyzed by the Cold War. Before the early 1950s, the UN General Assembly and ECOSOC had considered such questions as freedom of information and standards for professional conduct, including an international code of ethics for journalists—all highly political items. However, the international politics of the time did not allow for their elaboration, and the ECOSOC Subcommission on Freedom of Information and of the Press in the early 1950s failed to reach an agreement on anything of major significance. This period brought about only three instruments relevant to the present discussion: the Universal Declaration of Human Rights, the Genocide Convention, and the Convention on the International Right of Correction.

A signal for new political momentum was the Outer Space Treaty, adopted by the UN General Assembly in 1966, with a preambular reference to the UN Resolution 110 (II) condemning war propaganda. In 1972, the General Assembly passed a resolution that formally started the preparation of legal principles governing the use of satellites for direct television broadcasting. In the same year, the General Conference of UNESCO issued the Declaration of Guiding Principles on the Use of Satellite Broadcasting for the Free Flow of Information, the Spread of Education and Greater Cultural Exchange. Both the UN resolution and the UNESCO declaration made a point of national sovereignty suggesting that prior consent by the receiving country (through its government) was a precondition for such a new form of international communication. This naturally caused alarm among the advocates of the "free-flow" doctrine, leading to a controversy that has continued ever since at the UN Outer Space Committee.

Issues of space communication were not the only challenges to the old information order. Decolonization became recognized, by the early 1960s, not only as an independence movement in the Third World, but also as a set of principles in international relations—ultimately leading to the Declaration on the New International Economic Order (NIEO) by the UN General Assembly on May 1, 1974, followed by the Charter of Economic Rights and Duties of States by the same supreme body of the international community on December 12, 1974.

Parallel to this development, the concept of human rights was evolving from the 1948 Universal Declaration of Human Rights to a more definite set of principles codified as part and parcel of international law in the International Covenant on Civil and Political Rights and the

International Covenant on Economic, Social and Cultural Rights. These Covenants, adopted in 1966, had a direct bearing on information and communication—in a manner quite far from the simple free-flow doctrine. The same applies to regional conventions on human rights adopted in Western Europe as early as 1950, in the Americas in 1969, and in Africa later in 1981.

Apart from a progressive codification of human rights at large, the particular aspects of racialism and apartheid got their specific International Conventions (in 1965 and 1973), which contain articles with specific reference to mass communication. Other instruments again introduced a link between peace and international understanding, on the one hand, and the content of education, culture, and communication, on the other.

Consequently, the international context of information was quite "politicized" by the middle of the 1970s, and the foundations of NWICO were there already before it took the shape of a concept and a movement. It is these historical roots that help to understand why NWICO turned out to be a phenomenon of such importance and perseverance.

FORCES

An overview of history such as that just given makes it obvious that the main political force behind NWICO was the Non-Aligned Movement (NAM) representing the developing South or the Third World. Next to that was the socialist East (Second World). Together these two constituted a strategic alliance, which was not based on any official agreement and yet more often than not proved to be a delicate reality.

This "natural alliance" challenged the third main party in the geopolitical arena, the West (First World). To be precise, it was right-wing political forces in the West that were on the defensive and hostile, mainly on anticommunist grounds. At the same time, liberal and leftist forces in the West were mostly sympathetic toward the tide in history that could be seen behind NWICO. Manifestation of this were initiatives such as the Club of Rome-based "Reshaping the International Order" (Tinbergen, 1976) as well as early NWICO platforms provided by the Swedish-based Dag Hammarskjold Foundation (Development Dialogue, 1976) and the German-based Friedrich Ebert Foundation (Bielenstein, 1979).

As a matter of fact, we can list liberal and radical West—at least its intellectual elements—as the third force in support of NWICO after the South and East. At that time it was quite fashionable—today one might say "politically correct"—for media scholars to rally behind NWICO. In line with Nordenstreng (1993b), it can even be seen that there was a movement with two more or less converging tracks: political and intellectual.

On the other hand, none of the three forces behind NWICO was simple and united. NAM had internal frictions, with some of its members even at war (e.g., Uganda and Tanzania, later Iran and Iraq). Socialist East was divided not only between the U.S.S.R. and China, but also among its European group (Romania as the most deviant case)—not to speak of the dissidents in each country that stood against the whole system. Supporters in the West were based in political groupings, many of which (notably communists and social democrats) were enemies rather than allies. Especially orthodox East Europeans were often suspicious of the other two parties, as they were afraid of eroding the Marxist–Leninist ideology through ideas such as interdependence (one of the NAM principles). Actually, NWICO's main support in the socialist East was among its reformist and "liberal" elements—those who later promoted "glasnost."

Accordingly, it was a capricious gallery of forces rather than a solid coalition. All the same it was a reality—a reality widely recognized at the time of the Fourth NAM Summit in Algiers in 1973. It was there that 75 developing countries (the majority of UN membership) declared that "the activities of imperialism are not confined solely to the political and economic fields, but also cover the cultural and social fields" and demanded "concerted action in the fields of mass communication" (Nordenstreng, 1984, p. 9).

Indeed, if one has to choose a particular year, and a particular occasion, to signal the shift of geopolitical balance of forces to the side of the developing world, it would be 1973 and the NAM Summit in Algiers. What followed during the next three years until the Colombo Summit, including the articulation of NWICO, was politically preset already in 1973. (For a more comprehensive review of NAM and its record in this field before the Colombo Summit, see, e.g., Tran van Dinh, 1979.)

IDEAS

As far as the history of ideas is concerned, a central intellectual ingredient was the concept of freedom—how the value-loaded idea of press freedom was suddenly brought under a critical light. The address by Finland's President Kekkonen at the UNESCO symposium on TV-program flow was a typical case of freedom being problematicized or deconstructed (Nordenstreng & Varis, 1974). Powerful input to a critical look came from Herbert Schiller's (1976) account of the genesis of the U.S. free-flow doctrine as an instrument of cultural domination. A sharp look at the same issue from the South was provided by a veteran journalist in India, D.R. Mankekar, in his books *One-Way Free Flow* (1978) and *Whose Freedom? Whose Order?* (1981).

Parallel to questioning the traditional bourgeois notion of freedom, a new concept was introduced by a liberal French media expert, Jean D'Arcy: the Right to Communicate (Fisher, 1982; Fischer & Harms, 1983; Harms & Richstad, 1977). It was an attempt to meet the intellectual and political challenge of the time, with a Western human rights bias. However, it was met with only lukewarm reception in Western political circles, except in countries such as Sweden (which introduced it into UNESCO's program in 1974). Instead, it garnered increasing support in the developing world, where it was welcomed as a new collective right defending cultural sovereignty. In fact, for some time it served as a serious candidate for the leading intellectual idea in the global media debate— pushed by the East-West Center in Hawaii—but it never succeeded in reaching the same momentum as NWICO.

Obviously the Right to Communicate was bound to remain secondary to NWICO because the latter was more clearly a Third World concept —a logical extension of the New International Economic Order (NIEO). Both NIEO and NWICO had a politically powerful common denominator: the idea of self-reliance (Pavlic & Hamelink, 1985).

Because NWICO was from the beginning quite political by its nature, one easily overlooks what is perhaps the most essential in this concept: It simply locates the mass media within the framework of international law. As a matter of fact, the very concept of order was already included in the 1948 Universal Declaration of Human Rights: "Everyone is entitled to a social and international order in which the rights and freedoms set forth in this Declaration can be fully realized" (Article 28).

Therefore, an essential part of the NWICO content is composed of relevant instruments of international law. The first "inventory" of international law relating to the mass media—their freedoms and responsibilities—was done by Hilding Eek (Swedish Emeritus Professor of International Law) for the 1975 UNESCO meeting of experts to prepare the Mass Media Declaration. That report served as an eye-opener for many teachers and students of international communication, who were usually poorly read in international law. The present author was one of them and collaborated with Eek to edit it into a chapter in the reader *National Sovereignty and International Communication* (Eek, 1979). This reader (Nordenstreng & Schiller, 1979) included a whole part under the title "International Law: Codification of Fundamental Principles," with other chapters by respected U.S. authorities showing that the media and their freedom is indeed governed by a well established framework of international law. It was typical, then, that Kivikuru and Varis (1986), for example, had also a part on "legal aspects," and that there was a need for a sourcebook with a full text of relevant international instruments (Nordenstreng, Manet, & Kleinwachter, 1986). Recently Hamelink (1994) has followed the same "inventory" approach.

The actors in the NWICO debate were not only governmental bodies and academic experts, but nongovernmental organizations (NGOs) played an important role as well. The most significant NGO in NWICO matters was a loose coalition of international and regional organizations of working journalists (excluding editors and publishers), which was formed under the auspices of UNESCO in 1978 and remained active until 1990 (Nordenstreng, 1995; Nordenstreng & Topuz, 1989).

This "Consultative Club" gave first the "Mexico Declaration" in 1980 and then in 1983 issued the "International Principles of Professional Ethics in Journalism," reflecting the opinions of the majority of organized journalists in the world. Both of these documents shared the NWICO approach, and the 1983 Principles even spelled out one—the last of 10 principles—under the title "Promotion of a New World Information and Communication Order":

> The journalist operates in the contemporary world within the framework of a movement towards new international relations in general and a new information order in particular. This new order, understood as an integral part of the New International Economic Order, is aimed at the decolonization and democratization of the field of information and communication, both nationally and internationally, on the basis of peaceful coexistence among peoples and with full respect for their cultural identity. The journalist has a special obligation to promote the process of democratization of international relations in the field of information, in particular by safeguarding and fostering peaceful and friendly relations among States and peoples.

The concept of NWICO was compressed here to three sentences only, but they pretty well cover its essence. And it is worth noting that the speakers here are the nongovernmental professionals (through their representative organizations), who in many respects were more outspoken and uncompromising than respective governmental bodies such as UNESCO had been. In fact, the NWICO concept articulated in these professional principles was practically identical with the NAM version of the concept, although most of the Consultative Club members came from outside the NAM circle. This shows how pervasive and timely the concept was, at least until the early 1980s.

STAGES

Four different, although partly overlapping, stages can be discerned in the development of the global relation of forces since the early 1970s—in the field of communication policies as well as in the grand designs of world political strategies—until the late 1980s, when the fall of the Berlin Wall and the end of the Cold War opened a new chapter in history.

The first, occupying the early 1970s until 1976, was dominated by an offensive on the part of developing countries against the industrialized West, with East–West relations undergoing a calm process of détente. The second stage might be characterized as a Western counterattack of a self-defensive nature, which peaked around 1976–77. The third strategic situation emerged soon after the second and was highlighted on a number of occasions in 1978, including the adoption of the Mass Media Declaration of UNESCO. It can be described as a stage of tactical maneuvering in a spirit of compromise, or truce. The fourth stage followed soon after 1980 when Western countries took once more a course of confrontation, with corporate leadership.

The following review is based on the author's earlier works on the topic, notably *The Mass Media Declaration of UNESCO* (Nordenstreng, 1984, Ch. 1) and the *Sourcebook* (Nordenstreng et al., 1986). All quotes in the subsequent sections can be located in these sources.

Decolonization Offensive

By the early 1970s, the developing countries had accumulated a great deal of political power and economic potential, with the assistance of such organizations as NAM and OPEC. All this created a new relation of forces in the world arena, already under pressure from the socialist part of the world, leading to such manifestations as the oil crisis and the UN declaration on NIEO—all of which worked against the vested interests of the Western world order. Another corollary to this offensive of the 'underdog' against the West was a polarization of the Arab–Israeli conflict, reflected not only in a war between the parties, but also in the UN resolution by which the majority of the international community defined Zionism as a form of racism.

In this situation, it appeared that a new chapter in world history was in the making, and it was not by chance that the phrase "new order" became popular. After all, it implies a radical analysis of the world; the concept of order points at a global structure not far from Lenin's theory of imperialism (Nordenstreng, 1986). Beyond this, it suggests a radical program to change the world; the notion of new may well be interpreted as a call for war against the "old order." Consequently, the basic pattern was that the West was on the defensive, and the developing countries, supported by the socialist countries, were on the offensive.

As a political program and an intellectual concept, decolonization was well established by the early 1970s. But before 1973, the idea of decolonization was not applied in an articulated and authoritative manner to the sphere of information and culture. This occurred systematically in NAM platforms during 1976: first in a symposium on information in Tunis (April), then in a conference of information ministers in New Delhi (July), and finally in the Summit in Colombo (August).

Western Counterattack

This time a counterattack was mobilized in the West with the aid of old and new mass media lobbies and the publicity provided by the international news agencies and the commercial media themselves. Targets of attack were the Non-Aligned News Agency Pool (NANAP) and other manifestations of the information struggle in the South. This mobilization reaction also targeted UNESCO. First, a campaign was mobilized against the Intergovernmental Conference on Communication Policies in Latin America and the Caribbean, organized in San José, Costa Rica in July 1976. Later, in October–November 1976, attention was concentrated on the General Conference of UNESCO in Nairobi, Kenya, where, according to Western media coverage, the life or death of press freedom was to be determined by a draft of the Mass of Media Declaration.

The seriousness of this counteroffensive in the mass media field is indicated by the fact that it was not only a campaign waged through daily and weekly press coverage but strongly supported by committed lobby organizations such as the International Press Institute (IPI) and the Inter-American Press Association (IAPA). Furthermore, more or less academic studies and books began to appear in support of this counteroffensive (e.g., Righter, 1978). However, these conservative voices by no means dominated the community of communication research; the bulk of scholars in the field either remained uncommitted (and quite ignorant of the issues involved) or went along with the academic reorientation toward new progressive perspectives.

This counteroffensive from the West, like the previous strategic stage when the Western powers were generally on the defensive, was by no means a matter of communication politics only, but fundamentally a question of overall international politics. At this stage, the dominant Western line also became harder in a number of other issues, in which its interests were at stake—from world economy (UNCTAD and so-called North–South dialogue) to ideology (East–West relations). In particular, the Soviet–U.S. relations deteriorated from the relaxed state of détente that had dominated the first half of the 1970s.

At this time, around 1976–1977, the U.S. Senate Committee on Foreign Relations began to prepare special reports and organize hearings on the topic. To be precise, these activities were no longer typical manifestations of the second stage of a counterattack. Although certainly motivated by the same fundamental interests, they advocated a new and more flexible approach—a strategy of selective accommodation to, and active partnership with, the forces confronting the West. Especially outspoken in this respect is the Kroloff and Cohen report, which began by observing: "Whether we like it or not, there will be a 'New World Information Order,'" and continued:

> Worldwide the 'New World Information Order' could be good or bad. As the situation now stands, the United States has more to lose than any other nation as the "Order" becomes a fact. It should be noted, however, that the United States need not be a loser if appropriate actions are taken.

Indeed, the third stage of strategic designs of the 1970s was shaped very soon after the second one, but for some time it was largely masked by the loud propaganda of the second stage. In fact, before and during the General Conference of UNESCO in Nairobi in 1976—while the Western press and private broadcasting interests kept campaigning against UNESCO—Western diplomats were busy suggesting deals to the developing countries. The political purpose was to play down the draft Mass Media Declaration, which by that time had become a symbol for a consideration of the principles and contents of the mass media within an anti-Western context. To this effect, leading Western governments offered material help for the mass media infrastructures in the developing countries.

By and large, the new strategy followed the old formula: "If you cannot beat them, join them!" Also, the formula of "divide and rule" was employed in response to the fact that it had been precisely the united front of the developing countries, backed by the socialist countries, which had brought about the political defeats for the West during the first stage.

And the time proved to be opportune for this Western initiative—in general as well as in the field of communication. For a number of reasons the developing countries no longer appeared to be committed to their earlier militant stand—at least not at a high price or against lucrative offers for "help" and "cooperation." Consequently, the initiative shifted largely to the Western side, which generated various formulas for accommodation, particularly with "moderate" developing countries.

Such a strategic line was well elaborated by the time of the General Conference of UNESCO in Paris in 1978. An outspoken statement of this strategy was given by the head of the U.S. delegation, Ambassador John E. Reinhardt (an African-American), who in his address contrasted "restrictive declarations" against "positive cooperation" and made a call for "a more effective program of action," including "American assistance, both public and private, to suitably identified regional centers of professional education and training in broadcasting and journalism in the developing world," as well as "a major effort to apply the benefits of advanced communications technology, specifically communications satellites, to economic and social needs in the rural areas of developing nations." There was little new in this program, but its launching at UNESCO as a kind of political demonstration gave rise to the concept of a "Marshall Plan of Telecommunications," muted by those developing world representatives who were not quite convinced of the sincerity of U.S. intentions.

Obviously the U.S. "carrot" was designed to play down—if not bury—the Mass Media Declaration, as well as other "political" manifestations of the new order. However, the fact that the Declaration was finally adopted, only three weeks after launching this "Marshall Plan," shows that the Western strategy did not quite succeed. It did not stop the developing countries, with the help of socialist countries, from pushing "restrictive declarations." It helped the Western side only as a leverage in the bargaining process over the formulations of the Declaration. At this period of accommodation, the United States did not deploy its "stick"—for example, by threatening to withdraw from UNESCO as it had done two years before in approaching Nairobi.

A major effort in this struggle, waged according to the latest strategy of flexible accommodation and partnership, was done at the same 1978 UNESCO General Conference. The U.S. delegates, accompanied by representatives of Australia and France, joined some outstanding advocates of the developing countries (notably from moderate Sri Lanka, Tunisia, and Venezuela) in order to find a compromise between the "Marshall Plan" project and another idea put forward by the developing countries to set up a special fund at UNESCO for helping these countries in the development of their media infrastructures. The compromise reached was not far from the U.S. approach, whereby the new order is reduced to a relatively simple transfer of know-how and technology from the "information rich" to the "information poor," within an overall "free-flow" context. This led two years later to the establishment of the International Program for the Development of Communication (IPDC).

Another compromise on the same U.S.–Third World basis, adopted by consensus at the same session, concerned the International Commission for the Study of Communication Problems, which had been established in 1977—with the chairmanship of Sean MacBride—to help in overcoming the controversies accumulated around the Draft Declaration in 1975–76. This resolution appreciated the interim report that the Commission had prepared for the General Conference and invited, among other things, the members of the Commission "to address themselves, in the course of preparing their final report, to the analysis and proposal of concrete and practical measures leading to the establishment of a more just and effective world information order." Although this resolution did not contain explicit "free-flow" references, it obviously met the Western interest in alluring the developing countries to turn attention away from fundamental principles and content considerations (such as the Draft Declaration) to practical cooperation (such as the "Marshall Plan").

In this situation, it goes without saying that, when the developing countries were eager to seek a consensus, it did not mean that they simply would have sold short their principles and subscribed to a U.S.-designed position. On the contrary, neither did they turn down a historical opportunity to obtain material support for the setting up and maintenance of their media infrastructures—if not yet in terms of open checks, at least in authoritative promises. As Bogdan Osolnik (1979), who was a Yugoslavian delegate to the 1978 General Conference, put it, those advocating the new order "feel that various types of assistance are not enough and that what is needed is a fundamental restructuring of relationships, the elimination of all forms of inequality and foreign domination through the powerful media of contemporary communications" (p. 26).

Truce: Progress Through Compromise

Although the positions were divided, the compromise reached in Paris in late 1978, notably through the adoption of the Mass Media Declaration by consensus, continued to provide a framework for dialogue and even further agreements between the parties concerned. The first time the 1978 outcome of the UNESCO consensus was put to a diplomatic test was the adoption of a resolution on questions of information at the General Assembly of the United Nations in New York, only three weeks after the compromise was sealed at UNESCO. The political significance of the UN Resolution 33/115, adopted by consensus, was that the Paris formula was now endorsed by the highest authority of the international community. Under the title "International Relations in the Sphere of Information and Mass Communications," the General Assembly not only "recalled" the Mass Media Declaration and other relevant decisions of UNESCO's General Conference, but also referred to the UN resolutions concerning NIEO, as well as to the decisions and recommendations on information of NAM.

Since this resolution of December 1978, the UN General Assembly has adopted a resolution every year on questions of information, mainly endorsing the developments at UNESCO and suggesting practical measures to promote the information activities of the UN itself (through UN Information Centers, publications, radio programs, etc.). These resolutions have been prepared in the framework of a special working group, institutionalized in 1979 to a permanent UN Committee on Information. However, neither this Committee nor its parent body, the General Assembly, has performed a particularly innovative role in the NWICO process.

At UNESCO, the first landmark after the Paris compromise was in Kuala Lumpur (Malaysia), where the Intergovernmental Conference on Communication Policies in Asia and Oceania (the second regional conference after San José) met in February 1979. There the Paris formula was confirmed with the participation of not only 18 developing countries (some with quite different political orientations—from Pakistan and Indonesia to Afghanistan and Vietnam), but also 3 Western industrialized countries (Japan, Australia, and New Zealand; the United States attended only as an observer) as well as the Soviet Union and China. Moreover, this conference took a position considerably closer to the political line of the NAM than that of UNESCO's General Conference a few months before.

At this stage it became clear that support of NWICO was not limited to the intergovernmental platforms of NAM, UN, and UNESCO, but was extended to professional, academic, cultural, and even religious circles. As a matter of fact, the Pope himself appealed in June 1980 that "a new order of international relations be established on the basis of an ethics of justice, respect for the human person, recognition of the sovereignty of every nation, and solidarity." The Catholic as well as the Protestant churches regarded the ethics of communication as a particular extension of Christian ethics in general. It so happened that the original demands for a new order closely coincided with overall Christian aspirations, as demonstrated in an editorial of *Media Development* ("Toward a new international order," 1980, p. 1), the journal of the World Association for Christian Communication:

> Information and communication are much more than "commodities" or "consumer goods", a concept promoted by the West. They are essential needs for person-in-community and communities-of-persons. All people want and need to enrich their lives by sharing information and ideas with people and societies. Both content and form of communications must therefore respond to genuine communication needs of the people in a society.

Given such wide support to the primary ideas of the new order, it is not surprising that the MacBride Commission also ended up with its report *Many Voices, One World* (1980) promoting the overall approach "towards a new, more just and more efficient world information and communication order," to use the words of its subtitle. It is to be noted, however, that although the MacBride report confirmed the need for a comprehensive approach to communication problems, in which technology and infrastructures are closely linked with socio-economic policies and political principles, and in which freedom and responsibility are understood as indivisible, the concept of NWICO remained vague and indeed undefined. These weaknesses were instantly exposed by a group of academics, who were supporters of NWICO but annoyed about the MacBride report's compromising line (Hamelink, 1981).

The same critical approach exposed crucial differences of opinion between the members of the MacBride Commission itself. Thus, for example, Gabriel Garcia Marques and Juan Somavia (from Colombia and Chile, but both living in exile) made the following point in their dissenting opinion in *Many Voices, One World* (1980, p. 281):

> The insistence on the need to develop communication infrastructures in the third world countries is correct and necessary, but it should not be overstated. It is not possible to solve contemporary communication problems through money and training alone. The idea of a "Marshall Plan" for the development of third world communications is inappropriate and will tend to reproduce Western values and transnational interests in third world societies. Actions in this field should be carefully selected so as to reinforce minority power structures within third world countries or serve as a vehicle for cultural domination.

The U.S. Position.

Since Paris 1978, the destiny of NWICO became more and more of a central problem for U.S. foreign policy. This is clearly shown by a hearing on "UNESCO and freedom of information," held in the House of Representatives, Committee on Foreign Relations (Subcommittee on International Organizations), on July 19, 1979. In this forum, Reinhardt made another outspoken statement, this time as the Director of the U.S. International Communication Agency. Addressing the question, "Where is the new order going to take us?", he told the House, among other things:

> There have been some preliminary definitions issuing from the Non-Aligned Movement that, frankly, we find unacceptable. They would entail such things as a wholesale withdrawal of radio frequencies from current users, and a possible abolition of international copyright for published work entering the Third World. Here again we resist.
>
> But this resistance can and must be contained within a broader posture of creative engagement in the elaboration of the "New Order" idea. That is not simply because the idea has now been accepted by UN consensus. It is because the momentum behind the effort to redress neocolonial status in the world, to remedy historic disparities and dependencies as they are called, is in any event irresistible. Our own history and sense of mission are favorably inclined to this evolution. We might have been able to divert or defer the evolutionary pressure for a while, but eventually it would break through. And we are in far better condition to shape the future course of the "New Order" as co-architects than we would be if we were following a policy of detachment.

Thus Reinhardt still believed that it was worthwhile "to make the New World Information Order resemble as much as possible the order prevailing in our own 'new world'—the United States of America." By and large, such a line of cooperation and accommodation continued in official U.S. policy until the end of the Carter Administration (January 1981). It was supported by the outcome of the significant World Administrative Radio Conference (WARC 79) of the International Telecommunication Union (ITU), which met in Geneva from September to December 1979. WARC 79 was perceived in advance to pose to the United States a heavy "new order challenge," but "after some give-and-take, the US came away largely satisfied," as *Business Week* put it (March 3, 1980).

If the liberals went along with the NWICO movement—more or less reluctantly—the conservatives for their part became more and more vocal in their displeasure with the whole idea. As expressed by Congressman Dante B. Fascell, a "threat has emerged in international forums over the last few years as communist ideologues have combined with many Third World leaders in a concerted effort to frame what has been termed as a 'New World Information Order'" (Fascell, 1980, p. 12). *Time* magazine let it be understood that "a First Amendment war is shaping up on a global scale," since the new order, "as some Third World zealots would define it, directly threatens press freedom as Americans and Europeans conceive it" (October 6, 1980).

Moreover, there was a growing disillusionment over the feasibility of what might be called the "Reinhardt strategy," in which UNESCO occupies a central position as a forum of constructive bargaining and cooperation. The most outspoken criticism of strategy of flexible accommodation came from the British Managing Director of Reuters, Gerald Long, who delivered an illuminating speech in New York in May 1980:

> UNESCO's aims are clear: It seeks money from those countries that have developed the technology of media communications and that are for the most part committed to the view that information is an essential component of freedom and makes plans to use that money to transfer media technology to the countries that do not have it, while encouraging them to use the technology to control information for purposes of government. We are being asked to put up the money and provide the technical, human, and operational resources to spread throughout the world that very view of information that is most repugnant to us. The fact that such a program has not already been rejected out of hand shows that we would be wrong to underestimate the political skill of Unesco. (Nordenstreng, 1984, p. 44)

Despite hesitation, an International Program for the Development of Communication (IPDC) was endorsed by UNESCO's General Conference in Belgrade in October 1980, additionally "taking note of the declarations and recommendations of the Intergovernmental Conferences on Communication Policies held at San José in July 1976, Kuala Lumpur in February 1979, and Yaounde in July 1980," as well as "stressing that this international program, aiming to increase co-operation and assistance for the development of communication infrastructures and to reduce the gap between various countries in the communication field, must form part of the efforts for the establishment of a new, more just and more effective world information and communication order." For the United States IPDC was a compromise that could be seen to meet the Western interest "to de-emphasize normative prescriptions for information flows and to stress structural solutions or information imbalances—thereby promoting improved equality through conditions of freedom," as Reinhardt characterized it.

It is remarkable indeed that the United States and other leading Western powers went along with IPDC as finally formulated. After all, the outcome gave substantial ammunition to those opposing UNESCO from a conservative point of view. However, seen in a historical perspective, the West could hardly do anything but join the consensus, given its five-year-old strategy of flexible accommodation in favor of a technical assistance approach.

UNESCO in Belgrade.

The 21st session of the UNESCO General Conference in Fall 1980 was historical, not only because it formally established the IPDC, but also because it brought together all aspects of the great debate of the 1970s, including its most controversial elements concerning the conceptual and political substance of NWICO. Two resolutions, specifically related to the issue of a new information order, were passed in Belgrade. One of these was resolution on the MacBride Report. Patient and painful negotiations between and within various geopolitical groupings led to consensus around that resolution, which no doubt was politically the most significant outcome of Belgrade:

(a) This new world information and communication order could be based, among other considerations, on:

(i) elimination of the imbalances and inequalities that characterize the present situation

(ii) elimination of the negative effects of certain monopolies, public or private, and excessive concentrations

(iii) removal of the internal and external obstacles to a free flow and wider and better balanced dissemination of information and ideas

(iv) plurality of sources and channels of information

(v) freedom of the press and information

(vi) the freedom of journalists and all professionals in the communication media, a freedom inseparable from responsibility

(vii) the capacity of developing countries to achieve improvement of their own situations, notably by providing their own equipment, by training their personnel, by improving their infrastructures, and by making their information and communications media suitable to their needs and aspirations

(viii) the sincere will of developed countries to help them attain these objectives

(ix) respect for each people's cultural identity and the right of each nation to inform the world public about its interests, its aspirations and its social and cultural values

(x) respect for the right of all peoples to participate in international exchanges of information on the basis of equality, justice, and mutual benefit

(xi) respect for the right of the public, of ethnic and social groups, and of individuals to have access to information sources and to participate actively in the communication process

(b) This new world information and communication order should be based on the fundamental principles of international law as laid down in the Charter of the United Nations. (Nordenstreng, 1984, p. 49)

It is not difficult to see that, under paragraph (a), a great deal of diplomatic trading has resulted in favoring the Western "free-flow" position. However, all of these 11 points are merely "among other considerations" on which the new order *could* be based. Under Paragraph (b), however, is a brief but crucial statement on which the new order *should* be based. The latter endorses the general position that the fundamental principles of international law constitute a clearly defined basis for all international relations, including those in the field of journalism and mass communication. Accordingly, not only did all the Member States (including the United States at the time) approve the idea of defining the new order, but its overall orientation was fixed to the UN principles of international relations. This may not appear, at first glance, as a particularly significant position, but on closer examination it is the most essential element of the whole resolution.

The other resolution concerning NWICO, proposed in Belgrade somewhat unexpectedly by Venezuela, was on "measures to initiate studies necessary for the elaboration of principles related to a New World Information and Communication Order." This short document, which came to be known as the "Venezuelan resolution", begins by "recalling" the Mass Media Declaration, the recommendations of the three regional Intergovernmental Conferences, as well as other relevant resolutions of

UNESCO and the UN since 1978 and makes the point that "it would be desirable and beneficial for all sectors concerned if a clear and practical definition were drawn up of the principles and aims underlying the concept of a New World Information and Communication Order, as already expressed in various forums such as Unesco and the Non-Aligned Movement and in meetings of professional organizations." Its operative part:

> Invites the Director-General to take immediate steps to initiate studies with a view to drawing up the fundamental principles underlying a new world information and communication order and exploring the possibility and desirability of such studies serving as a basis for a Declaration on the Establishment of a New World Information and Communication Order.

Hardly revolutionary, but still the resolution met strong opposition among the Western delegations, which obviously were afraid of another unpleasant history such as the Mass Media Declaration. Yet this "time bomb" was adopted in the Program Commission by 51 votes in favor, 6 against, and 26 abstentions (those voting against were the United States, Canada, the United Kingdom, Switzerland, Japan, and New Zealand).

By and large, the balance of Belgrade (1980) repeated the main characteristics of Paris (1978): a fragile compromise with notable exceptions, surrounded by a good deal of public controversy. This time the coverage of UNESCO proceedings in the Western mass media was indeed quite heated and biased. In fact, the public response to Belgrade reflected divisions deeper than those exposed after Paris, comparable only to the fierce campaign before and during Nairobi (1976).

However, those close to the U.S. government (Carter Administration) did not express a totally skeptical view of Belgrade. For example, Sarah Goddard Power, Deputy Assistant Secretary for Human Rights and Social Affairs, made it known soon after Belgrade that "we were able to continue the process of turning Unesco away from Soviet-inspired ideological approaches to communications questions and to establish a communications development clearinghouse which institutionalized, for the first time, our practical, non-ideological approach."

The Soviet assessment of the outcome of Belgrade was, as might be expected, diametrically opposed to the U.S. point of view. Yuri Kashlev, executive secretary of the U.S.S.R. Commission for UNESCO, summarized the situation under these terms: "This was a major victory for the socialist and developing countries. The offensive against the positions of imperialism in a highly important field of ideology continues."

That this evaluation spoke not only for the Soviet Union, but reflected a wider perspective shared to a great extent by NAM, is demonstrated in a Yugoslavian review on the General Conference. Ivo Margan, Vice-

President of the Federal Executive Council, and Head of the Yugoslavian delegation to the Conference, argued that the decisions in Belgrade "rounded off ten years of work of the non-aligned movement in the struggle for the democratization of international relations, particularly in the field of information." In his analysis, the General Conference marked "a victory of the progressive and, it may be said, revolutionary approach, and the struggle of the non-aligned movement, publicly to assert in this sphere of international life the rights of individual states, as opposed to the monopoly held by a number of agencies of the advanced countries . . . effecting a form of 'information imperialism'."

Corporate Offensive

If the balance of Belgrade appears to be somewhat confused in light of the first reactions, the picture took a more definite shape during the next few months. The socialist and non-aligned positions, such as those quoted earlier, by and large remained as the final reading of that side's view on promoting the new order. But the political reaction of the leading Western powers rapidly shifted towards a neoconservative approach. A penetrating analysis from the latter point of view was offered soon after Belgrade by Rosemary Righter (1980, p. iii):

> Increased state intervention in the gathering and dissemination of news will be a reality of the 1980s. A larger role for governments is implicit in the concept of a 'new world information order', already accepted in principle by all Unesco states. That role will be further developed through the formulation of government policies mobilizing the media in the service of national unity, cultural sovereignty and political goals. News-as-instrument is coming of age.

Righter regretted the strategy of accommodation, which had placed Western countries "on the defensive, again trying to buy time." But she saw signs that "the events at Belgrade, in the aftermath, may finally provoke Western realization that it must stop this slow erosion of the freedom of the press and of the flow of news and ideas." She concluded:

> If a common Western strategy were to emerge from Belgrade, it would possibly throw in question Western participation in Unesco's communications program in all its aspects. For it was finally clear that cooperation, promised or performed, would not take the edge off the ideological challenge to the very concept of a free press.

The reaction was made even more serious by the fact that, according to a report in *The New York Times* (May 24, 1981), "Western news organizations will no longer be perceived as fighting alone in the name of press freedom and democracy" but that how "they will be allied with powerful business whose interests in maintaining the status quo are unabashedly materialistic." Moreover:

> The West had failed to understand fully that the demands were part of a broad drive to increase the developing countries' share of all resources. They seek a new economic order that would rewrite the rules of international trade and finance in their favor, the West fears. "It's not about information. It's about politics, high politics," said Peter Blaker, the British Minister for United Nations affairs.

Such reactions soon escalated into a new campaign in which "gloves come off in the struggle with UNESCO," as the title of this newspaper article reads. This time, it was not only a propaganda campaign in support of diplomatic bargaining. What happened was, rather, a fundamental change in the Western strategy—from accommodation back to confrontation. It was a historical reappraisal because ever since Nairobi (1976), and, in particular, after the Kroloff and Cohen (1977) report, the official Western approach, as recorded at UNESCO and the UN, remained fairly consistent until the end of 1980. This approach had been an integral part of the foreign policy of the Carter Administration.

The fact that Reagan took over from Carter at this stage obviously gave encouragement to a radical change in strategy—from a flexible liberal line to a hard conservative one. However, it would be too simplistic to explain the reorientation of the Western approach in terms of the change in the U.S. Administration alone. After all, the Western strategy had never been particularly coherent and united, even within the U.S. community of mass media experts. Rather, the change was due to a long-standing discord and disillusionment, which by this time had accumulated to the degree of enforcing a new offensive approach to the international information arena.

A prelude to a new stage of confrontation was displayed at UNESCO in February 1981. On that occasion, the international and regional organizations of professional journalists (the Consultative Club) were supposed to establish an international commission for the protection of journalists. The idea dates back to an initiative of the International Federation of Editors-in-Chief from 1957, and since 1970 it was promoted especially by the IPI as a response to the disappearance of 17 foreign correspondents in Cambodia (UNESCO, 1980). However, the Consultative Meeting on the Protection of Journalists, as well as a working paper prepared for it, came under heavy attack by the IPI, IAPA, the International Federation of Newspaper

Publishers (FIEJ), and the World Press Freedom Committee, supported by the government representatives of leading Western powers, particularly those from the United States. An intensive diplomatic and public campaign resulted in the admission of the "gang of four" (as the Western press organizations came to be known) in the Consultative Meeting, which then could not agree even on a modest communiqué at the end of divisive debate.

From Talloires to the White House.

Three months later—half a year after Belgrade—63 delegates from 21 countries gathered in Talloires (France) at the "Voices of Freedom Conference of Independent News Media," organized by the Tufts University's Fletcher School of Law and Diplomacy in cooperation with the World Press Freedom Committee. The organizers explained why the Talloires conference was held:

> For seven years a debate has been conducted in the councils of Unesco and other international organizations over the media and proposed curbs of press freedom. Those who advocate these controls have pressed for the creation of a so-called New World Information Order which is as yet undefined.
> In response the Free world media decided to take initiative and to announce the principles to which a free press subscribes....
> At this session for the first time Western and other free newspapers, magazines and broadcasters took a united stand against the campaign by the Soviet bloc and some Third World countries to give Unesco the authority to chart the media's future course.

Accordingly, as noted by Rosemary Righter in *The Sunday Times* (May 24, 1981), "after 10 years of losing ground in this long-simmering controversy, western governments are at last formulating a common strategy to reverse the trend towards state interference in the exchange of news and information and its content." And Talloires turned out to be something that Leonard Marks described as "the Magna Carta of the free press." In the West this was widely perceived as a relief—in the context of an understanding, perpetuated by influential Western lobbies and media, that the new order would be "a step toward Big Brother control over human lives similar to that pictured in George Orwell's frightening novel," as the *U.S. News & World Report* (June 15, 1981) put it. The outcome was the Declaration of Talloires.

As summarized by the organizers of the conference, the Talloires participants "urged to abandon attempts to regulate global information and strive instead for practical solutions to Third World media advancement." Seen in the perspective of the media debate of the 1970s, this means, first, to turn attention away from a normative consideration of the content of communication and the sociopolitical objectives that the media are supposed to serve and, second, to invite the media of the developing countries to cooperate with the private sector of the industrialized West in setting up, training, and maintaining their media infrastructure and personnel; in other words, "trading ideology against cooperation," as Rosemary Righter fittingly put it.

Thus Talloires was not a frontal attack against everything put forward by the new order movement. Rather, it was an updated version of the Marshall Plan approach that the Western powers employed at UNESCO from 1976 to 1980. It was logical, therefore, that among the Talloires participants there were some coming from the developing countries (notably such "moderates" as Jamaica, Egypt, and Malaysia).

By and large, philosophically and politically speaking, the notion of press freedom in the Talloires doctrine is virtually identical with the classic notion of free enterprise. It is natural, then, that the Talloires participants were "leaders of independent news media"—mostly owners or managers of private media enterprises and leading journalists working for them, that is, representatives of proprietors' interests, rather than professional journalists' interests.

The Declaration of Talloires ends with a statement that exposes the overall bias of the document: "Press freedom is a basic human right." This is simply not true. First, it is the individual ("everyone") and not the media ("press") that is under international law the subject and "owner" of the "right to freedom of opinion and expression." Thus freedom is granted to citizens and not to institutions such as press enterprises. Second, the human right in question "carries with it duties and responsibilities" and in no case can it be exercised contrary to the vital interests of the international community, above all the preservation of peace and security.

After Talloires, the next steps in an escalating confrontation were taken within the U.S. government. Hearings were organized by the Committee on Foreign Affairs of the U.S. House of Representatives. There the Assistant Secretary of State, Elliot Abrams, had this to say:

> We oppose interpretations of a New World Information Order which seek to make governments the arbiters of media content. We oppose interpretations which seek to place blame for current communications imbalances on the policies of Western governments and media. We oppose interpretations which seek to translate biases against the free market and free press into restrictions on Western news agencies, advertisers and journalists. Attempts to justify such restrictions as a necessary adjunct of the development process are spurious. The potential can be achieved only with freedom of choice in the information field. We reject any linkage of a New World Information Order

with the New International Economic Order and the radical restructuring of the international economic system which it includes.

The debate in the House of Representatives produced a resolution to the effect of withdrawing the U.S. contribution to UNESCO's budget (about 25% of total) "if that organization implements any policy or procedure the effects of which is to license journalists or their publications, to censor or otherwise restrict the free flow of information within or among countries, or to impose mandatory codes of journalistic practice or ethics." This "Beard amendment" received an unusually high level of support from the President of the United States. In a letter dated September 17, 1981, addressed to the Speaker of the House of Representatives, President Ronald Reagan wrote:

> We recognize the concerns of certain developing countries regarding imbalances in the present international flow of information and ideas. But we believe that the way to resolve these concerns does not lie in silencing voices nor restricting access to the means of communication, but in encouraging a broad and rich diversity of opinion. Efforts to impose restrictions on the activities of journalists in the name of issuing licenses to 'protect' them, and other restrictions of this sort that have been proposed by certain members of Unesco, are unacceptable to the United States. We strongly support—and commend to the attention of all nations—the declaration issued by independent media leaders of twenty-one nations at the Voices of Freedom Conference, which met at Talloires, France, in May of this year. We do not feel we can continue to support a Unesco that turns its back on the high purposes this organization was originally intended to serve.

Uncompromised NWICO position.

The new offensive launched under the name of Talloires was met by the advocates of NWICO with less spectacular presentations but without any notable compromising. The first reaction from the Non-Aligned Movement came only a few days after the "Voices of Freedom" had been raised in Talloires. The NAM Intergovernmental Council for the Coordination of Information happened to meet in Georgetown (Guyana) in May 1981, on which occasion the Council expressed "its full support for the activities of Unesco concerning the promotion of the New International Information Order" and, by the same token:

> rejected the simultaneous campaign of destabilization launched by Transnational Power Centers against the International Organization since the end of 1980, in the understanding that these global attacks

by the big news agencies and corporate enterprises are truly aimed at preventing the implementation of the New International Information Order and its fundamental principles, as stated in the V and VI Summit Conferences of the Non-Aligned countries in Colombo and Havana respectively.

The socialist countries of Eastern Europe were equally vocal in denouncing Talloires and expressing support to UNESCO. Reflecting the uncompromised NAM position, a Yugoslavian comment in *Review of International Affairs* (No. 760, 1981) called the Declaration of Talloires "at best surprising and an anachronism for these times . . . openly for the first time against the new international information order being sought by the non-aligned and developing countries and the immense majority of mankind they encompass." Soviet reactions displayed a more dramatic picture of the "information war" declared in Talloires—with its originators "often been caught red-handed in collaboration with the CIA," as *Moscow News* (No. 28, 1981) put it.

But it was not only the official position of NAM and the socialist countries that upheld an uncompromised position about NWICO. Also the professional journalists, through their Consultative Club representing NGOs of working journalists from all parts of the world, made it known that they rendered broad support to NWICO. At their meeting in Baghdad in early 1982, the international and regional organizations of professional journalists stressed that, although the new order is based on respect for international law and the UN Charter, it does not mean the establishment of "government censorship" or "licensing of journalists," as the Western campaign accused.

Another platform in support of NWICO at this crucial stage emerged in India under the auspices of the NAMEDIA Foundation, established by influential journalists and publishers who took the same approach as the previously quoted Mankekar. It sponsored the first NAMEDIA Conference in New Delhi in late 1983, opened by Prime Minister Indira Gandhi and addressed by NWICO veterans such as Masmoudi and MacBride. The atmosphere was uncompromised but concerned—not only because of the attack against NWICO, but more fundamentally because of the U.S. interventionist line around the world, with the latest in Nicaragua.

An outstanding demonstration of the worldwide support to NWICO among mass media professionals was the formulation of International Principles of Professional Ethics in Journalism. Issued in the name of 400,000 working journalists of the Consultative Club in November 1983—in the aftermath of the Talloires offensive—it balanced between various traditions of journalism, including the classic Western professionalism and the new Third World school associated with NWICO. Commenting these principles on behalf of the International Organization of Journalists

(IOJ), the present author said at the UN Committee on Information (New York, June 1985) and at the UNESCO General Conference in Sofia (October 1985):

> We are not afraid of combining freedom with such a responsibility that is dedicated to what might be called "United Nations ideology". As a matter of fact, speaking about freedom, we have noticed, in studying the history of French revolution and reading again the classics of libertarian thought, that the original, genuine doctrine of freedom of speech and freedom of the press was far from an abstract value void of socio-political substance. On the contrary, liberty was an ideological instrument in the hands of the raising bourgeoisie in its struggle against the old feudal order. The new information order outlined at that time for example by John Stuart Mill in his famous essay "On Liberty" determined freedom of expression to be a crucial value, not because of freedom as such, but because of its potential benefit for the common good of mankind.

At the Sofia General Conference the Consultative Club also issued a statement in the name of 400,000 working journalists throughout the world, reassuring that in their opinion UNESCO "has never suggested measures detrimental to freedom of information; on the contrary, UNESCO has contributed to a historical movement towards a higher level of freedom through its support for a new world information and communication order." This message departed sharply from the opinion of the media proprietors' NGOs (FIEJ, IPI, etc.), which had typically dominated the press coverage of UNESCO, portrayed as an enemy of freedom particularly because of its support to NWICO. Given the news value of such a statement in the middle of a mounting anti-UNESCO campaign, it even made a headline in the *International Herald Tribune*.

UPDATE

Although the concept of NWICO led an uncompromised life within the NAM as well as among many representative NGOs, its destiny in the universal intergovernmental forums of UNESCO and UN was more complicated and compromised. Along the 1980s, it became under increasingly heavy pressure from the Western governments, led by the Reagan Administration. Despite all the maneuvering and blackmail—including the U.S. and UK withdrawal from UNESCO—the concept survived until the end of the 1980s.

In 1983, UNESCO's General Conference requested the Director-General to give special attention among other activities to those:

> which will facilitate an in-depth analysis of the concept of a new world information and communication order, seen as an evolving and continuous process, so as to strengthen the bases upon which such an order conducive to a free flow and better balanced dissemination of information might be established.

This compromise formulation, adopted by consensus (including the United States), invited conceptual analysis and thus confirmed that the concept is worth pushing. However, reference to "an evolving and continuous process" implied that what was at issue is no fixed order with definite parameters but rather an overall course of development. This point, insisted by the Western side as a precondition for any reference to a new order, had come to signalize an anti-NWICO position in the political process around international communication. And yet, taken literally, the phrase could also be understood as neutral reference to an obvious state of affairs that does not necessarily compromise the original idea of NWICO.

The next General Conference of UNESCO, held in Sofia in 1985, no longer had the United States among the member states because it had withdrawn at the end of 1984. The U.S. withdrawal could not be justified on the basis of the previously-quoted "Beard Amendment" because there was no evidence of UNESCO restricting the free flow of information. It was a political decision that had more to do with a general turn away from multilateralism, that is, from the UN platforms that followed the principle: one state, one vote. The United States simply disapproved being voted down by a majority, and its departure from UNESCO was a warning signal to the international community that it may do the same in more vital bodies of the UN. As well put by a former Carter Administration official in his criticism of Reagan's move, UNESCO was "the Grenada of the UN"—referring to the U.S. invasion of that small island as a show of force.

In Sofia, a hard diplomatic struggle took place around these issues as the Western side tried to stop not only the elaboration of principles but even all studies and reflection concerning NWICO and related topics. Finally, a consensus was reached (including the United Kingdom, which soon thereafter left UNESCO), which essentially preserved the line followed throughout the 1980s. Thus, UNESCO would continue the "collection and analysis of information dealing with the development of the concept of a new world information and communication order, seen as an evolving and continuous process," while "broadening the study base when necessary." One of such activities was a symposium to review the effect of the 1978 Mass Media Declaration—an exercise carried out under this author's coordination between 1986 and 1988. This symposium served as a demonstration of how the tide was turning against NWICO and how the corporate offensive was getting more and more intensive (Nordenstreng, 1993c).

A notable chapter in the NWICO debate and struggle at this stage was the UN–UNESCO Round Table on NWICO, which was first convened in Igls (Austria) in September 1983 and a second time in Copenhagen in April 1986. It was a forum for expert discussions on the issues involved, without high-profile diplomacy or ambitions to achieve any concrete results. These occasions were indeed quite businesslike platforms, no doubt helping to demystify the political tensions and dogmatic positions that had accumulated around the topic.

A third UN–UNESCO Round Table never took place, even after the UN Committee on Information had given a green light to it. This time it was UNESCO that pulled out, around 1987, when M'Bow was replaced by Federico Mayor as its Director-General, and it became obvious that under his direction UNESCO would make a U-turn in matters of communication. Suddenly UNESCO, the earlier facilitator of NWICO debate, lost its interest in NWICO and even began to suppress the debate—resorting instead to the old "free-flow" approach.

In addition, the UN consensus was gone in the middle of 1980s, as demonstrated by the annual resolution on information: The reading in December 1985 was 121 in favor, 19 against, with 8 abstentions. Those standing against the overwhelming majority were the Western countries. Their latest tactic was to first enter consensus at UNESCO, with quite diluted political substance as a consequence of some "trading ideology against co-operation" and to then bring this consensus at the UN for ratification. There was an irony in this situation, whereby the same countries that withdrew from UNESCO or threatened to do so because of its "politicization," now insisted that UNESCO resolutions, rather than proceedings at the UN, should be the basis for discussing NWICO.

The developing countries did not fall into this trap because they realized that it is precisely the conceptual and political substance that gives them leverage as well as practical assistance. NWICO meant political currency to buy infrastructure—political currency not to be prematurely exhausted. It was obvious that there would have been no IPDC unless the movement toward NWICO, with instruments such as the Mass Media Declaration, would first have stirred up the Western interests to react with schemes such as the "Marshall Plan." So why give it up? (In reality IPDC did not succeed in mobilizing adequate assistance to meet the vast needs.)

But NWICO was not just a tactical instrument of diplomacy to turn some more money in favor of the developing countries. It was also and above all a manifestation of a fundamental course that was taking shape in the international community. Accordingly, NAM continued its traditional line with NWICO (see, e.g., NAM & NIICO, 1988). Seen in such a historical context, it was indeed "an evolving and continuous process"—until the early 1990s.

Meanwhile, a number of NGOs got together at the MacBride Round Table on Communication in Harare (Zimbabwe) in October 1989. This was a strategic move to carry on the NWICO tradition, in the "ecumenical" spirit of the MacBride Commission, as a coalition of professional and academic supporters of the idea without political pressures from governments or intergovernmental organizations. Yet NAM served as a friendly partner with Zimbabwe's Minister of Foreign Affairs addressing the Harare Round Table (the host country was at the time also President of NAM).

The MacBride Round Table was mostly an initiative of the present author—both as a social activist and as the IOJ President—and the closest collaborators in convening the first Round Table in Harare was Charles Chikerema, President of the Federation of Southern African Journalists from Zimbabwe, and Nikhil Chakravartty, President of the NAMEDIA Foundation from India. Our immediate goal was to overcome the discontinuation of the UN–UNESCO Round Table—to ensure that the NWICO debate would be carried on—but we were inspired also by a more general idea of creating NGO coalition as an expression of the grassroots voice and as a mobilizer of the professional and citizen associations in support of NWICO. Today one may see that there was indeed a general trend away from governments and official political actors toward the so-called "civil society"—not only regarding NWICO but also in several other sociopolitical matters.

In the 1990s, the NWICO debate gradually disappeared from intergovernmental platforms and remained visible only in the NGO and academic communities typically represented in the MacBride Round Table. In UNESCO, NWICO was not supposed to be even mentioned, and the UN General Assembly just recognized "the call in this context for what in the United Nations and at various international forums has been termed a new world information and communication order, seen as an evolving and continuous process" (Gerbner et al., 1993, p. xii). NAM for its part lost a good deal of steam when one of its central members, Yugoslavia, disintegrated, and the "collapse of communism" brought a fundamental change to the bipolar world where NAM had entered as the third force.

Moreover, a completely new version of the new order was introduced by President George Bush as a vision for the U.S. strategy in the post-Cold War world, particularly in the Persian Gulf War against Iraq in early 1991. Suddenly the United States was promoting the concept of a New World Order—including an information order dominated by the CNN—and the United States was not at all concerned about its "politization" or poor definition. Before this, Schiller and others had sarcastically observed that a new information order had in fact been established—by the transnational corporations. Indeed, we can say that by the early 1990s, NWICO "came about—in reverse" (Gerbner et al., 1993, p. xi). Cees Hamelink (1995, p. 31) offers a gloomy update on this development:

> The enemies of the egalitarian democratic ideal are those forces that actively shape the new world order that is currently emerging—largely in response to the collapse of Communism. The new world order poses a serious threat to the project of an egalitarian democracy since it exacerbates existing inequalities and results in a deep erosion of people's liberty to achieve self-empowerment. Since the new world order is not welcome everywhere, it also provokes a fierce opposition in forms of national, ethnic and religious fundamentalism that—ironically—equally threaten the prospect of an egalitarian democratic arrangement of world communication

All this makes the narrative of the great debate quite paradoxical. Not only did the new world order came about in reverse, but also the collapse of communism brought a tragic shift in former socialist countries: The reformist forces behind NWICO—and glasnost—were run over by emerging new corporate elites.

Yet, NWICO as an idea did not disappear. Although the political context has drastically changed, the issues involved remain more or less the same. This is obvious when reading the declarations on promoting "independent and pluralistic media," which UNESCO has produced in regional conferences since 1995 (Windhoek, Alma Ata, Santiago, and Sana'a; see UNESCO, 1996). Moreover, prospects opened by a global information society and its challenge to national sovereignty (see Nordenstreng & Schiller, 1993), instead of burying, will only revive the NWICO debate. However, it may no longer be called NWICO; the terminology and rhetoric is changing, but the substance will mostly remain and just be complemented by new elements of technological and social development. The emerging perspective under the conditions of ever-growing media concentration, on the one hand, and cultural "balkanization" of communities, on the other, is well captured by the title of the first publication of the MacBride Round Table: *Few Voices, Many Worlds* (Traber & Nordenstreng, 1992).

The latest political signals come from NAM, reminding both that this platform of the South is still alive and that it has not abandoned NWICO as a concept. The Fifth Conference of Ministers of Information of Non-Aligned Countries, held in Abuja (Nigeria) in September 1996, passed its final declaration to the UN Committee on Information (UN document A/51/372). The following two paragraphs open the section entitled "Establishment of the New World Information and Communication Order":

> The Ministers agreed that the struggle for the new world information and communication order should be intensified in spite of the end of the cold war, since the challenges and realities that informed the call for the order were still prevalent.

> The Ministers noted the continued imbalances and inequalities in the field of international information and communication. They highlighted the serious implications that the negative situation portended for non-aligned countries and stressed the urgent need to establish a new world information and communication order on the basis of the principles of independence, progress, democracy and mutual cooperation.

The XII Summit of the Non-Aligned Movement, held in Durban (South Africa) in September 1998, confirmed this position in its final document, which includes among others the following paragraphs:

> The Heads of State or Government... expressed their concern over the undisguised attempts of some countries to eliminate the concept of a new equitable world information and communication order and stressed that the establishment of a new world information and communication order aimed at ensuring impartiality and balance in the information flow, improving the information and communication infrastructure and capacity of the developing countries through the transfer of advanced information technology and expanding their access to information is more imperative than ever before, particularly for the maintenance of international peace and security.
>
> The Heads of State or Government reaffirmed their commitment to South-South cooperation in the field of information based on the principle of collective self-reliance. They recognised the profound impact that the major developments taking place in the information technology has on the economies of developing countries which will lead to furthur marginalisation in the globalised world economy... (see, e.g., Website http://southmovement.alphalink.com.au/southnews/NAM-finaldoc.htm, part on economic issues, section on information and communication, paragraphs 368 and 371).

In light of statements like this, we cannot conclude that the great media debate is over, and the ideas highlighted by the MacBride Commission (including NWICO) are dead. But the terms of the debate have changed, with globalization increasingly serving as a framework (See, e.g., Golding & Harris, 1997; Herman & McChesney, 1997). Although UNESCO has no longer played a central role in promoting the debate, the UN has produced at least one significant report: *Our Creative Diversity* (1995) by the World Commission on Culture and Development (chaired by former UN Secretary-General Javier Perez de Cuellar). Its significance, seen against the limits and possibilities for a global communication policy, is well analyzed by Raboy (1998).

Obviously, there is a lot to be learned from the great media debate—by all parties involved (the present author has drawn some conclusions in the textbook unit mentioned in the beginning of this chapter).

But equally obvious, there is no end for a global media debate; it goes on with increasingly vocal voices from the civil society channeled by NGOs such as AMARC (Community radio), Vidéazimut (alternative video) and the MacBride Round Table (policy), and inspired by initiatives such as the Cultural Environment Movement, the People's Communication Charter and a media monitoring system (Nordenstreng & Griffin, forthcoming).

REFERENCES

Bielenstein, D. (Ed.). (1979). *Toward a new world information order: Consequences for development policy*. Bonn: Institute for International Relations and Friedrich-Ebert-Stiftung.

Development Dialogue. (1976). *Information and the New International Order* (collection of papers). Uppsala: Dag Hammarskjîld Foundation.

Eek, H. (1979) Principles governing the use of the mass media as defined by the United Nations and UNESCO. In K. Nordenstreng & H. Schiller (Eds.), *National sovereignty and international communication* (pp. 173-194). Norwood, NJ: Ablex.

Fascell, D.B. (Ed.). (1980). *International news*. Beverly Hills & London: Sage.

Fisher, D. (Ed.). (1982). *The right to communicate: A status report* (Reports and Papers on Mass Communication No. 94). Paris: UNESCO.

Fisher, D., & Harms, L.S. (Eds.). (1983). *The right to communicate: A new human right*. Dublin: Boole Press.

Galtung, J., & Vincent, R.C. (1992). *Global glasnost: Toward a new world information and communication order?* Cresskill, NJ: Hampton Press.

Gerbner, G., Mowlana, H., & Nordenstreng, K. (Eds.). (1993). *The global media debate: Its rise, fall, and renewal*. Norwood, NJ: Ablex Publishing.

Golding, P., & Harris, P. (Eds.). (1997). *Beyond cultural imperialism: Globalization, communication and the new international order*. London/Thousand Oaks/New Delhi: Sage.

Hamelink, C. (Ed.). (1981). *Communication in the eighties: A reader on the MacBride Report*. Rome: IDOC International. (Reprinted in Whitney, C., Wartella, E., & Windahl, S. (Eds.), *Mass communication review yearbook* (Vol. 3, pp. 237-287). Beverly Hills/London/New Delhi: Sage, 1982.)

Hamelink, C. (1994). *The politics of world communication: A human rights perspective*. London: Sage.

Hamelink, C. (1995). The democratic ideal and its enemies. In P. Lee (Ed.), *The democratization of communication* (pp. 15-37). Cardiff: University of Wales Press.

Harms, L.S., & Richstad, J. (Eds.). (1977). *Evolving perspectives on the right to communicate.* Honolulu: East-West Center.

Herman, E. S., & McChesney, R. W. (1997). *The global media: The new missionaries of corporate capitalism.* London and Washington: Cassell.

Kivikuru, U., & Varis, T. (Eds.). (1986). *Approaches to international communication: Textbook for journalism education.* Helsinki: Finnish National Commission for Unesco.

Kroloff, G., & Cohen, S. (1977). *The New World Information Order: A report to the Committee on Foreign Relations, United States Senate* (mimeo).

Mankekar, D.R. (1978). *One-way free flow; neo-colonialism via news media.* New Delhi: Clarion Books.

Mankekar, D.R. (1981). *Whose freedom? whose order? A plea for a new international information order by Third World.* New Delhi: Clarion Books.

Many voices, one world; Communication and society, today and tomorrow. (1980). Paris: UNESCO.

NAM & NIICO. Documents of the non-aligned movement of the New international information and communication order (1986–1987). (1988). Prague: International Organization of Journalists.

Nordenstreng, K. (1984). *The mass media declaration of UNESCO.* Norwood, NJ: Ablex.

Nordenstreng, K. (1986). Defining the new international information order. In G. Gerbner & M. Siefert (Eds.), *World communications: A handbook* (pp. 28-36). New York & London: Longman.

Nordenstreng, K. (1993a). Legal status and significance. In G. Gerbner, H. Mowlana, & K. Nordenstreng (Eds.), *The global media debate* (pp. 57-67). Norwood, NJ: Ablex.

Nordenstreng, K. (1993b) New information order and communication scholarship: Reflections on a delicate relationship. In J. Wasko, V. Mosco, & M. Pendakur (Eds.), *Illuminating the blindspots: Essays honoring Dallas W. Smythe* (pp. 251-273). Norwood, NJ: Ablex.

Nordenstreng, K. (1993c). The story and lesson of a symposium In G. Gerbner, H. Mowlana, & K. Nordenstreng (Eds.), *The global media debate* (pp. 99-107). Norwood, NJ: Ablex.

Nordenstreng, K. (1995). Journalist: A walking paradox. In P. Lee (Ed.), *The democratization of communication* (pp. 114-129). Cardiff: University of Wales Press.

Nordenstreng, K., & Griffin, M. (Eds.). (1999). *International media monitoring.* Cresskill, NJ: Hampton Press.

Nordenstreng, K., Manet, E.G., & Kleinwachter, W. (1986). *New international information and communication order: Sourcebook.* Prague: International Organization of Journalists.

Nordenstreng, K., & Schiller H.I. (Eds.). (1979). *National sovereignty and international communication*. Norwood, NJ: Ablex.
Nordenstreng, K., & Schiller, H.I. (Eds.). (1993). *Beyond national sovereignty: International communication in the 1990s*. Norwood, NJ: Ablex.
Nordenstreng, K., & Topuz, H. (Eds.). (1989). *Journalist: Status, rights and responsibilities*. Prague: International Organization of Journalists.
Nordenstreng, K. & Varis, T. (1974). *Television traffic—A one-way street?* (Reports and Papers on Mass Communication No. 70). Paris: UNESCO.
Osolnik B. (1979). Unesco: The mass media declaration. *Review of International Affairs*, No. 690, 26.
Our Creative Diversity; Report of the World Commission on Culture and Development (1995). Paris: UN/UNESCO.
Pavlic, B., & Hamelink, C.J. (1985). *The new international economic order: Links between economics and communications* (Reports and Papers on Mass Communication No. 98). Paris: UNESCO.
Raboy, M. (1998). Global communication policy and the realization of human rights. *Journal of International Communication, 5*(1-2).
Richstad, J., & Anderson, M.H. (Eds). (1981). *Crisis in international news: Policies and prospects*. New York: Columbia University Press.
Righter, R. (1978). *Whose news? Politics, the press and the third world*. London: Burnett Books.
Righter, R. (1980). Unesco strengthens its programme for the press. *Intermedia*, No. 6.
Schiller, H.I. (1976). *Communication and cultural domination*. White Plains, NY: International Arts and Sciences Press.
Sreberny-Mohammadi, A., Nordenstreng, K., Stevenson, R., & Ugboajah, F. (Eds.). (1984). *Foreign news in the media: International reporting in twenty-nine countries* (Reports and Papers on Mass Communication No. 93). Paris: UNESCO.
Tinbergen, J. (1976). *RIO: Reshaping the international order—A report to the Club of Rome*. New York: Dutton.
Traber, M., & Nordenstreng, K. (Eds). (1992). *Few voices, many worlds: Towards a media reform movement*. London: World Association for Christian Communication.
Tran van Dinh (1979). Nonalignment and cultural imperialism In K. Nordenstreng & H. I. Schiller (Eds.), *National sovereignty and international communication* (pp. 261-275). Norwood, NJ: Ablex.
UNESCO (1980). *The protection of journalists* (New Communication Order No. 4). Paris: Author
UNESCO (1996). *Basic texts in communication 1989-1995*. Paris: Author.
Yadava, J.S. (Ed.). (1984). *Politics of news. Third world perspective*. New Delhi: Concept Publishing.

Yadava, J.S. (Ed.). (1984). *Politics of news. Third world perspective.* New Delhi: Concept Publishing.

14

"Many More Voices, Another World"
Looking Back at the MacBride Recommendations

with comments by

Allan Hancock and Cees J. Hamelink

In assessing how far these conclusions and recommendations have been realized since they were first formulated in 1980, we have to set them in context, as they are very much part of the political climate of their time. They came at a point when UNESCO was firmly committed to the concept of a New World Information and Communication Order and associated itself quite unequivocally with the MacBride report (however much it has since retreated from that position). Yet already within the text, there are portents of both the imminent NWICO conflict and the events of 1989.

In the introductory section, the polarities that are present throughout the Report are a discernible commitment to communication as a basic human right, linked to the concept of a free flow of information on the one hand and a causal link to planned communication policies (to bring such rights into being) on the other. It was this notion of causality that produced the original formula of a "free and balanced flow of information."

Later this became a focus for contention, leading to the series of redefinitions that were eventually brought to a close by the consensus of the 1989 General Conference of UNESCO: a 'free flow of information at international as well as national levels, and its wider and better balanced dissemination, without any obstacle to the freedom of expression.'

Throughout the text, the recommendations reflect a fragile accord (one that is confined to each principle as it is developed, rather than seeking an overall consensus on the document). The recommendations do not—and could not—fuse together to form a coherent philosophy, even a unified perception of communication. In fact, the footnotes of dissent (each mirroring an official rather than an individual position) are one of their most illuminating features.

It should be realized that the report has two audiences: one targeted, the other more general. The first audience—UNESCO and the UN system—could be expected to pay close attention to the Report's conclusions, and indeed many of its recommendations were put into effect, or at least begun to be, in subsequent years. The second audience, when it listened at all, did so selectively, picking out certain elements that were congenial and ignoring others that were not.

All this is borne out when we take the recommendations section by section.

Strengthening Independence and Self-Reliance (Recs. 1-41)

The Commission took its cue on communication policies from a longstanding UNESCO line of sectoral policy documents. These were intended as comprehensive statements of goals and strategies in its mandated fields of education, culture, and science and were normally the product of a series of regional consultations and intergovernmental policy conferences. They were very much in the tradition of centralized policy and planning, relying on intergovernmental negotiation pursued through the UN system and culminating in formal declarations of belief and intent. In practice, very few communication policies ever materialized, virtually no communication policy councils were ever formed to establish a democratic platform for discussion, and the policy statements produced by the intergovernmental conferences were mostly miscellaneous documents, 86% of whose recommendations were of an operational character (many of these being endorsements of existing institutions or strategies).

The specific recommendations made in this section (Recs. 2-4) either underwrote or highlighted favored initiatives of UNESCO and the UN. Although the recommendation on national languages rather innocently failed to anticipate the intensity of future debates on cultural diversity and the claims of minorities, it did endorse a series of projects for technology adaptation in support of linguistic work, that continued for a number of years in UNESCO (especially computerized adaptations). The emphasis on "education for all" was a clear forerunner of the basic education program that was the theme of the 1990 Jomtien Conference and has recently had its most articulate expression in "Learning: The Treasure Within" (the Report of the International Commission on Education for the 21st Century, chaired by Jacques Delors). The Delors Report makes it clear, however, how remote the goals of eradicating illiteracy still are.

---

1. Strengthening Independence and Self-Reliance
Communication Policies
All individuals and people collectively have an inalienable right to a better life that, howsoever conceived, must ensure a social minimum nationally and globally. This calls for the strengthening of capacities and the elimination of gross inequalities; such defects may threaten social harmony and even international peace. There must be a measured movement from disadvantage and dependence to self-reliance and the creation of more equal opportunities. Since communication is interwoven with every aspect of life, it is clearly of the utmost importance that the existing "communication gap" be rapidly narrowed and eventually eliminated.

We recommend:
1. Communication be no longer regarded merely as an incidental service and its development left to chance. Recognition of its potential warrants the formulation by all nations, and particularly developing countries, of comprehensive communication policies linked to overall social, cultural, economic and political goals. Such policies should be based on inter-ministerial and interdisciplinary consultations with broad public participation. The object must be to utilize the unique capacities of each form of communication, from interpersonal and traditional to the most modern, to make people and societies aware of their rights, harmonize unity in diversity, and foster the growth of individuals and communities within the wider frame of national development in an interdependent world.

2. As language embodies the cultural experience of people all languages should be adequately developed to serve the complex and diverse requirements of modern communication. Developing nations and multilingual societies need to evolve language policies that promote all national languages even while selecting some, where necessary, for more widespread use in communication, higher education and administration. There is also need in certain situations for the adaptation, simplification, and standardization of scripts and development of key-

boards, preparation of dictionaries and modernized systems of language learning, transcription of literature in widely-spoken national languages. The provision of simultaneous interpretation and automated translation facilities now under experimentation for cross-cultural communication to bridge linguistic divides should also be envisaged.

3. A primary policy objective should be to make elementary education available to all and to wipe out illiteracy, supplementing formal schooling systems with non-formal education and enrichment within appropriate structures of continuing and distance learning (through radio, television and correspondence).

4. Within the framework of national development policies, each country will have to work out its own set of priorities, bearing in mind that it will not be possible to move in all directions at the same time. But, as far as resources allow, communication policies should aim at stimulating and encouraging all means of communication.

Strengthening Capacities (Recs. 5-10)

Although it is debatable to what extent the international system, and individual governments, took note of these recommendations, they had a very specific echo in UNESCO: beginning with the intergovernmental conference held in Paris in 1980, that led to the creation of the International Program for the Development of Communication (IPDC). The Intergovernmental Conference on Activities, Needs and Programs for Communication Development—a cumbersome title, commonly abbreviated to DEVCOM—actually took place in April 1980, before the Twenty-First Session of UNESCO's General Conference endorsed the conclusions of the MacBride Commission. But the Commission's meetings, papers produced by its members, and especially the controversy surrounding the limited interim version of the Report all fueled the debate on UNESCO's future communication program.

The IPDC has had a checkered history (its funding has been largely inadequate, especially its core instrument, the Special Account); nevertheless, over a decade and a half it has been the most notable and visible mechanism in support of developing country communication channels. For most of its history, it has also been treated as a protected reserve, allowed to develop outside political controversy (with one exception being the production of the first World Communication Report, that led to a vote on the Report's List of Contents, carried out by roll call so as to identify publicly the position of each Council member).

However, the recommendations in this section, which are outside the competence or influence of the international system, have fared less favorably (the appeal to let radio take priority over television is a particular case in point).

Strengthening Capacities
Communication policies should offer a guide to the determination of information and media priorities and to the selection of appropriate technologies. This is required to plan the installation and development of adequate infrastructures to provide self-reliant communications capacity.

We recommend:
5. Developing countries take specific measures to establish or develop essential elements of their communication systems: print media, broadcasting and telecommunications along with the related training and production facilities.

6. Strong national news agencies are vital for improving each country's national and international reporting. Where viable, regional networks should be set up to increase news flows and serve all the major language groups in the area. Nationally, the agencies should buttress the growth of both urban and rural newspapers to serve as the core of a country's news collection and distribution system.

7. National book production should be encouraged and accompanied by the establishment of a distribution network for books, newspapers and periodicals. The stimulation of works by national authors in various languages should be promoted.

8. The development of comprehensive national radio networks, capable of reaching remote areas should take priority over the development of television, that, however, should be encourage where appropriate. Special attention should be given to areas where illiteracy is prevalent.

9. National capacity for producing broadcast materials is necessary to obviate dependence on external sources over and beyond desirable program exchange. This capacity should include national or regional broadcasting, film and documentary production centers with a basic distribution network.

10. Adequate educational and training facilities are required to supply personnel for the media and production organizations, as well as managers, technicians and maintenance personnel. In this regard, co-oper-

ation between neighboring countries and within regions should be encouraged.

Basic Needs (Recs. 11-18)

These recommendations were drawn from, and in their turn nurtured, a vigorous communication debate mobilized by the nongovernmental community, research associations, religious organizations, and many independent programs. Development support communication was initiated, not in UNESCO, but in UNDP and FAO (with Erskine Childers's original Project Support Communication unit in Bangkok shaping its parameters and the FAO Development Support Communication unit active along parallel but distinctive lines). The development support communication dialogue has continued, sometimes fitfully, in the years since MacBride, in particular, through a series of Round Tables working for improved interagency coordination—the latest taking place in 1998 (not to be confused with the series of Round Tables on the MacBride Report!)

Community media, and the community press in particular, attracted the greatest attention and were a special preserve of UNESCO. They still form a significant part of UNESCO's communication program (the emphasis is now on community radio) and—like many operational projects—have survived political vicissitudes because they respond to a basic dilemma of modern communications technology—how to address and involve small, community-based audiences when the principal raison d'etre of the media is to provide a mass audience vehicle, profiting from economies of scale. There has been a recurrent return to concepts of alternative media (in many ways seen as clones of alternative technologies and alternative development strategies) in an attempt to resolve this dilemma. There is also a strong, often didactic literature on community channels, including the many attempts to provide access channels as part of mass media systems, rather than looking for an alternative framework. All this has been regularly supported within the IPDC, perhaps even more so by UNESCO's Regular Program (that has been over the years a flexible vehicle for innovative piloting and experiment). The dilemma remains unresolved, however, and currently more hopes for reconciling individual or community aspirations and the mass audience are invested in forms of electronic access.

The principle of media education was taken up with enthusiasm by UNESCO (building on a strong tradition already in existence in a number of Western countries, including the United Kingdom, France, and Australia, and leading to various publications and an international conference held in France in 1990). But the UNESCO initiative was cut short by the mistrust of media education activities expressed at the time of the 1989 UNESCO General Conference, when, in searching for a consensus on how to eliminate the NWICO concept and terminology, media education was held by the professionals to be overcritical of their interests.

It is Recommendation 18 that appears to date the text most obviously. Throughout the MacBride report a dominant motif is that responsible communication development must come about through political decision making; investment finance will contribute, if at all, through tax levies. In the event, communication development, responsible or not, has mostly been funded commercially, with the financiers holding an equity in media infrastructures, usually as part of mixed ownership and consortium financing patterns, integrating the media into overall product and service development strategies. This could not have been foreseen at the time of the MacBride Commission (or if foreseen, would have been considered avoidable, and vigorously deplored). Even the idea of using low-cost communication technologies (Rec 14) was treated as a means of promoting community participation, and not (as it eventually turned out) as a spinoff from popular technology production for domestic, small business and entertainment uses. UNESCO has continued with the low-cost technology agenda, but with limited results (nevertheless, some of its initiatives, like low-cost FM transmitters, have had a decided impact on community radio).

Basic Needs

All nations have to make choices in investment priorities. In choosing between possible alternatives and often conflicting interests, developing countries, in particular, must give priority to satisfying their people's essential needs. Communication is not only a system of public information, but also an integral part of education and development.

We recommend:

11. The communication component in all development projects should receive adequate financing. So-called "development support communications" are essential for mobilizing initiatives and providing information required for action in all fields of development - agriculture, health and family planning, education, religion, industry and so on.

12. Essential communication needs to be met include the extension of basic postal services and telecommunication networks through small rural electronic exchanges.

13. The development of a community press in rural areas and small towns would not only provide print support for economic and social extension activities . This would also facilitate the production of functional literature for neo-literates as well.

14. Utilization of local radio, low-cost small format television and video systems and other appropriate technologies would facilitate production of programs relevant to community development efforts, stimulate participation and provide opportunity for diversified cultural expression.

15. The educational and informational use of communication should be given equal priority with entertainment. At the same time, education systems should prepare young people for communication activities. Introduction of pupils at primary and secondary levels to the forms and uses of the means of communication (how to read newspapers, evaluate radio and television programs, use elementary audio-visual techniques and apparatus) should permit the young to understand reality better and enrich their knowledge of current affairs and problems.

16. Organization of community listening and viewing groups could in certain circumstances widen both entertainment and educational opportunities. Education and information activities should be supported by different facilities ranging from mobile book, tape and film libraries to programmed instruction through "schools of the air".

17. Such activities should be aggregated wherever possible in order to create vibrant local communication resource centers for entertainment, education, information dissemination and cultural exchange. They should be supported by decentralized media production centers; educational and extension services should be location specific if they are to be credible and accepted.

18. It is not sufficient to urge that communication be given a high priority in national development; possible sources of investment finance must be identified. Among these could be differential communication pricing policies that would place large burdens on more prosperous urban and elite groups; the taxing of commercial advertising may also be envisaged for this purpose.

Particular Challenges (Recs. 19-21)

These challenges reflect a specific agenda, very topical within the UN system, that depended ultimately upon the involvement of the transnational corporations. The idea of using kenaf, for example, as an alternative source for paper production was much touted among the press associations (notably FIEJ), and led to a minor IPDC project, but not much more. The idea of telecommunications tariff reduction had a longer and more formal history, as a combined initiative of UNESCO and the ITU. A working group met in 1979/1980, and was followed by some regional meetings, but a full report on the issue was not published until 1986. A global satellite experimental project did much to create a basis for interregional broadcasting exchanges and the ITU (Maitland) Report, 'The Missing Link' (1985) highlighted the Third World's difficulties. The Maitland report recommended more investment in telecommunications in developing countries and more resources for training and transfer of technology. Higher priority had to be given to investment in telecommunications; the effectiveness of existing systems had to be improved; financing arrangements had to recognize that foreign exchange is scarce in many developing countries, and the ITU should play a more effective role in this field. In response the ITU established the Centre for Telecommunications Development (CTD) in 1985, that was expected to contribute in a significant way to telecommunications development. However, it failed to meet this expectation, to a considerable degree because of the limited and sporadic funding that it received.

Successive WARC conferences (World Administrative Radio Conferences, where frequency allocation takes place) did little to make the distribution of the electromagnetic spectrum more equitable; the ITU was too politicized, and telecommunications was too well recognized, by the eighties, as having major economic significance for the future. Some initial concern shown by the telecommunications industry produced funding for development projects through PROJECT SHARE; this has now been transformed into such approaches as sponsorship, the offer of funding or subsidy to selected educational projects in developing countries, or the kind of partnership arrangement proposed by the World Bank in its INFODEV project (a project fund based on industrial support and matching finance). While the ITU and UNESCO, together with other UN agencies, are again meeting in working groups to consider the social consequences of the new information and communication technologies, developmental needs and even the communication rights that these involve, UNESCO's operational program is more cautious: it speaks of 'advice on the appropriate conditions for access to telecommunications facilities for educational purposes, taking account of both market considerations and developmental priorities'

(UNESCO Approved Program and Budget for 1996-1997).

Particular Challenges

We have focused on national efforts that must be made to lead to greater independence and self-reliance. But there are three major challenges to this goal that require concerted international action. Simply put, these are paper, tariff structures and the electro-magnetic spectrum.

We recommend:
19. A major international research and development effort to increase the supply of paper. The worldwide shortage of paper, including newsprint and its escalating cost impose crushing burdens upon struggling newspapers, periodicals and the publication industry, above all in the developing countries. Certain ecological constraints have also emerged. UNESCO, in collaboration with FAO, should take urgent measures to identify and encourage production of paper and newsprint either by recycling paper or from new sources of feedstock in addition to the wood pulp presently produced largely by certain northern countries. Kenaf, bagasse, tropical woods and grasses could possibly provide alternative sources. Initial experiments are encouraging and need to be supported and multiplied.

20. Tariffs for new transmission, telecommunication rates and air mail charges for the dissemination of news, transport of newspapers, periodicals, books and audio-visual materials are one of the main obstacles to a free and balanced flow of information. This situation must be corrected, especially in the case of developing countries, through a variety of national an international initiatives. Governments should in particular examine the policies and practices of their post an telegraph authorities. Profits or Revenues should not be the primary aim of such agencies. They are instruments for policy-making and planned development in the field of information culture. Their tariffs should be in line with larger national goals. International action is also necessary to alter telecommunication tariffs that militate heavily against small and peripheral users. Current international consultations on this question may be brought to early fruition, possibly at the October 1980 session of the 154 nation International Telegraph and Telephone Consultative Committee, that should have before it specific proposals made by a UNESCO-sponsored working group on "Low Telecommunication Rates" (November 1979). UNESCO might, in cooperation with ITU also sponsor an overall study on international telecommunications services by means of satellite transmission in collaboration with Intelsat, Intersputnik and user country representatives to make proposals for international and regional co-ordination or geostationary satellite development. The study should also include investigation of the possibility and practicalities of discounts for transmission of news and preferential rates for certain types of transmission to and from developing countries. Finally, developing countries should investigate the possibility of negotiating preferential tariffs on bilateral or regional basis.

21. The electro-magnetic spectrum and geostationary orbit, both finite natural resources, should be more equitably shared as the common prop-

erty of mankind. For that purpose, we welcome the decisions taken by the World Administrative Radio Conference (WARC), Geneva, September-November 1979, to convene a series of special conferences over the next few years on certain specific topics related to the utilization of these resources.

SOCIAL CONSEQUENCES AND NEW TASKS

Integrating Communication into Development (Recs. 22-23)

Recommendation 22 was directed more toward UNDP than UNESCO and was planted in fertile ground. Up to the end of the 1970s, (under pressure from Erskine Childers' Development Support Communication Service), for a time communication was indeed identified as an essential component of development projects. However, UNDP shifted ground shortly afterward, and the concept has never been seriously considered by the World Bank. It was left for UNESCO, FAO, and significantly UNICEF to continue the tradition. At the end of the decade, when the "Human Development Report" was conceived, UNDP returned to many of its earlier values, but even then communication was not singled out. Only in the public information field (Para 23), and in the practice of news agencies like the Inter Press Service, was there continuity of effort, in part because the recommendation had been tailormade for its implementers.

Integrating Communication into Development
Development strategies should incorporate communication policies as an integral part in the diagnosis of needs and in the design and implementation of selected priorities. In this respect communication should be considered a major development resource, a vehicle to ensure real political participation in decisionmaking, a central information base for defining policy options, and an instrument for creating awareness of national priorities.

We recommend:
22. Promotion of dialogue for development as a central component of both communication and development policies. Implementation of national policies should be carried out through three complementary communication patterns; first, from decision-makers towards different social sectors to transmit information about what they regard as necessary changes in development actions, alternative strategies and the varying

consequences of the different alternatives; second, among and between diverse social sectors in a horizontal information network to express exchange views on their different demands, aspirations, objective needs and subjective motivations; third, between decision-makers and all social groups through permanent participatory mechanisms for two-way information flows to elaborate development goals and priorities and make decisions on utilization of resources. Each one of these patterns requires the design of specific information programs, using different communication means.

23. In promoting communication policies, special attention should be given to the use of non-technical language and comprehensible symbols, images and forms to ensure popular understanding of development issues and goals. Similarly, development information supplied to the media should be adapted to prevailing news values and practices, that in turn should be encouraged to be more receptive to development needs and problems.

Facing the Technological Challenge (Recs. 24-27)

Although there was a good deal of research interest in the social consequences of the new information technologies (including an international program of research studies orchestrated regionally by UNESCO), their results were no more than marginally incorporated in technology design. In the communication field, little was done at a national, governmental level; development was left primarily to industry and the multinationals, with governments entering the picture only at the point of approval or regulation. For most of the 1980s deregulation was the norm, and it was only in the 1990s, as a counterreaction to experience, that a more sensitive approach to regulation was achieved.

The monopoly situation referred to by Recommendation 27 both intensified and became more complex (even when the report was written, it was more complex than it appeared, with technology development often the result of protected defence applications). Legislative reform, when it occurred, was rarely in the interests of developing countries. Only those countries that managed to scramble on to the backs of the industrialized nations, transforming themselves (through advantageous marketplaces and labor forces) into a second-tier status, accommodated to the world system. The poorer countries, and virtually the whole of Africa, have seen the gap between them and the industrialized countries widen further.

Facing the Technological Challenge

The technological explosion in communication has both great potential and great danger. The out come depends on crucial decisions and on where and by whom they are taken. Thus, it is a priority to organize the decision-making process in a participatory manner on the basis of a full awareness of the social impact of different alternatives.

We recommend:

24. Devising policy instruments at the national level in order to evaluate the positive and negative social implications of the introduction of powerful new communication technologies. The preparation of technological impact surveys can be a useful tool to assess the consequences for life-styles, relevance for under-privileged sectors of society, cultural influence, effects of employment patterns and similar factors. This is particularly important when making choices with respect to the development of communication infrastructures.

25. Setting up national mechanisms to promote participation and discussion of social priorities in the acquisition or extension of new communication technologies. Decisions with respect to the orientation given to research and development should come under closer public scrutiny.

26. In developing countries the promotion of autonomous research and development should be linked to specific projects and programs at the national, regional and inter-regional levels, that are often geared to the satisfaction of basic needs. More funds are necessary to stimulate and support adaptive technological research. This might also help these countries to avoid problems of obsolescence and problems arising from the non-availability of particular types of equipment, related spare parts and components from the advance industrial nations.

27. The concentration of communications technology in a relatively few developed countries and transnational corporations has lead to a virtual monopoly situations in this field. To counteract these tendencies and international measures are required, among them reform of existing patent laws and conventions, appropriate legislation and international agreements.

Strengthening Cultural Identity (Recs. 28-30)

Perhaps the logical outcome of these recommendations (or at least an evaluation of their worth) is the publication of the Report of the World

Commission on Cultural Development "Our Creative Diversity" in 1996. Even at the time of the MacBride Report, there was much ambiguity in the understanding of communication as opposed to cultural policies. The ambiguity was itself culturally founded; there were those nations, essentially Latin, to whom culture was a main descriptor of social processes (and for whom communication was defined as a cultural industry), whereas other nations (essentially Anglo-Saxon) had a less far-reaching conception of culture.

The Report of Perez de Cuellar's World Commission treats communication quite extensively and updates thinking on many of the issues raised by the MacBride Report. This is not surprising because the perspective of the Perez De Cuellar report is holistic: It sees development as vectored by culture, with cultural processes as forces that search out unity in diversity and pluralism. In contrast the remarks made by the MacBride Commission on advertising content and practices read like an early agenda-setting exercise, a prelude to a debate that has since widened in the face of forms and techniques of advertising that the Commission would have had difficulty in predicting.

Strengthening Cultural Identity

Promoting conditions for the preservation of the cultural identity of every society is necessary to enable it to enjoy a harmonious and creative inter-relationship with other cultures. It is equally necessary to modify situations in many developed and developing countries that suffer from cultural dominance.

We recommend:

28. Establishment of national cultural policies that should foster cultural identity and creativity and involve the media in these tasks. Such policies should also contain guidelines for safeguarding national cultural development while promoting knowledge of other cultures. It is in relation to others that each culture enhances its own identity.

Comment by Mr. S. MacBride:

"I wish to add that owing to the cultural importance of spiritual and religious values and also in order to restore moral values, policy guidelines should take into account religious beliefs and traditions."

29. Communication and cultural policies should ensure that creative artists and various grassroots groups can make their voices heard through the media. The innovative uses of film, television or radio by people of different cultures should be studied Such experiments constitute a basis for continuing cultural dialogue, that could be furthered by agreements between countries and through international support.

30. Introduction of guidelines with respect to advertising content and the values and attitudes it foster in accordance with national standards and practices. Such guidelines should be consistent with national development policies and efforts to preserve cultural identity. Particular attention should be given to the impact of children and adolescents. In this connection, various mechanisms such as complaint boards or consumer review committees might be established to afford the public the possibility of reacting against advertising that they feel inappropriate.

Reducing the Commercialization (Recs. 31-33)

These recommendations are perhaps the least recognizable in today's media landscape. Everywhere public communication systems are under siege, compelled to find new revenue sources that, if not directly commercial, are service driven. This is not to say that in a number of societies measures have not been taken to favor voluntary contributions, provide tax incentives, and so on, but their impact has been limited and mostly retroactive. Future trends are more likely to emphasize sponsorship and lottery contributions, with traditional sources of funding (e.g., licensing) declining further. The comment by Elie Abel is very much a precursor of this situation.

Reducing the Commercialization of Communication

The social effects of the commercialization of the mass media are a major concern in policy formulation and decision-making by private and public bodies.

We recommend:
31. In expanding communication systems, preference should be given to non-commercial forms of mass communication. Promotion of such types of communication should be integrated with the traditions, culture, development objectives and socio-political system of each country. As in the field of education, public funds might be made available for this purpose.

32. While acknowledging the need of the media for revenues, ways and means should be considered to reduce the negative effects that the influence of market and commercial considerations have in the organization and content of national and international communication flows.

Comment by Mr. E. Abel: "At no time has the commission seen evidence adduced in support of the notion that market and commercial considerations necessarily exert a negative effect on communication flows. On the contrary the commission has praised elsewhere in this report courageous investigative journalism of the sort that can be sustained only by independent media whose survival depends upon their acceptance in the marketplace, rather than the favors of political leaders. The commission also is aware that market mechanisms play an increasingly important role today even in so-called planned economics."

> 33. That consideration be given to changing existing funding patterns of commercial mass media. In this connection, reviews could be made of the way in that the relative role of advertising volume and costs pricing policies, voluntary contributions, subsidies, taxes, financial incentives and supports could be modified to enhance the social function of mass media and improve their service to the community.

Access to Technical Information (Recs. 34-38)

Access to technical information is not purely a matter of principle: For access to be effective, it must include infrastructures and especially the ability to process a volume of information that is increasing exponentially. Since 1989, the volume of technical information flow has increased enormously, especially between the West and East, including much historical and scientific information that had earlier been protected. The nature and organization of the information that exists on the Internet would have been unrecognizable to the MacBride Commission, as would the anarchic structure within that it circulates (quite the opposite of information and communication policies). The current debate is more about supervising access to technical information (and restricting various kinds of offensive or potentially harmful information) than it is about accessibility.

Many of the ideas founded on national structures and frontiers are clearly no longer as relevant as they were to the MacBride Commission: Technically, at least, they have been bypassed. Just as limiting however are constraints created by economic conditions, status, and the costs of intercommunication.

Access to Technical Information

The flow of technical information within nations and across national boundaries is a major resource for development. Access to such information, that countries need for technical decision-making at all levels, is as crucial as access to news sources. This type of information is generally not easily available and is most often concentrated in large techno-structures. Developed countries are not providing adequate information of this type to developing countries.

We recommend:

34. Developing countries should pay particular attention to: (a) the correlation between education, scientific and communication policies, because their practical application frequently overlaps; (b) the creation in each country of one or several centers for the collection and utilization of technical information and data, both from with the country and from abroad; (c) to secure the basic equipment necessary for essential data processing activities; (d) the development of skills and facilities for computer processing and analysis of data obtained from remote sensing.

35. Developed countries should foster exchanges of technical information on the principle that all countries have equal rights to full access to available information. It is increasingly necessary, in order to reduce inequalities in this field, to promote co-operative arrangements for collection, retrieval, processing and diffusion of technological information through various networks, regardless of geographical or institutional frontiers. UNISIST, that provides basic guidelines for voluntary co-operation among and between information systems and services, should further develop its activities.

36. Developing countries should adopt national informatics policies as a matter of priority. These should primarily relate to the establishment of decision-making centers (inter-departmental and inter-disciplinary) that would inter alia (a) assess technological alternatives: (b) centralize purchases; (c)encourage local production of software; (d) promote regional and sub-regional co-operation (in various fields, including education, health and consumer services).

37. At the international level, consideration should be given to action with respect for (a) systematic identification of existing organized data processing infrastructures in various specialized fields; (b) agreement on measures for effective multi-county participation in the programs, planning and administration of existing or developing data infrastructures; (c) analysis of commercial and technical measures likely to improve the use of informatics by developing countries; (d) agreement of international priorities for research and development that is of interest to all countries in the field of informatics.

38. Transnational corporations should supply to the authorities of the countries in that they operate, upon request and on a regular basis as specified by local laws and regulations, all information required for legislative and administrative purposes relevant to their activities and specifically needed to assess the performance of such entities. They should

also provide the public, trade unions and other interested sectors of the countries in that they operate with information needed to understand the global structure, activities and policies of the transnational corporation and their significance for the country concerned.

PROFESSIONAL INTEGRITY AND STANDARDS

Responsibility of Journalists (Recs. 39-43)

The battle against NWICO was fought primarily by (and between) two groups: journalists and politicians. It was a preview of a battle that is being contested just as fiercely today, with the proliferation of media agendas in political life. In reality, the polarities confronted by NWICO—free flow and balance, freedom and responsibility—are perennial themes in the media and democracy debate. Under the Chairmanship of Sean MacBride (with a number of journalists also on the Commission) it is not surprising that detailed attention was paid to journalistic issues, and it is probably in this field that the greatest progress has been made (certainly in UNESCO, in which the professional debate has dominated activities in the communication sector).

The content of Recommendation 39 may remain valid in some societies, but overall the status of the journalist has been enormously enhanced (even if status is not necessarily synonymous with social standing). This set of recommendations nonetheless describes an ideal environment, that may be encountered in the course of journalism education programs, but is clearly fragmented in reality.

At the same time, it is important to note the emphasis placed on these recommendations on voluntary codes and councils (part of the consensus that was already being formed within the Commission to reconcile the professionals and the politicians, at a time when the real hostilities of the NWICO debate had not yet begun).

Responsibility of Journalists

For the journalist, freedom and responsibility are indivisible. Freedom without responsibility invites distortion and other abuses. But in the absence of freedom there can be no exercise of responsibility. The concept of freedom with responsibility necessarily includes a concern for professional ethics, demanding an equitable approach to events, situations or processes with due attention to their divers aspects. This is not always the case today.

LOOKING BACK AT THE MACBRIDE RECOMMENDATIONS

We recommend:

39. The importance of the journalist's mission in the contemporary would demands steps to enhance his standing in society. In many countries even today, journalists are not regarded as members of an acknowledged profession and they are treated accordingly. To overcome this situation, journalism needs to raise its standards and quality for recognition everywhere as a genuine profession.

40. To be treated as professionals, journalists require broad educational preparation and specific professional training. Programs of instruction need to be developed not only for entry-level recruits, but also for experienced personnel who from time to time would benefit from special seminars and conferences designed to refresh and enrich their qualifications. Basically, programs of instruction and training should be conducted on national and regional levels.

41. Such values as truthfulness, accuracy and respect for human rights are not universally applied at present. Higher professional standards and responsibility cannot be imposed by decree, nor do they depend solely on the goodwill of individual journalists, who are employed by institutions that can improve or handicap their professional performance. The self-respect of journalists, their integrity and inner drive to turn out work of high quality are of paramount importance. It is this level of professional dedication, making for responsibility, that should be fostered by news media and journalists' organizations. In this framework, a distinction may have to be drawn between media institutions, owners and managers on the one hand, and journalists on the other.

42. As in other professions, journalists and media organizations serve the public directly and the public, in turn, is entitled to hold them accountable for their actions. Among the mechanisms devised up to now in various countries for assuring accountability, the Commission sees merit in press or media councils, the institution of the press ombudsman and peer group criticism of the sort practiced by journalism reviews in several countries. In addition, communities served by particular media can accomplish significant reforms through citizen action. Specific forms of community involvement in decision-making will vary, of course, from country to country. Public broadcasting stations, for example can be governed by representative boards drawn from the community. Voluntary measures of this sort can do much to influence media performance. Nevertheless, it appears necessary to develop further effective ways by that the right to assess mass media performance can be exercised by the public.

43. Codes of professional ethics exist in all parts of the world, adopted voluntarily in many countries by professional groups. The adoption of codes of ethics at national and in some cases, at the regional level is desirable, provided that such codes are prepared and adopted by the profession itself—without governmental interference.

Toward Improved International Reporting (Recs. 44-49)

The operational base for the recommendations in this section has been transformed by a satellite-based news revolution that was unforeseen (at least in its magnitude) at the time of the MacBride Commission, and that replaced, in fairly short order, the traditional pattern of nationally assigned foreign correspondents reporting on their country of assignment. The arrival of CNN and the emergence of parallel systems such as BBC Worldwide changed the organizational basis of international television; the fall of the Berlin Wall achieved the rest. Major problems today lie not so much in the reporting of the industrialized world as a whole, but reflect differences within industrialized broadcasting systems, in which certain networks have international interests and others are almost exclusively domestic by virtue of their target audiences.

Towards Improved International Reporting

The full and factual presentation of news about one country to others is a continuing problem. The reasons for this are manifold; principal among them are correspondents' working conditions, their skills and attitudes, varying conceptions of news and information values and government viewpoints. Remedies for the situation will require long-term, evolutionary action towards improving the exchange of news around the world.

We recommend:
44. All countries should take steps to assure admittance of foreign correspondents and facilitate their collection and transmission of news. Special obligations in this regard, undertaken by the signatories to the Final Act of the Helsinki conference, should be honored and, indeed liberally applied. Free access to news sources by journalists is an indispensable requirement for accurate, faithful and balanced reporting. This necessarily involves access to unofficial, as well as official sources of information, that is, access to the entire spectrum of opinion within any country.

Comment by Mr. S. Losev:
This paragraph doesn't correspond to the Helsinki Final Act [see section 2—information, point (c)], contradicts the interests of developing nations, and therefore is completely unacceptable and I object to it being included. I suggest replacing this recommendation with the following text: "all countries should take appropriate measures to improve the conditions for foreign correspondents to carry out their professional activities in the host countries in accordance with the provisions of the Helsinki Final Act and with due respect to the national sovereignty and the national identity of the host country."

45. Conventional standards of news selection and reporting, and many accepted news values, need to be reassessed if readers and listeners around the world are to receive a more faithful and comprehensive account of events, movements and trends in both developing and developed countries. The inescapable need to interpret unfamiliar situations in terms that will be understood by a distant audience should not blind reporters or editors to the hazards of narrow ethnocentric thinking. The first step towards overcoming this bias is to acknowledge that it colors the thinking of virtually all human beings, journalists included, for the most part without deliberate intent. The act of selecting certain news items for publication while rejecting others, produces in the minds of the audience a picture of the world that may well be incomplete or distorted. Higher professional standards are needed for journalists to be able to illuminate the divers cultures and beliefs of the modern world, without their presuming to judge the ultimate validity of any foreign nation's experience and traditions.

46. To this end, reporters being assigned to foreign posts should have the benefit of language training and acquaintance with the history, institutions, politics, economics and cultural environment of the country or region in that they will by serving.

47. The press and broadcasters in the industrialized world should allot more space and time to reporting events in and background material about foreign countries in general and news from the developing world in particular. Also, the media in developed countries—especially the "gatekeepers," editors and producers of print and broadcasting media who select the news items to be published or broadcast—should become more familiar with the cultures and conditions in developing countries. Although the present imbalance in news flow calls for strengthening capacities in developing countries, the media of the industrialized countries have their contribution to make towards the correction of these inequalities.

48. To offset the negative effects of inaccurate of malicious reporting of international news, the right of reply and correction should be further considered. While these concepts are recognized in many countries, their nature and scope vary so widely that it would be neither expedient nor realistic to propose the adoption of any international regulations for their purpose. False or distorted news accounts can be harmful, but the voluntary publication of corrections or replies is preferable to international normative action. Since the manner in that the right of reply and correction as applied in different countries varies significantly, it is further suggested that: (a) the exercise of the international right of reply and correction be considered for application on a voluntary basis in each country according to its journalistic practices and national, legal framework; (b) the United Nations, in consultation with all concerned bodies, explore the conditions under that this right could be perfected at the international level, taking into account the cumbersome operation of the 1952 Convention on the International Right of Correction; (c) media institutions with an international reach define on a voluntary basis internal standards for the exercise of this right and make them publicly available.

49. Intelligence services of many nations have at one time or other recruited journalists to commit espionage under cover of their professional duties. This practice must be condemned. It undermines the integrity of the profession and in some circumstances, can expose other journalists to unjustified suspicion or physical threat. The Commission urges journalists and their employers to be on guard against possible attempts of this kind. We also urge governments to refrain from using journalists for purposes of espionage.

Protection of Journalists (Recs. 50-51)

UNESCO did indeed pursue the agenda proposed in Recs. 50 and 51, but in this field it—and the professional organizations—have gone even further, including such projects as the database on journalists' freedom of expression (IFEX) and the militant activities of such organizations as Article 19 and "Reporters without Frontiers." This is an area singled out not only by the 1989 UNESCO General Conference and subsequent communication programs, but also by the activities of the IPDC and the series of seminars on media independence and pluralism that began in Windhoek in 1991 and are still in progress. It is a relatively recent phenomenon that the journalists themselves have become explicit targets for attack and murder by warring fractions (e.g., in former Yugoslavia, Somalia, and Rwanda).

Protection of Journalists

Daily reports from around the world attest to dangers that journalists are subject to in the exercise of their profession: harassment, threats, imprisonment, physical violence, assassination. Continual vigilance is required to focus the world's attention on such assaults on human rights.

We recommend:

50. The professional independence and integrity of all those involved in the collection and dissemination of news, information and views to the public should be safeguarded. However, the Commission does not propose special privileges to protect journalists in the performance of their duties, although journalism is often a dangerous profession. Far from constituting a special category, journalists are citizens of their respective countries, entitled to the same range of human rights as other citizens. One exception is provided in the Additional Protocol to the Geneva Conventions of 12 August 1949, that applies only to journalists on perilous missions, such as in areas of armed conflict. To propose additional measures would invite the dangers entailed in a licensing system since it would require some body to stipulate who should be entitled to claim such protection. Journalists will be fully protected only when everyone's human rights are guaranteed.

Comment by Mr.S. MacBride: "I consider this paragraph quite inadequate to deal with what is a serious position. Because of the importance of the role of journalists and others who provide or control the flow of news to the media, I urge that they should be granted a special status and protection. I also urge that provisions should be made to enable a journalist to appeal against a refusal of reasonable facilities. My views on these issues are embodied in a paper entitled The Protection of Journalists (CIC Document No.90) that I submitted to the Commission; I refer in particular to paragraphs 1-17 and 35-53 of this paper."

51. That UNESCO should convene a series of round tables at which journalists, media executives, researchers and jurists can periodically review problems related to the protection of journalists and propose additional appropriate measures to this end.

Comment by Mr. S. MacBride: "I urge that such a Round Table be convened annually for a period of five years; I refer to paragraphs 50-57 of my paper on The Protection of Journalists (CIC Document No.90)."

DEMOCRATIZATION OF COMMUNICATION

Human Rights (Recs. 52-54)

The content of these recommendations is at the other end of the spectrum, illustrating well the imbalances within the MacBride Report itself. In UNESCO today, the Declaration on the Media is rarely mentioned, and the separation of individual and collective rights is no longer actively pursued. In the new programs of UNESCO, many of the same themes and issues have been validated, but with a totally different understanding and vocabulary.

These recommendations really have to be read in a dual light: remembering (and trying to make sense of) the fact that concepts of peace and international understanding, that once formed part of the rhetoric of the Cold War and were largely identified with the Soviet bloc, have now been given a new and different meaning through concepts like the Culture of Peace. In navigating this territory, it is wiser to look for definitions and examples at each step, to see that set of human rights, what international understanding, and that peace is being pursued.

Human Rights

Freedom of speech, of the press, of information and of assembly are vital for the realization of human rights. Extension of these communication freedoms to a broader individual and collective right to communicate is an evolving principle in the democratization process. Among the human rights to be emphasized are those of equality for women and between races. Defense of all human rights is one of the media's most vital tasks;

We recommend:
52. All those working in the mass media should contribute to the fulfillment of human rights, both individual and collective, in the spirit of the UNESCO Declaration on the Mass Media and the Helsinki Final Act, and the International Bill of Human Rights. The contribution of the media in this regard is not only to foster these principles, but also to expose all infringements, wherever they occur, and to support those whose rights have been neglected or violated. Professional associations and public opinion should support journalists subject to pressure or who suffer adverse consequences from their dedication to the defense of human rights.

53. The media should contribute to promoting the just cause of peoples struggling for freedom and independence and their right to live in peace and equality without foreign interference. This is especially important for all oppressed peoples who while struggling against colonialism, religious and racial discrimination, are deprived of any opportunity to make their voices heard within their own countries.

54. Communication needs in a democratic society should be met by the extension of specific rights such as the right to be informed, the right to inform, the right to privacy, the right to participate in public communication—all elements of a new concept the right to communicate. In developing what might be called a new era of social rights, we suggest all the implications of the right to communicate be further explored.

Removal of Obstacles (Recs. 55-58)

In spite of Mr Losev's gloomy comment, this is an area in which much has been achieved in response to the mood of the times and the collapse of totalitarian regimes. Since 1989, secrecy and censorship measures have been constantly attacked, in large part due to a burgeoning tradition of investigative reporting. However, what has been achieved has mostly affected journalism (Rec 56); the situation regarding media concentration and monopolistic practices (Recs. 57-58) is blurred. Independence and autonomy are normally championed in relation to freedom from governmental influence and control: economic and editorial independence are less visible on the agenda. Today's burning issue is journalistic invasion of privacy.

Removal of Obstacles
Communication, with its immense possibilities for influencing the minds and behavior of people, can be a powerful means of promoting democratization of society and of widening public participation in the decision-making process. This depends on the structures and practices of the media and their management and to what extent they facilitate broader access and open the communication process to a free interchange of ideas, information and experience among equals, without dominance or discrimination.

We recommend:
55. All countries adopt measures to enlarge sources of information needed by citizens in their everyday life. A careful review of existing laws and

regulations should be undertaken with the aim of reducing limitations, secrecy provisions and other constraints in information practices.

56. Censorship or arbitrary control of information should be abolished [see comment by Losev] In areas where reasonable restrictions may be considered necessary, these should be provided for by law, subject to judicial review and in line with the principles enshrined in the United Nations Charter, the Universal Declaration of Human Rights and the International Covenants relating to human rights, and in other instruments adopted by the community of nations [see comment by MacBride].

57. Special attention should be devoted to obstacles and restrictions that derive from the concentration of media ownership, public or private, from commercial influences on the press and broadcasting, or from private or governmental advertising. The problem of financial conditions under that the media operate should be critically reviewed, and measures elaborated to strengthen editorial independence.

58. Effective legal measures should be designed to: (a) limit the process of concentration and monopolization; (b) circumscribe the action of transnationals by requiring them to comply with specific criteria and conditions defined by national legislation and development policies; (c) reverse trends to reduce the number of decision-makers at a time when the media's public is growing larger and the impact of communication is increasing; (d) reduce the influence of advertising upon editorial and policy and broadcast programming; (e) seek and improve models that would ensure greater independence and autonomy of the media concerning their management and editorial policy, whether these media are under private, public or government ownership [see comment by Abel].

Comment by Mr.S. Losev: "This whole problem of censorship or arbitrary control of information is within the national legislation of each country and is to be solved within the national, legal framework taking due consideration of the national interests of each country."

Comment by Mr. S. MacBride: "I also wish to draw attention to the provisions of Article 10 of the European Convention for the Protection of Human Rights that I consider as wholly inadequate. I urge that Articles 13 and 14 of the Inter American Convention on Human Rights (1979) are much more comprehensive and effective than the equivalent provisions of the European Convention. The matter is discussed in paragraphs 26-29 of my paper on the Protection of Journalists (CIC Document No.90)."

Comment by Mr. E. Abel: "Regarding (a) and (c), anti-monopoly legislation, whether more or less effective is relevant only in countries where a decree of competition can be said to exist. It is a travesty to speak of measures against concentrations and monopolization in countries where the media are themselves established as state monopolies, or operate as an arm of the only authorized political party. Regarding (b) transnational corporations are expected to comply with the laws of the countries in that they do business. Regarding (d) where it can be shown to exist, the influence of advertisers upon editorial content or broadcast programming would warrant careful study. But a sweeping demand that such influence be reduced without pausing to examine or attempting to measure that influence in particular circumstances, is a symptom of ideological prejudice."

Diversity and Choice (Recs. 59-61)

Diversification and decentralization have taken root (if only because new commercial opportunities are often to be found at a more local level), but this has not yet been accompanied by a genuine measure of participation. The problem is partly mechanistic (and is shared by democratic systems as a whole, not limited to the media). Individual and community participation are to a great extent incompatible with the modus operandi of the mass media.

This being said, the recommendations made by the MacBride Report in this section are curiously specific. It can certainly be argued (Rec 59) that more abundant information is now reaching a wider public from a plurality of sources, but this is only a minor component of public participation. For some years (Rec 60), right up to the Beijing Conference of Women, there has been a growing action program to reduce the specific difficulties encountered by women in communication: both as professionals and in terms of women's image. UNESCO has played a full role in this exercise, combining research with practical initiatives (e.g., in a series of regional symposia that culminated in a Toronto meeting). The concerns of a number of minorities, grouped together without much discrimination in Recommendation 61, have also had their share of attention, although a good deal of it has been token, if well-meaning.

Diversity and Choice
Diversity and choice in the content of communication are a pre-condition for democratic participation. Every individual and particular groups should be able to form judgments on the basis of a full range of information and a variety of messages and opinions and have the opportunity to share these ideas with others. The

development of decentralized and diversified media should provide larger opportunities for a real direct involvement of the people in communication processes.

We recommend:

59. The building of infrastructures and the adoption of particular technologies should be carefully matched to the need for more abundant information to a broader public from a plurality of sources

60. Attention should be paid to the communication needs of women. They should be assure adequate access to communication means and that images of them and of their activities are not distorted by the media or in advertising.

61. The concerns of children and youth, national, ethnic, religious, linguistic minorities, people living in remote areas and the aged and handicapped also deserve particular consideration. They constitute large and sensitive segments of society and have special communication needs.

Integration and Participation (Recs. 62-65)

The spirit of much of this section has been realized, although often in ways radically different from what was cited by way of illustration. What has been achieved has been largely due to developments in information technology, but it has not been matched by any significant progress in management styles and practices. The management of democratic decision making has hardly begun to refine its models in light of technological change. Practical mechanisms for social action have not caught up with social theory, and management theory, in turn, cannot cope with the rapidity of change of technology (particularly when this implies extremely rapid obsolescence and more often than not a change in basic concepts and analyses). This is a problem remarked most recently by the Delors Commission (Report of the International Commission of Education in the 21st Century) in the context of educational development; the theoretical promise of the new information technologies is in fact constrained by our ability, within society, to assimilate, adapt, and deploy this potential.

Integration and Participation
To be able to communicate in contemporary society, people must dispose of appropriate communication tools. New technologies offer them many devices for individualized information and entertainment, but often fail to provide appropriate

tools for communication within their community or social cultural group. Hence, alternative means of communication are often required.

We recommend:
62. Much more attention be devoted to use of the media in living and working environments. Instead of isolating men and women, the media should help integrate them into the community.
63. Readers, listeners and viewers have generally been treated as passive receivers of information. Those in charge of the media should encourage their audiences to play a more active role in communication by allocating more newspaper space, or broadcasting time, for the views of individual members of the public or organized social groups.
64. The creation of appropriate communication facilities at all levels, leading towards new forms of public involvement in the management of the media and new modalities for their funding.
65. Communication policy-makers should give far greater importance to devising ways whereby the management of the media could be democratized—while respecting national customs and characteristics— by associating the following categories: (a) journalists and professional communicators; (b) creative artists; (c) technicians; (d) media owners and managers; (e) representatives of the public. Such democratization of the media needs the full support and understanding of all those working in them and this process should lead to their having a more active role in editorial policy and management.

FOSTERING INTERNATIONAL COOPERATION

Partners for Development (Recs. 66-68)

This is something of an inbred section, reflecting a home-based UN agenda. Recommendation 67, for example, is a clear blueprint for the establishment of what eventually became the IPDC. Other recommendations, that call for interagency dialogue and common programming, were less productive (this is the section most clearly associating UNESCO and the UN with the new orders of economy and communication), that were to provide a focus for tensions in the years to come.

Partners for Development

Inequalities in communication facilities, that exist everywhere, are due to economic discrepancies or to political and economic design, still others to cultural imposition or neglect. But whatever the source or reason for them, gross inequalities should no longer be countenanced. The very notion of a new world information and communication order presupposes fostering international co-operation, that includes two main areas: The international dimensions of communication are today of such importance that it has become crucial to develop co-operation on a worldwide scale. It is for the international community to take the appropriate steps to replace dependence, dominance and inequality by more fruitful and more open relations of inter-dependence, and complementarity, based on mutual interest and the equal dignity of nations and peoples. Such co-operation requires a major international commitment to redress the present situation. This clear commitment is a need not only for developing countries but also for the international community as a whole . The tensions and disruptions that will come from lack of action are far greater than the problems posed by necessary changes.

We recommend:

66. The progressive implementation of national and international measures that will foster the setting up of a new world information and communication order. The proposals contained in this report can serve as a contribution to develop the varied actions necessary to move in that direction.

67. International co-operation for the development of communications be given equal priority with and within sectors (e.g. health, agriculture, industry, science, education, etc.) as information is a basic resource for individual and collective advancement and for all-round development. This may be achieved by utilizing funds provided through bilateral government agreements and from international and regional organizations, that should plan a considerable increase in their allocations for communication, infrastructures, equipment and program development. Care should be taken that assistance is compatible with developing countries' priorities. Consideration should also be given to provision of assistance on a program rather than on a strict project basis.

68. The close relationship between the establishment of a new international economic order and the new world information and communication order should be carefully considered by the technical bodies dealing with these issues. Concrete plans of action linking both processes should be implemented within the United Nations system. The United Nations, in approving the international development strategy should consider the communications sector as an integral element of it and not merely as an instrument of public information.

Strengthening Collective Self-Reliance (Recs. 69-74)

Most of these recommendations also reflect personal agendas, some of that materialized, whereas others failed. Positive mechanisms that did move forward (although often with considerable difficulty and with financial constraints) included news agency development, broadcasting and news exchanges, networking projects associating researchers, documentalists, and professionals. The majority of them took place within the framework of the IPDC and of UNESCO's own program; a fair number have survived, although often in a changed form.

Strengthening Collective Self-reliance
Developing countries have a primary responsibility for undertaking necessary changes to overcome their dependence in the field of communications. The actions needed begin at the national level, but must be complemented by forceful and decisive agreements at the bilateral, sub-regional, regional, and inter-regional levels. Collective self-reliance is the cornerstone of a new world information and communication order.

We recommend:
69. The communication dimension should be incorporated into existing programs and agreements for economic co-operation between developing countries.

70. Joint activities in the field of communication, that are under way between developing countries should be developed further in the light of the overall analysis and recommendations of this Report. In particular, attention should be given to co-operation among national news agencies, to the further development of the News Agencies Pool and broadcasting organizations of the non-aligned countries as well as to the general exchange on a regular basis of radio, TV programs and films.

71. With respect to co-operation in the field of technical information, the establishment of regional and sub-regional data banks and information processing centers and specialized documentation centers should be given a high priority. They should be conceived and organized, both in terms of software and management, according to the particular needs of co-operating countries. Choices of technology and selection of foreign enterprises should be made so as not to increase dependence in this field.

72. Mechanisms for sharing information of a non-strategic nature could be established particularly in economic matters. Arrangements of this nature could be of value din areas such as multilateral trade negotiations, dealing with transnational corporations and banks, economic forecasting, and medium and long-term planning and other similar fields.

73. Particular efforts should be undertaken to ensure that news about other developing countries within or outside their region receive more attention and space in the media. Special projects could be developed to ensure a steady flow of attractive and interesting material inspired by news values that meet developing countries' information needs.

74. Measures to promote links and agreements between professional organizations and communication researchers of different countries should be fostered. It is necessary to develop networks of institutions and people working in the field of communication in order to share and exchange experiences and implement joint projects of common interest with concrete operational contents.

International Mechanisms (Recs. 75-78)

This final section is unashamedly parochial. Recommendation 71 asks for increased funding for communication (achieved, but not permanently, and not to the scale required to implement the Report); a separate communication sector in UNESCO (established, but much later in 1990), better coordination between the various UN agencies (still on the agenda, with only marginal improvement), and a satellite-based UN public information system (never achieved, and probably not within the bounds of probability). Recommendation 78 was an alternative formulation for what was to become the IPDC, and the Western reaction to this proposal (made by Commission member Mustapha Masmoudi) is unambiguously stated in the comments provided by Betty Zimmerman and Elie Abel. In effect, the Intergovernmental Conference (DEVCOM) held in April 1990 arbitrated between the two concepts and opted for the U.S. model of a coordinating agency.

International Mechanisms
Co-operation for the development of communications is a global concern and therefore of importance to international organizations, where all Member states

can fully debate the issues involved and decide upon multi-national action. Governments should therefore attentively review the structures and programs of international agencies in the communication fields and point to changes required to meet evolving needs.

We recommend:
75. The Member States of UNESCO should increase their support to the Organization's program in this area. Consideration should be given to organizing a distinct communication sector, not simply in order to underline its importance, but to emphasize that its activities are interrelated with the other major components of UNESCO's work—education, science and culture. In its communications activities, UNESCO should concentrate on priority areas. Among these are assistance to national policy formulation and planning, technical development, organizing professional meetings and exchanges, promotion and co-ordination of research, and elaboration of international norms.

Comment by Mr. M. Lubis: "I strongly believe that the present set-up in UNESCO (Sector of Culture and Communication) is adequate to deal with problems of Communication."

76. Better co-ordination of the various communication activities within UNESCO and those throughout the United Nations System. A thorough inventory and assessment of all communications development and related programs of the various agencies should be undertaken as a basis for designing appropriate mechanisms to carry out the necessary consultation, co-operation and co-ordination.

77. It would be desirable for the United Nations family to be equipped with a more effective information system, including a broadcast capability of its own and possibly access to a satellite system. That would enable the United Nations to follow more closely would affairs and transmit its message more effectively to all the peoples of the earth. Although such a proposal would require heavy investment and raise some complex issues, a feasibility study should be undertaken so that a carefully designed project could be prepared for deliberation and decision.

Comment by Mr. M. Lubis: "I am of the opinion that the present communication potential of the UN system has not been effectively and efficiently used and managed. And I cannot foresee for a long time to come that the UN system will be able to speak with one voice on the really relevant issues of the world, disarmament, peace, freedom, human rights. However, I support the suggestion about a feasibility study, contained in the same paragraph."

Comment by Mr. S. MacBride: "I would point out that the phenomenal growth of international broadcasting highlights the absence of a UN International Broadcasting System. Some thirty countries broadcast a total of 12,000 hours per week in one hundred different languages. I urge that the UN should establish a broadcasting system of its own that would broadcast 24 hours around the clock in not less than 30 different languages. See my paper on The Protection of Journalists (CIC Document No.90, paragraph 46) and the paper on International Broadcasting (CIC Document No.60)."

78. Consideration might be given to establishing within the framework of UNESCO as International Centre for the Study and Planning of Information and Communication. Its main tasks would be to: (a) promote the development of national communication systems in developing countries and balance and reciprocity in international information flows; (b) mobilize resources required for that purpose and manage the funds put at its disposal; (c) assure co-ordination among parties interested in communication development and involved in various co-operation programs and evaluate results of bilateral and multilateral activities in this field; (d) organize round tables, seminars, and conferences for the training of communication planners, researchers and journalists, particularly those specializing in international problems; and (e) keep under review communications technology transfers between developed and developing countries so that they are carried out in the most suitable conditions. The Centre may be guided by a tripartite co-ordinating council composed of representatives of developing and developed countries and of interested international organizations. We suggest UNESCO should undertake further study of this proposal for consideration at the 1980 session of the General Conference.

Comment by Ms. B. Zimmerman: "Although I agree that a co-ordinating body in the field of communication development could serve a useful purpose. I cannot support this precise recommendation. All members of the Commission did not have the opportunity to discuss thoroughly the advantages and disadvantages of various objectives and structures for such a co-ordinating body. As a UNESCO Intergovernmental Conference is to be held in 1980 to cover that topic. I feel the Commission should welcome the careful study that the UNESCO Conference is in a position to give the matter, rather than offering any recommendation at this time."

Comment by Mr. E. Abel: "This proposal is premature, unnecessary and unwise. The design of an appropriate mechanism for promoting and co-ordinating communications development demands more time and resources than this Commission possesses. Essentially the same proposal here advanced was one of two submitted to a UNESCO experts meeting in November; neither one was endorsed. The question is on the agenda for an intergovernmental meeting at UNESCO in April. The

UN General Assembly has now taken a strong interest in the matter and has requested the Secretary-General to intervene. As it stands, this proposal can only deter the necessary co-operation of both the competent UN bodies and the developed nations whose co-operation is indispensable to further progress."

Comment by Mr. S. MacBride: "I suggest that if any steps are taken in this discretion prior consultation and accord should be reached with journalists' organizations and NGOs involved in the mass media."

Towards International Understanding (Recs. 79-82)

These are model recommendations, timeless and unimpeachable. UNESCO has always focused its attention on peace building; it is embodied in its founding charter. The language of address often remains identical even when philosophies and preferred mechanisms differ (a source of confusion to the outside world, that does not invariably recognize the cyclical nature of political life). This situation has not changed.

Towards International Understanding

The strengthening of peace, international security and co-operation and the lessening of international security and co-operation and the lessening of international tensions are the common concern of all nations. The mass media can make a substantial contribution towards achieving these goals. The special session of the United Nations General Assembly on disarmament called for increased efforts by the mass media to mobilize public opinion in favor of disarmament and of ending the arms race. This Declaration together with the UNESCO Declaration on fundamental principles concerning the contribution of the mass media to strengthening peace and international understanding, to the promotion of human rights and to countering racialism, apartheid and incitement to war should be the foundation of new communication policies to foster international understanding. A new world information and communication order requires and must become the instrument for peaceful co-operation between nations..

We recommend:
79. National communication policies should be consistent with adopted international communication principles and should seek to create a climate of mutual understanding and peaceful co-existence among nations. Countries should also encourage their broadcast and other means of international communication to make the fullest contribution towards peace and international co-operation and to refrain from advo-

cating national, racial or religious hatred and incitement to discrimination, hostility, violence or war.

80. Due attention should be paid to the problems of peace and disarmament, human rights, development and the creation of a new communication order. Mass media both printed and audiovisual, should be encouraged to publicize significant documents of the United Nations, of UNESCO, of the world peace movements, and of various other international and national organizations devoted to peace and disarmament. The curricula of schools of journalism should include study of these international problems and the views expressed on them within the United Nations.

81. All forms of co-operation among the media, the professionals and their associations, that contribute to the better knowledge of other nations and cultures, should be encouraged and promoted.

82. Reporting on international events or developments in individual countries in situations of crisis and tension requires extreme care and responsibility. In such situations in the media often constitute one of the few, if not the sole, links between combatants or hostile groups. This clearly casts on them a special role that they should seek to discharge with objectivity and sensitivity.

The recommendations and suggestions contained in our Report do not presume to cover all topics and issues calling for reflection and action. Nevertheless, they indicate the importance and scale of the tasks that face every country in the field of information and communication, as well as their international dimensions that pose a formidable challenge to the community of nations.

Our study indicates clearly the direction in that the world must move to attain a new information and communication order—essentially a series of new relationships arising from the advances promised by new communication technologies that should enable all peoples to benefit. The awareness already created on certain issues, such as global imbalances in information flows, suggests that a process of change has resulted and is under way. The power and promise of ever-new communication technologies and systems are, however, such as to demand deliberate measures to ensure that existing communication disparities do not widen. The objective should be to ensure that men and women are enabled to lead richer and more satisfying lives.

15

Sean MacBride: A Short Biography

Jorg Becker and Kaarle Nordenstreng

It is difficult to adequately appreciate the life and work of the Irish statesman Sean MacBride (born in Paris on January 26, 1904), without making oneself familiar, at least on a general level, with Irish culture, history, and politics. Having finally won formal independence from England in 1921 after a long civil war, Ireland was among the latecomers in Europe to attain nationhood. If the paradigm of colonial relationships has any validity within Europe, then it could be applied to the history of this country. Foreign dominance versus national independence, foreign versus national language and culture, a small peripheral country versus a great power, economic dependence and underdevelopment versus industrialization and modernization, Catholic versus Protestant Christianity, a strategy of violent opposition to the foreign power versus a policy of peaceful change—these are the conditions that marked MacBride's understanding of politics.

This vicious circle of contradictions and problems, so well known in the countries of the Third World, was and still is particularly intensified in Ireland by the as-yet-unsolved problem of the province of Ulster, a problem that preoccupies all Irish politicians. One of the results of this very typical and explosive Irish situation is that socialists of all shades have been, and are still, keenly interested in Ireland. Lenin developed his theory of nationalities and of the two-class culture with explicit reference to the writings of the Irish socialist James Connolly, and up to this day there is still a bitter dispute in Ireland as to whether MacBride was a "leftist" or a "rightist" (see Golman, 1971).

From the time of his birth onward, Sean MacBride's life was influenced by Irish politics. His father, John MacBride (1865–1916), was an active participant in the violent and infamous 1916 Easter Rising by Irish nationalists. At his execution by a firing squad on May 5, 1918, he refused to have his eyes bound. Sean MacBride was, however, even more influenced by the political views of his mother, Maud Gonne (1865–1953). She was a political activist all her life. She was also a famous actress and a friend of the poet W. B. Yeats (1865–1939). She too suffered directly and physically for her support of the national struggle for independence: In 1918, she had to spend six months in a Dublin prison.

After his schooling, Sean MacBride worked as a freelance journalist in Paris, after which he studied law at University College Dublin and later opened a legal practice in Dublin. He was an active participant in the War of Independence and took part in negotiations with the London government on the new Anglo-Irish Treaty, to which he was then opposed. In 1936, he became Chief of Staff of the Irish Republican Army (IRA), but left on the enactment of the new Irish Constitution in 1937, which he said made it possible to achieve national objectives by political means. At the same time he was called to the Bar, and in the following years made a name for himself by defending IRA members and other political prisoners.

In 1946, Sean MacBride founded a new republican party, Clann na Poblachta. In the 1948 election this party succeeded in defeating the government of the conservative Fianna Fail party, led by Eamon de Valera, which had been in power uninterruptedly since 1932—in that time Ireland's great economic misery had become more and more visible. In the new coalition government, MacBride was Minister for Foreign Affairs. Although Clann na Poblachta was the smallest party in the new government, the policies of the coalition government were influenced on two points by MacBride: He kept Ireland out of NATO and was able to commit a large section of the other government members to the traditions of republican social radicalism dating from the 1930s. In the next general election Clan na Poblachta lost almost all its seats; MacBride, however, held onto his position up until the mid-1950s.

After various election defeats MacBride retired from Irish politics at the beginning of the 1960s. Throughout his life, however, he devoted himself to the defense of human rights, especially in cases of their violation. This interest in human rights and peace drew him more and more into the arena of international politics. Of all the tasks he was entrusted with, and of all the international marks of honor he received, the following deserve particular attention:

1961–1974	Founder member and Chairman of Amnesty International
1963–1971	General Secretary of the International Commission of Jurists

1968–1974	Chairman, Special Committee of International Non-Governmental Organization on Human Rights
1969–1974	Executive Chairman, later President, of the International Peace Bureau, Geneva
1973–1976	Commissioner for Namibia with the rank of Assistant Secretary General of the United Nations
1974	Nobel Peace Prize
1977	Lenin Peace Prize
1978	American Medal of Justice
1977–1980	President of the UNESCO International Commission for the Study of Communication Problems

It was Sean MacBride's involvement in movements for human rights and peace that led him to be concerned with questions of communication. Trying to influence public opinion on these issues, he could not help facing the strategic role of the mass media. Also, like many others, he realized that communication is an increasingly important human right of its own that needs protection. Moreover, he saw how linkages were growing between arms and media industries.

Sean MacBride was a perfect choice for UNESCO, that was given a mandate by its General Conference in Nairobi in 1976 to set up a high-level commission "to study the totality of communication problems in modern societies." As an elder statesman, both in governmental and non-governmental circles, he was at that time free from official roles and duties. However, he continued to be an active—and highly respected—participant in professional and citizen movements.

The MacBride Commission's task was not easy, given the international controversies surrounding media policies—and the mandate that was almost overambitious. MacBride himself explains in the Preface of the final report *Many Voices, One World* that his "concern from the beginning was how to achieve a balanced, non-partisan, objective analysis of today's communication scene and how to meet the challenge of reaching the broadest possible consensus in our views on the major issues before us" (p. xvii). This was achieved fairly well with the assistance of an able Executive Secretary, Asher Deleon from Yugoslavia. (As a matter of fact, Deleon was recruited first and he approached MacBride after Director-General M'Bow proposed MacBride as possible chairman.) This can be stated today, with the benefit of hindsight, although at first many thought that the report was not much more than an eclectic and poorly analyzed reservoir of raw material for a proper study (see Hamelink, 1980).

It is no doubt MacBride himself was a crucial factor in keeping the Commission together and thus in endorsing the point "that structural changes in the field of communication are necessary and that the existing order is unacceptable to all." The point is made in his Preface to *Many Voices, One World* with the following elaboration:

> There is obviously no magic solution to efface by a single stroke the existing complicated and inter-connected web of communication problems. There will be many stages, strategies and facets in the patient step-by-step establishment of the new structures, methods and attitudes that are required. Thus, the "New World Information and Communication Order" may be more accurately defined as a process than any given set of conditions and practices. The particulars of the process will continually alter, yet its goals will be constant—more justice, more equity, more reciprocity in information exchange, less dependence in communication flows, less downwards diffusion of messages, more self-reliance and cultural identity, more benefits for all mankind. (p. xvii)

After the Commission's work was completed, MacBride spoke on the report to several audiences, including WACC and IOJ, highlighting topics such as media concentration, newsprint shortage, foreign broadcasts, and his favorite topic—protecting journalists.[1] He also wrote a Preface or Foreword to at least six books on communication published during the 1980s.[2]

A central theme throughout these writings is what Sean MacBride used to characterize as a "shift in the center of gravity of power from governments, from established authorities to public opinion." In an address to WACC and the British Council of Churches in 1982, he put the case as follows:

> People are much better informed. They read more. This, coupled with radio and television, means that they are in a position to form judgements much more readily than ever before. As a result, public opinion has been acquiring increased influence in the world. No government in a democratic country, or even under a dictatorship, would dream of taking a major decision without sounding public opinion, hence the development of public opinion polls.

---

[1] MacBride's own position on the protection of journalists is elaborated in Document No. 90 of the Commission (issued in a mimeo by UNESCO in 1980).

[2] These books are in chronological order, Hoffman (1981), Becker (1985), Traber (1986), Nordenstreng, Kleinwachter, and Manet (1986), Masmoudi (1986), Becker (1988), and Preston, Herman, and Schiller (1989).

> An example is the Vietnam War. Probably for first time in the history of the world, we have a situation in that full-blown war is stopped in mid-stream by public opinion in the United States and all over the world, without either side having won or lost. Then followed Iran. The Shah was overthrown by public opinion. You may not like Khomeini, who replaced the Shah, but I think the fact to register is that this was done by public opinion, formed by a few tapes dictated by an old man sitting in a house near Paris. They led to the overthrow of what was probably the most powerful military regime in the world. (MacBride, 1983, p. 6)

We may only wonder what MacBride would have said if he had still lived to witness the "velvet revolution" in Czechoslovakia, the downfall of Ceausescu in Romania, and all the other changes in Eastern Europe after 1989, including the collapse of the Soviet Union in 1991. Certainly he would have joined those who based their analysis on the concept of civil society; however, he would hardly have celebrated the accompanying naive thrust in private enterprise and market forces (with a general shift of political balance to the right). These changes followed similar spectacular events in the transition to democracy in South America, in which every country (with the exception of Paraguay, that only underwent a political facelift) has shaken off the dictatorships of the 1980s. In the 1990s, a citizenship movement also began in many countries of Africa, in which people clamored for a multiparty government and sociopolitical freedom. South Africa is a promising case, whereas Somalia and Ruanda serve as warning examples of the complications involved.

In this connection it is worth noting what MacBride wrote back in November 1986, commenting on "socialist countries and other one-party states that are at least in theory responsible to the dominant party":

> Firstly, freedom to obtain, receive, communicate, or disseminate information and news is a fundamental human right that cannot be denied to their own public without weakening their own system of government. Secondly, in the present advanced state of communication and technology, it would be illusory for the government of a one-party democratic state to proceed on the basis that it can withhold news or views from its own people. Any attempt to suppress or delay information or views that are available outside their country, is not only bound to fail, but will ultimately weaken its own political authority. It is by far better that it should be the first to present the news to its own people and that it should make its own comment on the news. Total or partial suppression (or even delay) of the news or views can only result in weakening the credibility or political authority of the government involved. Thirdly, the absence of a critical opposition and adequate parliamentary safeguards in one party states often leads to bureaucrat-

> ic inefficiency and sometimes even to corruption. The best safeguard against such abuses are a free press and audio-visual media capable of investigating complaints by the public and of voicing criticism of the administration, thus assuming the role of ombudsmen on the part of the public. It is hoped that in view of the tremendous changes that have been taking place in the areas of communication, the governments and authorities in one-party states will review their policies and attitudes in regard to freedom of expression and communication.
>
> We are living through a period of very rapid and considerable evolution in the field of communication and also, indeed, in the area involving the formation and influence of public opinion. This is a period during that there should be a re-assessment by one-party states including socialist states—of their own policies in regard to freedom of expression and information. Failure to make such a re-assessment would be to ignore the tremendous changes that have taken place and that are continuing to take place. The process that is going on in the Soviet Union is quite promising in this respect. (quoted in Nordenstreng, Kleinwachter, & Manet, 1986, p. iv)

The same Foreword of 1986 also highlighted the problem of secret services, "sometimes interwoven with the control of the organs of communication with the public" (p. iv). He returned to this theme in what remained his last intervention on communication issues (Preston, Herman, & Schiller, 1989), published after his death in 1989, but the main point in this Preface was the overall use of the mass media for destabilizing governments, mainly in the Third World. Faithful to his honest and straightforward line, MacBride did not hesitate to single out the U.S. government and media as parties with a particularly doubtful record in this respect. Typical of his principled approach is what he wrote toward the end of his life about UNESCO and its former Director-General (and he really knew what he was writing):

> The Campaign against UNESCO and its Director-General was reminiscent of McCarthyism. Of course, the Western powers were not really so committed to UNESCO's objectives regarding its educational and scientific program for Third World countries; the betterment of education, the elimination of illiteracy, and the development of scientific expertise in the underdeveloped areas of the world were not regarded as top priorities for the United States. Hence UNESCO was to be brushed aside.
>
> The fact that the then Director-General, Amadau-Mahtar M Bow, was a black African, and a French-speaking African at that, did not endear him to the American establishment. And here I would pay tribute to Mr. M'Bow for his courageous leadership of UNESCO over two terms of office. (quoted in Preston et al., 1989, pp. xi-xii)

Sean MacBride died on January 15, 1988 and is buried in the Republican plot in Glasnevin cemetery in Dublin. His varied political career and his many scattered lectures and publications have not yet been scientifically reviewed or adequately acknowledged.

REFERENCES

Becker, J. (1985). *Information technology and a new international order.* Lund: Studentlitteratur.
Becker, J. (1988). *Paper technology and the Third World.* Braunschweig: Friedr. Viewig & Sohn (Deutsche Gesellschaft fur Technische Zusanmenarbeit).
Golman, L. I. (Ed.). (1971). *Karl Marx and Friedrich Engels: Ireland and the Irish question.* Moscow.
Hamelink, C. (Ed.). (1980). *Communication in the eighties: A reader on the "MacBride Report".* Rome: IDOC International.
Hoffman, E. (1981). *Medienfreiheit? Anspnuch und Wirklichkeit.* Schotten: Verlag der Studien von Zeitfragen.
MacBride, S. (1983). The desperate imperative. *Media Development, 2,* 3-7.
Masmoudi, M. (1986). *Voie libre pour monde multiple.* Dar el Amal: Economica.
Nordenstreng, K., Kleinwachter, W., & Manet, E. (1986). *New international information and communication order: Sourcebook.* Prague: International Organisation of Journalists.
Preston, W., Jr., Herman, E. S., & Schiller, H. I. (1989). *Hope & folly: The United States and UNESCO, 1945-1985.* Minneapolis: University of Minnesota Press (Institute for Media Analysis).
Traber, M. (Ed.). (1986). *The myth of the information revolution: Social and ethical implications of communication technology.* London: Sage.
UNESCO (1980). *Many voices, one world: Communication and society, today and tomorrow.* London/New York/Paris: UNESCO.

APPENDICES

MacBride Round Table Statements

The eight statements of MacBride Round Tables on Communication to date are reprinted here. Statements are from the Round Table meetings in Harare (1989), Prague (1990), Istanbul (1991), Sao Paulo (1992), Honolulu (1994), Tunis (1995), Seoul (1996), and Boulder (1997). No statements were released after the Dublin (1993) and Amman (1998) meetings. These statements add weight to the thesis that the principles of the NWICO are as valid today as they were in 1980. They also underline the fact that the *MacBride Report* is a benchmark in the history of culture and communication of the 20th century.

Appendix A

THE HARARE STATEMENT

The MacBride Round Table on Communication met in Harare, Zimbabwe, October 27–29, 1989, to assess the state of global communication 10 years after the publication of the report of the International Commission for the study of Communication Problems, chaired by Sean MacBride. The Round Table was convened by the Federation of Southern African Journalists in collaboration with the International Organization of Journalists (IOJ) and the Media Foundation of the Non-Aligned (NAMEDIA). Thirty-five communication professionals and specialists from 14 countries and 18 nongovernmental organizations participated in the Round Table and issued the following statement:

> The Round Table reiterated the principles on which the New World Information and Communication Order (NWICO) was based and underlined its importance for the present and the future, at local, national and international levels. The changes which have occurred in the world since the MacBride Report was published make the search for NWICO even more compelling. The Report's title, "Many Voices—One World" encapsulated the contemporary reality of an increasingly interdependent world on the one hand, and recognized the diversity of cultures and value systems on the other. This calls for common action as well as pluralism and decentralization.
>
> In analyzing the role of mass media in national affairs and international relations, the Round Table took cognizance of the rapid changes in communication technologies and their impact on national sovereignty, economic growth, and cultural identity, as well as on the development of individuals and communities. The Round Table was particularly con-

cerned with the emerging forces in the search for cultural emancipation. Cultural ecology is now an indivisible and central part of the global communication debate.

Recognizing the diversity of cultures, social systems and communication traditions, the Round Table emphasized the challenges and opportunities which this poses to the mass media. It was noted that the mass media could play a more decisive role in furthering the democratic process, in the realization of people's rights to self-determination and in the quest for peace and international understanding. As Sean MacBride stated "there has been a change in the centre of the gravity of power in the world—from government to public opinion, to the public sector."

The Round Table was convinced that the operation of the mass media, both at the national and international levels, should be determined primarily by professional media personnel, committed to the public interest, without undue government or commercial influence. Professionalism in the media must be associated with the idea of a free and responsible press. This calls, increasingly, for professional autonomy of journalists as well as public accountability. Questions of communication ethics and public morality are now central issues in international communication. This underlines the importance for more intense dialogue between and among professional and nongovernmental organizations, and concerned citizens.

The importance of the MacBride Report is further underlined by the fact that ten years after its publication it is now clear that the debate on NWICO was not over one single issue but was related to the entire structure of world communication resources. It included such vital areas as international law, telecommunications, international trade and tariffs, transnational data flow, intellectual and artistic property rights, and the individual's right of privacy.

The Round Table noted that economic and technological disparities still characterize the current international system. The rapid advances in communication technologies in the affluent parts of the world have widened the gap between the "haves" and "have-nots." Urgent investment is needed to improve the weak communication infrastructure in many developing countries. Appropriate technologies must be developed in the countries of the South, and bilateral and multilateral programs should be initiated to remedy these disparities and imbalances. Such measures can be accelerated and accomplished only by harnessing knowledge, which requires systematic research in all areas of communication.

Furthermore there is a great need for education and training of media personnel at all levels. The Round Table emphasized that such efforts must be made with a great deal of cultural sensitivity, leading to authentic indigenous forms of communication practices.

Recent technological developments and the globalisation of communication systems necessitate the creation of a multilateral regulatory framework for international communication. Towards this end the UN system should be better coordinated. There should be closer collaboration between such organizations as the United Nations Committee on Information (UNCI), United Nations Educational, Scientific and Cultural Organization (UNESCO), International Telecommunication Union (ITU), World Intellectual Property Organization (WIPO), General Agreement on Tariffs and Trade (GATT), United Nations Conference on Trade and Development (UNCTAD) and other bodies.

In all these efforts, participation is the key. This includes access to the media, people's right of reply, and their involvement in the decision-making processes. All these are basic elements of the right freedom of expression.

The core of the MacBride Report lies in the conviction that communication is a basic human right. Communication is both an individual human need and a social necessity—constituting the nervous system of society.

In pursuance of these and other questions, further MacBride Round Tables should be organized at regular intervals. To mobilise existing international resources, a network of interested non-governmental organizations is needed to promote dialogue on and advance new initiatives towards "a new, more just and more efficient world information and communication order."

Harare, 29 October 1989

Appendix B

THE PRAGUE STATEMENT

The second MacBride Round Table of nongovernmental organizations, meeting in Prague, Czechoslovakia, September 21–22, 1990, discussed current and future communication problems in light of the changes that had recently occurred in international relations and in the social lives of many individual countries. The Round Table was attended by 30 communication professionals and academics from 20 countries representing 19 international and regional organizations or institutions. It was hosted in the ancient city of Prague by the International Organization of Journalists (IOJ).

> The Round Table sent a message to the third conference of Ministers of information of Non-Aligned Countries (COMINACIII), meeting in Havana, Cuba, September 25–29, 1990.
>
> The Round Table was greatly indebted to Czechoslovakia, a country whose policy of respecting freedom and pluralist democracy made it the first such event that was entirely in the hands of nongovernmental organizations. The debate on the New World Information and Communication Order (NWICO) has thus returned to where it started. It is now in the arena of professional organizations, of communication researchers, and, most importantly, in the arena of grassroots movements representing ordinary men, women, and children who are directly affected by our current cultural and communication environment.

The Round Table noted with deep satisfaction the progress made in the freedom of public communication in many parts of the world. For the first time it was almost possible to discuss NWICO in an atmosphere free of the old ideological polarization of the power blocs. Free from, but not unconscious of the victimization of UNESCO, participants felt that the time had come to reassess and explore in depth the original meaning of NWICO.

Now that new freedoms have been won, the question that needs to be answered is, "freedom for what?" or in the words of the MacBride Report, "Communication for what?" The Round Table noted that the industrialized countries of both East and West have increasingly one thing in common: a sheer lack of idealism and a lack of vision of the society they wish to build. The developed world is now inhabited by increasingly valueless societies.

In the euphoria over the end of the Cold War, which has had disastrous consequences on the nations of the South for a long time, the Round Table was concerned about the state of communication in the majority of developing countries. The rapid development of communication technology, which has drastically increased the capacity for information in industrialized countries, has bypassed many countries in the South. Essential technical infrastructures for communication are still not available there or are inaccessible to most of the people. Instead, foreign communication enterprises have, in alliance with many governments and elitist interests, created an artificial commercial culture that is accessible only to an affluent few. This trend prevents the achievement of cultural emancipation and sound development policies.

To reverse this situation, South–South cooperation is imperative. This calls for new structures to promote collective self-reliance and solidarity. At the same time, a new basis and new methods of North–South cooperation must be found to ensure greater equality and more genuine partnership. This should lead to the promotion of authentic cultural values, deepening the respect for human rights and dignity and strengthening the urgent concerns about women and youth.

UNIVERSAL PROCESS OF NWICO

The Round Table noted that the principles and main recommendations of the MacBride Report are as valid today as they were 10 years ago. They are as relevant for developing countries as for developed ones, even those entering the so-called postindustrial era. As Bogdan

Osolnik, a former member of the MacBride Commission attending the Round Table stated, "the NWICO is a universal process which not only includes countries of the Third World but can only be realized on a global level." More than ever, new thinking about national communication policies for the 1990s and beyond is now needed, reflecting both the promises and perils of the present juncture. The new thinking should encompass different structures of democratic and pluralistic media that transcend the danger of both state and commercial monopolization and are under public control.

The meeting in Prague coincided with the 10th anniversary of the 21st General Conference of UNESCO in Belgrade. The fact that on that occasion 153 countries formally adopted the aims and principles of the new communication order is now a heartening memory. Since then many issues have been debated and reflected on in conferences and reports, notably at the first MacBride Round Table in Harare. But the Prague Round Table felt that some specific points needed urgent attention:

- The Round Table and its associated organizations should continue to mobilize public opinion, especially through the media, about the principles and recommendations of the MacBride Report. Although the MacBride Report has already created widespread awareness of global imbalances in communication flows, greater awareness is definitely needed of the negative effects of these imbalances on the development of the countries of the South.

- There is continuous need to promote the initiatives and efforts that are taken in the South to redress the situation and to struggle for more participation in regional and global communication. This includes efforts to improve South–South communication, especially on a regional level, and the promotion of existing initiatives.

- In an era in search of greater democracy and respect for human rights, the right to communicate should be promoted as one of the fundamental principles of a democratic order. The right to communicate is in the words of Sean MacBride, "the very foundation of other human rights."

- The ideas of NWICO should be contextualized in the various regions. They should be applied in accordance with specific cultural values, historical traditions, and the social needs of particular countries and regions.

- Media professionals should study the ideas of NWICO and appropriate them as their own. To this end a number of measures should be taken by professional organizations, such as publishing of study guides and brochures, organizing special seminars, and making awards to those who excel in the implementation of NWICO values.

- Professionals and academics should also promote serious media criticism by linking together various projects and institutions engaged in analyzing the media coverage of events and issues relating to peace, development, and other global problems. Such systematic monitoring of media performance by the media professionals and communications researchers—instead of governments—was one of the proposals made by Sean MacBride as a followup to the Report.

- A specific perspective on women and women's issues is needed because their voices have not been sufficiently heard in the movement for a NWICO. Although women are still underrepresented in the field of communications, in most countries there is a significant development of women's alternative media that may constitute new media models and new approaches to grassroot organizations. Women should be encouraged to join the NWICO movement, and future Round Tables should have more women participants with topics of special interest to them on the agenda.

- UNESCO, which at one time played a pivotal role in the conceptualization of the NWICO, and later became paralyzed in this respect, should regain its role as a catalyst for new thinking and new actions in the field of communication now that the international climate is changing.

- In the current search for a new world order, it should be remembered that ordinary people still feel threatened. They are still afraid of armed conflicts, social unrest, environmental catastrophes and various manifestations of fanaticism related to race, religion, cultural, and ethnic identity and economic deprivation. In the spirit of the MacBride Report, the mass media should be reminded that their most urgent task is to address these problems and mobilize public opinion for their solution.

Prague, 22 September 1990

Appendix C

THE ISTANBUL STATEMENT

The Third MacBride Round Table met at the end of a conference on "Newsmedia and International Conflict," which critically assessed the roles the mass media played during the war in the Persian Gulf. It took place in the ancient city of Istanbul, Turkey, at the crossroads of East and West, North and South, on June 21, 1991. Thirty participants from 14 different countries and 18 nongovernmental organizations endeavored to pursue the thoughts and values of the New World Information and Communication Order (NWICO) as advanced by the Non-Aligned Movement and inspired by the ideals of the late Sean MacBride. The Group made the following observations on the current state of communication and mass-mediated culture:

> We observe with growing concern the rapidly increasing concentration, homogenization, commercialization, and miniaturization of national and world cultures. The principles of the MacBride Report, "Many Voices, One World," have been countered:
>
> - by the virtual monopoly of global conglomerates over the selection, production and marketing of information and entertainment products, including crucial scientific and technical data and informational rights;

- by the transnational industrial–media complex under its American military protectorate;
- and by the weakening of multilateral relations and international organizations.

This trend has further widened the inequities of resources within and amongst nations.

We are confronted, therefore, with media coalescing into a centrally manufactured symbolic and cultural environment. That environment permeates every home in and ever-growing number of countries. It is displacing parents, schools, communities, publics and even nations as the originator of messages and images that define our lives and our relationships with each other. It serves marketing strategies and government priorities that are increasingly beyond the reach of democratic policy-making.

Great efforts must now be made to develop a culture of non-violence, of dialogue and negotiations, practicing the art of democracy, and promoting a culture of peace. This effectively means to demilitarize cultural products and processes.

Politically, alternative systems of peace and security need to be established, both on the global and regional levels. The United Nations, and especially UNESCO, should play a central role in this, thus becoming what they were always meant to be, peace-making and peace-keeping bodies.

The challenge before us is to build new peoples' coalitions and constituencies that can help regain a significant measure of participation in cultural policy-making, nationally and internationally.

The coalitions should include a broad range of public groups, social movements, and organizations. They should enlist media professionals, citizen activists, consumer groups, women's minorities, religious, labor, environmental and other organizations in the new cultural struggle.

The democratization of communication should build on the strength of national coalitions entering into international co-operation on the basis of independence, equality and mutually beneficial objectives. The new frontier for the advancement of human values and rights is the cultural frontier. It is there that the principles of the MacBride Report have to be recognized as more essential than ever.

In pursuance of these and other relevant objectives, the MacBride Round Table will publish a collection of documents, support the development of and communication amongst groups concerned with media democratization, and organize future meetings to facilitate the work of the Round Table and related coalitions.

Istanbul, 21 June 1991

Appendix D

THE SÃO PAULO STATEMENT

Guarujá near São Paulo in Brazil was the setting of the fourth MacBride Round Table on international communication, held on August 21, 1992. This meeting reminded participants of the 500-year-long invasion of Latin America and the Caribbean by Europe and North America. We witnessed some of its disastrous consequences: the "street children" of São Paulo, the culture of violence, and the environmental degradation that had recently been the focus of the Earth Summit in Rio de Janeiro, Brazil's second largest city.

We were reminded of the cycle of poverty that now characterizes most countries in the South and many in the North and of the convulsion taking place in the Balkans and parts of the former Soviet Union. Daily we read about new threats of war and internecine strife in the Middle East and elsewhere.

Against this backdrop, 53 communications practitioners and academics from 22 countries, many representing NGOs, reflected on the state of public communication and the roles policy makers and media workers could play in the face of such problems. These are our conclusions:

1. Peace

Peace and international understanding were at the very heart of the thoughts and actions of the late Sean MacBride. The report, Many Voices, One World [1980, Recommendation 79] urges the mass media "to refrain from advocating national, racial or religious hatred, and incitement to discrimination, hostility, violence and war." It states, "A new world information and communication order requires and must become the instrument for peaceful co-operation between nations" [ibid].

It is an irony of history that, although the urgency of peace for human development has increased since the MacBride Report was published, the NWICO—a promoter of peace—was discarded by many governments and treated with derision by influential media establishments.

Present-day wars have taken a heavy toll on civilians, among them journalists carrying out their professional duties. In the former Yugoslavia alone, in the first seven months of 1992 at least 48 journalists were killed. In 1991 (according to "Reporters sans Frontieres") at least 72 journalists in 21 countries met a violent death for what they had written or for exercising their profession.

For much of his life as an international statesman, Sean MacBride was particularly concerned about the protection of journalists. He proposed that UNESCO convene an annual round table "to review problems related to the protection of journalists and propose . . . appropriate measures to this end" [Recommendation 51].

Although tribute should be paid to several NGOs which have advanced the cause for the safety of journalists, this topic still needs to be taken up again at the highest intergovernmental level.

The conflicts in the former Yugoslavia and elsewhere are but symptoms of a wider and deeper malaise, namely the disregard for human rights and the callous indifference to the abysmal living conditions of millions of people. Are we entering a new phase of history in which human dignity is trampled underfoot by the culture of violence: the indiscriminate violence in ethnic, racial, religious and nationalist conflicts, the "precision bombing" in regional and global confrontations, and the subtle strangulation of the South through economic relations and trade wars?

2. Culture

In the quest for peace, justice and development the role played by culture has often been disregarded. In the current (UNESCO-proclaimed) Decade of Culture, policy makers and media workers should analyse the way mass media shape and change cultural environments. This is nowhere more evident than in the countries previously subject to a monolithic and ideologically guided cultural policy, and in the countries of the South now overrun by the cultural industries of global capitalism. Both in the former socialist countries of Eastern Europe and in the South there are movements of cultural assertion, embracing old cultural identities and forging new nationalist loyalties. In this situation, new cultural policies are urgently needed, especially to foster cultural identities that are tolerant of and non-threatening to other peoples.

Almost everywhere in the world new cultural environments should be developed in which multi-ethnic, multi-faith, and multicultural societies can flourish. New cultural policies should also pay special attention to the rich cultural life of ordinary people, especially women, whose cultural expressions have often grown out of long traditions of living in peace and harmony. Just as urgent is the need for all countries to counter the widespread culture of violence with a "culture of peace" promoting human dignity for all peoples.

3. Civil Society

Social movements are crucial for the process of democracy in general, and, in particular, for democratizing communications. Many social movements encapsulate NWICO values and can therefore play a paradigmatic role. Such movements include those dealing with the environment, feminist and women's issues, disarmament and peace, adult literacy, adult education, and cultural democracy. All are the natural allies of media reform movements.

Social movements are at the heart of what constitutes civil society, a concept implying that citizens have rights and duties which are not conferred on them by the State, but which are universal and part of the human condition. In this context, the "right to communicate," a key concept of the NWICO, should be viewed not just as a right citizens demand of governments, but rather as an inalienable right held by them as members of civil society.

Institutions of public communication were originally at the heart of civil society, and one of the tasks of the 1990s is to make them once again civil society's champion. At a time when they are considered primarily "industries," it must be stressed that the mass media are a "social property." They exist for the sake of the public and owe their autonomy to the autonomy of civil society. Civil society is thus by definition a media reform movement. It is only through an invigorated civil society that a genuine public sphere can be built, that is, one which is accountable to the public rather than one absorbed by the State or capitalist market economy, or a combination of the two.

4. Imbalances in Information Technology

Information and communication technology are currently growing at an unprecedented pace. So is the variety of their uses and applications. This situation is characterized by:

- the concentration of high-tech hardware and software firms in North-Atlantic countries, especially the U.S. and Japan;
- the relative decentralization of information technology applications;
- the spread of micro-computers and the reduction of equipment costs.

The adoption of digital technology in telecommunications by the South is constrained by heavy financial costs. In addition, there has been increasing deregulation of telecommunication services and continued intrusion of transnational corporations. An alternative and less costly solution for the development of all means of telecommunication infrastructure would be the use of satellites; unfortunately, they are controlled by power elites.

Special attention must be paid to system design, data processing and software development, all labour intensive processes, which increasingly have been relocated to the South. Once again, cheap labour is paying for the technological advances of the rich. However, there are also impoverished classes in the North, which, like many developing countries, are deprived of information technology. In addition, there is increasing competition between poor European regions and some countries of the South to win their share in information technology industries.

Governments have by and large lost control over the development and application of information and communication technologies. Transnational corporations can either bypass governments or are in collusion with them to ensure greater profits from their "markets."

Various strategies should be devised to harness information technology in such a way that it benefits ordinary people. This means analysing communication technology in the context of people's needs, especially in the countries of the South. It further means monitoring and exposing structures and activities of transnational corporations, a task that is all the more urgent now that the United Nations is primarily promoting the TNCs as "engines of growth" throughout the world. NGOs in both the South and the North have to be mobilized to bring pressure on both the United Nations and national governments so that information technology serves the people's ends.

5. Women and Communications

The Round Table recognized that the previous activities associated with the NWICO did not pay sufficient attention to women's particular needs and perspectives in communications. If the renewed NWICO movement is to move forward in a non-elitist direction, women must be given their due.

What this means, first of all, is acknowledging that women's values are more likely to promote the so-urgently-needed culture of peace. Simply put, women are seldom found among the decision and policy-makers who send people to war. Women frequently make up both the rank-and-file and the leadership of peace movements, although the latter is rarely reflected in the mass media.

Our rampant culture of violence has had particular effects on women, who are not only especially vulnerable to physical violence in times of war, but who are also subject to daily violence and intimidation in so-called "normal" conditions. In this situation, increasingly recognized by intergovernmental and nongovernmental organizations, the mass media and mass culture play a primary role by promoting images of violence towards women.

Women's concerns in communications have, however, gone well beyond the traditional attention paid to negative, stereotyped images in the mass media and discrimination in employment in the media industries. For instance, women have a new agenda with regard to the vital issue of communication technology, which includes: the possibility of gender discrimination built into the very conceptualization of communication technology, the hierarchical structure and binary logic of informatics, felt to be laden with gender-specific values, a critique of information technology built upon a larger epistemological critique of the enlightenment notions of progress and rationality embodied in science and technology. Many women also want to make greater use of communication technology, for example, for building feminist data networks or simply for fostering greater exchanges of information. For these women the primary issue is not a critique of technology, but rather access.

It is above all women, as a social movement, that has greatest relevance to the NWICO. Women as a whole, regardless of their class, ethnic and racial differences, have not been able to participate in the most essential communication process: naming reality. Women are part of another culture, the culture of silence, that also affects the poor, the manual laborers, the marginalized, the minorities, the alienated youth, the lower castes, the people with dark skin, the various peoples from the South "demonized" in the Western press, in short, the mass media's "non-people." A "NWICO for the 1990s" will only be meaningful to the extent that it gives voice to all of these groups.

Appendix E

THE HONOLULU STATEMENT

The 6th MacBride Round Table on Communication was held in Honolulu, Hawaii. This was an appropriate multicultural and multilingual setting, a home to "many voices in one world." Honolulu, through the contributions of the East-West Center and the University of Hawaii, Manoa, also played a major role in the evolvement of the concept of the Right to Communicate, which was to become a central pillar of the MacBride Report.

The Round Table meeting lasted for three full days (January 20–23, 1994) and much of that time was devoted to the study of communication equity, both within nations and internationally, focusing especially on the perspective of marginalized groups and societies. In this it followed a tradition established in the 1970s when research played a crucial role in a process leading up to the formulation of the MacBride Commission's report *Many Voices, One World*. Based on the reflections of more than 40 research papers, several discussion groups and many other significant interventions, the participants wish to address a number of issues.

Empowerment of Women and Grassroots' Organizations

> Previous Round Tables have referred to the concerns of these groups of people, and emphasized the need for their cultural and socio-political emancipation. The mass media could play an important role in assisting and publicly legitimizing this process. But women, as well as other "minorities" (which in some places are, if fact, majorities), and grassroots and citizens' organizations of all kinds, must seize their own communication power and develop alternative media. Comparatively inexpensive technology, like video, on-line computer links and desk top publishing, can facilitate this development.

One of the main functions of the study of international communication problems, as summarized in the MacBride report, is the necessity for an ongoing process of democratization in society as a whole and the mass media in particular. This however, presupposes the active participation of women and grassroots organizations whose views, contributions, and aspirations are usually ignored by the mass media, and who are largely excluded from the socio-political decision making processes at national and international levels. No genuine civil society and no functioning public sphere are possible without the active participation of all marginalized groups.

Rights of Indigenous Peoples and Their Cultures

The Round Table noted the United Nations Declaration of the International Year (1993) and the Decade (1994-2003) of the World's Indigenous People.

The Round Table recognized:

- that the lives, languages and cultures of indigenous peoples are at great risk of extinction amidst today's revolution in communication technologies;
- that the indigenous peoples of the world are marginalized from communicative links in the world and within countries and that therefore they remain at great risk under pressures from the State, capital and other groups.

The Round Table accepted favorably the report of the working group on indigenous peoples. The working group report appeals for the dedication of funding from communication resources, and calls upon media industries, educational institutions and the MacBride Round Table itself for greater commitment to the support of programs to enhance the status of indigenous peoples.

"Information Superhighway": Efficiency Versus Equity in Information Flows

Meeting immediately after the 16th conference of the Pacific Telecommunications Council, the technological scenario of an "information superhighway", as proposed by the Clinton Administration, provided the backdrop for some of the Round Table's discussions. While the U.S. National Information Infrastructure (NII) plans remain substantially unclear, they aim at creating a more efficient flow of information through integrated system digital networks (ISDN). Similar to the construction of interstate highways under the Eisenhower Administration, the metaphor of "electronic superhighways" promises higher volume of communication flows, but not necessarily greater equity.

Similar "information superhighways" are likely to be constructed by the European Union, Japan, and other major economies. The "information superhighways" will inevitably bypass poorer regions. No "information superhighway" is planned for the developing world, nor are exits or entries likely to be available to marginalized communities. Many questions remain. Who sets and collects the tolls on the "superhighway"? Who establishes the highway code, and polices traffic? Will there be public transportation and equal access for all?

It is likely that the new information highways will widen the gap between the information rich and information poor, both within individual countries and between rich and poor regions of the world, to such an extent as to render it unbridgeable in the foreseeable future.

The Round Table considers the establishment of reliable and affordable telephone systems, to which ordinary people can have ready access, as a high priority for developing countries. The telephone is also the linchpin for access to most of the new information technologies such as fax and electronic mail. The efforts of the ITU and organizations like PTC to "close the gap" are greatly appreciated.

DIALOGUE WITH UNESCO, ITU AND GATT

The research papers presented at the Honolulu Round Table amply demonstrate that the issues addressed by the MacBride Commission are still there, and that the problems identified in the Commission's recommendations have barely been addressed, let alone resolved. On the contrary, many international problems have compounded themselves and are ever more intractable.

Media practitioners and academics are continually reminded of the unresolved nature of most of these issues. It is no coincidence that attendance at the annual MacBride Round Table has grown steadily, with over one hundred people from some twenty countries attending the Honolulu meeting.

All of this prompted us to reflect on the leadership which UNESCO once held in the study of global communication problems. Given, however, the convergence of telecommunication and mass media, and the future "information superhighways," the ITU and GATT play an increasingly pivotal role. We plead for coordination and consistency in the efforts of all intergovernmental organizations, and for close and timely consultations with nongovernmental organizations.

We believe it is time that UNESCO should reactivate its resources, and renew its commitment, towards democratization of global communication structures. But, this is only possible if the U.S., U.K. and Singapore governments rejoin UNESCO. We urge these governments to take practical steps as soon as possible towards full membership in UNESCO.

The next MacBride Round Table will be held March 9-11, 1995 in Tunis, Tunisia. The Tunisian Association of Communication (ATU-COM) will serve as host. The meeting will examine the means of access and distribution of an "electronic superhighway" system and the safety of journalists on life-threatening assignments. In addition, the three Working Groups on Gender, Indigenous People, and Grassroots' Organizations, established by the Round Table in Honolulu, will continue their work at the Tunis meeting.

Appendix F

THE TUNIS STATEMENT

The 7th MacBride Round Table, held in Tunis, was in many ways a journey home to Africa for a movement that owes a great debt to this region. It is to the Algiers Non-Aligned Summit in 1973 that many look for the origins of the struggle for a new and more equitable communication order. Tunisia also was one of the non-aligned countries to spearhead the struggle for a new international order in the fields of culture and communication. It was here, 20 years ago, that the first concrete instrument was established, Non-Aligned News Agencies Pool. And it was here that the Non-Aligned Symposium on Information in 1976 articulated its aspirations toward more equitable and fair global communication structures and flows.

The venue of the 7th MacBride Round Table therefore offered welcome reminders of the cultural and political movement, which led to the UNESCO commissioned report *Many Voices, One World,* popularly known as the MacBride Report, and indeed of the contribution of the diverse cultures of Africa. Over 70 participants from 18 countries at the 7th MacBride Round Table, meeting from March 16 to 18, 1995, were the guests of the Tunisian Association of Communication (ATUCOM). Its president, Mustapha Masmoudi, was one of the MacBride commissioners, and participants greatly benefited from his extensive experience and wise leadership.

AFRICA FACES THE INFORMATION HIGHWAY

The main theme of the meeting was Africa and the Information Superhighway, or the implications of the next generation of information technology for this vast continent. The point of departure for discussion was obvious: as put recently by an African diplomat to the UN General Assembly, "While industrialised countries are already talking about an Information Superhighway, in most of the developing countries that highway has not been paved." There is a strong possibility that much of the African coastline will be ringed by glass fibre cables. But, except for some large cities, the land mass of Africa is likely be untouched by an information highway for a long time to come. More than 70% of Africa's population live in villages with no electricity and no telephone connections, nor are they likely to have them in the foreseeable future. Besides, these villagers have so little spending power that they are of little interest to the big players of the information highway. The highway planners are interested only in Africa's affluent city dwellers who are already in possession of a telecommunication infrastructure, thereby further widening the gap between the rich and poor.

So it is vitally important that the media and political debates on the information society do not distract attention from the basic communication needs in Africa, far more mundane but all the more essential for that.

AFRICA'S COMMUNICATION AGENDA

For the Third World and Africa particularly, the information superhighway must have a public lane that integrates the various media, including traditional channels, in a way that promotes Africa's development. Thus the communication agenda for Africa that emerged at the MacBride Round Table contrasts sharply with high-level debates and promises emanating from Washington, Brussels, and Tokyo:

- Radio, the only affordable mass medium for most people, must be extended, improved in quality and diversified in content, particularly in its educational programs.

- A more reliable and less expensive telephone network should be established as a matter of urgency and gradually extended to rural areas; an inter-African telecommunication system needs to be developed under the auspices and with the support of the International Telecommunications Union (ITU).

- The current problems caused by the steep increase in paper prices need to be addressed lest the effects on African education and book production be catastrophic.

- An independent press committed to democratic accountability needs to be strengthened.

- The training and education of journalists in all parts of Africa remain an urgent and ongoing task.

Africa may have lost its "strategic" significance for the West since the end of superpower rivalry. Now would be the time to show honest and active solidarity with the hard pressed peoples of this continent, starting from their real needs and not from the global strategic needs of the corporate-driven North.

THE ROLE OF THE INFORMATION SUPERHIGHWAY

The information society comes into perspective when viewed against these basic communication needs. Yet it would be a mistake for Africa to ignore the possibilities, and risks, of the new global networks. The challenge is to push debate beyond the question of simply gaining access to the superhighway to that of defining an information society that is relevant to real African needs and building it up from that base. There are ways in which it can complement and reinforce the impact of more traditional communication initiatives addressing basic needs; and it can offer entirely new instruments to many struggling with the many demands of African economic and social development. For instance, existing Internet African services could form a mutual organisation to share information, coordinate services, and collaborate on service extension. Or information networks could be used to gather and distribute international market and trading information, to support local cooperatives, and to reduce the slice of the commercial intermediaries based usually in the North.

The rural dimension of African society, encompassing 70% of the population, must also be to the forefront. Reaching out to rural communities to enhance dialogue and favor access to information, using appropriate techniques and technologies (not necessarily the most advanced), must be a goal of development projects, whether sponsored by international organizations, NGOs, governments, or the private sector.

The opening for such refocusing of the information society on real needs is found in pledges to public access, universal service, and development in the South, contained in government and intergovernmental statements. The G7 Summit in Brussels in February 1995 commits its participating governments to "promoting universal service to ensure opportunities for all to participate" and to "encouraging the dialogue on worldwide cooperation" such that industrialized countries will work toward the participation of developing countries in the global information society.

Of course, significant measures to achieve these worthy aims are nowhere to be found in the fine print, in which common concrete actions for the information society are put forward. The direct implication throughout is that their fate will lie with liberalized markets and deregulated and privatized industries, as the motive force and main instruments of change.

Yet these are not only insufficient: Many observers are concerned that market forces, left unfettered, will significantly increase the gap between the have's and the have-not's. If laudable words are to translate into positive action that seriously addresses shortcomings in the proposed implementation of the global information society, then much work remains to be done. If such promises are left unfulfilled, if powerful countries are not forced to honor their commitments, then calls for universal access and development priorities are likely to diminish to inaudible whispers under the din of "market realities" and "trickle-down" benefits. A leader article in the *Economist* magazine recently offered an off-hand dismissal of those calling for a more equitable interpretation of the information society: "There is already a clamor to turn access to cyberspace into another "entitlement." When that clamor becomes too loud to ignore, then maybe some of the promissory notes will be called in and paid up.

With these issues in mind, the Round Table issued a specific call to action in relation to the development of the information society in Africa. This follows as the second part of this Statement.

WOMEN MUST BE HEARD

The Tunis Round Table also discussed the roles of women and grass-roots organisations for the strengthening of democracy in Africa and elsewhere. The democratic process depends on a viable civil society, organized in citizens' groups, social movements, human rights' and women's organizations. Democracy declines and may disintegrate when its processes are usurped by politicians and their parties—as has been demonstrated in some parts of Africa and elsewhere. In many cases the mass media systems have accelerated the decline, primarily the agents of government or politicians rather than the voice of civil society as a whole. Women's organizations in particular must make themselves heard by pressuring the mass media and/or by finding a voice of their own in alternative media.

The recent Social Summit in Copenhagen heard that 70% of the world's poor are women, and the central role of women in struggling to survive poverty and nurture new generations is finally receiving some recognition. In relation to the empowerment of women in the communication field, the Round Table emphasized the need to strengthen efforts already underway and to expand their role, inter alia, through access to the media and through participation in the management and operation of newspapers and radio stations in both urban and rural areas. In the sphere of traditional communication, attention was drawn to the importance of folk theater, storytellers, choirs: Their role is pivotal in promoting active communication centred on cultural values.
A new agenda is also being constructed by women on the vital issue of communication technology, covering such topics as the possibility of gender discrimination built into the very conceptualisation of communication technology; the hierarchical structure and binary logic of informatics, laden with gender-specific values; and a critique of information technology built on a larger epistemological critique of enlightenment notions of progress and rationality embodied in science and technology.

JOURNALISTS IN SITUATIONS OF VIOLENCE AND WAR

Sean MacBride was especially concerned with the danger faced by journalists in their work. The loss of journalists' lives in the last few years has shown the need for better protection in situations of violent conflicts; 1994 was the worst year on record with the killing of 122 reporters, photographers, and editors while carrying out their work. The International Red Cross and other human rights organizations, and above all governments and authorities directly involved in such conflicts, must find new means and ways of securing greater safety for journalists. Such considerations, however, should be supplemented by efforts of journalists and news gathering organisations towards more honesty and fairness in war reporting.

The Tunis Round Table referred to one of the oldest documents on international communication, namely the UNESCO Declaration of 1978 on Fundamental Principles concerning the contribution of the Mass Media in strengthening Peace and International Understanding, to the Promotion of Human Rights, and to countering Racialism, Apartheid, and Incitement to War. Although Apartheid has now officially been abolished, thanks to the biggest social movement of the last two decades, all other issues of the UNESCO Declaration remain unresolved. They remain a responsibility of the mass media for years to come.

Appendix G

THE SEOUL STATEMENT

The 8th MacBride Round Table, held in Seoul from the 24th to the 27th of August 1996, attracted more than 200 participants to its sessions and workshops, and a further 200 to the first Asian Alternative Video Festival. The theme was: Communication and Culture: Identity, Plurality and Equality. Converging from a total of 24 different countries, ideas were shared among academics, researchers, NGOs, and senior representatives of the International Telecommunications Union (ITU) and the Arab League of Educational, Culture and Science Organisations (ALECSO).

> The last number of years has seen a rising number of Declarations, Statements, Resolutions, Charters etc. issuing from conferences and other gatherings on the right to communicate, and on alternative and democratic media. The MacBride Round Table itself adds annually to the tally. Yet these statements are symptomatic of some very significant, and potentially far reaching, developments in the area of communications and media.
>
> There is a growing number of gatherings around media issues, partly, at least, because of rising interest among NGOs. And others, such as international aid funders and UN agencies, are displaying renewed interest, many alerted to the importance of media by the much-heralded "Information Society." Furthermore, these gatherings are more conscious than before of the existence and growth of an external, global constituency, interested and involved in media and communication issues, to which they can address themselves. Increasingly, these declarations raise matters and target audiences that cut across different forms of media, appealing to sectors beyond the immediate interest of

the gatherings issuing them, suggesting the recognition of a deeper affinity between the different sectors and media activities.

Thus, perhaps more important than the statements themselves is what they say about the movement for the democratisation of media and communication. The movement is growing, it is becoming self-aware at a global level, and it is crossing traditional media boundaries. It is in this context that the MacBride Round Table situates itself.

The Round Table over the years, has mirrored these trends within its own development. In the past few meetings, it has debated issues as diverse as the Information Society, alternative video, indigenous people's communication, and gender equality. But then, given its genesis in the UNESCO Commission, it is no surprise that the Round Table is broad-based and concerned with a wide range of issues. The Round Table has also seen a growth in the participation of NGOs in annual meetings and the development of close relations with a number of them, nationally, where the Round Tables have been held, but also internationally and across a range of media. Indeed, the Round Table has constituted itself as an NGO, and is currently discussing with the International Telecommunications Unions how this oldest of UN organisations can open its doors to NGOs.

The MacBride Round Table in Seoul significantly reinforces these trends. The Round Table was held in parallel with, and initiated, the Asian Alternative Video Festival '96, the first of its kind, which was attended by video NGOs from around Asia and by an enthusiastic local and international audience. And the diversity of issues debated, in presentation sessions and workshops, was greater than perhaps ever before.

The Seoul Round Table offered considerable evidence of the coming of age of new responses to communication and media issues at a global level. Enriching and transforming old debates with fresh evidence and ideas from a variety of sources, the meeting demonstrated both that the imbalances of the past persist across the different media and geographies; and that new approaches to solving them are emerging from diverse quarters.

Asia was largely on the sidelines of debates on communication that raged during the 1970s and 1980s, but today it offers some invaluable lessons in moving forward into the late 1990s and beyond. The first such lesson is obvious: A global movement for media equity and democratic communication structures cannot afford to exclude any regions or interests. A debate conducted among the minority with power, even accompanied by claims to be acting on behalf of those excluded, can result in no lasting progress.

Building on this, the Round Table illustrated that solutions to media and communication imbalances must be tailored to the characteristics and challenges of each region, and within regions, to the often more extreme contrasts between different areas and populations. Asia is a diverse region within a diverse world. Analyses of problems, and ways and means of solving them, are not available off the shelf, no matter the political complexion. While guided by the same core democratic, participative and equitable principals, analysis and response must relate to the variety and complexity of lived experience.

A number of practical concerns and implications were drawn from these considerations:

1. Responses to media commercialisation and homogenisation originating *at local level* can play a central role in a new media and communication environment.

In the context of global forces that threaten national cultures and identities, a local level of response may be just as, or more, effective as a state led defence of national culture. While resistance to wholesale commercialisation and commodification of communication is essential at all levels, rebuilding political and cultural identity can begin at the community (including communities of interest) and local level. Often alongside a process of (neo-) liberalisation, community radio, alternative video and access television, community Internet and computer networking, and alternative printed press are gaining strength. These democratic forms of media offer a fresh basis to construct a shared identity, one less reliant on national symbols—or rather one that can renew them from the ground up.

2. In addition to supporting such local and community media, however, there is a need to *democratise* the processes by which communication and media policy, dealing mainly with "mainstream media," are being formulated and implemented. When devised and conducted behind closed doors, even within governments with at least some claim to democracy, communication policies can be compromised in a number of ways.

The workshop on Press Censorship suggested strongly that democratic laws and practices in the media tend to lag behind those governing political and electoral institutions, seriously undermining the legitimacy and progress of the latter. And feeding back onto itself, the issue is poorly reported in the media, nationally but also, and especially, internationally where powerful geo-political interests and media concentration come into play.

3. A further, and related, concern is *censorship* of the use of the new technologies. Ample evidence was presented regarding the media of "cyberspace" and video in many countries of Asia and elsewhere. Alongside traditional forms of media oppression, new authoritarian forms are emerging sometimes through the abuse and misapplication of legitimate political and social concerns regarding, for instance, the right to individual privacy and the control of pornography. Internationally, the issues of intellectual property rights and copyright, for instance, fall into the same category. Coupled with concerns on censorship is the general danger under which journalists work in many parts of the world. In the Middle East, Europe, Latin America, Africa and Asia, and elsewhere, journalists regularly work in life threatening situations. Better protection of journalists is desperately needed to help ensure a continued free flow of information in our society.

4. Progress made at the Round Table towards building *alliances* among video NGOs and among the communication scholars, offers tangible evidence, reinforced in presentations across a number of communication areas, of the value of collaboration beyond the national level—while again underlining the need for sensitivity to local differences. The practical benefits for such collaboration can translate down to the very local level, as well as up to global level. Locally, tracking the activities and strategies of transnational corporations between different Asian countries as they affect the lives of workers; recording them on video for mutual exchange, discussion and response; and exploring appropriate vehicles for transnational regulation and accountability worldwide, were recognised as essential. When industry goes global, so also must labour—and this has obvious applications across all regions.

5. At international *policy* level, also, the value of broad alliances of different alternative media and communication advocacy groups was emphasised. Of immediate relevance are global and regional government sponsored plans to build a new information and communication based society, for example, the Asia-Pacific Information Infrastructure (APII) promoted by advanced Asian countries, the Global Information Infrastructure (GII) of the USA and allies, and the Information Society of the European Union. There is no doubting the progress in core infrastructure in more developed countries, or that there are potentially great benefits everywhere. Yet insistent and repeated rhetoric of APEC, G7, OECD, EU, among others, claiming to affirm the priority of universal service and the need to avoid disparities between the "information rich and information poor," functions only to obscure the absence of any serious attempt to address these issues. There is willingness neither to concede on the centrality of competition in building this 'brave new world' not to acknowledge the central role of significant transfers to address marginalised communities—often the majority. Following the old advertising maxim, repetition will eventually wear down resistance—and mainstream media also play a central role in this.

All can agree on the current imbalances and inequalities of access to, and adequate training in the use of, communication and information technologies such as basic telephony, the computer and the Internet. The right to communicate in the 21st century will be fundamentally related to the world's ability to address these inequalities.

The task of devising and promoting alternative policies to the neo-liberal orthodoxy is urgent, and building alliances between different concerned media and communication groups would be a major step towards creating the necessary scope and scale of ideas and resources. At least at national level, some legal sovereignty stills remains and the institutions exist, or can be readily created, to implement universal service policies that serve the needs of all. However, a much greater task lies ahead for international institutions such as the ITU and UNESCO, in the face of the growing influence of the corporate sector among intergovernmental organisations. Nevertheless, particularly encouraging is the recent initiative of the UN Administrative Coordination Committee to pursue the concept of the Right to Communicate right across the UN system, with the ITU as the central agency.

CONCLUSION

When constraints tightly delimit room for manoeuvre, Declarations, Resolutions and other such statements sometimes take the place of action. In the interregnum between the suppression of intergovernmental media debates in the mid 1980s and the recent rise of new movements for democratic media and the Right to Communicate more firmly rooted in experience, this was probably unavoidably the case. Now, the MacBride Round Table is just one among an increasing number of organisations and events fuelled by widespread concern regarding the current direction of media and communication. The Round Table cannot pretend to cover the huge range of issues involved. But the emerging issues echo those of other meetings. In short, the conclusions of the Round Table are:

- The international debate on democracy and equity in communication, clearly growing in strength and depth, must fully explore and acknowledge significant variations within and between different regions of the world, before an effective common strategy can be developed.

- Responses at a local and grass-roots level, in the form of democratic, alternative and developmentally-oriented media, may play a major role in countering the process of globalisation and homogenisation of media and culture.

- The democratisation of the process of devising and implementing mainstream media policy, at national but also international level, must be a priority.

- Especially among the new media of video and "cyberspace," the introduction of new authoritarian forms of censorship in nominally democratic political systems is emerging as an issue of especial concern.

- The benefits of alliance building, a growing trend among NGOs and scholars, can enrich local activities and efforts and, at international level, can contribute to the development of more equitable and democratic communication and to the establishment of the Right to Communicate.

Particularly satisfying was the decision of video NGOs in Asia to collaborate more closely in a number of concrete areas; and of the research scholars to form an Asian Communication Studies Network, a first meeting of which will be held in Australia during 1997.

Appendix H

THE BOULDER STATEMENT

The Ninth MacBride Round Table, hosted by the University of Colorado School of Journalism & Mass Communication, was held in Boulder, Colorado, USA, on October 1-2, 1997. The Round Table was held in association with the 12th colloquium of the European Institute for Communication and Culture on Community Citizenship. Most papers are available at the MacBride Website, at http://tdg.uoguelph.ca/~drichard/macbride/.

Over 50 participants, mainly from the North American academic community, were in attendance and the program included some 20 papers, workshops, and two keynote speakers, Steven Bates who spoke on "Realigning Journalism with Democracy: The Hutchins Commission, Its Times, and Ours," and Saskia Sassen who spoke of "The State and the New Geography of Power." Community and alternative media attended in strength, as did critical media analysts and representatives of national and international NGOs. Those present shared both an awareness of the great challenges facing us and some optimism, summarized by more than one speaker in Antonio Gramsci's famous words 'pessimism of the intellect and optimism of the spirit.'

The MacBride Round Table reflects two historical developments toward the end of the 20th century: the growing societal influence of privately owned media, and a power shift from governments toward civil society. This nongovernmental platform was established at the end of the 1980s when it became clear that the intergovernmental UN system, particularly UNESCO, was incapable of supporting the intellectual and political dialogue emanating from the emancipatory movements of the 1970s, notably the International Commission for the Study of Communication, chaired by the late Sean MacBride.

THEMES ADDRESSED

The Round Table theme, "Global Media and Global Responsibility: A Time to Choose," points to a crucial turning point: Must we acquiesce to total market domination, or can we assert an alternative view? This was explored in three intensive sessions.

The first took a critical look at the New World Information and Communication Order (NWICO) and its legacy. It was addressed from the Perspectives of American media ideology, of Latin American traditions, and generally the developing countries adjusting to the new information age.

Second, several papers reviewed current trends in mass media around the world, ranging from journalism in the age of globalization to the use and abuse of the concept of the Information Society. The third area focused on alternative and participatory media, reporting several experiments and studies, and including a video session by Paper Tiger Television's DeeDee Halleck and Michael Eisenmenger.

Stephen Bates, literary editor of the *Wilson Quarterly*, addressed the gathering on the second day of the Round Table. It is now 50 years since the Hutchins Commission published its report "Free and Responsible Press." Dr. Bates reviewed the conditions that led to the setting up of this unique exercise of reflecting the role of the media in society, the work of the Commission, and the lukewarm, even hostile, reception it met within the media industry of the day. Round Table participants noted similarities between this U.S. exercise of the 1940s and the global work of the MacBride Commission 30 years later. Although the changing times have naturally made some of the Hutchins Commission's analyses and proposals obsolete, many of them remain valid—perhaps even more so than at its time—under the contemporary conditions of global communications.

One aspect raised by the Hutchins Commission that has become ever more central is the need to develop media literacy and media criticism.

As observed in a paper by Sakae Ishikawa of Japan, the new communication environment is entering an age of overload, as people become overwhelmed by a flood of information that may or may not be true.

A GLOBAL MEDIA MOVEMENT

The Round Table heard how, in the United States, the various elements exist on the ground to support a new phase of growth in community and alternative media. Key conditions are already in place: the training capacities, the facilities, and an active personnel. What is missing, perhaps, is a crucial element that could, in practice, bind these together and energize them. An important parallel can be drawn at the international level, where such conditions may be present in greater force.

The various components of an international movement on media and communications that can challenge the current neoliberal orthodoxy, seem to be emerging. The creation of a global social movement—largely absent from the NWICO—requires a number of factors, among them a core constituency of on-the-ground activists who recognize their affinities and can mobilize in concerted actions; an understanding of the key global issues of the day and of the arenas in which they are fought out; and the capacity to get their message out both to natural allies in progressive movements and to the general public.

While operating at several levels—local, national, and international—such a movement would work on two broad fronts. On the one hand, alternatives to current homogenised and commodified media must be further supported, in participative forms, producing a diversity of output— not to displace mass media, but to create a truly democratic space in which everyone has the right to participate in whatever active or passive manner they wish. On the other hand, the mass media and transnational institutions of corporate power and domination over world information must be challenged in their own terms and on their own ground. Public media policy and institutions, too, must be opened out to democratic participation.

Some elements of a movement are more clearly present than others. There is certainly growing activism in alternative media, such as radio, access television, and internet use, across the world. A long tradition thrives of articulate voices raised in criticism of the current state and trends of the media, from academia to lobby groups to certain UN Commissions and reports.

Furthermore, these are beginning to recognize their common cause and build bridges. Within the various strands, national and international organisations are already well established. Nationally, coalitions of several strands of the movement are appearing: The Round Table heard of national organisations in countries as diverse as the United States, Ireland, and South Africa that bring together all forms of alternative media and media activists. The creation of such groups as the Platform for Cooperation on Democratisation and Communication in London in 1996 and growing support for the People's Communication Charter, point to a willingness to cooperate across the board, bringing together diverse constituencies in pursuit of a common mission.

Indeed, a major outcome of the 9th Round Table was the unanimous endorsement of the Charter, will add the Round Table to the select group of the Charter's "Founding Parents." The Third World Network, AMARC, Vidéazimut, the Cultural Environment Movement, WACC, and others have already approved the Charter through their respective procedures.

Further evidence of a growing movement can be seen in plans for a series of major international meetings during 1998, the 50th anniversary of the Universal Declaration of Human Rights.

Yet there are also elements that clearly need serious attention if a global movement of any consequence is to emerge.

Among these are the need for a self-reflexive critical capacity on what the movement is about, tackling such basic questions, discussed at the Round Table, of whether participative media really do empower people and in what ways; whether civil society organizations and movements can themselves embody the democratic and participative principles they espouse; and what realistic alternative structures and institutions can be proposed.

Sharing of research results, a deep understanding of the core problems, and nuanced reflection on their contradictory impact, will be needed if strategic interventions are to be pursued effectively. At the same time, key issues at the international level must be explored in depth, such as the shift away from the UN system toward a trade paradigm in media and communications; and the implications of trends in copyright and intellectual property rights.

SOME IMMEDIATE TASKS

The Round Table was keenly aware that grand schemes and declarations cannot substitute for action, and many concrete ideas and approaches were raised. An immediate strategy across a set of different fronts is clearly needed, and mutual support and coordination among the growing number of initiatives and organizations was seen as critical to ensuring current energies are not dissipated. Participants enthusiastically shared information on many activities already underway and proposed collaborative action in others, among them:

Research to assess the real impact of alternative media, to explore the relevance of emerging technologies, and to deepen understanding of activities outside the wealthy countries.

The building of a broad-based social movement, self-reflective and self-critical and sustaining a clear common agenda.

The need for an international nongovernmental platform to cover global regulatory agencies (ITU, WTO, etc.) and democratic forms of governance.

About the Authors

Jeffrey C. Ady is associate professor of communication at the University of Hawaii, Manoa, with emphasis in organizational and intercultural communication studies.

Michael Basil is assistant professor of mass communication and journalism studies at the University of Denver and works in the area of mass media effects.

Jorg Becker is professor of communication at Marburg University, Germany, and specializes in international and development communication.

Dennis Davis is Professor of Communication and Director of International Programs in the College of Communications at Pennsylvania State University. His specialty is mass communication theory, new media literacy, and political communication.

Johan Galtung is professor of peace studies in various universities in Europe, Japan, and the United States and is presently based in France. In communication he may be best known for his seminal study of news structure.

Cees J. Hamelink is professor of international communications at the University of Amsterdam, and former President of the International Association for Media and Communication Research (IAMCR). His work is on communications ethics and technology.

Allan Hancock is former director of the Communication Division at UNESCO and works as a consultant in media policy.

Wolfgang Kleinwaechter is director of the NETCOM Institute Leipzig. His work includes regional development and the information society, and the Right to Communicate.

Igor E. Klyukanov is assistant professor of speech communication at the Pennsylvania State University.

Poka Laenui (Hayden F. Burgess) is director of the Institute for the Advancement of Hawaiian Affairs, Wai'anae, Hawaii.

Kaarle Nordenstreng is professor of journalism and mass communication and the University of Tampere, Finland. He works on international communication policy and ethics.

Michael Ogden is assistant professor of communication at the University of Hawaii, Manoa with a specialty in telecommunications and policy.

Seán Ó. Siochrú is research director at NEXUS Europe, a research agency based in Dublin, Ireland, and founder and chairperson of Community Media Network.

Ramona R. Rush is professor of communications at the University of Kentucky. Her work is on international and intercultural communications, ecological communications, women and communications, and conflict resolution.

Hemant Shah is a associate professor of communication and journalism at the University of Wisconsin, Madison, where he specializes in development journalism.

Majid Tehranian is professor of international communication at the University of Hawaii, Manoa, and director of the Toda Institute.

Michael Traber is former director of research and publications at the World Association of Christian Communication (WACC), in London.

Richard C. Vincent is associate professor of international communication at the University of Hawaii, Manoa. He specializes in the study of international communication and policy, media processes, and news analysis.

Author Index

A

Abel, E., 224, 225, *231*, 283, 295, 296, 301, 303
Ajami, F., 23, *60*
Allen, D., 78, 82, *87*
Ambrosi, A., 140, *154*
Anderson, M. H., 235, *267*
Appadurai, A., 33, *60*, 174, *182*
Appelman, D., 124, *135*
Appleby, S., 45, *62*
Apter, D., 174, 178, *182*
Aronowitz, S., 174, *182*
Attali, J., 24, 46, *60*

B

Bagdikian, B., 105, *135*
Barlow, J., 126, *135*
Barnet, R. J., 39, *60*
Barnett, T., 213, 219, *221*
Bartholomew, D., 123, *135*
Bartley, R. L., 23, *60*
Baumann, M., 81, 84, *87*
Becker, J., 310, *313*
Bell, D., 24, 31, 32, *60*
Bender, G., 117, *137*
Benedikt, M., 106, *135*

Bennett, W. L., 161, 162, 163, *167*
Berman, J., 125, *137*
Beuve-Mery, H., 224, 225, *231*
Bevans, C. I., 192, *198*
Bielenstein, D., 238, *265*
Biesada, A., 115, 116, 118, 127, *135*
Binyan, L., 23, *60*
Book, E., 192, *198*
Boulding, K. E., 54, *60*, 85, *87*, 206, *212*
Brandt, W., 27, *60*
Branscomb, A., 114, 124, *135*
Brislin, R., 218, 219, *221*
Brown, C. J., 94, *100*
Brown, R., 99, *100*
Bruck, P., 181, *182*
Butalia, U., 180, *182*

C

Campbell, J., 73, *87*
Campeanu, P., 224, *231*
Carey, J. W., 227, *231*
Cerf, V., 109, 110, 113, 115, *135*, *136*
Chamberlain, B. E., 94, *100*
Chomsky, N., 162, *168*
Christians, C. G., 156, 162, 166, *167*

Clark, J. W., 210, 211, *212*
Cleveland, G., 192, 193, 194, *199*
Coate, J., 122, *136*
Cohen, S., 254, *266*
Commission for the Study of Communication Problems, 170, *182*
Connolly, F., 124, 128, *136*
Cook, G., 121, *136*
Cronkhite, G., 211, *212*
CRTNET, 54, *60*
Curtis, T., 225, *231*

D

d'Arcy, J., 96, *100*, 240
Dalton, R. J., 175, *182*
Dare, O., 180, *182*
Davis, D. K., 157, 158, 159, 160, 162, 163, 165, *167*, *168*
Dayan, D., 50, *60*
Development Dialogue, 238, *265*
Diamond, J., 204, *212*
Dilawari, S. R., 172, *182*
Docherty, T., 24, *61*
Downing, J., 180, *182*

E

Eapen, K. E., 180, *182*
Eek, H., 240, *265*
Ekenzo, E. M., 224, 225, *231*
Elgin, D., 123, 128, *136*
Eliasoph, N., 181, *182*
Elmer-DeWitt, P., 113, *136*
Encanto, G., 172, *182*
Engels, F., 94, *101*, 214, *222*
Entman, R. M., 162, *167*
Epstein, E. J., 161, 163, *168*
Etizioni, A., 24, *61*
Ewen, E., 32, *61*
Ewen, S., 32, *61*
Eyerman, R., 178, *182*

F

Fackler, P. M., 156, 162, 166, *167*
Fair, J. E., 173, *184*
Falk, R., 218, *221*
Faludi, S., 77, *87*
Fascell, D. B., 249, *265*
Ferre, J. P., 156, 162, 166, *167*
Fisher, D., 224, *231*, 240, *265*
Fishman, M., 163, *168*
Fiske, J., 180, *182*
Flood, K., 87, *87*
Flourney, D., 50, *61*, 172, 182
Folbre, N., 79, *87*
Foucault, M., 30, 33, *61*, 215
Frank, A., 218, *221*
Frankfort, H., 35, 36, *61*
Frederick, H. H., 54, *61*, 85, *87*
French, M., 71, *87*
Friedman, J., 215, 216, 221, *221*
Fuchs, L. H., 195, *199*
Fukuyama, F., 23, 30, 31, *61*

G

Gallagher, M., 68, *87*, 82
Galtung, J., 5, 6, *21*, 54, *61*, 81, 82, 85, *87*, 163, *168*, 178, 179, *182*, 187, 204, 205, 209, 211, *212*, 218, 235, *265*
Gans, H., 160, 161, 162, 163, *168*,
Garcia, L., 117, *136*
Gayatri, G., 173, *185*
Gelb, N., 229, *231*
Gerbner, G., 229, *231*, 235, 262, *265*
Gibson, W., 106, *136*
Giddens, A., 157, *168*, 172, 173, *182*
Gimbutas, M., 75, *87*
Golding, P., 123, *136*, 170, *182*, 213, 219, 220, *221*, 264, *265*
Golman, L. I., 307, *313*
Gore, A., 54, 99, *100*, 118, 127, 130, *136*
Graber, B., 163, *168*
Greenbaum, J., 110, *136*
Greenwald, J., 125, *136*
Gregory, D., 172, *183*
Griffin, M., 265, *266*
Gross, L., 229, *231*
Gunter, B., 163, *168*
Gutierrez-Villalobos, S., 82, *87*

AUTHOR INDEX

H

Habermas, J., 33, *61*, 215
Hamelink, C. J., 32, *61*, 85, *87*, 147, *154*, 213, 217, 218, 219, *222*, 240, 248, 262, *265*, *267*, 309, *313*
Haque, M., 173, *183*
Harasim, L., 106, *136*
Harms, L. S., 223, *231*, 240, *265*, 266
Harris, P., 213, 219, 220, *221*, 264, *265*
Harvey, D., 24, *61*
Heilbroner, R. L., 36, *61*
Henderson, H., 84, 86, *87*, 88
Herman, E. S., 162, *168*, 264, *266*, 310, 312, *313*
Hertog, J., 82, *87*
Hertzler, J., 207, *212*
Hillis, D., 112, *137*
Hiltz, S. R., 114, *136*
Hitler, A., 26, 48, 55, *61*, 74
Hobson, J. A., 18, *21*, 38, *61*
Hobson, S. G., 18, *21*
Hoffman, E., 310, *313*
hooks, b., 75, *88*
Huntington, S. P., 23, 24, 30, 31, 32, 46, 47, *61*
Husted, F. M., 192, *199*

I

International Directory of Development Journalists, 180, *183*
International Labour Organization (ILO), 189, *199*
International Organization of Journalists (IOJ), 216, *222*
International Telecommunication Union (ITU), 99, *101*
International Work Group for Indigenous Affairs (IWGIA), 188, *199*

J

Jackson, J., 111, *137*
Jacobson, T. L., 181, *183*
Jameson, F., 174, *183*
Jamias, J. F., 176, *183*
Jamison, A., 178, *182*
Jasinski, J., 159, 165, *167*
Jokiel, L., 190, *199*
Juergensmeyer, M., 45, *61*

K

Kapor, M., 105, 121, 124, 125, 126, 128, *137*
Karnow, C., 124, *137*
Katz, E., 50, *60*
Kay, A., 112, *137*
Kehow, B. P., 52, *61*
Kennedy, P., 24, *61*
Kim, J., 204, *212*
Kincaid, D. L., 207, *212*
Kirat, M., 180, *183*
Kirschner, B., 123, *137*
Kivikuru, U., 240, *266*
Kleinwachter, W., 94, 96, 99, *101*, 240, 242, *267*, 310, *313*
Koetter, F., 39, *62*
Krause, G., 95, *101*
Krol, E., 52, *61*, 107, 113, *137*
Kroloff, G., 254, *266*
Kuechler, M., 175, *182*
Kunst, M., 78, *88*
Kuykendall, R. S., 192, *199*

L

Lapham, L., 125, *137*
Lash, S., 24, *61*
Lazarsfeld, P. F., 228, *231*
Lee, P., 54, *61*
Lee, Y. C., 51, *62*
Lenin, V. I., 38, 55, *62*, 242, 307
Lerner, D., 171, *183*
Lévi-Strauss, C., 214, 215, 216, 217, *222*
Levy, M., 163, *168*
Lewis, P., 139, 140, *154*
Libset, S. M., 37, *62*
Lieberman, D., 111, *137*
Liska, J., 211, *212*
Littman, J., 125, *137*

Losev, S., 224, 225, *231*, 289, 294, 295
Lubis, M., 224, 225, 302, *231*
Luke, S., 173, *183*

M

MacBride, S., 27, *62*, 224, 225, *231*, 245, 258, 283, 292, 295, 303, 304, 307-313, 318, 341, 350
Mahbubani, K., 23, *60*
Maitland, D., 25, *62*
Manca, L., 180, *183*
Mandel, E., 24, *62*
Manet, E. G., 240, 242, *267*, 310, *313*
Mankekar, D. R., 239, *266*
Marcus, G., 174, *183*
Marquez, G. G., 224, 225, *231*
Martín-Barbero, J., 216, *222*
Marty, M., 45, *62*
Marx, K., 94, *101*, 153, 214, 216, *222*, 224
Masmoudi, M., 224, 225, *231*, 258, 301, 310, *313*, 337
Masuda, Y., 24, 32, *62*
Mattelart, A., 32, *62*, 228, *231*
Mazlish, B., 24, *62*
Mazumdar, A., 176, *183*
McChesney, R. W., 264, *266*
McCombs, M. E., 228, *231*
McDaniel, D., 172, *183*
McFadden, T., 107, *137*
McKay, F., 173, *183*
McLuhan, M., 59, 224, 225, *231*
McPhail, T., 50, *62*
Melucci, A., 174, *183*
Merton, R. K., 228, *231*
Meyers, M., 181, *183*
Meyrowitz, J., 172, 173, *184*
Miedzian, M., 72, 73, *88*
Milner, A., 215, 220, 221, *222*
Milton, J., 92, 93, 94, 95, 97, *101*
Mohr, L., 140, *154*
Morgan, M., 229, *231*
Mowlana, H., 216, 219, 220, *222*, 235, 262, *265*

Mueller, M., 226, *231*
Muller, R. E., 39, *60*
Murdoch, G., 123, *136*
Murphy, B. K., 169, *184*

N

NAM, 261, *266*
NIICO, 261, *266*
Naess, A., 71, *88*
Nagai, M., 224, 225, *231*
Negroponte, N., 105, *137*
Newton, H., 108, *137*
Noelle-Neumann, E., 228, *231*
Nordenstreng, K., 54, *63*, 218, *222*, 235, 236, 238, 239, 240, 241, 242, 249, 259, 260, 262, 263, *265*, *266*, *267*, 310, *313*

O

Ogan, C., 173, *184*
Ogden, M., 128, *137*
Omu, F. I. A., 224, 225, *231*
Orr, D., 72, 78, 83, *88*
Osolnik, B., 224, 225, *231*, 246, *267*, 322
Oteifi, G. E., 224, 225, *231*

P

Pageot, 192, *199*
Pai, S., 50, *62*
Passin, H., 171, *184*
Patterson, T. E., 162, 163, *168*
Pavlic, B., 240, *267*
Peck, M. S., 79, *88*
Pelton, J., 117, *137*
Penty, A. J., 18, *21*
Perry, S., 104, *137*
Phillips, K., 123, *137*
Pieterse, J. N., 173, 174, 178, *184*
Poole, G., 126, *137*
Porat, M., 24, 32, *62*
Postman, N., 161, 162, *168*
Preston, W., Jr., 310, 312, *313*
Pronk, J. P., 224, 225, *231*
Pye, L., 171, *184*

Q

Quarterman, J., 109, 110, *137*

R

Raboy, M., 140, *154*, 264, *267*
Ratan, S., 111, *138*
Rheingold, H., 104, 105, 106, 107, 108, 109, 112, 118, *138*
Richstad, J., 223, *231*, 235, 240, 266, *267*
Righter, R., 243, 253, 255, 256, *267*
Roach, C., 203, 205, 208, *212*, 217, *222*
Robertson, R., 24, *62*
Robinson, J. P., 163, 167, *168*
Rogers, E., 170, 171, *184*
Rosen, J., 165, 166, *168*
Rowe, C., 39, *62*
Roy, C., 189, *199*
Ruben, B., 204, *212*
Rush, R., 68, 69, 71, 72, 75, 77, 82, 85, 86, *87*, *88*, 173, *184*

S

Sagan, C., 209, *212*
Sahlins, M., 214, 215, 216, 221, *222*
Samarajiwa, R., 170, *184*
Schement, J. R., 225, *231*
Schiller, H. I., 32, *62*, 228, *231*, 239, 240, 262, 263, *267*, 310, 312, *313*
Schmidt, A., 215, *222*
Schramm, W., 171, *184*
Schudson, M., 161, *168*
Schwartz, E., 123, *138*
Servaes, J., 170, *184*
Seymour, C., 114, *138*
Shah, H., 81, *88*, 173, 177, 178, 179, 180, 181, *184*, *185*
Shaw, C., 230, *231*
Shaw, D. L., 228, *231*
Shiller, D., 161, *168*
Siebert, H., 81, 84, *87*
Signorelli, N., 229, *231*
Singer, M., 24, 59, *62*
So, A., 32, *62*

Soja, E. W., 33, *62*
Somavia, J., 224, 225, 248, *231*
Sparks, C., 203, 205, 208, *212*
Sreberny-Mohammadi, A., 235, *267*
Stapleton, R., 123, 124, *138*
Stecklow, S., 52, *63*
Steinem, G., 75, *88*
Stenger, N., 107, *138*
Sterling, B., 108, 109, 110, 112, 113, 116, *138*
Stevenson, R., 235, *267*
Stewart, R., 172, *182*
Stix, G., 113, 121, *138*

T

Tarjanne, P., 25, 53, *63*
Tawney, R. H., 36, *63*
Tehranian, K., 24, 33, 42-44, 56, *63*, 78, 85, *89*
Tehranian, M., 24, 32, 33, 40, 45, 46, 55, 57, 59, *63*, 78, 85, *89*, 170, *185*
Thomas, P., 213, 214, 219, 221, *222*
Thurston, L. A., 194, 198, *199*
Tinbergen, J., 238, *267*
Toffler, A., 24, *63*, 123, *138*, 225, *232*
Topuz, H., 241, *267*
Toregas, C., 123, *138*
Traber, M., 54, *63*, 263, *267*, 310, *313*
Trachtenberg, A., 38, *63*
Tran van Dinh, 239, *268*
Tuchman, G., 163, *168*
Tunstall, J., 228, *232*
Turoff, M., 114, *136*
Tusa, J., 229, *232*

U

Ugboajah, F., 235, *267*
UNESCO, 254, 263, *268*, 310, *313*
United Nations Development Program, 25, *63*
United States Senate, 192, *199*
Urry, J., 24, *61*

V

Van Tassel, J., 123, *138*
Varis, T., 239, 240, *266, 267*
Varley, P., 123, *138*
Verghese, B. G., 176, *185*, 224, 225, *231*
Verhelst, T., 174, *185*
Vincent, R., 54, *61, 68*, 81, 82, 85, *87*, 163, 178, 179, *182*, 204, 205, 209, 211, *212*, 217, 218, *222*, 229, 230, *232*, 235, *265*

W

Wallerstein, I., 32, *63*
Wartenberg, T. E., 181, *185*
Weber, M., 36, 37, 46, *63*, 224
Webster's New World Dictionary, 74, *89*
Webster, A., 176, *185*
Webster, S., 124, *128,* 136
Wells, A., 228, *232*
Westin, A., 123, *138*
White House, 116, 121, 122, *138*
Widavsky, A., 24, 59, *62*
Wilden, A., 204, 207, *212*
Williams, A., 221, *222*
Winer, D., 126, *138*
Winner, L., 225, *232*
Witlox, N., 78, *88*
Wittig, M., 123, *138*

Y

Yadava, J. S., 235, *268*

Z

Zakon, R., 129, *138*
Zimmerman, B., 224, 225, *231*, 301, 303

Subject Index

A

Abkhasians, 59
Abrams, Elliot, 256
aborigines, 189
Abuja (Nicaragua), 263
academics; *see* research community
accuracy of information, 72
activists (communication), 55
advertising, 10, 39, 41, 50, 74, 80, 152, 161-162, 256, 276, 283, 295-297, 344
Aeropag, 93, 96, 98, 100
Aeropagitica, 92-93, 95
Afghanistan, 247
Africa, 35, 38, 45, 51, 180, 219, 225, 238, 245, 281, 309-310, 335-339, 344
Afro-Americans, 16, 53, 245; *see also* people of color
agenda setting, 59, 228
agriculture, 14, 25, 35-36, 188-189, 275, 299
aid (and incentives), 18, 275-276, 283-284
Alexandria, 36
Algeria, 42, 180
Algiers, 239, 335
alternative media; *see* media, alternative media
AMARC, 139-140, 145, 265, 350
Amazon, 189
America Online (AOL), 51, 110
American Association of Higher Education, 128
American Indians, 191
American Medal of Justice, 307
American Telephone & Telegraph Co. (AT&T), 49, 52, 118, 129-130
Amin, Idi, 74
Amnesty International, 306
Amsterdam, 36
Anarchism, 9
Anglo-Irish Treaty, 306
annexation, 192-198
Apartheid, 339
APEC, 46, 344
Arafat, Yasser, 50
Arab-Israeli conflict, 242
Arab League of Educational, Culture and Science Organizations (ALECSO), 341
Arab world, 38

Archie, 112
Arctic, 189
Argentina, 110
aristocrats, 5
Arnet, Peter, 51
ARPANET, 108-109, 129-130; *see also* United States, Pentagon
Article 19 organization, 291
ASEAN (Association of Southeast Asian Nations), 39, 46
Ashby's law, 10
Asia, 38, 51, 110, 180, 188-190, 342, 344
Asian Alternative Video Festival, 341-342
Asian Communication Studies Network, 346
Asia-Pacific Economic Cooperation (APEC), 39
Assam, 176
Association for Progressive Communication (APC), 54-55, 139-140
Athens, 93
Australia, 42, 55, 110, 189, 245, 247, 275, 346
Austria, 261
Automatic teller machines (ATMs), 113, 123

B

Baghdad, 36, 51
Balkans, 38, 325
Bangladesh, 189
banking, electronic, 123
Barcelona, 36
barriers to entry, 38, 98, 278-279, 316
Barthes, Roland, 215
Bates, Steven, 347-348
"Beavis and Buthead," 57
Beijing, 36
Beijing Conference on Women, 296
Belgium, 192

Belgrade, 250-253, 321
Belize, 122
Berlin, 58, 95, 242
Bermuda, 122
bias, 163, 235, 256
Bill of Rights, 126, 128
bisexual, 77
BITNET, 129-130
Blacks; *see* Afro-Americans
Bliley, Rep. Thomas, 120
Boas, Franz, 214
Bolivia, 55
Bombay, 58
Bono (rock musician), 57
books; *see* media, books
Boomerang Effect, 205
Bosnia, 28, 40, 59, 326
Boucher, Rep. Rick, 199
Boulder (Colorado), 314, 347-351
Bourdieu, Pierre, 215
Brandt Commission, 27
Brave New World, 126
Brazen Rule, 209
Brazil, 40, 55, 85, 189, 325-330
Bremen, 192
British Broadcasting Corporation (BBC), 50-51, 229, 289
Bretton Woods Agreement, 38
British Council of Churches, 308
broadcasting; *see* media, broadcast
broadcast news; *see* media, broadcast
British Telecom, 49
Bruges, 37
Brussels, 99, 336-337
Buddhism, 31
Buenos Aires, 99
bureaucracy, 18, 74, 78, 157-162, 169, 173, 309-311
Burma, 42, 50, 189
Bush, President George, 27, 51, 262

SUBJECT INDEX

C

Cable News Network (CNN), 46, 50-51, 59, 262, 289
cable television; *see* media
California, 190
Cairo, 36, 58
Calhoun, J. C., 192
Cambodia, 254
Canada, 55, 110, 122, 189, 191, 252
Cape Town, 84
capital, 3-21, 37, 40-41, 56, 59, 74, 80, 123, 187, 189, 191, 332
capitalism; *see* Free Market
Caribbean, 325
Carter, President Jimmy, 254
Carter Administration, 249, 252, 254, 260
Castro, Fidel, 51
Catholic, 37, 93, 247, 305
Ceausescu, Nicolae, 309
cellular phone; *see* mobile phone
censorship, 94, 97, 104, 258, 294-296, 343, 346
center, the, 24-25, 58, 219, 317-353
center-periphery, 24-25, 58, 219, 315-351
Central America, 188, 191
Chakravartty, Nikhil, 262
Chamoru, 190
Chief State Officers (CSOs), 7, 10-11, 17
Chikerema, Charles, 262
Childer, Erskine, 279
children, 72-73, 79, 283, 297, 319-320, 325
Chile, 248
China (PRC), 6, 14, 27, 31, 39-42, 45, 48-50, 131, 188, 192, 225, 239, 247
Christianity, 30-31, 45, 157, 247, 305
Chittagong Hills Tracts, 189
Church of England, 37
City University of New York, 129

civilizations, 23-66
civil rights/liberties, 77, 79, 114, 124
civil society, 3-21, 55, 59-60, 68, 70, 85-87, 91-101, 187, 189, 191, 211, 224, 227, 262, 265, 309, 327, 332, 338, 347-349, 351
Clann na Poblachta, 306
Clinton Administration, 46, 50-51, 59, 115-118, 121, 126-127, 333
Clinton, President Bill, 117, 120
Coca-Cola, 35, 39, 46, 204
Cold War, 23-24, 30-32, 38, 97, 107, 155-156, 237, 242, 263, 293
post Cold War, 31-33, 46, 112, 155-168, 262
Colombia, 248
colonialism, 26-27, 187-202, 236, 242, 305
Colorado, 347-351
communication flow; *see* news flow
communism, 24, 30, 41, 48, 161, 262-263
communitarian-democracy, 24, 45, 210-211
communitarianism, 26-27, 43, 45-46
community-oriented media; *see* media, community oriented
Commonwealth of the Northern Marianas Islands, 190
Computer Science NETwork (CSNE), 129
computers; *see* media, computers
CompuServe, 51, 110, 130
conflict resolution, 76-77, 83
Confucian, 30-31, 209
conservative, 32, 238, 243, 249, 253-60, 305, 309
Constantinople, 36
consumers/consumption, 13, 15-16, 20, 39, 41, 71, 80, 104, 135, 143-148, 152-153, 158-162, 214, 247, 281, 284, 323-324
Continental Cablevision, 52

SUBJECT INDEX

convergence (of media technologies), 104, 205, 207, 334
Copenhagen, 261, 338
copyright, 49, 119, 248, 282, 316, 344, 348; *see also* intellectual property
Corporate executive officers (CEOs), 7, 12, 17, 113
corruption, 16-17, 19
cosmology, 8
Costa Rica, 42, 55
cottage industry, 24
Cox, 125
crime, 124, 163
Cross Times, 84
Crusades, 32, 36
Cuba, 27, 42, 45, 55, 319
Cultural Environment Movement, 265, 350
Cultural Revolution, 14
culture, 5, 35, 51, 55, 70, 72, 75, 77, 92, 99, 131-132, 156-162, 165-167, 174-181, 187-222, 228, 236, 239, 243, 248, 251, 253, 270, 276, 278, 282-283, 290, 298, 302, 303, 305, 315-316, 319, 323-324, 326-327, 329, 331, 338, 341, 343
CUSeeMe, 112
Cultivation Theory, 229
cybermalls, 104
cyberoutlaws, 115
cyberights, 81-101, 104
cyberspace, 91-138, 338, 344, 346; *see also* Internet
Czechoslovakia, 55, 309, 319-322

D

"Dallas," 147
Danforth, Sen. John C., 119
data bases; *see* media, data bases
Decade of Culture; *see* UNESCO
deconstruction, 30
Deep Dish, 145
Deleon, Asher, 307

Delhi, 36
Delors Report (Report of the International Commission of Education in the 21st Century), 271, 297
Delphi, 51-2
democracy, 9, 12, 15-16, 19, 24, 26, 30-31, 33-34, 40-41, 45, 47, 57, 60, 69, 72, 80, 83, 93-94, 103, 115, 121-124, 126, 128, 132-133, 135, 139-154, 169-170, 203-212, 218, 225-226, 239, 263-264, 293-294, 296-297, 309, 316, 319, 321, 324, 327, 336, 338, 345-347, 349-350
Deng Xiaoping, 6
Denmark, 191-192
Dependency Theory, 29, 214
deregulation, 110, 280, 328, 337
Derrida, Jacques, 215
de Valera, Eamon, 306
DEVCOM, 272, 301
development, 20, 32, 57, 140, 145, 152, 169-185, 189, 225-227, 230, 235-265, 269-303, 320-321, 326, 333, 336-337, 345, 348
Development Support Communication Service, 279
digital media; *see* media, digital
direct broadcast satellites (DBS); *see* media, DBS
discourse, 11, 18, 21, 24, 26-31, 51, 56-57, 59, 73, 163, 181, 209, 213-216, 218, 220, 227-228, 230, 263, 317, 324
disease, 76
Disney World, 43
distance learning, 272, 276
Dole, Gov. Stanford, 194
Dublin, 306, 311-312
Duke University, 129
Durban (South Africa), 264

SUBJECT INDEX 365

E

1870s, 162
EARN (European Academic and Research Network), 129
Earth Summit, Rio de Janeiro (1992), 325
East, The, 24, 204, 238, 242-243, 284, 320
Eastern Europe, 18, 30, 58, 156, 239, 258, 309, 326
East Timor, 189
East-West Center, 331
ecology, 67-89, 189
economics, 3-66, 75, 79-81, 94, 100, 104, 139-154, 162, 170-171, 176, 189, 191, 215, 217, 219-220, 227, 230, 236, 239, 243, 245, 247, 254, 264, 275-277, 285, 290, 298, 301, 315-316, 322, 326, 333
Economist, The, 49, 338
education, communication, 83
education, journalism, 83, 303, 336
Eek, 240
Egypt, 36, 42, 256
Eighteenth Century, 4, 36
Eisenhower Administration, President Dwight D., 52, 333
Eisenmenger, 348
electro magnetic spectrum, 119
Electronic Frontier Foundation, 121, 127-128
electronic mail; *see also* E-mail, electronic mail, media,
Eleventh Century, 36
elites (countries and people), 26, 55, 71, 85, 92, 161-162, 169, 172, 276, 310, 328-329
empires, 35, 38
employment, 19, 43
England; *see* Great Britain
Enlightenment, 3, 25, 30, 36, 39, 214
environment, 13, 45, 58, 70, 81, 85, 189, 322, 326

equity/equality, 25, 52, 57, 79, 82-83, 112, 126, 133-134, 179, 207, 210, 213, 235-307, 315-351
espionage, 113, 291
ethics; *see* journalist, professional ethics
ethnicity, 45, 156, 161, 187-202, 219, 263, 297, 322, 327
Europe, 3, 15, 18, 33, 36-42, 51, 58, 110, 189, 191, 221, 238, 249, 305-306, 325, 328, 344
European Convention for the Protection of Human Rights, 295
European Union (EU), 39, 46, 53, 333, 344
Exon, Sen. Jim, 120

F

facsimile/fax; *see* media, facsimile
FAO, 279
fascism, 96
feminism, 70, 72, 78, 83, 86
feudalism, 3, 36-37, 56, 93, 164
Fianna Fail, 306
Fido Net, 55
FIEJ; *see* International Federation of Newspaper Publishers
File transfer protocol (FTP), 112
film; *see* media, film
Finland, 239
First Amendment; *see* United States, First Amendment of Constitution
First World, 24, 32, 38, 48
Florence, 36
folk theater, 338
Fordism, 56
Ford, Sen. Wendell, 119
Fourteenth Century, 36
Fourth World, 24
France, 37-38, 45, 192, 228, 240, 245, 255-257, 275
Frankfurt, 58
Frankfurt School, 216

freedom/liberty, 94, 104, 121, 133-134, 209, 221, 240, 249, 251, 259, 263, 293-294, 320
freedom of expression; *see* freedom of speech
freedom of speech, 6, 41, 160, 223, 230, 248, 259, 270, 291, 293, 309-310, 319
freedom of the press, 92, 94, 249, 251, 253, 255-256, 259, 286, 293, 319
free flow; *see* news flow/information flow
free market, 9 18, 24, 27, 30, 32-33, 36-41, 45-46, 70-71, 78, 80, 83, 85, 105, 113, 152-153, 155-162, 166, 169, 194. 214, 218, 226, 229, 256-257, 284
French revolution, 174, 259
Friends of the Earth, 55
fundamentalism, 45

G

Gaia (goddess of the Earth), 75, 83
Gallup, George, 128
Game Theory, 209-210
Gandhi, Prime Minister Indira, 48, 80, 258
"gang of four," 255
Gannett, 198
Gatekeeper Theory, 118, 290
Gauhati, 176
gays, 16, 77
General Agreement of Tariffs and Trade (GATT), 38, 98, 333-334
General Atomics, 118, 130
General Systems Theory, 204
Geneva, 18, 249, 307
geopolitical, 24, 238-239, 343, 347
Georgia (U.S.), 122
Georgetown (Guyana), 257-258
Geneva Convention; *see* League of Nations
Germany, 38, 45, 55

Glasnevin, 311
global/globalism, 20, 24, 27, 31, 33, 38-40, 45-47, 58-60, 68-72, 77, 79-87, 91-92, 97, 99, 106, 140-141, 143-145, 151-152, 216-219, 235, 242, 249, 255, 263-264, 277, 317, 320-321, 326, 333, 335, 337-338, 342-345, 348-349, 351
global glasnost, 211
Global Information Infrastructure (GII), 344
Global Information Infrastructure Initiative (GIII), 98
Global Information Society, 99
Gonne, Maud, 306
Gramsci, Antonio, 220
grassroots media; *see* media, grass roots
grassroots movements, 139-154, 319, 331-332, 334, 338, 345
Great Britain, 18, 37-38, 55, 110, 122, 129, 191-192, 215, 218, 229, 249, 252, 254, 260, 275, 305-306, 308, 334
Greece, 93, 96, 100
Greenpeace, 55
Grenada, 260
Group of 77, 27-28, 49
G7, 28, 49, 98, 337, 344
Guarujá, 325
Gulf War; *see* Persian Gulf War
Gundishapur, 36
Gutenberg, Johan, 92, 100
Guyana, 257-258

H

hackers, 114
Haiti, 24, 28, 31, 42
Halleck, DeeDee, 348
Hamburg, 192
Harare, 262, 314-317, 319, 321
Harvard University, 216
Hawaii, 109, 119, 122, 187-202, 331-334

Hawaiian National Broadcasting
    Corp., 197
Hawaii Investors, 190
Hawaii Public Radio, 198
health care, 132-133, 171, 189, 275,
    286, 299
Hegelian, 31
Helsinki Final Act, 289, 293
Helsinki Citizens' Assembly, 20
Hindu, 31, 107
Hindustan Times, 176
history, 8, 18, 23-66, 92, 95-96, 98,
    155, 166, 172, 174, 177, 188, 214,
    219, 235, 238, 242, 248, 272, 284-
    285, 290, 305, 309, 321, 326
Hilton Hotels, 39
Hobbesian, 31
Holiday Inns, 46
Hollings, Rep. Ernest, 119
homeless, 74
Hong Kong, 25, 54, 192
Honolulu, 103, 316, 331-334
Honolulu Advertiser, 198
human rights, 4, 8, 45, 55, 68, 91-
    101, 210, 235-304, 306-307, 309,
    316-317, 320-321, 326-339
Human Rights Declaration; *see* United
    Nations, Human Rights
    Declaration
hunger strikes, 15
Hussein, Saddam, 27, 31, 51
Hutchins Commission, 347-348
Huxley, Aldous, 126

I

IBM Corporation, 118, 130
imperialism, 27, 33, 37-38, 203-212,
    228, 239, 242, 253
India, 40, 42, 45, 51, 176, 180, 188,
    239, 258, 262
Indian Council of North America
    (CISA), 191
indigenous people, 174, 189-202,
    316, 332, 334, 342

Indo-European, 75
Indonesia, 247
Indra's Net, 107
Industrial Age, 94
industry, 4, 25, 40, 45, 48, 54, 59, 68,
    171, 189, 218, 226, 242, 247, 256,
    280-281, 289-290, 309, 320, 324,
    327-328, 332, 336-337; *see also*
    industrialization
inequity; *see* equity
Infoban, 103
information (super) highway, 52-53,
    68, 103, 118, 122, 124, 126, 332-
    338, 341
Information Society Theories, 29,
    32, 151, 220, 337-338, 341-342,
    344, 348
Igls (Austria), 261
Inouye, Sen. Daniel, 119
Integrated System Digital Networks
    (ISDN), 52, 333
intellectuals, 178, 180, 238, 240, 242
Inter-American Press Association
    (IAPA), 243
intergovernmental organizations
    (IGOs), 6, 20, 47, 49, 60, 144,
    150-151, 270, 303, 326, 329, 334,
    345, 348, 351
International Association for Mass
    Communication Research
    (IAMCR), 323
International Chamber of
    Commerce (Paris, 1920), 18, 20
International Commission for the
    Study of Communication Problems;
    see MacBride Commission
International Commission of
    Jurists, 306
*International Directory of
    Development Journalists*, 180
International Federation of Editors-
    in-Chief, 254

International Federation of Newspaper Publishers (FIEJ), 255, 259, 277
International Herald Tribune, 49, 259
International Indian Treaty Council, 191
International Labour Organization, 188-189
International Monetary Fund (IMF), 27, 38, 144, 151
International Non-Governmental Organization on Human Rights, 307
International Organization of Journalists (IOJ), 216, 258-259, 262, 308, 315
International Peace Bureau, 307
International Press Institute (IPI), 243, 254, 259
International Program for the Development of Communication (IPDC), 236, 245, 249-250, 261, 272, 274, 291, 298, 300-301
International Publisher Association, 49
International Radio Telegraph Convention (Berlin, 1906), 95
International Red Cross, 339
International Telecommunications Union (ITU), 98-99, 151, 249, 277, 317, 333-334, 336, 341-342, 345
    World Administrative Radio Conference (WARC), 79, 249, 277, 279
    World Telecommunication Development Conference (Buenos Aires, 1994), 99
International Telegraph and Telephone Consultative Committee, 278
International Telegraph Convention, 95

International Year of the World's Indigenous People (1993), 191
Internet, 46, 50-52, 92, 97-98, 100, 103-139, 285, 339, 343, 345, 349; *see also* cyberspace
Internet 1996 World Exposition, 131
Internet Protocol (IP), 108; *see also* TCP/IPs
Internet Relay Chat, 112
INTERNIC Information Services, 118
Inter-Press Service (IPS), 145, 279
Invisible Hand, 4
Iran, 28, 36, 40, 42, 48, 50, 239, 309
Iran-Iraq War, 40
Iraq, 28, 31, 40, 42, 239, 262
Iraqi war in Gulf; *see* Persian Gulf War
Ireland, 305-311, 349
Irish Constitution, 306
Irish Republican Army (IRA), 306
Isahan, 36
Ishikawa, Sakae, 348
Islam, 30-32, 219-220
isomorphism, 205
Istanbul, 304, 323-324
Italy, 37-38, 45, 192

J

Jackson, Michael (rock musician), 46
Jamaica, 256
jamming (radio signals), 97
Japan, 5-6, 14, 38, 40, 42, 51, 53-54, 110, 114, 247, 252, 333
Jefferson, Pres., Thomas, 121
Jeffersonian, 48, 105, 128
Jerusalem, 50
Johnson, Rep. Tim, 120
Jomtien Conference, 271
journalism/journalists, 19, 80-81, 83-84, 103, 155-186, 235-304, 308, 322, 326, 329, 336, 339, 344, 347, 351; *see also* "the press" and UNESCO: "Consultative Club"

education of; *see* education, journalism and language/culture barrier, 290
licensing, 257-259
professional ethics and responsibilities, 162, 257, 286-291, 316, 322, 326
protection of journalists, 254-255, 291-292, 295, 326, 334, 339, 344
justice/judicial, 11, 14, 40, 76-77, 80, 193

K

Kamehameha I, 192
Kamehameha III, 192
Kashlev, Yuri, 252
Kekkonen, President, 239
Kenman, George, 32
Kennedy, President John F., 21, 123
Kenya, 55, 85
keyboard cowboys, 115
Khrushchev, Nikita, 207
Kluckholm, Clyde, 216
Korea, 38, 40; *see also* North Korea and South Korea
Kroeber, Alfred, 215-216
Kroloff and Cohen report, 244, 254
Kuala Lumpur, 247, 250
Kurds, 58
Kuwait, 54

L

labor, 8, 13, 17, 33, 49, 55, 171, 226, 281, 286, 324, 329, 344
language barrier; *see* journalists
languages, 45, 99, 228, 271-272, 280, 290, 297
  English, 37, 50, 194
  French, 37, 310
  German, 37
  Hawaiian, 194
  Latin, 37
  Hindi, 51
  Italian, 37
  Japanese, 50
  Polish, 50
  Spanish, 50
Latin America, 38, 45, 51, 145, 180, 325, 344, 348
League of Nations, 95, 192, 236
Geneva Convention Concerning the Use of Broadcasting in the Cause of Peace, 95
left, the, 9, 33, 238, 305
Leninism, 239
Lenin Peace Prize, 307
lesbians, 77, 86
Less Developed Countries (LDCs), 27-29, 38, 41, 53-54, 58
liberal, 26, 29, 32, 214, 238, 249, 254, 305
liberalization of markets, 144, 151-153, 337, 343; *see also* neoliberalization
Libertarian, 160-161, 163-165, 167, 169
libraries, 53, 276
Library of Congress, 54
Liliuokalani, Queen, 193
Lisbon, 28
literacy, 111, 271-273, 276, 310, 327, 348
localism, 24, 27, 40, 43, 46, 139-154, 166, 177-179, 181, 217, 229, 343
Locke, John, 85
London, 36, 58
Long, Gerald, 249
Los Angeles, 25, 58
Louvre, The, 122

M

MacBride, John, 306
MacBride Commission, 27, 170, 218, 223, 228, 230, 235-306, 307-308, 314-351
MacBride Report, 27-28, 213, 217, 223-232, 235-304, 307-308, 314-351
  Draft Declaration, 245-246

SUBJECT INDEX

MacBride Round Tables, 262-263, 265, 314-351
  First; Harare, 262, 314-317
  Second; Prague, 216, 314, 319-322
  Third; Istanbul, 314, 325-330
  Fourth; Guarujá (São Paulo), 314, 325-330
  Sixth; Honolulu, 103, 314, 331-334
  Seventh; Tunis, 314, 334-339
  Eighth; Seoul, 314, 341-346
  Ninth; Boulder, 314, 347-351
M'Bow, Dir. Gen. Amadou-Mahtar, 261, 310
McCarthyism, 310
McDonald's Corporation, 39, 46
McKinley, President William, 194
Madonna (rock musician), 35, 46
magazines; *see* media
Malaysia, 189
Manila, 58
manufacturing, 29
Many Voices, One World; see MacBride Report
Mao Tse-tung, Chairman, 6
Margan, Ivo, 252-253
market, 8, 13, 16, 19, 24, 30, 36, 38, 41, 53, 80, 85, 96, 99, 105, 118, 134, 141, 144, 152-153, 156, 160-161, 194, 277, 281, 283, 309, 316, 323, 326-327, 337-338, 343
Marks, Leonard, 255
Marques, Gabriel Garcia, 248
"Marshal Plan" of Communication/Telecommunications, 245, 248, 256, 260
Marxism, 26-27, 29-30, 32, 80, 205, 215, 226
Mass Media Declaration; *see* United Nations
materialism, 214, 216
Mayor, Federico, 261

Maternalism, 74, 189, 215, 217, 219, 221
MCI Telecommunications Corporation 110, 118, 130
media, 12, 50, 55, 59, 67, 74, 82-86, 94-95, 140-186, 203-212, 214, 217, 219, 225, 227-229, 235-306, 307, 321, 323-327, 329-336, 338, 341-346, 348-351; *see also* mass media
  alternative, 82, 139-154, 265, 322, 331, 338, 341-351
  audiocassettes, 50
  books, 92-94, 144-145, 273, 276, 336, 351
  broadcast, 11, 43, 50, 52-53, 55, 95, 105, 116, 125, 133, 139, 141, 144-147, 151-153, 162, 197-198, 228-230, 244-246, 248, 265, 272-273, 275-276, 290, 295, 300, 302, 304, 336, 338, 343, 349
  cable television, 52-53, 55, 104, 115, 128, 133
  community-based, 139-154, 265, 274, 343, 348-349
  computers, 43, 52-53, 103-138, 145, 225-226, 229, 285, 328, 331, 343, 345, 349
  copy machines, 50
  databases, 53, 104, 115, 128, 133
  desk top publishing, 145, 333
  digital, 103-138, 328
  Digital Audio Broadcasting (DAB), 144
  Direct broadcast satellite (DBS), 51, 96, 144
  electronic mail (e-mail), 85-86, 111, 333
  facsimile/fax, 50, 85, 224, 333
  film (movies), 53, 105, 141, 145, 152, 228, 273, 276, 300
  grassroots, 149, 170, 210, 247
  magazines (including news magazines), 11, 55, 105, 145, 162, 273, 278

multimedia, 43, 53, 125, 226
newsletters, 145, 331
newspapers, 11, 43, 53, 55, 80, 83-84, 94, 103, 105, 141, 152, 162, 164-165, 176, 197-198, 229, 255, 273, 276, 278, 290, 295, 298, 336, 338, 343
portable video, 50, 139, 141, 145, 152, 226, 265, 331, 343-344, 346
radio; *see* media, broadcast
satellites, 50, 96-97, 117, 144-145, 151, 245, 277-279, 288, 302, 328
television; *see* media, broadcast
underground, 49
VCRs, 55, 85
video on demand, 125
media conglomerates; *see* TMCs
media effects research, 155-168, 223-232
Media Foundation of the Non-Aligned (NAMEDIA); *see* Non-Aligned Movement
media monitoring, 265
Mediation and Conflict Training for Journalists Project (MPJ), 84
Mega Sound, 51
melting pot model, 206
Merit Network, Inc., 130
Mexico, 14
Mexico City, 58
Middle Ages, 36
Middle East, 325, 344
military, 17, 38-39, 77, 97, 107, 113, 194-195, 197, 307, 309, 326
Mill, John Stuart, 259
MILNET, 109, 129
minorities, 13, 15-17, 53 77, 81, 123, 134, 161, 219, 228, 293, 296-297, 324, 329, 331, 342
Mitsubishi, 49
mobile telephones, 53
modernity, 8, 24-25, 29, 33-43, 45, 47, 58-59, 67, 155-185, 219
Mondiale Satellite Channel, 145

monopoly, 7, 40, 134, 253, 281, 295, 321, 323
Montesquieu, 6
Morella, Rep. Constance, 119
Morgan, Lewis Henry, 214-215
Moscow News, 258
movies; *see* media, film
"Mr. Rogers' Neighborhood," 229
multinationals; *see* TNCs
murder, 71, 73-74, 254-255, 291-292, 295, 326; *see also* journalists, protection of
Murdock, Rupert, 51-52
Music Television (MTV), 43, 46, 50-51, 57
Muslims, 220
Mussolini, Benito, 55
mythology/myths, 72-73, 75, 79, 83, 107, 174, 227
1920s, 95
1930s, 95
1940s, 237-238, 348
1950s, 237-238, 242
1960s, 32, 96, 163, 169, 237
1970s, 96, 103, 114, 162, 191, 236, 238, 241-242, 244, 348
1980s, 96-97, 103, 162, 191
1990s, 103, 113

N

Nairobi, 85, 252, 254, 307
NAMEDIA Foundation (India), 258, 262, 315
Namibia, 307
narrative; *see* discourse
National Research and Education Network (NREN), 130
nationalism, 27, 31, 37, 39, 43, 46, 48
National Rifle Association, 14
national security, 97, 100
Nazism, 96
"Neighbors," 147
Net, the; *see* Internet
net surfing, 112

Neve Rheinische Zeitung, 94
New Age philosophy, 48
New Delhi, 176, 258
New International Economic Order (NIEO), 27-28, 237, 240-242, 246, 254, 257, 299
news agencies, 144-145, 243, 254, 256-258, 273, 289, 300; *see also* TNAs
news flow/information flow, 58-59, 112, 118, 155-185, 203-212, 235-304, 308, 316, 321, 335, 337, 344, 348
New International Information Order (NIIO), 208, 236, 245, 249, 253, 258
news magazines; *see* media
newspapers; *see* media
news agency pool; *see* Non Aligned Movement, news agency pool
New World Economic Order; *see* New International Economic Order
New World Information and Communication Order (NWICO), 27-28, 54, 59-60, 82, 235-304, 308, 314-351
UN-UNESCO Round Table on NWICO, 261-262, 274
new world order, 23-24, 26, 28, 33, 57-58, 155, 236-237, 242, 245, 247-251, 262, 335
New York, 18, 25, 40, 55
New York Times, 97, 254
New Zealand, 42, 131, 247, 252
NHK, 51
Nicaragua, 258
Nigeria, 180, 263
Nineteenth Century, 4, 36, 38, 55, 92, 161
Nixon, President Richard, 123
Nobel Peace Prize, 307

Non-Aligned Movement, 238-239, 242-243, 246-248, 252-253, 257-259, 261, 263, 323, 335
Conferences
Fourth Summit, Algiers (1973), 239, 335
Fifth Summit, Colombo, 239, 243, 258
Sixth Summit, la Havana, 258
Twelfth Summit, Durban, South Africa, 264
Intergovernmental Council for the Coordination of Information, Georgetown, South Africa (1981), 257-258
Ministerial Meetings
New Delhi, 243
Fifth, Abuja (Nigeria), 263
Ministers of Information of Non-Aligned Countries (COMI NACIII), 319
NAMEDIA Foundation; *see* NAMEDIA Foundation
Tunis Symposium on Culture and Information (1976), 243, 335
Non-Aligned News Agency Pool (NANAP), 300, 335
Non Government Organizations (NGOs), 6, 47, 49-50, 54-55, 59-60, 76, 85, 139-140, 149-151, 216, 241, 258-259, 262, 265, 274, 304, 307, 317, 323, 326, 328-329, 334, 346-348, 351
normative, 30, 162
North, the, 24, 27, 81, 219, 243, 278, 315, 351
North America, 40-2, 188-189, 191, 238, 245, 249, 325, 347
North American Free Trade Area (NAFTA), 39
North Atlantic Treaty Organization (NATO), 306
North Korea, 28, 42
Norway, 109, 129, 192

SUBJECT INDEX

NSFNET, 109-110, 116, 130-131; *see also* United States, NSF
nuclear weapons, 17, 98

O

obscenity, 117, 344
OECD, 151, 344
Office of Hawaiian Affairs (OHA), 197
oil, 27, 242
Oklahoma City, 58
"one world," 85
Organization of Petroleum Exporting Countries (OPEC), 27
Orwell, George, 255
Ottoman Empire, 38
Oxfam, 55
Ozal, President Turgut, 51
Oz (land of), 107

P

Pacific Asia Council of Indigenous Peoples (PACIP), 190
Pacific Islands, 187-202
Pacific Telecommunications Council (PTC), 332-333
Pakistan, 247
Palestine Liberation Organization (PLO), 49
Palestinians, 59
papacy, 3, 37, 247
paper production and affordability, 277-278, 336
Paper Tiger Television, 348
paradigms/paradigm shifts, 56-57, 70-73, 82-83, 170-171, 220, 350
Paraguay, 309
Paris, 18, 36, 122, 244-248, 252, 259, 309
Parsons, Talcott, 216
Patriarchy, 8, 67-89
peace, 24, 27, 37, 40, 46, 55, 58, 68, 77, 81, 83, 97, 170, 256, 264, 293, 301-303, 306, 316, 321, 324-327, 329, 339, 349-350

peace studies, 78
Pearl Harbor, 195
pendulum principle, 208
people of color, 71, 134, 161, 219, 310, 322, 326
People's Communication Charter, 265
Perez de Cuellar, Sec.-Gen. Javier, 264, 282
Periphery, 24-25, 32-33, 50, 58, 86, 219-220, 305, 315-351; *see also* Center-Periphery
Persian Gulf, 40, 323
Persian Gulf War, 24, 27-28, 40, 50, 262, 323
personal computers (PCs); *see* media, computers
Pinochet, Gen. Augusto, 228
Platform for Cooperation on Democraticisation and Communication, London (1996), 349
Plekhanov, Georgei, 215
poor, the, 74, 86, 245, 316, 328-329, 333, 336, 338, 344
postal system, 35, 192, 275
postcolonial, 26
postindustrial, 24, 29, 32, 48, 320
postmodernity, 24-25, 33, 35, 39, 46-48, 51, 57, 59, 155-185
poststructuralism, 215
power relationships, 5, 7-8, 15, 17, 21, 28, 32-33, 36, 45, 56, 59, 67-89, 96-97, 114, 126, 129, 144, 155, 157, 173-174, 181, 215, 240, 243, 246, 248, 257-258, 303, 320, 328, 337, 342-343, 347-349
Prague, 304, 319-322
premodernity, 59
Pressler, Sen. Larry, 120
press pool; *see* Persian Gulf War
press, the; *see* journalism
Principle of Multiple Collective Action, 211

print media; *see* media, newspapers
privacy, 135
Prodigy, 51, 110
progressivism, 174, 243
PROJECT SHARE, 277
Protestant, 3-4, 37, 45, 247, 305
public broadcasting, 133, 198, 288
public journalism, 165-167
public opinion, 308-310, 316
Pulsar, 145

R

radio; *see* media, broadcast
Rand Corporation, 49, 107
Rabin, Yitzhak, 50
Radek, Karl, 215
"Rambo," 229
rap music, 51
rape, 71
Readers Digest Syndrome, 206
Reagan Administration, 259
Reagan, President Ronald, 254, 260, 338
Reformation, 36
Reinhardt, Ambassador John E., 244, 248-249
religion, 3-4, 8, 11, 27, 31, 40, 45-46, 49-50, 55-58, 60, 72, 74-75, 180, 190, 195, 219, 275, 283, 293, 297, 322, 324, 326-327
Renaissance, 36
Reporters Without Frontiers, 291
research community, 71, 76-77, 80-81, 83, 103, 111, 118, 129-130, 155-168, 223-232, 238, 243, 247, 280-281, 301-302, 323, 325, 333, 344, 346-347, 349, 351
responsibilities of journalists; *see* journalists, responsibilities
Reuters, 249
revolutions, 174
rhetoric; *see* discourse
right to communicate, 91-101, 118, 152-153, 160, 169-185, 218, 223, 240, 251, 293-294, 309, 321, 323, 327, 331, 345-346
right to listen; *also see* communication recipients
Rockefeller, John D., 49
Rockefeller, Sen. John, 119
rock music, 57
Romania, 309
Rome, 36-37, 238
Roosevelt, President Franklin D., 55, 123
Rosen, Jay, 165, 167
Rousseau, Jean-Jacques, 48
Rushdie, Salmon, 57, 218
Russia, 27, 38, 40, 45, 48-49, 98
Rwanda (also territory of Ruanda), 291, 309

S

Saami, 188
Sadat, Anwar, 50
Saipan, 190
salad bowl model, 206-207
São Paulo, 316, 325-330
Sassen, Saskia, 347
Saudi Arabia, 50, 54, 131
Scandinavia, 188
Second World, 24, 39, 238
Segal, Baba, 51
Seoul, 316, 341-346
Serbia, 28
"Sesame Street," 229
Seventeenth Century, 4, 36, 92
sex ,10, 57, 67-89; *see also* sexuality
Shah of Iran, 309
Shiites, 58
Shopping for a Better World, 17
Silicon Graphics, 125
Singapore, 25, 41, 54, 334
Sixteenth Century, 25, 36, 157
soap operas, 229
social democracy, 3-4
socialism, 3-4, 18, 20, 45, 161, 236, 238, 242, 244, 253, 258, 309-310, 326

Social Summit (Copenhagen), 338
Sofia, 260
Somalia, 24, 28, 31, 40, 42, 59, 291, 309
South, the, 24, 27-28, 81, 219, 238-239, 243, 263-264, 315-351
South Africa, 42, 84, 110, 264, 309, 349
South America, 188, 191, 238, 309
South Korea, 25, 41, 45, 341-346
sovereignty, 195, 197, 315
Soviet bloc, 5-6, 238-239, 255, 293
Soviet Union, 23-24, 30-32, 39-42, 45, 188, 206, 215, 228, 239, 243, 247, 252, 258, 309, 325
former Soviet Union, 24, 31, 85
Spain, 37
spamming, 130
spirituality, 72, 75
sports, 77
Sri Lanka, 42, 245
Stalin, Joseph, 74
Star TV, 50-1
the State, 3-21, 26, 35-38, 41, 45, 50, 57, 59-60, 85, 152-153, 169, 178, 181, 187, 189, 191, 206, 218, 264, 295, 300, 310, 327, 332
state control of media; *see* State
status quo; *see* elites
Steiner, Rudolf, 6
stereotyping, 77, 161, 329
Stevens, Rep. Ted, 119
Steward, Julian, 215
Sting (rock musician), 57
stockholders, 12
storytellers, 338
"street children," 325; *see also* children
structuralism, 214-218, 220
Sunday Times, 255
surveillance, 228
sustainable development, 20
Sweden, 55, 192, 240
Switzerland, 9, 192, 252

T

Tahiti, 192
Taiwan, 25, 41, 45, 54
Tallories, 255-258
Tanjug News Agency, 300; *see also* Non Aligned Movement
Tanzania, 239
Tatans, 59
TCI, 125
technocrats, 158
technological determinism, 173, 223-225
technology, 23, 26, 29, 33, 35-38, 40-41, 43, 49, 53, 55-58, 70, 85, 94-95, 97, 103, 114, 124, 132, 173, 190, 223-232, 245, 247, 264, 281, 286, 296, 300, 302-303, 316-317, 328-329, 331-333
new communication technology (including telecommunications) 40, 50, 53-54, 85, 93, 96-100, 103-138, 141, 144, 156-162, 204, 211, 223-232, 237, 249, 264, 274-278, 281, 284, 297, 300, 302, 303, 315-317, 320, 328-331, 332-333, 335-336, 339, 344-345, 350
Tehran, 58
Telecommunications Act; *see* United States, Telecommunications Act
Telecommunications Policy Roundtable, 127, 132
telecommuting, 122
telegraph, 94-5, 278
telephone, 53, 107, 117, 125, 172, 333, 336, 345
television; *see* media, broadcast
telnet, 112
Tennessee, 54
terrorism, 15-16, 58
Texas, 122
think tanks, 32, 49

Third World, 24, 27, 32, 38-39, 48, 169-185, 236-268, 305, 310, 320, 336
Third World Network, 350
Thirteenth Century, 18, 36
Thoreau, Henry David, 48
Tiananmen Square, 50
Tibet, 49
Tibetans, 59
Timbuktu, 36
Time magazine, 249
Time Warner, 125
Tokyo, 58, 336
Toronto, 296
totalitarianism, 45
tourism, 50
trade, 38-39, 47, 326
trade unions, 12
transborder information flow, 95, 104
Transmission Control Protocol/Internet protocol (TCP/IPs), 108-109, 118, 129
transnational corporations (TNCs), 6, 20, 39, 41, 47, 49, 60, 104-105, 143-144, 262, 280, 282, 295, 301, 323-324, 328, 337, 344
transnational media corporations (TMCs), 47, 60, 74, 96, 141, 161, 295, 323, 349
transnational news agencies (TNAs), 144, 243, 256, 258; *see also* news agencies
Tufts University, Fletcher School of Law and Diplomacy, 255
Tunis, 314, 334-339
Tunis Association of Communication (ATUCOM), 334-335
Tunisia, 245, 334-339
Turkey, 51, 323-324
Twelfth Century, 18, 37
Twentieth Century, 38, 55, 79, 347
Twenty-First Century, 67, 85, 110, 134, 345
Twigg-Smith, Thurston, 198
two-way flow, 92, 170, 280

U

UCLA, 129
Uganda, 239
Uighurs, 59
Ulster, 305-306
UNCTAD; *see* UNESCO
UNESCO, 28, 82, 98, 151, 235-303, 310, 317, 324, 326, 333-334, 339, 342, 345, 348
  Bard Amendment, 258-260
  "Consultative Club," 241, 254, 258
  Consultative Meeting on the Protection of Journalists, 254-255
  Decade of Culture, 326
  General Conferences
    Nineteenth, Nairobi, 243-244, 252, 254, 307
    Twentieth, Paris, 244-246, 248, 252
    Twenty-First, Belgrade, 249-255, 321
    Twenty-Second, Paris, 259
    Twenty-Third, Sofia, 260
  Intergovernmental Conference on Communication Policies in Asia and Oceania, 247
    Kuala Lumpur (1979), 250
    Yaounde (1980), 250
  Intergovernmental Conference on Communication Policies in Latin America and the Caribbean
    San José, Costa Rica (1976), 243, 247, 250
  International Principles of Professional Ethics in Journalism (1983), 241, 258
  Mass Media Declaration (1978), 96, 242, 244, 252, 260, 292-293
  Mexico Declaration (1978), 96, 242, 244, 252, 260, 292-293
  Paris Compromise, 246-247
  World Commission on Culture and Development report (1995), 151

SUBJECT INDEX

United Airlines, 45
United Arab Emirates, 54
United Kingdom (UK); *see* Great Britain
United Nations (UN), 18, 20, 27-28, 38, 59, 68, 85, 98, 188-189, 207, 235-268, 270-303, 307, 317, 323, 328, 341-342, 345, 348-350
  Administrative Coordination Committee, 345
  Charter (general reference), 258
  Charter, Article 23, 20
  Charter of Economic Rights and Duties, 237
  Committee on Information (UNCI), 246, 259, 261, 263, 317
  Conference on Freedom of Information, Geneva (1948), 237
  Conference on Trade and Development (UNCTAD), 243, 317
  Convention on the International Right of Correction, 237
  Corporate Assembly (UNCA), 20
  DBS Resolution (1982), 96
  Decade for World's Indigenous People (1994-2003), 332
  Decade for Women (Nairobi), 85
  Declaration of Guiding Principles on the Use of Satellite Broadcasting for the Free Flow of Information, 237
  Development Program (UNDP), 25
  Economic and Social Council (ECOSOC), 236-237
  General Assembly (UNGA), 20, 27, 190-191
  General Conferences, 246, 302
  Genocide Convention, 237
  Human Development Report, 279
  International Covenant on Civil and Political Rights, 237-238
  International Relations in the Sphere of Information and Mass Communications Report, 246
  Martinez-Cobo Report, 187
  Mass Media Declaration (1978), 96
  Outer Space Committee (COPUOS), 96
  Outer Space Treaty, 237
  Peoples Assembly (UNPA), 20
  Recommendation 67; *see* IPDC
  Resolution 33/115, 246
  Secretary for Human Rights and Social Affairs, 252
  Security Council, 27, 38
  UNICEF, 279
  Universal Declaration of Human Rights (1948), 237, 240, 350
  Universal Declaration of Human Rights, Article 4, 94
  Universal Declaration of Human Rights, Article 19, 96, 98, 294
  Working Group on Indigenous Populations, 189
  World Commission on Culture and Development, 264, 282
United States, 11, 16, 28, 31-32, 37-40, 45, 51-55, 72, 98-99, 103-138, 187-202, 207, 215-216, 228-229, 240, 243-260, 301, 309-310, 334, 344, 348-349
  Central Intelligence Agency (CIA), 258
  Communications Act of 1934, 116
  Communications Decency Act of 1995, 117, 120, 131
  Department of Defense, 109, 120
  Department of Education, 130
  Department of Energy, 104
  Drug Enforcement Agency, 131
  First Amendment of Constitution, 94, 117, 249
  High Performance Computing Act (1991), 116, 130

High Performance Computing and Communications Initiative (HPCCI), 116
House Committee on Foreign Relations, 248, 256
International Communication Agency, 248
National Aeronautics and Space Administration (NASA), 109
National Research Education Network (NREN), 116, 128
National Science Foundation (NSF), 109, 115, 118, 130-131
NII (National Information Infrastructure), 98, 115-156, 118, 121, 127, 132-133, 333
Pentagon, 97, 107; see also military
Pentagon's Advanced Research Projects Agency (ARPA), 108-109, 115; see also ARPANET
Secretary of State, 256
Secret Service, 131
Senate Committee on Foreign Relations, 243
Supreme Court, 190
Telecommunications Act of 1996, 105, 117, 120
withdrawal from UNESCO, 245, 260
United States Institute of Peace, 32
United States-Iraq conflict/war; see Persian Gulf War
universal service, 54, 133, 152, 285, 338
universities, 76-79, 81, 113, 130-131, 134
University College Dublin, 306
University of Colorado, 347
University of Hawaii, 26
University of Leicester, 235
University of Minnesota, 130
University of North Carolina, 129
University of Utah, 129
underrepresented nations and peoples organizations (UNPOs), 47, 49
urban, 32, 35-37, 40, 44, 60, 86, 273, 276, 238, 338
Uruguay, 55
USENET, 104, 115, 129
U. S. News & World Report, 255
U.S.S.R.; *see* Soviet Union
US West, 125
UUCP (Unix-to-Unix Copy Protocol), 129

V

"velvet revolution," 309
Venezuela, 245, 251
Venice, 36
Veronica, 112
videocassettes; *see* media, videocassettes
video games, 123
Vidéazimut, 139-140, 265, 350
Vietnam, 27, 38, 42, 45, 131, 247
Vietnam War, 309
violence, 10, 15-16, 40, 46-47, 72-74, 77, 81, 84, 156, 163, 229, 325, 329, 339
Voices of Freedom Conference of Independent News Media, 254-257

W

Wall Street Journal, 49
war, 46, 70, 96, 192, 195, 236, 249, 260, 292, 302-303, 322-323, 326, 329, 339
WAIS, 112, 130
WARC; *see* ITU
Washington, DC, 14, 118, 123, 127, 132, 190, 194, 336
weapons technology, 326-327
welfare, 74
West, the, 14, 24, 29-31, 45, 51, 114, 163, 169, 171-173, 176, 178, 180-181, 204, 214, 217, 219-220, 226, 230, 240-265, 275, 281, 284, 289, 315-351

West Papua, 189
West Virginia, 12
wire services; *see* news agencies
White, Leslie, 215
Whole Internet Users' Guide and Catalogue, 51-52
Wilson Quarterly, 348
Windhoek, 291
women, 13, 16-17, 67-89, 134, 293, 296-298, 303, 319-320, 322, 324, 327, 329, 331-332, 334, 338-339, 342; *see also* gender
Women's Institute for Freedom of the Press, 82
women's movement, 77, 79
women's studies, 77
World Association for Christian Communication (WACC), 247, 308, 350
World Bank (International Bank for Reconstruction and Development), 27, 38, 151, 279
INFODEV, 277
World Communication Report, 273
World Council of Churches, 49
World Council of Indigenous Peoples, 188, 191
World Economic Forum, 20
World Intellectual Property Organization (WIPO), 98, 317
World Press Freedom Committee (WPFC), 255
World Systems Theory, 29
World Trade Center, 40, 58
World Trade Organization (WTO), 144, 151, 351
World War I, 26
World War II, 26, 38, 172, 180
World-Wide Web (WWW), 104, 112; *see also* Internet

Y

Yanomami, 189
Yaounde, 250
Yeats, William Butler, 306
Yeltsin, President Boris, 18
Yugoslavia, 24, 31, 252-253, 258, 262, 291, 307, 326

Z

Zambia, 42
Zen and the Art of the Internet, 52
Zimbabwe, 262
Zionism, 242
Zndanov, Audrey, 215